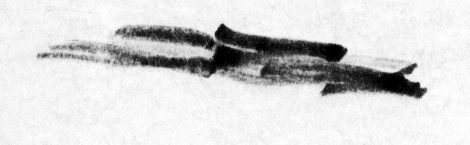

CAN THE SOVIET SYSTEM
SURVIVE REFORM?

CAN THE SOVIET SYSTEM SURVIVE REFORM?

SEVEN COLLOQUIES ABOUT THE STATE OF
SOVIET SOCIALISM SEVENTY YEARS AFTER
THE BOLSHEVIK REVOLUTION

Edited by
G. R. URBAN

Pinter Publishers, London and New York
in association with John Spiers

First published in Great Britain by
Pinter Publishers Limited
in association with John Spiers
25 Floral Street, London WC2E 9DS

British Library Cataloguing in Publication Data
A CIP catalogue record for this book is available
from the British Library

Library of Congress Cataloging-in-Publication Data

Can the Soviet system survive reform? : seven colloquies about the
state of Soviet socialism seventy years after the Bolshevik
revolution / edited and introduced by G. R. Urban.
p.   cm.
Includes index.
ISBN 0-86187-001-8
1. Gorbachev, Mikhail Sargeevich, 1931–   . 2. Communism—Soviet
Union.   3. Soviet Union—Politics and government—1982–   I. Urban,
G. R. (George R.), 1921–
HX313.G67C36   1989
335.43′0947–dc19   89-3731
                                                                     CIP

ISBN 0 86187 001 8

First published 1989

Printed and bound in Great Britain by
Biddles Limited, Guildford and King's Lynn

Contents

Preface

Two of the seven chapters in this symposium (my conversations with Max Kampelman and Alexander Zinoviev) predate Mikhail Gorbachov's election, in March 1985, as General Secretary of the Communist Party of the Soviet Union. They are, nevertheless, incorporated because they may help the reader to judge whether continuity, discontinuity, or some mixture of the two, is the defining characteristic of Soviet policies since Gorbachov's elevation. The conversations with Galina Vishnevskaya, Alain Besançon and Vladimir Bukovsky have not been updated for a similar reason. Some of the points they make, although overtaken by events, shed a revealing light on the evolution of Soviet behaviour precisely because they have been so overtaken.

This volume does not claim to be an exhaustive analysis of the Gorbachov reforms, much less of the Soviet system. It does, however, attempt to catch the atmosphere of transition in Soviet history between one variant of the system and another, both through the eyes of perceptive outside observers and those who speak to us with the authority of personal experience.

I am greatly indebted to Max Kampelman, Alexander Zinoviev, Galina Vishnevskaya, Alain Besançon, Vladimir Bukovsky, Giorgio Napolitano and Milovan Djilas for their candour and patient cooperation, to Encounter Ltd who published six of the seven dialogues, and to RFE/RL Inc. who initiated and broadcast these materials.

G.R.U.

Introduction

It is a commonplace but one well worth restating that, with a few exceptions in Classical Europe and, two thousand years later, along the North-West European seaboard and in North America, the vast majority of human beings have been wards under the rule of privileged minorities, despotic princes, vainglorious warlords, inequitable viziers and fanatical religious leaders over virtually the whole of recorded history. Oppression of one kind or another has been the normal thing in human affairs—it is parliamentary democracy that is revolutionary and has to be explained.

Twice in our century this 'normal thing' almost destroyed the young plant of representative democracy. Twice it assumed the shape of totalitarian dictatorship; but while National Socialism (and to a smaller extent Fascism) drew its appeal from the apotheosis of race and nation and had, consequently, only limited supra-national appeal, Marxism-Leninism addresses the whole of mankind and calls for a universal new beginning. It exploits the full gamut of our natural (and many of our unnatural) fears and phobias, and is as feverishly concerned with playing midwife to the Spirit of History as it is with the more mundane affairs of the distribution of wealth and even of brainpower. It does so in the name of an impassioned though ill-defined Utopia which draws its vocabulary from science but has penumbral associations with religion.

Liberal democracies have always found it hard to comprehend what makes totalitarian societies work. 'As is your sort of mind/ So is your sort of search', has always hampered their understanding. The master-key approach to history and society; the concept of the State as something larger and deeper than the sum of its parts and the ability of the State to inspire sacrifice; the permanent mobilisation of men in the service of seemingly impractical goals and their willingness to be so mobilised; the appeal of collectivism and the popularity of conquest have been foreign to the imagination of democrats.

In the 1930s, while Adolf Hitler was rapidly rearming, liberal democrats in Western Europe advocated unilateral disarmament. Defeat by the brown brand of totalitarianism was barely avoided and then at the cost of the demise of Europe as a force of world influence. For the cultural élite, parliamentary democracy was musty and unexciting. Its appeal to the intellect was weak, its appeal to the passions derisory. The temptation to betray it, first through a liaison with the Right and then with the totalitarian Left, was too strong to be resisted. Democratic discussion was all very well but it did not kill plutocrats or dispossess capitalists. Hitler and Stalin did. The enemy was brought within our walls, and parliamentary democracy had a narrow escape.

Marxism-Leninism confronts us, towards the end of the 20th century, with challenges that were unknown in 1917 or even in the 1950s. With war-like conflict virtually ruled out as an option in the nuclear age, Western students of the Soviet system must carefully now examine whether Soviet society and Russian political culture are open to reforms of a kind that would make the Soviet State a peaceable, responsible and civilised partner for global coexistence, and whether the reforms associated with the name of Mikhail Gorbachov are likely to be such reforms. This entails asking a number of questions that go beyond 'restructuring'.

Can the 19th century Utopia of Marx and its illegitimate offspring, Leninism, be turned into civil society? Can Communism refashion itself into a genuine pluralistic order that would, while still disallowing the free and open competition of political parties, nevertheless contrive to offer the citizen a broad sense of choice and participation? If so, isn't 'existing socialism' in a rather favourable position to develop a type of watered-down democratic order that would meet the Russian people's modest expectations, offering, at the same time, a model to other politically under-developed nations? Is the virtual bankruptcy of the Soviet economy a strong enough source of disaffection to make the ordinary Russian demand fundamental changes in the system? Or has the system come so close to satisfying the Russian people's quest for a lowly but risk-free egalitarianism that the prospect of a more prosperous but less secure life offers few attractions? Do the Russian people actually prefer their present state of unfreedom because they think it is *freedom*, or because they are comfortable with authoritarianism and regimentation in a way that passes Western understanding? If the latter, doesn't our notion of democracy and self-determination confer upon them the right to choose to live undemocratically, and upon us the obligation to respect that choice?

I do not propose to examine these questions in detail because they are discussed in the present volume. Suffice it to observe that the reformability of totalitarian systems is so far not endorsed by evidence. Hitler and Mussolini had to be defeated in war. The Communist countries, all of which find themselves, in the late 1980s, in profound economic and social crisis, have so far failed to come up with solutions. The two principals, the Soviet Union and China, are in turmoil, groping their way to an economically more efficient and socially more acceptable order without having yet found one. Poland is the permanent invalid of Eastern Europe, Romania the ultimate Stalinist deterrent, Czechoslovakia the cemetery of Communist reformation, while the Bulgarian Communist system lacks sufficient identity of its own to tell us much about the fortunes of 'socialism' one way or the other. Even reform-happy Hungary, where the 'human face' of the Communist system has been longest on display, is in the grips of a fresh crisis. Half-measures have proved almost as destabilising as no reforms at all, but the constraints of the system permitted of no others. Yugoslavia, with its political centrifugalism, nationality problems, economic debilitation and three-digit inflation offers any would-be reformer the perfect anti-model.

The chances of the reform of Soviet totalitarianism are particularly difficult to gauge. One popular view holds that 'Sovietism' agrees with the Russian people rather well because it is, *mutatis mutandis*, a successor to both Czarism and the 'Russian idea' of Slavophil provenance. It combines (it is said) grandiose rhetoric and a Messianic nationalism with the evasion of individual responsibility, inertia and apathy well known to us from the pen of Goncharov. Commander and those commanded connive in the silent understanding that the 'command is the message'. Once an

order has been given and taken, no more need be done
about it in practical life. A favourite tactic with any bureaucracy, this happy immobilism is said to occupy an especially
hallowed place in Russian life. If I decline to examine it
here it is not because it is untenable but because it is
unprofitable as a hypothesis. If it is true, the Soviet-Russian
way of life is cast in concrete and no more need be said
about it in the short and medium term.

What, then, are the chances of evolutionary reform within
the system? Soviet Communism, it hardly needs saying,
differs from all other authoritarian and totalitarian forms of
government in that it offers a seamless explanation of the
life of society and the place of the individual in it, as well
as rules of conduct to hasten the consummation of 'History'.
Individual men and women are seen as characters in a play
they have not written but cannot escape. Once the ordinary
citizen has been made to understand that his destiny is to
put himself in phase with the plot, he accepts it as a privileged form of freedom and serves it without regard to his
private inclinations or self-interest.

The lynchpin in this grand design is the industrial proletariat. Members of this under-privileged and 'increasingly
impoverished' class are the sole authentic agents of the
design of History. In them is vested the consciousness of
revolution and the power to achieve a classless society. Their
triumph eliminates conflict among classes and nations, at which
point the dialectic becomes irrelevant and is presumably
retired. As pathfinders to this irenical outcome, the proletariat
and its 'vanguard' speak with the moral authority of mankind.

Can a political philosophy of this kind reform itself
without forfeiting its title to legitimacy? Our first problem
with Marxism-Leninism is that it is not a political philosophy
at all. It is a social cosmogony combined with a doctrine of
salvation couched in the language of the popular science of
the 19th century. It offers a single key for unlocking any
door and answering any question human beings can meaningfully ask on this side of eternity. It offers wholeness,
satisfaction and hope—it decries individualism, fragmen-
tation and compromise. It is a secular faith in all but name
and thus intolerant of unauthorised interpretations. Revisionism, opportunism, left-deviationism, right-deviationism,
formalism, adventurism *et al.* have all been condemned in
their time as fateful heresies and punished accordingly.

This singular wholeness and idolisation of the ideology is enough to frustrate or severely limit the scope of any genuine reform of the system. It does not rule out *tactical* change because Leninism offers a broad enough body of quotations to repudiate the more repulsive or anachronistic features of Leninism *by* Leninism; but the results of so wavering an apostasy are bound to be uncertain and to fall short of any genuine reformation. 'Real-existing socialism' is all of a piece and can only survive as a monolith.

It is, therefore, difficult to agree with those Western observers of the Soviet scene who believe that Gorbachov's 'restructuring' is in fact an admission that the 'old' variety of the Soviet system has already expired and a new one is being raised on its ruins. This may well be what the General Secretary privately feels should be done, but it is not what he says or what the doctrinal foundations of Soviet Communism would permit him to say or to do. Gorbachov protests that he wants to change and strengthen the system *within* the boundaries of the system so that it can 'reveal its true potential'. We have no reason to doubt that that is exactly what he wants to do and all he can do. 'In October 1917,' he said in his festive oration on 2nd November 1987, 'we departed the old world and irreversibly rejected it. We are travelling to a new world, the world of communism. We shall never deviate from this road.' That he is, nevertheless, a revisionist and a heretic on a royal scale is the least of the charges that the orthodox keepers of the sanctum will probably level at him when the time is right.

There is, however, another and equally fundamental though long-term obstacle to the reform of the Soviet system—the changing character and gradual depletion of the industrial working class. The arrival, in 1917, of revolutionary Communism in underdeveloped and mainly agricultural Russia already required some twisting of the ideology. The hyphen inserted between Marxism and Leninism is testimony to the violence that had to be done to the Marxist canon. It was not clear how a revolution of the proletariat could occur in the virtual absence of a proletariat; nor how a state of 'socialism' much less 'communism' could be attained if the pre-existing conditions of a developed 'capitalism' and a 'bourgeois revolution' did, in fact, not exist as the ideology demanded.

Not to be deterred by theory, a coup d'etat was, neverthe-less, carried out. The dictatorship of the proletariat was declared to have come into existence; but it soon transpired that the dictatorship of the proletariat was to be a few determined men's dictatorship *over* the proletariat. The size and maturity of the Russian working class turned out to be inadequate to shoulder the responsibilities History had allegedly assigned to it. How, then, was History to attain its purpose?

The spirit of revolution, the Bolsheviks under Lenin now declared, was to be injected into the proletariat by 'progressive' elements drawn from outside the proletariat— by men of culture and historical inspiration (albeit also of bourgeois background) such as themselves. Their guardian-ship was to be temporary. It would cease when the working class was mature enough to be aware of its own interests. Seven decades on, the maturing process appears to be still unaccomplished.

This prestidigitation was Lenin's great contribution to Communist theory. It is, to this day, his claim to fame as the father of the 'vanguard' Party. Unelected, unrepresent-ative and unaccountable to the population or even the proletariat, the Party 'leads' society by virtue of its privi-leged understanding of the purpose of History and the moral authority conferred upon it by that understanding.

Stalin was, of course, aware of the problem of the missing proletariat. The forced march to industrialisation of the 1930s, and the coercive urbanisation of much of the peas-antry greatly increased the number of industrial workers, but these did not quite add up to a 'working class'. Those uprooted and often illiterate multitudes that were now forced to eke out a living in communal apartments in Soviet slums and shanty towns were only marginally closer to constituting a class-conscious industrial proletariat than the uprooted tribesmen in Yemen and Ethiopia constitute a proletariat in the late 1980s.

From 1917 to this day, the Soviet 'proletariat' has been a disinherited mass of displaced muzhiks whose 'proletarian' activities have been performed for it, using its name but without its consent, by the Communist Party. That proud breed of dignified workers whose civilised life-style and love of high culture would be second only to their dedication to the public good—the working class Marx had envisaged—

never materialised. The Party did. There was no room for both.

On the eve of the 21st century the proletarian base of Soviet society is threatened by a new and unforeseen danger—unforeseen, that is, by the keepers of the Bolshevik covenant. Stalin's own 'perestroika' of the 1930s demanded the rapid increase of the industrial labour force; Gorbachov's, however, demands its rapid decrease. If the reform of the Soviet economy is to succeed, the shift from material and labour-intensive industrial occupations to brain-intensive work in high technology and the service sectors will make the 19th century notion of the 'proletariat' increasingly antiquated and ultimately irrelevant. Gorbachov's intention to reform the system strictly within the confines of the system will then be challenged by the retreat and the gradual disappearance of the very backbone of Soviet Communism. This will probably make little practical difference to the immediate future of *perestroika*, but it will make it extremely hard for the reformers to justify what they are doing in terms of the ideology. How can a revolutionary society of the 'victorious proletariat' maintain its legitimacy when the proletariat is being phased out by a revolutionary science and technology? How can there be a dictatorship of the proletariat when the proletariat has decided to opt for the values, the culture and the life-style of the bourgeoisie—when, *horribile dictu*, Gorbachov's 'restructuring' tacitly *demands* that it should do so?

The Soviet leaders are not unaware of the dilemma. In his keynote address to mark the 70th anniversary of the Bolshevik revolution, Gorbachov said: 'The Western world is full of "theories" that the working class is disappearing. They write that it has already dissolved into the 'middle stratum', been socially reborn and so on and so forth. Of course, there are large and considerable changes in the working class, but the class-opponent is in vain lulling himself and trying to disorganise, disorientate and confuse the workers' movement. The working class now, in its new social frontiers, represents a numerically predominant force and possesses the potential to play a decisive role, all the more so at the sharp turning-points in history.'

This is whistling in the dark, and the General Secretary is too intelligent a man not to know it. By no stretch of the imagination can the proletariat 'within its new social frontiers' still be considered to be a proletariat—whether in Western Europe, the US or a future USSR. No German car-worker, French railway engineer or American lathe operator, with his outstanding earning power, well-equipped home, one or two motor vehicles and holidays abroad, would think of himself as a proletarian or conform to those patterns of behaviour that are supposed to be peculiar to the proletariat. A simple reading of the social history of our century tells us that, with certain untypical exceptions (such as the British), all the world's proletarians aspire to the state of the middle classes.

Not to realise this about the nature of the 'human factor', which Gorbachov and his team constantly invoke in support of 'restructuring', is to opt for yet another Communist Utopia of the kind Milovan Djilas discusses in this volume. Wherever the world may be heading, it is not toward a Marxist-Leninist model of society, whether of the old or of a more recent vintage. That the Soviet Union will, by the sheer fact of its existence, always be seen to be a source of encouragement for the rebellious and the disaffected is a very different thing from saying that the system has the wind of history in its sails, and that the name of that wind is the disinherited proletariat.

But Gorbachov and the ruling oligarchy are aware of their predicament and claim to have found an answer. It follows in the footsteps of what one might call the 'Marcuse-fallacy' which expired in 1968 and has so far managed to haunt us only on the pages of radical memoirists. This fallacy holds that even though the world's manual and industrial workers are no longer numerous, impoverished or class-conscious enough to provide the gunpowder for the revolutionary transformation of society, a grand substitute (or com-plement) has arisen in the shape of other radical forces— underprivileged blacks, radical clerics, alienated intellec-tuals, concerned environmentalists, unilateral disarmers, Marxisant Catholics, women's liberators, and, above all, 'third-worlders' as well as the actual unruly intelligentsia of the third world itself.

There is a modicum of truth in this claim, but no more. It is certainly true that these groups have an uncanny way of picking up causes that are damaging to the policies of democratically elected governments. It is also true that many of these causes coincide with or work to the benefit of Soviet ambitions. It is true, moreover, that some of these causes receive publicity wildly out of proportion with the strength of the disaffected, because members of the Western media themselves frequently belong to the alienated or purport to do so out of radical chic.

But it would be extremely far-fetched to infer that these groups could, with or without the 'old' proletariat, become an organisable force at the 'sharp turning points in history'. If the Communist myth of revolution requires an international revolutionary proletariat, this surrogate will do as a myth, but woe betide if Gorbachov and the other Soviet innovators mistake it for the reality.

It is, of course, imaginable that the Soviet reformers will surprise us with even more unorthodox pronouncements than they have done already. The prospect of a war-like clash between 'imperialism' and socialism has been dropped from the new (27th Congress) Party programme, as Gorbachov emphatically tells us in his book *Perestroika*. So has the doctrine that 'peaceful coexistence' with the capitalist world is a sharpened form of the international class-struggle. How these deletions can be made to square with Lenin's insistence that 'a funeral requiem will be sung over the Soviet republic or over world Capitalism' is not immediately obvious. By the same token, it is imaginable, although it would seem less likely, that the notion of the world-proletariat as the bearer of the purpose of History will eventually also be jettisoned or reformulated in so bland a manner that the arrival of universal socialism will, in effect, be relegated to the Greek calends. Few tears would be shed outside the Party circuit if this were to happen, for it would mean an open avowal that the Leninist dictatorship has, as Vladimir Bukovsky suggests in his contribution to this volume, quietly collapsed under the weight of its own absurdities.

But this is not what is most likely to happen. One cannot see any Soviet leader's experimentation with reform carrying him to a point where the self-questioning of the system would drive it to self-destruction. Nor can one see so spontaneous a quest for change coming from below that the reforms would eventually have to be harnessed to policies hostile to the survival of the system. The Russian masses may incline to anarchy as they always have done in history, but anarchism is not enough. The political will to overthrow the system, using the Gorbachov upheavals as its launching pad, is, certainly at the end of the 1980s, too weak and unfocused to be considered a serious propellant.

The reality is unspectacular yet heavy with foreboding. The Soviet Union is a ramshackle but functioning empire. It is underpinned by a system that provides it with a rationale and works well enough by Russian standards. Although built on untenable premises and utopian expectations as well as a record of great savagery, it is the only system hundreds of millions of Soviet citizens have known for the best part of three generations. It is one many of them detest, but it is not foreign to Russian culture or Russian ways of doing things. It offers an all-resolving doctrine and an all-powerful Saviour. With all its faults (or perhaps because of them), it is a system that has secured for the Russian people an honoured place among nations. The fear and respect of foreigners is the gift Communism has bestowed on a land of once lowly muzhiks. That great rendezvous with history that the Russian nation always sought but never attained under the divinely inspired Autocrats of all Russias has now come its way through a system that denies divine inspiration and decries the concept of nation. The point was not lost on Stalin. It is unlikely to be lost on his present successors.

The reformers do not, therefore, have too hard a row to hoe as hoeing goes in Russian history. True, the run-of-the-mill apathetic citizen would be happier without 'restructuring' because it means work and accountability. Yet he can be cajoled or blackmailed into toeing the line provided that living standards rise, the changes are gradual and certain familiar loopholes to play and outplay the system remain untouched. 'Authoritarian rule tempered by corruption' has deep roots in the Russian psyche and will not be easily abandoned. It is a grotesque but effective way of asserting human rights under adverse conditions. Where the state itself is the source of lawlessness, bribable officials and operators of the black economy are a liberating force of uncommon importance.

Where, then, is the Soviet Union heading under the heresiarchs of the late 1980s? I would not presume to look far into the future. Assuming, however, that the heresies survive even if the heresiarchs do not, it is possible to foresee a system that will be shorn of both the more repulsive instruments of totalitarian rule and much of its missionary ambitions and rhetoric. The single-party dictatorship will become more diversified and marginally more popular as it becomes more deeply entrenched in Russian values and the Russian past. Internationalism will weaken, xenophobia will grow. The Party will be assimilated as the Union's natural government and will need, and provide, less and less ideological justification for its rule. The public acceptance of the system as a participatory but non-liberal national-socialist state will increase.

Communism, if these forecasts are correct, will then reach its final stage of development in a feckless Russo-Corporatism—'socialist' in form, nationalistic in content, and Oriental in style—that will puzzle the world with alternating feats of realism and recklessness; liberalisation and repression; the desire to atone for a guilty past and the obsession to hide it. It will be a system Peter the Great, Nicholas I, Pobedonostsev, or Dostoevsky for that matter, would have no difficuly in recognising as a legitimate successor to what has gone before.

G. R. Urban

1. MAX KAMPELMAN
Negotiating with the Russians

From Helsinki to Madrid

URBAN: Critics of 'the Helsinki process' frequently suggest that it is wrong and demoralising to resume negotiations with a power that has violated, in almost every particular, an agreement it solemnly signed as recently as 1975. George F. Will wrote in *The Washington Post*:

> As the Western public becomes used to the sight of Western and Communist diplomats deliberating about freedom of expression, travel, trade unions and other matters, the public concludes that the people talking so earnestly, for so long, share a political vocabulary and frame of reference, so the Helsinki process spreads a fog of false, but soothing assumptions.

Others have argued, especially in Reagan Administration circles, that the very act of sharing a negotiating table with the Soviet Union—after the Soviet aggression in Afghanistan, the suppression of 'Solidarity', the accelerated build-up of the SS-20s, and the arrest of the Helsinki human-rights monitors—was an act of assuring the Soviet leaders that their international credentials stood unaffected, and that the West was prepared to deal with them as equals even if it could not grant them a clean bill of health. It was, as the *Neue Zürcher Zeitung* put it, an act of helping the Soviet Union to 'polish up its image' at a time when it was sorely tarnished.

At a more general level, critics have been warning us that this is no time to confer an extra dimension of respect and 'legitimacy' on the Soviet leadership—no time to mislead Western public opinion into thinking that compromise, give-

and-take, the spirit of live-and-let-live are part of the Soviet leaders' mental equipment, or that we could convert them to our ideas if only we mustered the better case and deployed the better argument.

Are the critics right in saying that the whole negotiating process, from Helsinki to Madrid, suffers from these faulty assumptions—that the psychology it generates undermines our public perceptions of what the Soviet Union is about and how it proposes to achieve its objectives?

KAMPELMAN: I share the diagnosis as to the totalitarian nature of the Soviet Union, but I disagree with the prescription. I believe in dialogue and negotiation. We recently completed the Madrid agreement during which we met with the Soviets for three years. That agreement did not demoralise our forces in the West, nor did it in any way 'polish up' the Soviet image. On the contrary, we were engaged in active political struggle for 'hearts and minds', and did a great deal more 'tarnishing' of the Soviet image than we could have done by absenting ourselves from the forum. It is not the negotiating process that confers the 'equal' status; it is Soviet military power that provides it. As to 'respect' and 'legitimacy', we effectively challenged both in a respectable international forum.

Let me also say that had we decided not to sit down and negotiate with the Soviets, we would have separated ourselves from the real forces in Western Europe, abdicated our responsibility to our European friends, and abandoned the field of political competition with the Soviet Union.

We would also have added credibility to the Soviet propaganda campaign which alleges that the United States is 'not interested in negotiating'. I have given this matter much thought, and I fail to see how it would have served our interests had we refused to sit down with the Soviet Union.

On the question of 'legitimacy'—that issue was decided by President Franklin D. Roosevelt in 1933 when the United States recognised the Soviet Government. The fact that one recognises a power by no means implies approval of its philosophy, or acquiescence in its policies, or legitimacy of its objectives. It is this important distinction that the free world must understand if we are going to be effective in competing with the Soviet Union. If we isolate ourselves from this battle by insisting on purity, on not sullying our hands, we put ourselves in a position where we become an irrelevance and add to the very power we are trying to contain.

We do recognise the Soviet leaders as the *de facto* rulers of a substantial part of the world. We recognise them as a significant military power. If that is what the word 'legitimacy' means, then we recognise that the Soviet Government has it. But it is a legitimacy based on police and military power alone, rather than 'the legitimacy of consent.'

Now, if we had sat down to negotiate with the Soviets and *not* raised their violations of Helsinki (and of SALT), then, of course, it could rightly be said that we were also legitimising the violations of the Helsinki agreement. But this is not what we did.

The challenge to us is to recognise the *de facto* legitimacy of Soviet power but to challenge the legitimacy of that power's behaviour. That distinction has to be understood, and I think we have the important task of educating Western public opinion to comprehend it.

URBAN: The question I am trying to explore is whether, by sitting down to talk with the Soviets as 'bona fide' neighbours, we are not telling the world that we share with the Soviets a moral universe as well as a planet.

KAMPELMAN: I repeat: that we recognise the Soviet system as an existing Government and to do business with it does not mean that we approve of it. We are engaged in a dynamic power-struggle with it for the future of certain forms of society (and, perhaps, the future of mankind). I find it difficult to believe that anybody who examines the record of our negotiations in Madrid can interpret it as a measure of approval of Soviet policies. What we have done, for example, in Madrid was consistently to criticise the Soviet Union for being an aggressive power, for violating its international commitments, for its anti-Semitism, and so on.

URBAN: I have been watching the American role, and especially your personal role, in the Madrid process with the greatest admiration. Week after week, for almost three years, you arraigned the Soviet Union in this 'world court in continuous session' (I think the phrase is yours) with lucidity and eloquence. Seldom before has the Kremlin's ideological duplicity been more tellingly exposed.

KAMPELMAN: But had we not gone to Madrid, the world forum would not have been open to us.

URBAN: Yes, but might it not be argued that your impressive rhetoric was a substitute for an active policy?

KAMPELMAN: If Soviet totalitarianism could be effectively changed by a wave of the wand or by non-participation in the negotiation process, it would have been far better to try to change it in that way rather than to make those 80 speeches that I was called upon to make. But I do not know what realistic alternative we had that would have been in our general interest. I spent many hours, believe me, analysing this problem and was unable to come up with an alternative that would have satisfied me.

What was the negotiating position we took? We decided to strengthen the Western Alliance by recognising that our West European friends, who share our values, were geographically in the forefront of confrontation with the Soviet Union; that they were concerned about a nuclear catastrophe; and that they were, therefore, in no position to 'ostracise' the Soviet Union—indeed they had been doing the very opposite.

Any effort by us to persuade them to ostracise the Russians—assuming that we were ourselves persuaded that this was the right way to proceed—would have failed. We would have (as I say) isolated ourselves, and to that extent weakened the Euro-American Alliance.

URBAN: Are you implying that, apart from the United States, the rest of the Alliance was on the other side of the fence? I suspect that the British Government might well have gone along with an alternative policy (perhaps 'masterful inactivity') even if certain other NATO members might not.

KAMPELMAN: I am concerned that there is not a single West European Allied Government that would have been willing to be held responsible for destroying the Helsinki process— which would have been the effect of non-participation. This

does not mean that our European Allies were unaware of
the nature of the Soviet Union, but that they understood
the importance of being perceived to be always willing to
talk and negotiate with the other side.

Consider NATO's 1979 'dual-track' decision on the
Pershing and Cruise missiles. At that time it was necessary
for the Alliance to reaffirm its willingness to enter into
discussions as a condition for going ahead with the military
deployment. In other words, the pressures for 'talking to
the Soviet Union' were there in 1979, that is *before* the
Madrid talks began. . . .

URBAN: You are really talking about the German Federal
Republic now, are you not?

KAMPELMAN: No—I am talking about Germany only as one
of several West European countries. It is a mistake to
assume that Bonn is alone in holding the views I describe.
Germany has considerable influence and has, in Herr
Genscher, a capable foreign-policy leader with a strong
mind. But the views the Germans entertain in this matter of
negotiation are common to France, Italy, the Scandinavian
countries and others too. I spent time in London and
discussed this matter with diplomats in the British Foreign
Office. I must assume they reflected the views of the Prime
Minister. Given all this, I recommended to the US Government that we put our weight behind the Helsinki-Madrid
process.

Containing and counteracting Soviet influence takes many
forms. I was anxious that we should not abandon the
political platform, the public opinion debate, the information front. I felt certain that Madrid could provide us
with the necessary forum to advance our Western interests.

URBAN: Critics do not quite share your view that Madrid
was a good forum for undermining Soviet influence.
Leopold Unger, for example, records a whole list of reasons
why the Madrid document is a two-edged sword. In reality,
he says, it is more likely to damage Western interests than
to promote them. He complains that the human-rights
discussions, due in Ottawa and Bern, which might prove
embarrassing to the Kremlin, have been put off until 1985
and 1986, whereas the Stockholm disarmament conference

is taking place right now, making it possible for the Soviet Union to promote its various 'peace' initiatives. Not once, he writes, is Poland mentioned in the 40-page Madrid document, although the conference took place in the shadow of Polish developments. Nor, he argues, is mention made of those persons in the Soviet Union and Poland who have been imprisoned for monitoring the observation of the Helsinki agreement.

KAMPELMAN: There may be a certain heroism in 'going down fighting', but I would much rather win battles. It is doing us all a disservice to minimise the fact that the Soviet Union found itself thoroughly on the defensive in Madrid. The Madrid process did not at all serve Soviet interests, unless we believe that just the fact of an agreement does so. I believe, for reasons I have detailed, that the Madrid concluding document, with its reiterated and expanded assertions of human values, is in our interests. The criticism that it did not in its text specifically name Poland or individual dissidents is inexplicable to me given the impressive effort made in their behalf by the West. We must not hand the Soviets a victory they have not won and do not deserve. This would be shooting oneself in the foot.

URBAN: What critics like George Will and Leopold Unger have been trying to argue is quite simple: don't trust a man who has repeatedly made a fool of you.

KAMPELMAN: I respect that view, but we do not in that sense trust them. The long-term objectives I share with George Will and Leopold Unger are: try to undermine Soviet totalitarian society, reducing its influence. We should hope for a thaw, a 'liberalisation' or humanisation of that system, if that is at all possible. Now, if those are our hopes, we must try to achieve them in ways that are open to us: and that means using the international political process. We are not involved in an abstract ideological crusade; we are involved in a political competition for power and influence.

Mind you, there *is* another position which says: it was all right to go to Madrid as long as we used the conference as a forum in which to hit them hard, but we should have stopped prior to the point of an agreement. I can understand that point of view; it is a valid theoretical alternative; but it does not, alas, have any relationship to reality. We could have followed that course if we were just writing a 'scenario', or if the Soviets had refused to satisfy some of our substantive requests at the negotiating table. Had we refused to concur in the final result once the essence of our demands was met, our good faith as negotiators would have been undermined, much to our damage.

Over the past year we have been deploying our Pershing and Cruise missiles, to help restore a certain balance of power, the new imbalances of which had so alarmed Chancellor Helmut Schmidt. Complete deployment is by now not just a military issue, it is also a symbolic feature of NATO's unity and determination. Certainly our European Allies told us that putting ourselves in a position where *we* were the ones who would not want to go ahead with negotiation and written agreements would make it much more difficult to make the deployment of these missiles acceptable to West European public opinion. We could not be unconcerned about that result.

URBAN: Some critics contend that the West could have said: 'We shall not come to terms with you based on the words of this agreement alone—we insist on your 110,000 troops getting out of Afghanistan.' Or, 'We insist that the 51 Helsinki monitors be released from jail.' Wouldn't these have been reasonable requests fully covered by the ten principles written into 'Basket 1' of the Helsinki agreement?

KAMPELMAN: Yes, these would have been legitimate demands. The 35 states that signed the Helsinki agreement assumed certain obligations about respecting the sovereignty of other nations and abstaining from aggression, not only against one another, but with respect to all countries of the world. Therefore, the Soviet invasion of Afghanistan was clearly in violation of the principles of the Helsinki agreement.

This was a controversial question. We *were* very much tempted to go down the road you indicate. In the end we came to the conclusion that insistence on Afghanistan and the imprisonment of the Helsinki monitors would have made it impossible to carry our Allies with us and thus take advantage of those substantial concessions which the Soviets had to make in the course of the negotiations. Rather than accomplishing a Western goal, we would have assisted the Soviets in the direction of accomplishing one of theirs: Western divisiveness. We did push for and achieve some 'gestures', but they were quite limited.

The absence of an agreement would have meant that there wasn't going to be a follow-up conference dealing with 'confidence-building measures' and 'surprise military attack.' The new provisions improving human-rights clauses would also have been lost. So we settled for the provisions and for less on performance. History will judge whether our call was correct.

The issues of Afghanistan and the Helsinki monitors were regrettably unattainable in the Madrid context. That is why the US introduced the issue of humanitarian gestures. Some humanitarian gestures (such as the release of the Pentecostals) have already been made by the Soviet side, and I hope more will follow.

URBAN: May I raise two points? You will recall that the Soviet invasion of Czechoslovakia did not stop *détente*. In 1968 *détente* suffered a temporary setback but picked up again soon after the suppression of Dubcek's Czechoslovakia and culminated in the Helsinki agreement. Why did this happen? Because, in the late 1960s and the 1970s, the will to have a substantial relaxation of tensions with the Soviet Union was shared on both sides of the Atlantic.

But in the early 1980s this was no longer so. *Détente* was and is substantially dead. Couldn't the invasion of Afghanistan and the suppression of Poland have been used by us as opportunities for suspending the negotiations 'until further notice'? You need not have alienated the European Allies by saying 'No' to the Helsinki process. It might have been sufficient to sit back and do nothing (as, in fact, you did for a limited period) pending a change in Soviet behaviour.

My second point is unrelated to the first but relevant to the question in hand. You once told me when we met in Madrid that you were unhappy about the apparently increasing divisions within NATO. You suggested that the President of the United States should consider proposing to the heads of all Allied governments a summit conference to consider 'what to do about NATO.' Were the formulations of the 1949 treaty still relevant? Did the Allies continue to see the Soviet Union as a threat to their independence and democratic social order? Should the United States still keep its forces in Western Europe? Did Europe want a different world-order from the one envisaged by the decision-makers of 1949?

In other words, you were expressing your concern about the drift within the European side of the Alliance, hoping to shock the Europeans into reconsidering their policies.

Now you seem to be referring to the rather dovish attitude of the West Europeans in the matter of the Helsinki process as your justification for not pursuing a crisper line towards the USSR. Isn't there a discrepancy between these two attitudes?

KAMPELMAN: I don't think there is. The suggestion I made to you in thinking aloud was that, if NATO was to continue to experience the strains from which it is now suffering, it was time for us to sit down to re-examine NATO's utility in its present form, either with a view to reaffirming it or with a view to reforming it. That is still a very relevant issue. On the other hand, NATO is not an institution which ever accepted dictation from the United States: dialogue between the member states must take place. Surely Americans have an obligation not only to say our piece but also to listen to our Allies.

After the imposition of martial law in Poland the NATO countries came back to Madrid (in February 1982) and said that they were not now going to do 'business as usual' and negotiate. We made it plain that we were going to use the Madrid forum to criticise the violations of the Helsinki Final Act by Polish repression and the Soviet pressure on Warsaw. And we did. After a few weeks of this, we agreed to a recess until November 1982. But the question you are raising is: Why did we come back in November and resume the negotiations?

The United States was returning to Madrid at the end of the agreed-upon recess, but we were widely and correctly seen as not wishing to be 'negotiating as usual.' Our European Allies disagreed with our apparent unwillingness to talk. They were telling us that public opinion in their countries required negotiations; that public opinion understood condemnation but it would not understand attending a conference and then not wanting to finish it constructively.

We then had a series of meetings among ourselves—first in Norway, then in Portugal, Luxembourg, and Brussels. These resulted in a proposal by our Allies that when we returned to Madrid we should resume the negotiations but not on a 'business-as-usual' basis. It was suggested that we reflect in our negotiating posture our outrage at Polish martial law through a series of new demands, such as a provision on free trade unions. It was on this basis that we went back to the negotiating table in Madrid in November 1982.

URBAN: Yet Poland is not mentioned in the Madrid agreement.

KAMPELMAN: Of course not. It was never considered by us that Poland would specifically be mentioned. You have to realise that in the Helsinki process nothing goes forward unless it is by consensus. Warsaw is one of the negotiating parties and, quite clearly, Poland would never agree to the mention of Poland in the Madrid document. We did not seek it, and it would have been foolhardy for us to have expected it. Our effort was rather to try to reflect the issues presented by the Polish experience, unmistakably but in a manner that had a chance of being adopted.

We did that in several ways. One was the trade-union provision in the final document; another was our amendment on religious freedom; there was also a series of further amendments resulting from the suppression of 'Polish pluralism.' The time to be specific about Poland by name was at the round-table. We did so. The meeting was the forum to influence public opinion. This was the political battlefield.

I supported that approach. We maintained Allied unity, and then went on to obtain Soviet textual concessions and produced a full document. I believe we were effective with European public opinion by pointing out that we went to Madrid to try to settle issues with the East through negotiations, but we highlighted the repressive nature of the Soviet Communist system during the negotiating process.

From Kissinger to Kampelman

URBAN: Would I be right in suggesting that the whole idea of putting our names to a negotiated agreement was to neutralise the so-called West European 'peace' movement and get those Cruise and Pershing missiles in place? You must have been conscious of the threatened 'hot autumn' and the 'freeze' movement in the United States. Weren't those the real targets of the Madrid compromise?

KAMPELMAN: They were important targets.

URBAN: A sop to European public opinion?

KAMPELMAN: No, not a 'sop', but an essential move to win over public opinion. Washington saw the Madrid document as a way of competing with the Soviets for West European public opinion—to help those elements who are friendly to us and deter those who are against us.

But the Madrid agreement went beyond this issue of deployment. We always have to bear in mind our ultimate problem—how best to deal with the Kremlin, how best to contain its influence and deter its expansionism. We endlessly discussed 'the nature of the Soviet system' and hammered out a Western view which we all share. We also have agreement among us in NATO on the need to undermine Soviet penetration if we possibly can, because we all share a sense of being threatened. But we are still left with the ultimate question of how to carry out our objectives. Of course, as we have said and commentators are repeating, the Soviets and the Poles are still suppressing free trade unions and doing reprehensible things. Repeating this does not address the basic challenge, important as it is to remind people about the facts.

The fundamental question is: what can we do about Soviet behaviour that can be effective? That is what preoccupies me. We cannot hope to influence Soviet policy without great military strength, and military strength cannot be had without the support of public opinion. If Madrid meant taking a step in lining up public opinion behind us, then we have achieved a great deal.

URBAN: Just before the Helsinki agreement was signed I published a hefty volume on *détente*. It was my considered view then that our approach to the Helsinki process rested

on some fundamental ideological misapprehensions. Some
of our opinion-makers said that the Soviet system was, for
all practical purposes, akin to our own: that the Soviet
leaders were Western-style politicians with foreign accents;
that the Soviet Union's long revolutionary history and
expansionism could somehow be undone by appending a
signature to a piece of paper. The act of negotiating a
document of good behaviour with a power that stood for
global revolution and the extinction of 'class enemies' and
'hostile social orders' was, I argued, a questionable
enterprise.

KAMPELMAN: At the time of Helsinki I also felt that it was
an unwise enterprise and said so.

It is too soon to tell what history will conclude about
the Helsinki process. My own view is that in Madrid we
successfully turned Helsinki around—to our advantage. We
learned to use the instrument. I believe it can work; and if
it does, I will say that I was wrong in 1975. The Europeans
I have talked to since—and *they* were the ones responsible
for 'Basket 3', not the Americans—never had any illusions
that changes could take place in the Soviet Union suddenly
or quickly, just because the Kremlin had signed a piece of
paper.

What they hoped was that civilised standards to strive for
would be established and norms of responsible behaviour
would be set. Those objectives have not been reached.
That fact does not, of course, mean that the norms are
unimportant. My point is that if the new generation of
Soviet leadership should come to believe that it is in its own
interest to begin to liberalise its system and that it can
survive some of this humanisation, then perhaps the standards established in 1975 in Helsinki and 1983 in Madrid
will prove to be useful.

We cannot, however, base the justification of Madrid on
that hope; nor on the hope that the Soviet leadership will
respond to moral considerations—they do not. They
respond to *power* considerations. But power considerations
may, if we create the right context, lead them to take some
of our moral requirements into account. I am not too optimistic about this—I only say that there is some possibility
that it might happen. So long as it does not, the standards

are available to be used by us in the international debate, in the 'war for hearts and minds'. This is very important.

In 1975, I thought that we had in Helsinki given an unnecessary triumph to the Soviet Union. My job in Madrid was to turn a possible earlier setback into a victory, I don't want to abandon the political struggle, and that is why I don't want to assume that we can't influence public opinion throughout the West and the Afro-Asian world. We have to do everything we can to get on the wavelength of public opinion so that they can hear what we are saying about the nature of the present Soviet régime.

Had there been a way of counteracting Soviet influence by non-participation and non-agreement, I might well have moved along that line. But there wasn't.

URBAN: Haven't we been through this kind of exercise before? When the appeasement of Hitler was the dominant strain in West European thinking, our politicians and media-men let it be known that Hitler was, at heart, a reasonable man—the sound of fury of his rhetoric were meant (it was said) for internal consumption; we could have peace with him if we satisfied legitimate German aspirations, and so on. Aren't we now making a similar error?

KAMPELMAN: You keep asking and returning to this question which I have already answered. There is a risk—but it is not an unreasonable one. In any case, we have not been saying that the Soviet leaders are nice chaps because they wear shirts and ties and know how to use cutlery. In Madrid we have been saying the opposite. We have been demonstrating in direct and clear language that the Soviet system is illiberal and repressive, and we have repeated it over and over again. If people choose not to hear that part of our message or to misunderstand it, I don't know what we can do about that. I believe our message has come across. That is why, just as the Madrid document was about to be approved, I made a very stern speech in Madrid (18 July 1983) in which I told the representatives of the Russian régime once again exactly where we stood with them. And I did it precisely because I didn't want Madrid to be the source of any euphoria in the West about the nature of

Soviet give-and-take. I didn't want anyone in the West to be misled by the idea that the leopard had changed its spots.

Now maybe what we did was not enough. Perhaps the risk you suggest is more than a risk—perhaps it is the reality. History will judge that. Personally, I have seen no signs of euphoria. In my opinion, our societies have a very sober understanding of the Soviet system. People are not saying that we have returned to a period of *détente*; much less do we have any Neville Chamberlains in our Western leaderships. But if you ask me: Is there a risk? Yes, there is a real risk of repeating the illusions of 1973–75, the illusions of a one-sided *détente*.

URBAN: May I remind you of Dr Kissinger's view? Henry Kissinger explains in his memoirs that his dual-track policy—strength on the one hand, and *détente* on the other—appeared to make no sense to the average American. Americans, he tells us, have no understanding of or liking for 'power politics' or even 'Realpolitik'. They could not see how you could pursue a tough policy towards the Russians on the one hand, as the pre-condition of talking peace, and cooperation on the other.

If American public opinion is really such that it cannot understand a sophisticated policy of that kind, then—Kissinger says—there is no hope that the United States can pursue a coherent policy in world affairs. Hasn't Kissinger's complaint some relevance to your own twin-track diplomacy?

KAMPELMAN: Yes, there was a lesson to be learned, and I think we have learned it.

In the 1970s the American President and his representatives consistently argued that peace was at hand. They spoke of this 'relaxation of tensions' as a magic formula which would usher in a new age. Now, if the current US leadership propounded a similar view, one might understand why the American public would make the same mistake, assuming that peace and reconciliation with the Soviet Union were around the corner. But this is not so. The American leadership and its negotiators have absolutely refused to mislead. Indeed, we kept insisting that there is *no détente* now. Of course, I cannot tell with absolute certainty that our double-track policy, offering diplomatic negotiations in a context of ideological candour, has been understood by the public, but I am convinced that proper leadership will produce a favourable public response. (The 1984 Presidential election results are surely a case in point.) Furthermore, if we pursued the military approach without trying to negotiate with the Russians at the same time, we would not only fail in Europe, but lose support in the United States as well.

URBAN: Is it not the case, though, that the American people will not support heavy expenditures on rearmament unless they are convinced that they are being threatened? Directly threatened, and also indirectly via client-states in the Western hemisphere? If the Kissingerian complaint is correct, and another public confusion over words is to be avoided, Washington may well be tempted to use a heavy brush to depict the character and intentions of the USSR.

KAMPELMAN: I don't find that confusion. I am not persuaded that Dr Kissinger fully understood American public opinion. That was not his strength. The Nixon administration over-sold *détente* and told the American people that peace was at hand. For one thing, it wasn't true. For another, the Soviet leaders were never really ambiguous about *détente*, although they tried their best to mislead us. We were living with wishes, not reality. Today American public opinion is again more realistic about the nature of the Soviet Union and the importance of the balance of armed power. The debate in Congress was whether we should have a 5 per cent or 8 per cent increase in our arms expenditure, but it is not a debate as to *whether* there should be an increase. And if we were not still having a troublesome unemployment rate, I don't think that debate would even be a serious one. True, there is a 'peace' movement in the United States, but even that movement now talks soberly about *verification* because it realises that the Kremlin régime cheats.

The essential point is the argument of deterrence—the argument that we need arms in order to make it unprofitable for the Soviet Union even to consider threats and adventures.

In Western Europe, deep-seated support exists for *Solidarity* and Polish pluralism. American public opinion, as well as that of Western Europe, has repeatedly stood up for the Sakharovs and Shcharanskys. We have to be careful, however, not to put ourselves into a position where it could be said of us that to support *Solidarity*, the noble Russian dissidents et al., means supporting 'war'. That is what the Russians are trying to communicate to Western Europe. We have to refute that position.

URBAN: A sophisticated argument. . . .

KAMPELMAN: And I hope it will work.

URBAN: But how certain are you that it will have an impact on the general public?

KAMPELMAN: All I know is that illusions about *détente* have apparently not been reawakened. I do not hear many people saying that the Soviets are being cooperative and peaceful. Both American and West European public opinion are well aware of the nature of Soviet totalitarianism and clearly understand the military threat, in spite of the nervous fear of war.

URBAN: I suspect the Europeans understand the Russians better than they do the Americans.

KAMPELMAN: I agree we are not understood, and that we contribute to not being understood. We also make mistakes. I would not want to defend the Caterpillar decision or the decision on the pipeline deal, because I believe that if economic warfare can be successful, we should not disdain it. I did not support our lifting of the grain embargo without getting anything in return. I have no objection to engaging in any kind of competition, short of a shooting war.

On the other hand, I have no liking for competitive contests I am likely to lose. If we had turned away from the negotiating table—if *we* had been the ones not coming to an agreement in Madrid—West European public opinion and the world press would have lambasted us for simply not wanting to have any dialogue with the Soviet Union, and that would have done great damage to Western unity and to missile deployment.

From Cold War to Bargaining

URBAN: May I now come to the actual text of the historic
Madrid agreement? I invite you to imagine what a political
prisoner somewhere in the Soviet Union might think of it.
Would he say: 'I am being mistreated in this clinic every
day—I am injected with drugs—my jailers abuse my human
dignity. Yet, until I heard about the Madrid agreement, I
was holding out, because I believed I had allies in the
Western world. But now it appears that the people who
have been sustaining my courage—the Americans, the
British, the French, and the other Western powers—have
sold out to my captors. If they themselves have had to come
to a compromise with the Soviet system, how can I hope to
defeat it? The Madrid document appears to have this
message for me: I'd better make my own compromise,
because all the cards are stacked against me. . . .'
   Is this what our unfortunate political prisoner would be
thinking?
   Or would he rather say: 'My only chance of getting out
of this hell is to exploit the pressures put upon my captors
by the Western nations in Madrid'?

KAMPELMAN: I believe you overstate the case, for I think
you will find both points of view prevalent. You know the
dissident movement as well as anybody is likely to know it.
But dissidents do not think or philosophise alike. They have
different view-points, and different degrees of sophistication.
   I have had a rather active exchange with dissidents in the
Soviet Union and their friends in the West. Some have been
saying to me: 'Why are you letting the Madrid meeting
come to an end? While it continues you are helping to
defend us on the human-rights issue. That continuation is
important.' I point out to them that we have arranged for
a number of follow-up meetings so that the accountability
process continues. Other correspondents in the Soviet
Union urge me to do everything possible to keep the
'Helsinki process' alive, because the Soviet authorities
would welcome an opportunity to blame us for destroying
it. Keeping the Helsinki values alive gives them hope.
   I can see how certain dissidents may feel that the fact of
a Madrid agreement has let them down, even though the

document reflects Western standards. That saddens me, but I understand it. They may think that they have been 'sold out' because Madrid ended and they are still in jail. Shcharansky's wife, for example, feels that we should not have agreed to anything until her husband was released.

I can, therefore, see both sides of the argument. We had to make our own call. At some point we had to make a decision, one based on the best information and the most responsible judgment we could muster. What we have done may disappoint some courageous dissidents, but it will please other sincere opponents of the Soviet régime. I could only do what my judgment and conscience led me to do.

URBAN: Don't you think that the two reactions I have tried to describe go for the captive nations as a whole with almost equal force? After all, they, too, are 'political prisoners', multiplied by the millions, and they, too, might say: It is time we made our peace with the Communist régime, seeing that the Western Governments, too, seem to have no alternative but to come to terms with it.' Or they might say: 'Our only chance of keeping or enlarging such areas of freedom as we have managed to carve out for ourselves is to hold the Communist régime to its words according to the Helsinki process.'

KAMPELMAN: I am sceptical that your first analogy would apply to the East European peoples. According to my reading, the East Europeans are extremely pleased that the Helsinki process has been kept alive, but there will be follow-up meetings on security, surprise military attack, human rights, and so on. They don't want a war of the Superpowers. Their preoccupation is with trying to get increased areas of liberty in their own societies, to improve their standard of living, and to challenge Soviet authority and repression.

For my own part, I cannot see myself encouraging anyone to go to jail. I don't want to spur anyone to be a martyr of totalitarian society. To do so, or not to do so, is primarily a decision that must stem from the individual's conscience. If an individual does make the decision to resist, I would want to congratulate him for his heroic qualities of character, but I don't want to encourage liberals and democrats and other protestors to sacrifice themselves.

As far as the global power struggle is concerned, Czechoslovakia, Hungary and Romania are members of the United Nations. They are states we have recognised; we have exchanged Ambassadors with them for many years. That in itself confers a form of legitimacy, as we discussed earlier; with the Soviet Union we crossed that threshold in 1933. We recognise them diplomatically, but we must be prepared at the same time to challenge the moral legitimacy of totalitarian régimes.

URBAN: But in a brutally power-political world might not compromises like that of the Madrid agreement be a hindrance to the success of your policies? In June 1983 Yuri Andropov, then the Soviet leader, said that our time is

> marked by a confrontation, unprecedented in the entire post-War period by its intensity and sharpness, between two diametrically opposed world outlooks, the two political courses of Socialism and Imperialism. A struggle is going on for the minds and hearts of billions of people on our planet.

I think we can safely subscribe at least to the latter part of that analysis, as indeed President Reagan and Mrs Thatcher, the British Prime Minister, have repeatedly done. . . .

KAMPELMAN: I agree with that. . . .

URBAN: But if that is so, isn't it in the Western interest to make sure that the peoples of Eastern Europe remain unreconciled to their fate and never allow Moscow or the local régimes to feel that their rule is anything but tenuous? In that case, mightn't Madrid have done us a disservice?

KAMPELMAN: Madrid has not done that. Indeed, Madrid has said to these people—particularly with the help of the Western radio stations (and other forms of communication)—that we hold their Governments accountable for the international agreements they have signed. We have for three years systematically mentioned the names of dissidents; we have raised issues of human rights in all East European countries; we have talked about the Charter 77 group in Czechoslovakia, and so on. Let's assume that the Helsinki process broke up. How would the peoples of Eastern Europe be any better off? They wouldn't even have this forum in which we can put pressure on the Soviets on behalf of our Western principles. There wouldn't be a standard to which we could hold the Soviets and by which to measure their behaviour. I have no doubt but that the end of Helsinki would be looked upon by the peoples behind the Iron Curtain as a blow.

More than that could be dangerous. We must be extremely careful not to suggest to the peoples of Eastern Europe that we would come to their aid if they rose against their Governments. This was, no matter how mistakenly, believed by the Hungarian revolutionaries in 1956. I don't want to see a replay of that saddening and tragic experience.

I am persuaded that the Helsinki process has been directly beneficial to the cause of freedom in Eastern Europe. The *Solidarity* movement in Poland demanded, as one of its first political demands, that the Helsinki agreement be republished in all its details. *Solidarity* obviously felt that the 'Final Act' gave them a banner, a stimulus, and indispensable arguments. I wonder whether *Solidarity*, or indeed the Pope's astonishing visit, could have taken place in the absence of the Helsinki agreement or the Madrid negotiations.

It's my hope that the East Europeans will be able to go on using the Helsinki process and take some encouragement from it. There is going to be a cultural forum in Budapest (and if any country wants to raise the issue of 'cultural genocide' in the Soviet Union that is an appropriate subject). There is going to be a meeting on human rights, and another on 'the reunification of families and human contact'. There will be a fourth on 'the non-use of force'. What an opportunity all these meetings will create for not allowing these issues to disappear from the table! This year we shall have yet another meeting to commemorate the tenth anniversary of the Final Act. That too will give us a chance to keep the process alive by which the Soviet régime can continue to be held accountable.

If I felt for a single moment that by not going to the negotiating table, or not coming to an agreement, we would have been more likely to humanise or liberalise the Soviet system, I would have been for it. But since that was not the case, I felt that we had to keep putting pressure on the Kremlin until they either quit the Helsinki process because they felt it was not in their interests, or observed it more punctiliously, and experienced the sharp criticism high-lighting their irresponsible behaviour.

URBAN: Having read your speeches at the Madrid confer-ence, I was surprised that the Russians sat there. Why did they not walk out on you? In the past, milder provocations sufficed to make them remove themselves from the nego-tiating table.

KAMPELMAN: What I said undoubtedly hurt them, but there was good reason why they didn't pull out. They did not want to be held responsible, at that point and in that place, for interfering with the process of negotiations. It would have interfered with their peace propaganda against Western deployment. They would have loved to have *us* not show up or pull out.

URBAN: So both parties recognised that the propaganda stakes were high, and that even self-respect and 'face' had to take second place to the politics of missile deployment?

KAMPELMAN: Yes, but we did not have to face the problem of 'face' or self-respect; we were on the offensive and the final agreement was consistent with our approach. I am convinced that the Soviet calculations went beyond the deployment issue. In the last phases of Madrid the Soviets took it for granted that the Pershing and Cruise missiles would begin to go into place, but they have by no means given up the struggle to try to divide the United States from its Allies, reduce NATO's military standing, and generally contribute to a disorientation in Western society. They do take a long historical view of all this—and I feel we must do likewise.

URBAN: Khrushchev once told the West: 'We will bury you.' But if the Soviets keep telling us self-righteously that they will bury us, why are they so indignant when President Reagan tells them that they are an evil empire? Even the most dyed-in-the-wool Soviet Communist (and there are not many of those left in the USSR) will understand that a man who threatens to kill me or 'bury' me will hardly be seen by me as a man of goodwill. I will see him as a person bursting with unpleasant intentions.

KAMPELMAN: There is no question that President Reagan's phrase hurt them very much.

URBAN: But how do you explain why a cynical power, deeply versed in Leninist amorality, should have reacted to the President's observation with such a display of hurt innocence?

KAMPELMAN: Well, historians and other scholars have made the important point that what we are dealing with in the Soviet Union is not only a Leninist ideological component but also a Russian component, and that Russian component is the one that so desperately seeks respectability. If you withhold that respectability you administer an insult to the Soviet system as a whole.

I agree with that analysis. I have also heard academic friends of mine underline the point that Russian history is an integral part of understanding Soviet behaviour. But I don't feel this is an argument that I can harness to our purposes. If we identify Soviet society with the Russian character, Russian history, and Russian culture, it will tend to make the West believe that it's easy to deal with these Soviets because they are really just Russians following their normal national interests: you can negotiate with them as you can with any other competing nation. You sit down and bargain with them and come to an agreement.

That is the danger. The fact is, of course, that it is not— or not only—the Russian ingredient that makes it difficult for us to negotiate with the Soviets, but the Leninist ingredient.

This desperate Soviet straining for respectability is genuine, whatever its source. Many of the Russian negotiators I meet find it incomprehensible that we should accuse them of all these terrible things: they want to be regarded as a world power that commands respect.

Well, I kept telling them privately (and not infrequently in public speeches) that if they seek respectability they must act in a responsible manner. I made this point repeatedly because I know that it counts with them. I am not saying that 'respectability' is a factor that has a *decisive* influence on their behaviour; but it does have some impact, and that helps to explain their indignant reaction to President Reagan's charge that they are a focus of evil.

The Importance of Being Patient

URBAN: Some parts of your Madrid agreement strike me as quite shaming for the Soviet Union, and I am really surprised that the Soviet negotiators put their names to it. I have especially in mind provisions dealing with the freedom (such as it is) of Western journalists and embassies to perform their missions in the USSR. For example, the agreement stipulates that the signatories will 'facilitate the normal functioning of their missions'; that 'access by visitors to these missions will be assured'; that 'journalists wishing to travel for personal reasons and not for the purpose of reporting shall enjoy the same treatment as other visitors from their country of origin'; that they will 'further increase the possibilities . . . for journalists . . . to establish and maintain personal contacts and communication with their sources'; that they will, 'as a rule, authorise radio and tele-vision journalists . . . to be accompanied by their own sound and film technicians'; that 'journalists may carry with them reference material, including personal notes and files, to be used strictly for their professional purposes'. And so on.

Did the Soviet negotiators not quite realise that they were signing a document that makes it abundantly clear that Soviet society is, in fact, not a very civilised society and is unlikely, short of a democratic rebirth, ever to earn our respect?

KAMPELMAN: *Of course* it is shaming for them . . . and disgraceful . . . and humiliating for them. And I think they know it.

In our committee meetings we used many illustrations to try to tell the Soviets why all these specific provisions were necessary. I remember quoting the specific case of a Belgian journalist who, when leaving Moscow, was not allowed to take his personal papers with him.

Unquestionably they were embarrassed, but they then went back to insisting on 'non-interference in internal affairs.' For three years they experienced public humili-ations. They hated it.

URBAN: We have indeed much written evidence that they really did hate it. For example, *Izvestiya* commented (on 14 September 1983) that the American delegation was 'under-mining the process of "détente" . . . sharply cranking up the arms race . . . reviving the cold war spirit and returning to the disgraceful "position of strength" policy. . . . It is with regret that one has to recall certain forces' demagogic rhetoric about human rights.' This sounds like an obvious reference to Ambassador Kampelman. Clearly, you did hurt them.

KAMPELMAN: I confess that it was our objective. But I repeat again, we did this in the hope of modifying their behaviour, in time; and, short of that, to do battle for the 'hearts and minds' that concerned Andropov.

URBAN: But you said the Russians protested that we had no right to interfere in their 'internal affairs'.

KAMPELMAN: They used that argument, but it was totally unpersuasive. It produced in Madrid a kind of chortle running through the meeting. It had no effect.

URBAN: Would you say that perhaps the most important point about the Helsinki and Madrid documents is precisely this: that they have introduced a concept into international law whereby a great many issues that used to be regarded as 'purely internal matters' for the sovereign state have become the subject of international obligation?

KAMPELMAN: Yes, new standards have been set, and that is a fundamental departure.

URBAN: The trouble is that the Helsinki and Madrid documents are not treaties. They are non-binding, and hence their provisions are 'soft-law' provisions.

KAMPELMAN: That is true, but what we have been trying to do is to turn an unenforceable document into a document with some enforceability through accountability. In other words: we took the non-enforceable Helsinki agreement—which the Soviets did not expect to have to live up to because it was not a treaty—and put a measure of accountability into it. What is more, we have put a measure of *continuing* accountability into it by making arrangements for the various follow-up meetings. We have tried to put some soul into what was just a dummy. We are in the process of turning it into a binding document by holding states accountable for their behaviour.

What Helsinki and Madrid have done is to say: 'Peace is more than just the absence of shooting. Peace is the totality of the relationships we have written into these two documents. A country that makes war on its own people cannot be trusted not to make war on its neighbours.'

Freedom and peace are indivisible. The strength of the Madrid proceedings is that we have taken something that some said was initially in 1975 a Soviet propaganda victory, and turned it round in the way I have just described. Doing so might, as you rightly observed, risk adding to the respectability and even legitimacy of the Communist régimes. We recognised that risk, and tried to counter it. The many pluses make the Helsinki process worth preserving.

URBAN: But I can visualise these very hard, cynical people in the Politburo saying to themselves: 'Of course we will sign this document, comrades. We can sign it with impunity because we are negotiating with bourgeois innocents who believe in some independent, non-class-related code of ethics. We, on the other hand, are guided by the Leninist principle of morality, which teaches that morality is what is good for the Revolution and the Party, and that is for us to decide. . . .' Can't you see the Russian comrades chuckling to themselves while uttering some such sentiment?

KAMPELMAN: Oh, I can see that possibility, but it is an unpersuasive rationalisation.

URBAN: Assuring themselves that 'of course Madrid means nothing'?

KAMPELMAN: I am not sure that they believe it means nothing; but naturally they might say that. Our task is to see to it that it *does* mean something.

Now I don't like to build international agreements on optimistic expectations, or use hope alone as the justification of our actions in a political struggle. Nevertheless, I am sustained by the hope that at some point somebody in the Soviet system will say: 'How long can we go on being isolated in this manner? Is Leninist doctrine, justifying 'wars of liberation' and 'revolutionary terrorism', relevant to a world that has nuclear arms and is threatened by nuclear extinction?'

If we go on putting pressure on the Soviet Union, making it clear that it would be highly unprofitable for the Kremlin to challenge us, somebody might very well say: 'Our goals are better served if we relax secret-police controls and let these Helsinki monitors go free.' Or: 'We'll loosen up the stakes a bit for the sake of a better understanding with the other side', etc. This is not, mind you, an expectation—merely a faint hope; but we are looking for a crack in the hard Soviet system. We have to keep pressing before there can be any turning-point to what Euro-Communists once accepted as 'an historic compromise'.

Let me put it this way: I believe President Reagan really wants the totalitarian Soviet system to end, but not by war. The Soviets want to 'destroy the system' in the bourgeois or 'imperialist' world, and are probably willing to do so by means of war if they can prevail. On the other hand, there are large numbers of anti-Soviet critics in America and Western Europe who don't want to think about an 'end' to the Soviet system because any such notion would have war-like implications in public opinion and would be considered highly irresponsible in the nuclear age. These people tend to say: 'We don't want to destroy the Soviet system. What we ought to try to do is to get it softened or weakened or liberalised from within. So what we really have to do is to undermine its influence, contain it and deter it, humanise it, perhaps isolate it, and constantly put pressure on it in the hope that cracks may develop.'

I respect this view even though it is not symmetrical with the ideological Soviet challenge to us.

URBAN: Going down the Madrid list of trade-union rights, safeguards for religious freedom, journalists' rights and so on—which of these, would you say, are the most important?

KAMPELMAN: The most significant are the new provisions on 'free trade-unionism' because they are immediately relevant to the developments in Poland. We need to proclaim the fact that, in the Madrid document, the totalitarian Soviet leadership and the Polish military authorities had to accept the principle of free trade-unionism because of Western pressure.

The Helsinki Final Act included no statement on trade unions. The Madrid document reflects our initiative stem-

ming from the suppression of *Solidarity*. It clearly states
that the participating countries

> will ensure the right of workers freely to establish and join trade
> unions, the right of trade unions freely to exercise their activities and
> their rights as laid down in relative international instruments.

URBAN: But this right is qualified by a provision that it 'will
be exercised in compliance with the law of the State.'
Doesn't this, potentially at least, undo much of the good
stemming from the first part of that provision?

KAMPELMAN: No, because if you read the provision you
have quoted to the end there follows a further qualification,
which says that the signatories will act 'in conformity with
the State's obligations under international law.' Now this
clearly refers to the conventions of the International Labour
Organisation which guarantee the free exercise of trade-
unionism.

Furthermore, the trade-union provision of the Madrid
agreement also calls upon States to encourage direct
contacts between trade unions and their representatives.
The West—which has always made the point that unions
freely organised in the West are not to be confused with
the totalitarian State-controlled organisations known as
unions in the East—was able to insist successfully that this
provision be applicable only to such unions as are indeed
freely organised by workers and are free to function under
ILO standards.

What we should be saying in our communication with
Poland (and the rest of Eastern and Central Europe) is that
the overwhelming force of Western public opinion is so
much in support of the principle of free trade-unionism that
the Soviet and East European Governments had no way
out but to acknowledge it in writing. Obviously it would be
an illusion for us to expect that they would now scrupulously
put it into practice. But I think we have moved a step
forward in civilising the international community. This is a
plus. There is a plus to be derived from the establishment
of standards, even if those standards are being ignored for
the moment. Whether ignoring those standards will be
permanent or not depends a great deal on how seriously we
hold governments accountable for not living up to them.

URBAN: Critics, however, might say: 'It is all very well to talk about standards. But here, for example, is the old Soviet Constitution associated with the name of Stalin, and indeed the new and present one, which sets standards so high and fair (and even "liberal") that no one in Westminster or on Capitol Hill could take great exception to them. Yet they have been more honoured in the breach than the observance. Not only that, but the Soviet Union has signed peace treaties with the East and Central European countries as well as various UN instruments, all of which it has continuously violated. Why, then, should the standards set in Helsinki and Madrid fare any better?'

KAMPELMAN: And such critics would be absolutely correct in saying that the standards set by all the instruments you have quoted have been ignored. But again I ask myself and responsible commentators: What are the alternatives to establishing standards and insisting on accountability?

If you establish the standards and permit those who violate them to escape unscathed, then you can be rightly accused of cynicism. I choose to believe, however, that by introducing the element of accountability you are putting some life into those standards. The standards we are talking about are those of the last 30 or 35 post-War years. They received a dramatic impetus through the Helsinki process, which defined peace as something that must have a human ingredient incorporated in it. We have to be patient about this. I don't mean to say that we should not be dissatisfied about the *results*; but I don't want impatience to lead us to the point of saying that the standards are useless, and therefore let's decry them as a failure and eliminate the whole negotiating enterprise.

I welcome the criticisms you have quoted. We have ourselves been most critical in Madrid by pointing out 'lack of compliance'. But we concluded from the lack of compliance that we should try to inject 'accountability'. Others who pointed out the lack of compliance have come to a different conclusion—arguing that the whole Helsinki process should be rejected because there is no way of ensuring that Soviet society will ever comply with the Helsinki provisions. Why then, they said, go through the charade? I understand this argument; but, at the same time, I disagree with it. I know of no superior alternative that satisfies our political needs. Furthermore, in spite of Soviet

recalcitrance, many of the Helsinki provisions are being
lived up to in some sectors of East European societies.

But, to go back to your point about the non-observance
of standards established in international treaties and indeed
in the Soviet Constitution, let me say this. Sometimes the
difference between defeat and victory is how one defines it
for oneself. I feel that too many of us who are strong
champions of democracy tend either to be so overwhelmed
by the power of the totalitarian world, or become so discour-
aged by the imperfect way in which we are dealing with
it, that we tend to *assume* defeat. This is regrettable and
dangerous, because assuming defeat will help to make it a
reality. Defeatism is a self-fulfilling prophecy.

Can the Soviets live with Compromise?

URBAN: You have referred to the conventions of the International Labour Organisation, but do they really guarantee
free trade-unionism? The regulations of the ILO are 'soft'
and unenforceable; whereas those of the State are hard and
enforceable. Some Western sceptics now say: 'Look what
our negotiators did in Madrid. They wrote a trade-union
provision into the agreement but acknowledged at the same
time that the State's law must be respected. That means
that they have supported what the State's law says about
trade-unionism in Poland, and that in turn means that the
Poles have suffered a defeat.'

KAMPELMAN: I would say that those Western observers who
say that sort of thing are *creating* the defeat. They may not
intend to, but they are providing a gratuitous victory for the
totalitarians and especially for the Polish military régime.
If one looks at the trade-union provisions of the Madrid
agreement and says: We made it very clear that the State's
laws must be consistent with international covenants, and
this in turn is an acknowledgment of the ILO which has just
condemned the Polish military authorities, and if you add
to all that that it is not *Solidarity* that has been defeated in
the eyes of the world but a military régime in Poland—you
then give heart to your Polish friends and turn your alleged
defeat into a measure of victory.

What I am saying is that much of whether a diplomatic

move of this kind is a success or a failure depends on how we choose to interpret it. There are too many people among us who, while sharing our general convictions, simply do not understand the importance of maximising political advantage. In a sense, all one can do with an international conference which is governed by the rule of consensus is to produce ammunition—but if somebody is to take that ammunition and shoot himself with it, alas, we can't stop him.

URBAN: Then the Helsinki and Madrid agreements, if they were to be taken seriously, would invalidate (among other things) the so-called 'Brezhnev doctrine', and make nonsense of the entire concept of the division of Europe.

The preamble to the 'Final Act' includes an all-important sentence. It says that the participating States 'will respect and put into practice, each of them in its relations with all the other participating states, irrespective of their political, economic or social systems as well as of their size, geographical location or level of economic development', the principles enumerated under the various sections of the agreement. One of these reads:

> The participating States will refrain in their mutual relations in general, from the threat or use of force against the territorial integrity or political independence of any State, or in any other manner inconsistent with the purposes of the United Nations and with the present Declaration. No consideration may be invoked to serve to warrant resort to the threat or use of force in contravention of this principle.
>
> Accordingly, the participating States will refrain from any acts constituting a threat of force or direct or indirect use of force against another participating State. Likewise they will refrain from any manifestation of force for the purpose of inducing another participating State to renounce the full exercise of its sovereign rights. Likewise they will also refrain in their mutual relations from any act of reprisal by force.
>
> No such threat or use of force will be employed as a means of settling disputes, or questions likely to give rise to disputes between them.

KAMPELMAN: Yes, the whole concept of 'Yalta' with its spheres of influence is invalidated by Helsinki because it looks upon every signatory as a sovereign State and it does not recognise 'blocs'. It rules out any spheres of influence. That is why the French, the Yugoslavs and the Americans said in Madrid that Yalta was directly contrary to the 'Final Act', and that Helsinki demolishes, on the principles just quoted, the Brezhnev doctrine. That should be highlighted by Western observers and analysts. To suggest the contrary, as some critics have mistakenly done, is particularly damaging because it enables the Soviet leaders to say: 'You see, even Western observers concede that Hensinki is the recognition of our sphere of influence in Eastern Europe!' People on our Western side who make these observations just do not understand the adverse implications.

URBAN: But what about the point that the Helsinki agreement legitimises the post-War frontiers of Europe and is a surrogate peace treaty?

KAMPELMAN: There appears to be a widespread assumption that this is so; but it isn't. Europe's post-War order was tacitly accepted much before the Helsinki agreement in 1975. The first proposal for a 'security conference' was made by Brezhnev in 1969. He was looking for a substitute for a peace treaty, but he had already by 1975 accomplished that goal in the Austrian *Staatsvertrag* and the various German treaties. Indeed, I saw a study the other day indicating that, after they had signed the German treaties, the Russians began to wonder whether they needed to go through with 'the Helsinki process' at all. They then conducted a serious debate as to whether they had to pay a price in terms of Human-Rights-in-'Basket-3' for something that they already had in hand. But the process had begun, and they felt they could turn it to their advantage. And this is what they have tried to do. They simply turned around and said: 'We have a provision here on "the inviolability of frontiers" that can only be changed by peaceful means—and that is a legalisation of our boundaries.' It is no such thing.

Of course, in Madrid, we didn't let them get away with it. They tried but we refuted their position. The US, for example, raised the Baltic issue again.

I have spent my life in political struggles, and I'm not interested in 'going down to defeat gloriously' so that I can be registered as some kind of martyr. Put simply and candidly, I want to win these battles. We have a formidable opponent; he must be contained and deterred. If you start out with a sense of defeatism you will be defeated. I feel a sense of optimism about the Helsinki process, and that is why I am not prepared to assume that the process itself is a Soviet accomplishment. It has been a Western victory, and the document reflects Western values.

URBAN: How difficult was it to get the Soviet side to accept some of the stipulations that you were anxious to get into the Madrid agreement? Take the trade-union provision— how did the Polish representatives react?

KAMPELMAN: They explained to us time and again that under no circumstances could they accept the provision because it would mean strengthening *Solidarity*. They realised why we were pushing, and said 'Absolutely no.'

But then they suddenly gave in. Why? Because, I'm convinced, we were adamant and used pointed arguments. Let me tell you this: There are 10 to 15 provisions in the Madrid agreement to which the totalitarians first said 'Absolutely no', and meant it. They didn't say it only to us—they said it to the neutrals too, and persuaded the neutrals that what we demanded was quite impossible to achieve. They went about explaining their refusal in very logical terms: 'How could you expect us to do something that runs directly counter to our system? Do you think the Helsinki agreement was meant to be a war against our system?' And so on. But then, lo and behold! they went ahead and accepted our formulations when they felt it necessary to do so in the face of Western unity.

URBAN: But, frankly, if the Helsinki agreement *were* to be scrupulously put into effect—wouldn't that mean in effect dismantling the entire Soviet system?

KAMPELMAN: In the short term, it would change the system in dramatic ways, but would not 'destroy' it. It would not necessarily do away with the supremacy of the Communist Party or central economic planning. It does not destroy their system to permit families to unite by emigration or move freely, or to release those political prisoners now behind bars or in psychiatric hospitals. Nevertheless, you are probably right in suggesting that their leaders are afraid that if the human-rights provisions of 'Basket 3' were properly complied with, then, after a ten-year period, they might have a very different social order. The challenge is whether the Soviet authorities will try to find a way to live with their commitments. They should begin the preparation to meet this challenge because the repression cannot last for ever. They must one day move to make that 'Historic Compromise'.

URBAN: Could they, for example, live with Point 8 of the 'Guiding Principles' of the Helsinki agreement, which provides for the equal rights and self-determination of all peoples?

> By virtue of the principle of equal rights and self-determination of peoples, all peoples always have the right, in full freedom to determine, when and as they wish, their internal and external political status, without external interference and to pursue as they wish their political, economic, social and cultural development.

If the various nations and smaller ethnic groups living in the Soviet Union were really given a chance to avail themselves of these provisions, the transformation of the Soviet State as we know it would probably not be too long in coming. But the chances of this happening are, shall we say, rather modest. After all, the Soviet Constitution makes similar provisions, including the right to secede from the USSR.

KAMPELMAN: My point is that we should not be silent about the provisions we have written into the Helsinki agreement. We should proclaim them in our public statements and broadcasts loud and clear, instead of simply saying: 'Oh, the Soviets just can't be expected to live up to this.' If they can't, this is their worry, not ours. They freely signed the agreements.

Our job is to tell the world that the Soviet authorities felt obliged to accept our provisions on human rights and the self-determination of peoples, and exploit these provisions to maximum effect in our public diplomacy. And if the Soviets are hypocritical about these provisions, then let this be manifest.

You see, nobody *forced* them to negotiate and finally sign the Helsinki document. What is clear is that it makes no sense to abandon a process that gives the West this signal libertarian advantage.

URBAN: How did the representatives of 'Solidarity' abroad, and indeed the Baltic exiles, react?

KAMPELMAN: They have, as far as I know, been saying that Madrid for them has been extremely helpful. This is what they have told me. In Washington we had a meeting of a Congressional Commission which citizen groups, including those from the Baltic groups in the USA, attended. The unanimous view which emerged was that the negotiations had struck a blow for freedom. The Latvians, Lithuanians and Estonians all felt that 'the Madrid process' should be preserved because it gave their peoples some hope.

URBAN: I've been struck by some of the language used in the Madrid document. Many of the words are 'weasel-words'. Civil Servants call it 'rubber language' because you can stretch it any way you like. This goes, of course, for Helsinki as much as for Madrid. Perhaps some examples are worth quoting.

The signatories will *'further strengthen'*; they *'declare their intention to'*; *'express their willingness'*; *'recognise the value of'*; *'agree to encourage'*; *'will consider the possibility offered by'*; *'will favourably deal with'*; *'declare their intention to consider'*; *'foster cooperation'*; *'favour the study of'*; *'favour the further expansion of'*, and so on.

Let me make two comments. First, formulations of this sort can mean anything or nothing. Incorporated as they are in a non-binding agreement, they seem to me to be not worth a great deal more than the paper they are written on.

Second, there is a case for saying that no Western democracy *can* make binding commitments in a document of this sort. I would argue that the vast majority of activities involved in the Helsinki process—the publishing of newspapers and books; educational ties; scientific cooperation; tourism, etc.—occur, on our side of the fence, in the private sphere and can therefore not be subject to the force of international agreements without a lot of controversial domestic legislation. That is why *we* have to use 'rubber language'.

But I would go on to argue that the use of this 'flexi-language' implies that Soviet society is like our own; that it, too, can only 'encourage' some theatre or other to perform a play, or 'recognise the value of' expanding tourism, etc. And we know, of course, that this is far from being true, because the USSR is a totalitarian society; what the Party-State says, goes. So the 'weasel-words' written into the agreement carry two dangers: first, they probably mean nothing; second, if they do mean anything, it is likely to be detrimental to us because they appear to put Soviet society on a par with our own.

KAMPELMAN: I thoroughly disagree that the words you quote are worthless. I do not understand the criticism. They do provide meaning, particularly as we put meat on the bones. The language and provisions reflect the fact that only words agreed by all could be incorporated. If we could have taken a vote where a majority of 27 to 8 emerged, the language would have been different. But it *had* to be a vote of 35 to zero. That being the case, we were looking for some forward movement in *our* direction. We had no illusions that we could do more than that, and that was what we achieved. We were trying (to use the term once again) to *establish standards* in our general attempt to civilise and humanise the totalitarian camp. The clarity of the language we obtained is therefore, in my view, particularly noteworthy and important.

Let me give you an example. The Helsinki 'Final Act' stated under Principle 7 that the participating States *'confirm the right of the individual to know and act upon his rights and duties in this field.'* Now, as we know, the Soviet authorities violated this provision by arresting and imprisoning the 'Helsinki monitors'. Our problem in Madrid was how to move forward from this position; how to make it technically more difficult for the Soviets to keep these monitors in prison and for them to make further arrests of this sort in the future. We could have tried to move forward by saying in our suggested text that: *'The Helsinki monitoring group shall be legal.'* But this wouldn't have worked.

Therefore, we decided to reformulate the Helsinki text in the following manner. The participating States

> recall the right of the individual to know and act upon his rights and duties in the field of human rights and fundamental freedoms, as embodied in the Final Act, and will take the necessary action in their respective countries to effectively ensure this right.

The new and significant part is that the States 'will take the necessary action. . . .'

This adds a requirement. Needless to say, it is not foolproof and cannot force compliance, but it tightens the vice.

There is also an additional reason why it would probably have been counter-productive for us to insist that the Helsinki monitors shall be recognised as legal. A suggestion of that sort was in fact made; and it was specifically proposed that our formulation should make it mandatory for the Helsinki monitoring group to attend the next follow-up meeting. I opposed it because I could see the Soviet Union establishing an *official* Helsinki monitoring group of its own, sending it to Vienna, and feeding us disinformation.

The Give-and-Take of Diplomacy

URBAN: We are back at our original problem. Can we negotiate with a global superpower whose words we cannot trust, whose entire ideology lifts amorality to the level of principle, and whose very reading of human nature and man's destiny is entirely different from our own?

KAMPELMAN: Our discussion boils down to a simple point. How does the free world counteract the Soviet political philosophy and undermine its strength, short of using violence? Is diplomacy a usable vehicle, or should diplomacy be out of bounds because it (theoretically) provides 'legitimacy'? That's the essence of the question. To cite one example: do we sign a treaty banning bacteriological weapons with the Soviet Union when we know perfectly well that the Soviets used chemical and bacteriological weapons in Afghanistan?

URBAN: If you were really putting that question to me, my answer would run along the following lines. Naturally we have to use diplomacy as a means, but we have to use it as only one of several weapons—as the Soviets do. The Soviet Union employs every conceivable pressure and influence— whether legal, illegal or directly subversive—to undermine the unity of the Western Alliance and soften the cohesion of our societies. *We* are not offering a counter-challenge on the same wide scale. We know how to wield the weapons of diplomacy reasonably well, but when it comes to information policy and political warfare we are less well equipped to do to the Soviet Union what it is doing to us. The reasons why this is so are well known, but the fact remains that we are at a disadvantage.

KAMPELMAN: I would like the West to be as good at *all* the things you mention as the Soviets are, if not better than they are. But I would not feel defeatist about the fact that

I cannot be 'as good as they are' at subversion, for example, because democracies just cannot use the same methods as dictatorships do, at any rate in time of peace. What helps us to restore the balance (and, as I strongly believe, more than restore the balance) is that we have a much better case, and our populations are much more loyal to decisions taken by our Governments than are those of the totalitarian régimes, especially at a time of crisis.

In any case, Allied unity in Madrid was quite conspicuous. For example, to mention the real, full names of victims of Soviet repression is, in my view essential. Whereas in 1977 (in Belgrade) the United States was the only country to mention the names of victims, in Madrid fourteen countries did so. Using this minor criterion, we have improved our solidarity fourteen-fold since Belgrade; and I hope we shall continue to do so.

URBAN: Did the Soviet negotiators say to you at any time: 'Why do you use this strong rhetoric? Why do you lambaste us every week? How can we negotiate an agreement with critics who insult our system and question our credibility?'

KAMPELMAN: Oh, yes—this was one of their recurrent themes. In private conversation, too, they would often say: 'Why do you let a few criminals stand in the way of peace between us? We don't want to fight a war with you, we want peace—yet you constantly raise the cases of these criminals and turn them into heroes.' They were referring to the dissidents and human-rights monitors, of course.

URBAN: Did you at any time suggest to them: 'If I didn't make these strong speeches I could never come to any kind of agreement with you because, given the atmosphere in Washington, strong words are the pre-condition of compromise. If your President wants a summit meeting with mine, you'll have to put up with our charges and critical observations . . . and then come to terms with us.'

KAMPELMAN: I never said anything of the sort because that would have minimised the genuineness and seriousness of our feelings. I did not make those speeches just for domestic political considerations. I made them because they accurately reflected our concerns. True, I was engaged in political competition for 'Heart and Minds' against the

Soviets, but I meant every word I spoke. Let me share an incident with you.

During the first few weeks of the Madrid meeting, I had asked some of our staff experts to put together some material on Soviet anti-Semitism. I then suggested to Judge Griffin Bell, who was my co-chairman, that he prepare a speech on the subject and deliver it to the conference.

I thought that a speech on anti-Semitism would be more effective coming from a Baptist than a Jew. Judge Bell was perfectly happy to do so; but the night before he was due to deliver it he called me to say that he was unexpectedly required to return to the United States and could not make the presentation. He suggested that I make it instead. I might have done so had it not been for the fact that I would have wanted a different kind of speech if I were to deliver it.

So I went to see one of the Soviet delegates with the text of the speech in my hand and said to him: 'We are going to deliver this speech today on Soviet anti-Semitism. But we will not deliver it at our formal meeting. Let me remind you that you have been telling me over and over again that we tend not to get results because we publicise our criticisms. All right; I am delivering the text of the speech to you rather than to the meeting. Send this to Moscow, and tell your superiors that we regard this as a test case—I will not make this speech, but will that produce some action? I will inform the State Department what I am doing; and if you can show us that as a result of this private diplomacy we can get results, then you have taught me something. . . .'

URBAN: And did you get any results?

KAMPELMAN: The Soviet delegate seemed to be appreciative. He took the text and said he would deliver it to Moscow. The Kremlin then apparently completely ignored our initiative. For about a year nothing was said; but a year later I made a fully documented and rather sharp statement about Soviet anti-Semitism, and it had, I know, a dramatic impact on the meeting.

When the Soviet delegate, white-faced, complained, I reminded him that I had given him an opportunity to demonstrate that private diplomacy could work where public rhetoric might not.

'Clearly it does not work,' I said. 'So we have to conclude
that all your exhortations that honey will get us more than
vinegar are so many empty words.' We had publicly
mentioned about 130 names of Soviet dissidents. I later
said to the Soviet delegate: 'Can you show me that those
thousands we have *not* mentioned are getting out of
jail. . . .'

I don't believe at all that quiet diplomacy is more likely
to achieve results with the Soviet Union than public outrage.
The Soviet leaders respond only to their perceived 'national
self-interest'.

To return to your original point, I could not have (as you
suggested) legitimately said to the Soviet delegation: 'We
have to use strong words to provide a political atmosphere
which makes an agreement possible.' It was for quite
another reason. The United States took the position from
the very beginning that we would be just as happy with an
agreement to *disagree*. What we did want to do was to
preserve 'the Helsinki process' by having a series of follow-
up meetings. . . .

Urban: What about domestic political considerations?

Kampelman: Was any of this intended to have any influence
on the 1984 elections? Not at all. Let me point out to you
that the Madrid conference evoked very little attention and
had very little coverage in the United States. Nevertheless,
your question is relevant.

I remember the Soviet delegates at one of our meetings
criticising me for holding press conferences. They alleged
that I was violating 'the rules of confidentiality'. Closed
meetings, they said, were closed meetings precisely because
we didn't want to have all the difficulties that publicity
entails. I at once responded by saying that my reason for
speaking to the press every time I spoke to the meeting was
because I represented a democratic society. The people
I represent, I explained, had a right to know what their
Ambassador was saying. I did not, however, use the press
conferences to divulge what position any other delegation
had been taking; I only reported what *I* had said.

Now that was, in a way, reflecting an American domestic
concern. But the main thrust of our articulations was to get
behind the Iron Curtain, to give heart to the dissidents, and
to influence Western public opinion in the missile debate.

URBAN: The US Presidential elections did not, then, weigh heavily with you?

KAMPELMAN: No. I am a Democrat, originally appointed by President Carter, and reappointed by President Reagan. I did not look upon my role as that of helping to re-elect President Reagan, just as I did not see my role in 1980 as that of helping to re-elect President Carter. That was not my job. My strength in Madrid was that I represented both Democrats *and* Republicans, a broad American consensus.

And I don't really think the President was motivated by domestic politics when he endorsed the Madrid formula. Madrid was a very small issue in American politics, and in any case mine was a bipartisan appointment. Indeed, one source of great strength in dealing with the Soviets was the fact that I was a Hubert Humphrey Democrat now representing a Republican Administration. I was able to say to the Russians: 'You must understand that this is an *American* position and not a Republican or a Democratic position. Personally I speak as a Democrat, but our commitment to the values I represent is a universal American commitment, not a political party commitment.'

One illustration. A group of Democratic Senators, six in all, were *en route* to call upon Andropov; and on their way to Moscow I met with some of them. I made a point of urging upon them that they must never allow the Soviets to feel that the American human rights commitment is a 'Reagan commitment'. The Soviets must never be allowed to run away with the idea that they would be 'off the hook' if the next Presidential elections produced a Democratic President.

URBAN: Could you, in your private discussions with the Soviet negotiators in Madrid, garner any special insights into the workings of the Soviet mind?

KAMPELMAN: Yes, let me give you an example. Some time ago I had a luncheon meeting on the subject of dissidents with leaders of the Soviet delegation. They took the usual Soviet line: 'Why-do-you-let-these-criminals-stand-in-the-way-of-peace-between-us?', etc. I decided to respond seriously, and carefully explained that human rights happened to be of very great importance in the United States. I tried to show them what we mean by human rights, and how we attempt to translate them into meaningful individual rights. Their head-of-delegation decided to reply in like-minded terms, and proceeded to talk about the Marxist-Leninist view of human rights—the class angle, the right-to-a-good-job, adequate health care, a comfortable old-age pension, and all the rest.

I listened to him patiently, and instead of arguing with him about this (which I had done at the plenary meeting) I said: 'Surely you don't believe any of this yourself?'

'Ah, but I certainly do! Why do you think I don't?'

'Because if you believed it you wouldn't be so adamantly opposed to our idea that an experts' meeting on human rights should be called after this conference. If you believed what you are saying you would vote for that meeting and present your full views there. Clearly you have no confidence that you have any kind of persuasive position to present. . . .'

Well, shortly thereafter, I was told by a member of the Soviet delegation that Moscow would in time agree to an experts' conference on human rights; and in fact it did.

URBAN: Still, one of the persistent problems in talking to the Russian people is that the Western notion of human rights does not make much sense to them. Some of this incomprehension appears to be rooted in Russian culture and history. Distinguished dissidents like Andrei Amalrik and Alexander Zinoviev have repeatedly told us in their books and articles that ideas such as 'individual liberty . . . human dignity . . . human rights' have only a weak, and in some cases a perverse, meaning in Soviet/Russian psychology and usage. Did you run into this semantic problem in your negotiations?

KAMPELMAN: One of the principal problems in dealing with the Soviet leadership is that they simply don't know what the rest of the world is like and have, therefore, no standards for making comparisons. However, our Western broadcasts are getting through to the people, and the audiences are learning.

I am not convinced that in this discourse (human rights, human dignity) there is so large a semantic gap between us that our ideas are forever destined to remain alien to them. I feel that there is something within every human being that strives for a measure of freedom and a measure of mutual respect. One guarantee that this is so is the continuing influence of Christianity. Another is the heritage of 19th-century Russian socialism and its great interest in French and German thought. Russia was gripped by a tremendous move for a form of democratic socialism much before the Bolsheviks came to power or were even present on the scene. Remember too that the original appeal of the Bolsheviks was also an appeal to justice and human dignity.

I suspect that this heritage and its contemporary restatement are still powder-kegs for the Soviet system. We are not, after all, dealing with people living in some primitive jungle who have had no exposure to the cultures of developed societies. We are dealing with a social order which is at least beginning to find out what the rest of the world is like. A controlled culture and totalitarian government can, for a time, choke off man's strivings; but these are never suppressed for long. I am confident that in the Soviet Union, too, these elementary human impulses are alive even though they may be hidden. I do not believe that the Russian character is *intrinsically* slavish, servile, or totalitarian.

During World War II, impressive historical and cultural analyses were made of 'the *German* character', from Luther to Hitler. They were near unanimous in showing that it was totalitarian. This was, of course, balderdash. The history of the German Federal Republic is the most eloquent proof that it was arrant nonsense. We must be careful not to make any similar generalisations about the Russians.

URBAN: May I sum up this conversation by saying that the Western world should, in your view, take on the Soviet Union at every level of political engagement except the level of military warfare, in the certain confidence that the West can prove to be at all levels more incisive, effective, and generally superior?

KAMPELMAN: Yes, we must be prepared to confront their challenges at every level: at the level of military preparedness, propaganda, diplomacy, social and economic programmes, political warfare, and indeed at the level of searching for peace. I don't want to abdicate any of these competitive fields to the Soviet Union.

At the same time it is essential for us to examine our interests independently. I don't think we should feel that because the Soviets are prepared to do *A* and *B*, *A* and *B* must, by definition, be contrary to our interests. There is a curious erratic tendency to say just that. For example, it has been said that, because the Soviet Union wanted us to enter the Second World War, *therefore* it was bad for us to enter the Second World War. We have to be very careful about this sort of contrariness.

I do not want to denigrate the position of those critics whom you have been citing. I must, however, say that I cannot accept their view. I do not shy away from the word 'confrontation'. But we seek understanding and peace. The Soviets feel that they are insulting us when they accuse us of being 'confrontational'. Let us openly say that we are prepared to be 'confrontational' if that is necessary to advance our values and interests, and our faith in maintaining peace through containment and deterrence. I want to confront them wherever I can, because their system is obviously hostile and dangerous. But I hope the Western world will now begin to analyse *how* best it can conduct the struggle in the '80s and '90s.

The first rule of winning any battle is to know the kind of threats, dangers, and provocations you are up against. I feel that in Madrid we made great strides in grasping the character of the Soviet system. I was talking to Jeane Kirkpatrick the other day, and I asked her: 'How do you address this whole problem of negotiating with the Soviet Union? Putting aside the military aspects (because we know well enough that military preparedness is essential), how do we engage the Soviet system?' 'Well,' she said, 'the first thing is correctly to identify the enemy.' I agree with that, and I think we are doing it. But is that enough?

Surely we must also see to it that we identify ourselves with the aspirations of the general public in the Western world, and their aspirations for security and peace. We must never be taken to be 'working for war' or 'provoking crises' which might lead to war. People want and expect civilised diplomacy and realistic negotiations. We have the difficult task of making sure that such diplomacy is not identified with capitulation—a delicate task, because negotiation means give-and-take. We can take comfort from the fact that in certain East–West agreements, and in the Madrid negotiations especially, we have taken a great deal more than we have given.

1984

2.   ALEXANDER ZINOVIEV
Why the Soviet system is here to stay

Only Insiders Understand

URBAN: You have challenged in your books and lectures virtually all Western interpretations of the Soviet system, offering a variety of arguments to show where they went wrong and why they proved inadequate. Your most spectacular challenge, however, is not to any particular scholarly reading of Soviet society, but to the Western observer's generic (as it were) ability to understand the Soviet system at all. Again and again you insist that, no matter how well a Western scholar may have immersed himself in Soviet history and ideology, no matter how sharp his wit or fertile his historical imagination, the Soviet system will for ever remain a closed book to him. To understand it and deal with it, you suggest, one has to be 'part' of the Soviet system. Only 'from inside' will it yield the necessary clues to truthful analysis.

ZINOVIEV: The terms of reference appropriate for the understanding of Western society are inadequate when it comes to analysing other types of society. A scholar using a Western conceptual framework may find it very difficult to make sense of Indian society in the 12th century, or Chinese society 500 years B.C. Soviet society, I contend, is basically different from Western society. Trying to understand it with any chance of success presupposes a specific conceptual framework, fresh mental models, and a new vocabulary. In other words, it postulates an entirely new theory and methodology.

Let me make this clear by giving you some examples.

Take the word '*party*'. On the face of it, the Communist Party of the Soviet Union is a 'party'. So is the Social Democratic Party in Germany or the Conservative Party in Britain. Yet the two are fundamentally different phenomena. The CPSU is not a 'party' in any Western sense of the word. It is not a political phenomenon. It is the motor and overseer of the ruling system. Nor can we say that the Soviet system is a '*political*' phenomenon.

URBAN: Not a political phenomenon?

ZINOVIEV: No. Communist society is not a political phenomenon, because 'politics', as that word is understood outside the Soviet Union, does not exist there. Politics, for a simple definition, may be described as a web of contentious relationships between largely independent actors for a slice of power or the whole of state power. The Communist Parties of Western Europe *are* political parties, at least while they are in opposition. It is also true to say that the relations of the USSR with the outside world are political relations. But once a Communist Party takes power, its political character is dissipated and the party assumes a social character. It restructures the whole of society, eliminating the very notion of any struggle for power or any possibility of independent forces arising (or surviving) to conduct such a struggle.

Now, it is for me axiomatic that for any scientific understanding of social phenomena to be possible you have to place yourself inside the society you are investigating. You have to identify with the conditions obtaining in it and adopt its terms of reference. What is more, you have to go back to its smallest unit and deduce your conclusions from what you have found there. A self-contained feudal estate or a capitalist unit of production is the only true nucleus for understanding feudal or capitalist society. The same goes for the Soviet system. You must understand its basic unit— the autonomous 'collective', which may be a working group in a university, a farming community, a school or whatever—before you can say anything useful about the Soviet system. And that, as I say, requires inside knowledge, a new set of conceptual tools, and a new vocabulary.

URBAN: I am a little unhappy about the idea that you have to possess 'inside knowledge' in order to understand Soviet reality. It is a claim which has been made in too many bad causes to be acceptable without further explanation. Nazi ideologists claimed that the special spirituality that made the German people ripe for a National-Socialist renewal was inaccessible to the minds of non-Germans. Similar claims were made by the Italian Fascists and a great many other prophets and defenders of the alleged uniqueness of this-or-that social order or 'national psyche'.

Nor does your emphasis on 'inside knowledge' quite accord with your claim that you are seeking a strictly scientific understanding of Soviet society. A chemist or physicist who claimed that his theory could only be understood and tested by dark-haired males, 179 centimetres tall, born in the village of Cuckfield in the year 1947 would be given short shrift by his colleagues.

ZINOVIEV: Your analogies do not stand. Communism is a new type of society, because it has fundamentally changed the character of social relations. Fascism and Nazism did not do that. Those were political régimes of a certain kind, but not new types of societies. It is therefore perfectly possible for, say, a British capitalist scholar to understand the nature of Italian Fascism without any special empathy; but he cannot, as long as he remains an outsider, understand Communist society.

URBAN: But you have said that 'political' society requires several independent actors vying with one another for political power. Now, in Hitler's National-Socialist society, or in Italy under Mussolini, there were no such independent actors. The Nazi and to a lesser degree the Fascist Parties were the motors and overseers of everything that went on in the state, exactly as the Communist Party is in the Soviet Union. No opposition was tolerated.

Why, then, do you say that Nazism and Fascism were 'political régimes' rather than societies comparable in many ways to Soviet Communism? What you appear to be clearly implying is the orthodox Soviet position: that Capitalism, Nazism, and Fascism belong, so to speak, to the same species, whereas Communism does not. The view in the West is, of course, the opposite. Many believe that Communist society, Nazi society, and Fascist society have much more in common with one another, precisely because they are One-Party totalitarian systems, than any of them has with, say, British parliamentary democracy or the French republic.

ZINOVIEV: Fascism was a 'political' phenomenon, even though it was a single-party phenomenon, because it did not involve the structural overhaul of society. It did not lead to a fundamental reorganisation of social relations despite the egalitarian, anti-aristocratic tendencies which were undeniably present in both the German and Italian variety. . . .

URBAN: . . . an old Soviet cliché! (if I may interrupt you for a moment). . . .

ZINOVIEV: Every society, whether ancient or modern, can only be understood within its own terms of reference. Our tools of analysis which are appropriate for the comprehension of ancient Egypt are not appropriate for the comprehension of feudal society in, shall we say, France in the 13th century. That is all I am saying.

Soviet society, too, demands a specific approach and a specific language, because it has brought about a qualitative transformation in the whole of society. I base my insistence on the need to understand Soviet society from within on certain post-Kantian and post-Hegelian ideas which stress the importance of identifying with the objects of your observation before comparing them with other phenomena or imposing value-judgments on them.

URBAN: No doubt you are thinking of Dilthey and his notion of 'Verstehen' . . .

ZINOVIEV: Yes, among others. We must first understand from within the basic cell of Soviet society—the autonomous community, or collective. Having done that, we must try to identify the laws that govern its interaction with other cells. We do, of course, start with those most easily identified and then proceed only gradually to the more complicated ones. The essential rule to remember is that we must not be sidetracked into premature comparisons. We must anchor our thinking in the basic characteristics of the Soviet system as self-contained, immanent phenomena. Having done that, we can at a later stage make historical comparisons with Fascist Italy, or whatever.

URBAN: I take your point. But why do you contend that a competent scholar in France or the USA cannot summon sufficient intellectual or imaginative power to get within the skin of the Soviet system? One of the very best histories of English literature was written by two Frenchmen (Legouis and Cazamian). Is it reasonable to claim that scholars like George Kennan, Merle Fainsod, Leonard Schapiro and Ronald Hingley have shown themselves incapable of making the intellectual-imaginative leap?

ZINOVIEV: The Soviet system is *sui generis*. It is extremely difficult to understand, even for people who have been born and bred in it. Please bear in mind that the time-lag between physical or social phenomena and the scientific under-standing of these phenomena can be unconscionably long. People existed for millions of years without understanding the nature of gravitation. Newtonian mechanics are a very recent discovery, and Einstein's relativity theory is even more recent. Capitalist society had existed for many centuries, but it was only in the 19th century that social science began to decipher the structure and describe the regularities of capitalist society. Communist society is very young indeed. Its whole history spans a mere 67 years. It is, therefore, difficult to take it in from the outside. Moreover, Western scholars approach it with their own educational background, their own values and mental models. All of this makes for distortions and incomprehension.

Consider, by contrast, my own fitness to comprehend Soviet reality. I was born in the Soviet system a few years after the October Revolution. I went to Soviet schools and universities and served in the Red Air Force during the War. I spent 30 years of my life studying Soviet society, designing my own logic and method to make that study profitable. I am probably the only man in the world who has developed his own sociological framework for the comprehension of Soviet society based on the experience of having lived in that society, met people at every rung of the social ladder—for several years I worked in a factory—and watched their mobility horizontally and vertically.

URBAN: And how would you summarise your theory?

ZINOVIEV: I do not claim that I have produced a complete and testable theory. I have merely laid the foundations of what might, in perhaps two or three centuries, be an overall scientific theory with a descriptive and prescriptive potential. An outline of my theory is given in my book *The Reality of Communism*.

URBAN: No doubt you will, nevertheless, want to give me some skeletal indication of your hypothesis as we go along. Let me, in the meantime, underline my unease at hearing you say that in order to comprehend and deal with Soviet society you have to be a part of it. I'm reminded of the absurd criminological argument that no judge who has not himself committed murder has the right to pass sentence on a murderer, because he cannot possibly identify with the psychological predicaments that turn a law-abiding citizen to homicide. A rough and ready analogy, you may well say; but it makes my point.

ZINOVIEV: Communist society is an empirical fact. Scientific investigation requires that we observe empirical facts for what they are. In Soviet society these can only be experienced from within.

URBAN: You are saying that they are not accessible to Western scholarship . . . that Western scholars cannot, because of the remoteness of their point of observation, write authentically about Soviet society.

ZINOVIEV: Perhaps they can—but so far they have not done so. Take, for example, the favourite Western reading of Soviet society, which comes direct from Solzhenitsyn— namely that the Soviet people regard the Party and Government as an alien system which they hate and are anxious to overthrow. It just does not correspond to the facts.

URBAN: Is Solzhenitsyn, in your view, entirely wrong in saying what he does . . . and what many Western observers have also been saying quite independently from and well before him?

ZINOVIEV: Of course he is.

URBAN: What, then, are the real facts, as you see them, about the Soviet people's attitude to the Communist system? Do they support the system as one of their own choosing?

ZINOVIEV: It is not for me to make political judgments of

that sort. Certainly, the system is accepted. My job as a scientist is to describe the system and make sense of it. If you want to find out how the Soviet people really relate to the Party and Government, you have to examine the structure of Soviet society; and that is what I have done.

I describe and analyse the empirical facts as I find them. Take a primary social group, a cell, for your starting point; and let your particular example be a scientific institute. You'll find that this primary group is itself an extremely complicated phenomenon. It'll have a director, assisted by a deputy director, and a group of senior collaborators. The institute will be divided into, let's say, five departments. Each of these will fall into several sub-groups, each with its own leader, staff, Party secretary and other functionaries. Furthermore, you will find that numbers will put certain restrictions on the effectiveness of each group. If your whole staff runs to one hundred, you will probably need ten groups to make the division of work, control, and leadership manageable. If several major groups cooperate for the attainment of some social or productive achievement, you will find that control retreats to small cabals within each group; and eventually a hierarchy of élites will come into existence, with specific characteristics and laws governing their relationship. These laws are tricky to determine, but they exist.

URBAN: What you are implying, I think, is that, far from Solzhenitsyn being right, the structure of Soviet society is in reality in substantial harmony with the wishes and mentality of the Soviet people.

ZINOVIEV: No. It is not a question of people's wishes but of social laws. The structures and correlations I observe do not depend on the human characteristics of the participants. The correlations I establish have the force of natural laws. They apply to every people and to any number of people—everywhere.

URBAN: You mean all Communist societies of the Soviet type?

ZINOVIEV: Yes, they apply wherever private property has been abolished and both industry and agriculture have been nationalised. Wherever these conditions really obtain, social structures identical with those we find in the USSR will inevitably come into being.

URBAN: A universal law?

ZINOVIEV: Yes—all laws of Communist society are universal laws, wherever Communism is reality.

URBAN: Are you comfortable with so Stalinoid an assertion?

ZINOVIEV: I am and have always been an anti-Stalinist. You know that. But I make this statement not as a Stalinist or anti-Stalinist, but as a scientist relying for my conclusions on empirical evidence.

URBAN: Whatever its scientific truth, I'm a little wary of your 'universal law', because Stalin's tyranny over East-Central Europe and his claim to the leadership of the world Communist movement were based on the assertion that the Soviet model of Communism was a universal model for Socialist/Communist societies. This entitles us to handle your 'law' with a measure of caution.

ZINOVIEV: The laws of Communism as expressed in Soviet society are universal laws, but their application and the results springing from them may vary. If you compare Communism as it is actually practised in the Ukraine, Georgia, and Russia you will find great differences. Indeed, Georgian Communism is more distant from the Muscovite variety than, shall we say, Polish Communism; and it stands to reason that the differences are explained by climate, national history, and other characteristics peculiar to a nation or a region. But if you disregard the accretions and consider Communist society in its pure, if you like, labora-tory condition, the laws of Communism will be seen to be valid at all times and everywhere. This does not invalidate the fact that life for the ordinary man is much better in Georgia than in Russia, or that a Hungarian is substantially better off in terms of housing, food supplies, culture and so on, than his opposite number in Czechoslovakia. But if you compare the organisation of a factory in Georgia, Czecho-slovakia, Hungary and Russia, you will find that they are structurally identical and that the social relations they generate are identical too.

URBAN: You seem to be stressing the importance of an abstraction: that under laboratory conditions Communism would assume identical forms wherever it was applied. To most of us, however, this abstraction is not very important, because we know well enough that, as long as society is made up of human beings (rather than robots or genetically engineered hominids), laboratory conditions will never be obtained. The human element will always intrude—diluting, corrupting, and rendering ridiculous any 'pure' form of Communism. Even Mao's abhorrently pure form of social engineering, the 'Cultural Revolution', did not escape that fate.

Personally I would put the emphasis on what you have said about Hungary, where food is plentiful, housing is (by Communist standards) in tolerable supply, culture is freer than in any other Communist country, and even some foreign travel is permitted. But these gains are due not, as you suggest, to national characteristics being imposed on Communist social structures (though Magyar know-how and sophistication do play a role)—but to the Hungarians' quiet determination to amend the Soviet book, revise the Soviet 'laws', and indeed turn their backs on both without openly saying so. And as my concern, and I take it your concern, is the welfare and happiness of the maximum number of men and women, and not the realisation of an abstract form of seamless Communism, I applaud the Hungarian experiment because it seems to me to be proof that the key to the success of Communism is—the *abandonment* of Communism.

ZINOVIEV: Naturally, if you take human society in the round, you have to take into account and allow for an almost infinite number of complications. But I am not concerned with the legacy of history, with culture or religion. As a logician and sociologist I describe, in abstract form, certain phenomena I have found to exist in Communist society. I describe Communism in its ideal state. I do not dispute that its realisation can be different in different countries. But my business is to construct a model, and for that to be possible I have to proceed step by step. In *The Reality of Communism* I attempt to describe my method.

I contend that any analysis of the Soviet system has to begin with generalisations. I posit certain general laws, and posit them in a language and logical order peculiar to my method. Having established these, I refine them by taking on board empirical evidence, so that I end up by obtaining a more or less complete picture of how Soviet society works—a painstakingly slow procedure.

Now, Western students of the Soviet Union, especially those hostile to the Soviet system, are in a hurry. They are ready with instant analyses and judgments. They variously allege that the Soviet system is 'totalitarian' in the sense of Nazi Germany; that it is 'unstable'; that it will fall prey to its inner contradictions, and so on. But these are opinions based on guesswork, incomplete knowledge or straightforward incomprehension. They reflect the needs of journalism and political propaganda. They do not accord with the reality as it appears to the eyes of a competent scholar. Mine is a scientific method which seeks to ferret out facts, not pass value judgments.

Model Methodology

URBAN: All this raises a very large question which we cannot tackle in this conversation: whether social science is a 'science', and whether any scholarship dealing with human beings can be or should be 'value-free'. Without stumbling into that particular jungle, let me say that many of your readers will doubtless regard your scientific neutrality towards the Soviet system as a tacit vindication of that system—on the not unreasonable argument that any value-free investigation of a system which has caused the violent death of millions, and the occupation and suppression of half the European continent, is a typical case of *la trahison des clercs*—and thus, in reality, not value-free at all. One might as well, they would argue, make a 'systems-analysis' of the Nazi concentration camps—their social structure, hierarchical organisation, their links with other organs of the National-Socialist system, etc.—without spilling ink on the unpleasant (and 'value-heavy') fact that the camps were there to gas, burn, starve, shoot, hang, and otherwise exterminate human beings.

I respect your insistence on the integrity and neutrality of 'science'. Nevertheless your dispassionate approach to a topic so heavy with suffering puts me slightly on my guard.

In 1984, can one say 'Soviet' without muttering 'Gulag' in the same breath?

ZINOVIEV: You are not the first to make this sort of accusation. But your criticism betrays a certain philistinism and is unjustified. The charges against me are usually couched in this form. In my scientific work I describe Soviet society as a normal phenomenon. My critics say (exactly as you have just said) that this implies approval of the Soviet system. But the inference is nonsensical. The concept of 'norm' carries no value-judgment. It is totally neutral. It stands for 'a standard for measure'. . . .

URBAN: . . . it does, in a general sense. But it also stands for 'rule for proper conduct' in ethics, and in axiology for 'standard for judging value' . . .

ZINOVIEV: But as I have clearly ruled out ethics and axiology from my investigations, we need not waste time on secondary meanings. 'Norm' in science is a neutral notion. When I say that Soviet society is a normal phenomenon, all I'm saying is that, *given the nature of Communist society*, Soviet society *is* a normal society; it is, after 67 years, in perfect harmony with the pure model of Communist society. Would my critics have raised their eyebrows if I had said: 'a poison snake with its fangs intact in the South Asian jungle is a normal phenomenon'? Clearly they would not. A poison snake in the streets of *London* would be an abnormal phenomenon, but not in India. Yet my statement about Soviet society is of the same sort. I discuss all this in more detail in *The Reality of Communism*, so I will explain it no further.

URBAN: Does 'normal' Communist society, then, require mass violence by the state as a normal condition of its existence?

ZINOVIEV: I am not concerned with the chaotic origins of Soviet society or the peculiarly Russian conditions between the two World Wars which coloured the emergence of Soviet society. I describe the structure of Soviet society as it is— not its accretions.

URBAN: If mass violence is an accretion, it is one that matters to ordinary human beings more than any other feature of Soviet society. However this may be, your comments on the alleged ineptitude of Western students of the Soviet Union nettle me. Take one of the most reliable (and respected) studies of the day-to-day workings of Soviet society, Merle Fainsod's 'Smolensk under Soviet Rule'. Here is a painstaking analysis of the Soviet system based on a mass of Soviet documents and written by an American scholar deeply versed in the culture of the Soviet Union and the Russian language. Would you say that Fainsod's picture of the Soviet system is inadequate or misleading?

ZINOVIEV: Factology is not enough. It is one thing to be versed in facts; it is another to discern social laws. Facts exist in abundance. The task of science is not to collect facts but to interpret them. In Newton's day everybody knew about apples falling, and everybody knew that there was some force keeping the planets moving about the sun and the moon in motion around the earth. But the force itself was invisible. Newton, however, could see behind these seemingly unrelated facts and showed that it was one and the same force—universal gravitation—that causes them all to happen. In trying to understand Soviet society, too, you have to start with a hypothesis and turn it into a scientific theory with a predictive potential as firm as Newton's law of mechanics.

Now, I ask you, how do the works of American Sovietologists measure up to these requirements? Can you show me a single Western book that has been able to predict any development in Soviet society—even the most primitive? People in the West who concern themselves with the Soviet Union are not scientists in the proper sense of the word, and therefore understand nothing.

URBAN: This is a sweeping statement. I don't want to argue with you on a point where your knowledge is extensive, but I do know that even the most dedicated quantifiers and model-builders among Western social scientists would hesitate to claim that any 'law' concerning the behaviour of human beings could have the predictive force of Newton's law of gravitation.

ZINOVIEV: In principle it can. I am concerned with the pure model of Communist society. The Western interpretations of Soviet reality are based on personal impressions, historical analogies, moral predilections, and other non-scientific factors. I reject these.

URBAN: You have intimated that the Western interpret-ation of Soviet society as 'totalitarian' occupies a prominent place on your blacklist. Yet this is a notion that people like George Kennan, Zbigniew Brzezinski, Carl J. Friedrich, Hannah Arendt, Karl Deutsch (to name but a few) have spent a long time thinking and writing about. And none had any doubt that Soviet society was 'totalitarian'. Were they all in error?

ZINOVIEV: Error is a strong word. They may not have been in error by their own standards; but I do not accept those standards. My theory leads me to a mathematical model of Communist society. Admittedly it will take hundreds of specially trained researchers to substantiate it over a long period of time, and even when it is completed, the gap between abstract truth and concrete application may well be a large one. Nevertheless, the laws emerging from my theory have the force of the laws of physics. They are objective universal laws.

URBAN: There appears to me to be an interesting contradic-tion in what you are saying. First you insist that Soviet society can only be understood from within. At the same time you claim that Soviet society is governed by testable universal laws. Doesn't your second claim make nonsense of the first? For what sort of a testable universal law is it that is accessible only to a group of privileged observers—those who, like yourself, have been born and nurtured in the Soviet system?

ZINOVIEV: I do not say that you have to have any special intuition to unearth the clues to Soviet reality, but I do say that you cannot get a handle on empirical evidence unless you are part and parcel of Soviet society.

URBAN: But isn't the net effect the same? It means that non-Soviet scholars are, by definition, debarred from under-standing Soviet society. Would a Western scholar be able to understand it if he adopted your methodology but worked from *outside* the Soviet system?

ZINOVIEV: My theory requires that the point of observation must be within Soviet society.

URBAN: Western scholars, then, have to take your theory on trust?

ZINOVIEV: No, my method is open to them, but whether they use that or some other method, they will have to take, for their starting point, a disinterested, empirical view of Soviet reality with the eyes of an insider. I have no dogmatic views about this. Experience will tell whether it is or is not possible. So far, I can see no indication that any Western scholar would be inclined to undergo a methodological sea-change. The methods they now use, if indeed they use any, are deplorable. Their judgments are chaotic.

Let me give you one example. Before the Second World War, Hitler's leadership had studied the facts. They understood the strengths and weaknesses of the Soviet Union better than the Soviet leadership itself. The Germans had the most excellent information services and thorough evaluation: they knew everything about Soviet industrial capacity; they knew the number of tanks and guns and aircraft we had and could produce; the nature of our supply system; the state of our railways and roads; the readiness of our units in the Red Army and Air Force; the size of our food reserves, and so on. Yet when it came to estimating our military potential and our ability to resist, Hitler and his lieutenants made some very fundamental mistakes which cost them the War.

URBAN: How would you define those mistakes?

ZINOVIEV: Well, they knew facts, but facts, as I said a moment ago, are not enough. They had no method for understanding and correlating the facts they had.

URBAN: Do you mean they failed to allow for certain intangibles such as the 'spirit of resistance' of the Russian people when attacked by an aggressor?

ZINOVIEV: Not at all. They failed to work out a scientific method whereby the facts about Russia's military and industrial potential could be correlated with a host of other factors and integrated in an overall formula. That could have given the Germans a reliable picture of the strengths and weaknesses of the Soviet system. They didn't do it. The Western countries, even Western Intelligence, make the same mistakes in our own time.

Soon after my expulsion from the Soviet Union, three Western gentlemen came to see me. 'Zinoviev,' they said, 'we have read your books and articles, and we admire your insights. We want you to give us your formula for the destruction of the Soviet system.'

Well, I told them: 'I don't object to being used by you. Anybody and everybody can use me. I'm politically indifferent. I could work for the Soviet authorities, and I could equally work for you. I'm a scientist, a university professor. I have obtained results. My sole ambition is that these results should be known in the world as "Zinoviev results" and my theory as "Zinoviev's theory of the Soviet system". You can use my theory in any way you like but, believe me, I don't want to destroy the Soviet system any more than I do the West. Now, if you want to know my theory, give me ten or fifteen gifted students. Arrange for them to spend three years under my guidance and make it possible that, in due course, these students can pass on their knowledge to further groups of young scholars. One of these will eventually work out a computer-model of the Soviet citizen and perhaps even of Soviet society.'

None of this pleased my three interlocutors. 'How long will all this take?' they asked. 'About five years,' I replied. This was far too long for them. They were in a hurry. They wanted me to produce a magic formula—at once. So they packed their bags and left. They failed to understand, as the Nazis had failed to understand before them, that obtaining a reliable formula requires a long, painstaking, scientific effort.

URBAN: This is a remarkable story. Your 'scientific' neutralism is in line with the thinking of the wartime German missile-experts. Some of them chose to go to the USA to continue their work, while others went to the Soviet Union to do the same. That the Soviet Union was as unfree a society as Hitler's had been did not bother them. Their sole interest was to construct bigger and better missiles.

But, to return to the Nazis' faulty assessment of the Soviet Union, Hitler was not alone in underestimating Soviet staying-power. In Britain and the USA, too, there were fears (many of them openly expressed) that the Soviet Union would prove no match for Hitler's superbly equipped and led forces. Nor were these fears unreasonable, seeing that the mighty USSR could barely, and then only at enormous cost, impose its will on tiny Finland in the 1939–40 Winter Campaign. But when Stalin eventually turned the tables on Germany, his successes were ascribed to Russian patriotism, his personal leadership, and US and British war supplies. Nobody, except Western Communists and other admirers of the Soviet system, said that Hitler or the West had underestimated the strength of Soviet society.

ZINOVIEV: Patriotism cuts both ways—it can carry a negative or positive charge. By the same token, the size of the Soviet war machine could have assumed negative as well as positive roles. Everything depends on a large number of non-military variables which flow from the nature of the Soviet system and are not easily understood and quantified. Hitler had no formula for their incorporation in his assessments of Soviet power. That is why he miscalculated. Today, Western Sovietologists make the same mistakes. Lacking an adequate method, they are incapable of forming a reliable estimate of the USSR's *overall* military potential.

URBAN: But let us, please, stay with my example for a moment. Western historians say that the USSR won the War for three main reasons. First, Hitler alienated a friendly Russian and Ukrainian population. When the German troops arrived in the Ukraine (so runs the argument) they were greeted as liberators. It was the general beastliness of Nazi policies towards the Slavs, and the particular brutality of the German occupation authorities on Soviet territory, that eventually stiffened Soviet resistance. Would you accept that?

ZINOVIEV: No, this factor played no role at all.

URBAN: The second factor is said to have been Stalin's appeal to Russian patriotism and nationalism; his enlistment of the spiritual power of the Orthodox Church; his evocations of Russia's great military feats in the past and the restoration of military ranks and insignia.

And the third factor is said to have been the massive contribution which the USA and Britain made to the Soviet war effort in the form of trucks, tanks, guns, aircraft, raw materials and other supplies.

Would you allow that these factors played a part?

ZINOVIEV: No—all these explanations are extremely wide of the mark—some, to be sure, are completely nonsensical. The historical process during the War was extremely complicated. Hitler made mistakes, Stalin made mistakes, Roosevelt made mistakes, and Churchill made mistakes. But, confining ourselves to the Soviet–German war, the mistakes made by those two sides broadly speaking cancelled out each other. What mattered (to repeat) was Hitler's misreading of the character and overall potential of the Soviet system. The tragedy is that Western observers and Western governments are now repeating Hitler's errors.

Recently I was invited to attend a conference on the nature of Soviet power. One of my co-participants was a distinguished Western military specialist. He knew every Soviet general's name in the higher echelons of the armed forces. He knew their functions, their departmental jealousies, the equipment of the various Red Army units, their peace-time and mobilisation strengths—he knew everything. The only thing he could not compute out of all this impressive information was the one thing that mattered: the overall power of the Soviet Union.

I assured him that if he lived in the Soviet Union he would find that most Soviet scholars were unable to name the members of the *Politburo*, much less the Central Committee. Yet they'd have a very precise idea of what the system was about. Why? Because they would understand that individuals did not matter in the Soviet system. What matters is the system itself, and that can be understood only through scientific study. Western Sovietologists have written volumes about the question of succession in the Soviet leadership. Yet, in the months preceding Khrushchev's dismissal they were unable to detect the slightest tremor in the Soviet landscape. Nor could they tell us anything useful about Brezhnev's succession. They widely tipped Chernenko as the most likely successor. The hallmark of science is its ability to predict. Western Sovietology is the work of charlatans.

URBAN: Have *you* been able to predict the behaviour of the Soviet system?

ZINOVIEV: Yes, I have. I cannot make mathematically precise predictions, but I can predict certain tendencies.

URBAN: For example?

ZINOVIEV: Let us suppose that the NATO countries or the USA alone occupy Iran or intervene in certain African countries. I can, by using my mathematical model of the Soviet Union as a world power, forecast the kind of counter-measures the Kremlin will take, such as moving into Pakistan, activating the Soviet–Syrian treaty, stepping up the pressure on South Africa, and so on.

URBAN: May I say that systems-analysts have a wonderful way of predicting the obvious. 'How will the US Federal Government allocate certain funds set aside for welfare programmes in disadvantaged areas?'—this was the subject of an expensive team-research project in my time at the University of Southern California. Two years and several hundred thousand dollars later, the research team came up with the astounding forecast that the Federal Government would build schools in black neighbourhoods where schools were in short supply, and hospitals in areas where medical care was insufficient! When the Federal Government did, eventually, announce its plan to build schools and hospitals where these were most needed, my systems-analyst colleagues had a knowing smile on their faces: 'We told you so. . . .'

Your forecast strikes me as being of the same sort. Any junior foreign-service officer in Britain or France *failing* to forecast the kind of Soviet moves you have predicted would have his chances of promotion seriously jeopardised.

ZINOVIEV: You make it sound all too simple. Building a mathematical model is a highly skilled and complicated busi-ness. I could teach you my method if we had a couple of years at our disposal—

URBAN: Are you implying that I'd be a slow or a fast learner?

ZINOVIEV: At two years you'd have to be a fast one.

URBAN: Could we, on the strength of your method, understand, for example, French society before the French Revolution—or after?

ZINOVIEV: You could use my scientific method for devising a theory about French society. But my own theory does not apply to French society. It applies to Communist society only.

URBAN: Will it, then, explain Chinese Communist society?

ZINOVIEV: No, it will not. Chinese society is not a purely Communist society. Soviet society is the classical pattern. Some of my theorems will, of course, cover China, Hungary, Romania and the other East European countries, but in general my theory applies to Soviet society only.

URBAN: But would you not agree that ten years of the Maoist Cultural Revolution brought China closer to the egalitarian Communist model than anything that has happened in the Soviet Union in its 67 years of history?

ZINOVIEV: I don't know Chinese society, so I will not talk about it. But there is yet another reason why my theory cannot be applied to China. According to my theory, every social system has limitations of scale. If the size of a system outstrips those limitations, two things can happen: it will either develop its own sub-systems of viable size and thus survive; or it will not, in which case it will destroy itself. I can prove with the certainty of a mathematical theorem that China cannot become an effective world power precisely because it has too large a population. A society of 1,000 million people is too unmanageable and unwieldy.

URBAN: What would you say is the optimal size for a society to be effective?

ZINOVIEV: About 200 million is enough. China could become a great state if it killed off at least half its population. There are certain hard, testable mathematical correlations which give us the upper (and lower) limits of an effective society. There are, of course, many other mathematical correlations too, which I could teach you if you chose to become my student for a while. For example the calculus of the system's decision-making ability, of its stability, the parameters of risk-taking by the leadership, and so on. Unfortunately, some weaknesses remain in my theory so that I cannot adequately explain everything I'd like to explain.

URBAN: Did you predict the Soviet move into Afghanistan on the strength of your computations?

ZINOVIEV: Yes, I did, in a talk to the American Club in Munich.

URBAN: Why was the world not alerted to your prediction?

ZINOVIEV: That I cannot tell you.

URBAN: What you have, then, given us is a theory that is (1) essentially accessible to Soviet residents only; (2) specific to the Soviet type of Communist society; and (3) specific to the size of Communist society that happens to be the size of existing Soviet society. All this puts me on my guard—especially as your claim to be 'scientific' has an old ring of 19th-century scientism about it.

You have, as a Soviet man, observed Soviet society with enormous empathy—and wit—for 30-odd years, and written about it in great detail with mordant humour and great sophistication. I would have thought *that* was your great contribution to the debate about Soviet society—not some mathematical model specific to the Soviet Union, to Soviet men, and in the last analysis, perhaps only to one Soviet man: yourself.

ZINOVIEV: You are absolutely wrong there. Mine is a rigorous theory based on first-hand experience; and I feel I have the right to speak in terms of my theory because it concerns the life and death of mankind. The Soviet Union has become a very serious enemy of the Western world and we have to spend time, energy, and money to perfect our understanding of that enemy. It may well be that the uses of my theory will be limited to one single occasion. That would not upset me in the slightest.

The Soviet Union resembles in most of its features a mechanical system. Most facts about Soviet society can be counted and fed into a computer. When the danger of war arises, we are, on the strength of my theory, in the fortunate position of being able to 'take the measure' of the Soviet system in the literal sense. Suppose the next war were to be a nuclear war: it is of fundamental importance for us to know whether the Soviet or the Western system has the greater capacity for survival.

URBAN: And you can tell us which. . . .

ZINOVIEV: It can be done. Oh yes, it can. Our contemporary computers are not equal to the task, but as soon as we have one that can digest several hundred variables—it will be done.

URBAN: How do you quantify morale, dedication, the force of nationalism?

ZINOVIEV: It is difficult, but it can be done.

Of Russian Pride and Ethnic Prejudice

URBAN: Take a practical example. General Sir John Hackett, in his well-known book *The Third World War*, predicts that, after a limited nuclear exchange and a stalemated conventional war in Central Europe, the Soviet Union will break up into its constituent parts under the impact of national separatism. Now, how would you quantify the Ukrainian, or Lithuanian, or Uzbek wish for national independence?

ZINOVIEV: This is a ridiculous scenario. General Hackett wants the Soviet Union to disintegrate, and he predicts events in accordance with his own wish.

URBAN: Are you saying that the spirit of national independence does not exist in the non-Russian parts of the USSR?

ZINOVIEV: Yes, I am.

URBAN: That it does not exist at all?

ZINOVIEV: It exists, but it is too weak to matter. You have to see things as they really are. With the sole exception of the small Baltic republics, which (especially Estonia and Latvia) are in fact German by tradition and culture, the other non-Russian nations and nationalities are net *beneficiaries* of the Russian connection. Offer an ordinary Ukrainian or Azerbaidzhani the possibility of secession from the Soviet Union—he will refuse it! You will, of course, always find tiny minorities of nationalists and dissidents who think otherwise, but the vast majority will have nothing to do with national independence. It would cost them too dear.

URBAN: You sound like a Habsburg defender of the status quo in, shall we say, 1914.

ZINOVIEV: Not at all. I speak of a status quo which is genuinely accepted. Take the Azerbaidzhanis. Many of them live in Moscow and Leningrad, holding down privileged positions, occupying sumptuous homes, sending their children to privileged schools, and so on. They 'live off the land' of the Russians. For them Russia is a colony.

URBAN: Is the Russification of the non-Russian republics, of which so much has been written, also a myth in your view?

ZINOVIEV: Absolutely. The non-Russian republics have not been 'Russified' in the old imperial sense of the word. On the contrary: one of the most significant features of the October Revolution was the colonisation of *Russia* and the Russian nation. The Bolsheviks were afraid of the submerged masses of the Russian people. They found it more convenient to uproot groups of Ukrainians, Tatars, Georgians, and so on, and base their rule on these much more manipulable *déraciné* minorities. Even today when this anti-Russian trend is being reversed, in Moscow, Leningrad, and the other major Russian cities you will find that at least half the senior élite in the Party, Government, and public administration are not Russians. If you look at the list of Soviet writers, generals, or academicians rather few of the names will be Russian. The rest will be typical names of Ukrainians and so on.

Until not so many years ago the Russian people were the underdogs of the Soviet empire, as indeed they had been underdogs under the Czars too. They were peasants bound to the villages, tilling the land, supplying the armed forces with cannon-fodder and, generally speaking, performing the lowly, menial tasks at servitors' rates. The result is that the great majority of people running our country and setting the tone of its culture—whether in literature, music, jurisprudence or science—come from non-Russian ethnic stock. After the Revolution some three million of the Russian intelligentsia were slaughtered. Then, with the 1928–32

Collectivisation campaign, about 15 million Russian peasants—the basic stock of our nation—perished. It is only now that the Russian people are being slowly emancipated and allowed to compete for the more influential posts. But, until quite recently, the Governments of Russia were not *Russian* Governments. There have, in fact, been no Russian Governments in Russia (or the Soviet Union) since Peter the Great. Our Czars since Peter were, to say the very least, Germanised by marriage.

It is, then, safe to conclude that every minority nation or nationality has been enjoying a privileged position in comparison with the Russian people—that they have regarded Russia as their colony. For example, every nation and nationality has its Academy of Sciences. There is no Russian Academy of Sciences.

URBAN: This is true of the Communist Party too. All Republics have their own Communist Parties, but there is no Russian Communist Party.

ZINOVIEV: Yes, perfectly true.

URBAN: But then knowledgeable scholars like Leonard Schapiro have argued that this is because the dominant organisation, the Communist Party of the Soviet Union, is in fact the *Russian* Communist Party.

ZINOVIEV: This is quite untrue. The CPSU has never been a Russian phenomenon.

Today in the Soviet Academy of Sciences only about 10 per cent of the Academicians are Russian, whereas Russians make up half the total Soviet population. The same goes for the Central Committee, the KGB, the Army, and so on. Right through the Soviet élite, the Russian people is badly under-represented. So is its culture in the Soviet Union as a whole.

URBAN: This certainly runs counter to almost all the written and spoken evidence I have seen on the subject. For ten years under Brezhnev all members of the Secretariat of the Central Committee were Russian, even though Russians account for only about 60 per cent of the Party's membership. Volumes have been written about the Russification of the Central Asian Republics, the Baltic States, the Ukraine.

I will not review the evidence, for it is too well known. Would you say it is *all* nonsensical?

ZINOVIEV: Indeed I would, and I do. These republics have not been 'Russified' in any meaningful sense of the word.

URBAN: Is the reverse, then, the case?

ZINOVIEV: Yes, it is. If you go to the Soviet Union with certain *a priori* conceptions in mind, you will always find evidence to endorse them.

URBAN: But isn't it also true that if you come *from* the Soviet system with a certain mathematical model in mind, you will always find facts to endorse *that*?

ZINOVIEV: If your *a priori* conception is that national conflicts will destroy the Soviet system, you will come back with a thick file of 'evidence' showing that those conflicts actually exist. Some Western scholars believe that alcoholism will be the death of the Soviet Union. One nonsense is as good as another.

URBAN: But you will surely allow that linguistic Russification exists?

ZINOVIEV: Absolutely not. All Soviet citizens are indeed taught Russian. But this cannot be called 'Russification'. You may have been misled by a recent demonstration in Georgia which is now widely quoted as showing that there is widespread resentment among Georgians of the Russian language and of the Russian people. But this is not true. It is now established that only some of those demonstrators had any command of the Georgian language. All Georgians, however, speak Russian—and so they should, in their own interest. For when a Georgian goes to Moscow to sell his produce, or speculate on the black market, or publish his book, he needs Russian, not Georgian. Georgia is a small republic. Russian is the *lingua franca* of the Soviet Union.

URBAN: As you seem to be speaking with the authentic voice of imperialism, let me point out that in British India too—where the English language was genuinely accepted both as *lingua franca* among Indian tribes and nationalities, and as a passport to education, professional advancement, and business success—it was widely argued by the British that good public administration and India's own economic

interests were better served within the British Empire than
they would be outside it. Yet, when the chips were down,
the British-educated Indian intelligentsia preferred Independence to economic advantage and good administration, and
caused the British to leave.

What I am saying is that no matter how persuasive the
economic or cultural self-interest of your Georgians may
be, you cannot expect them not to want to assert their
national independence just because, on sober calculation,
they might be economically better off under Russian rule,
going to Russian schools, etc., than they would be under
their own. Nations do not act so rationally—as we well
know from the disintegration of the colonial empires after
the War.

ZINOVIEV: But your assertions about Russification are
absurd. The Russian language is generally accepted in the
Soviet Union—

URBAN: So was (and is) English in India. . . .

ZINOVIEV: —but the adoption of Russian is not Russification. I can confidently assert that the opposite is closer
to the mark. Take the Ukraine, which I know well (I was
a frequent visitor there as an examiner of doctoral candidates). All educated Ukrainians speak Russian; they also
speak Ukrainian. Russians have not colonised the Ukraine.
Indeed, it is virtually impossible for a Russian to get a job
in the Ukraine, whereas in Russia about 60 per cent of
leading posts are held by Ukrainians. There was a time
when 70 per cent of Soviet academicians were Jews, whereas
Jews account for only about 1 per cent of the Soviet population. When I was suggested for election to the Academy
as a Russian, the Academy's official line was that in principle
more Russians should now be admitted. I was closely ques-
tioned by an interview board as to whether I was a Jew or
a Russian. I am, as you know, a Russian, but despite the
Academy's official line, a Jew was elected. And I'm inclined
to ascribe this to what I have already told you: the Soviet
leaders are at heart afraid of the Russian people. They are
more at home with uprooted minorities.

URBAN: How, then, do you explain Stalin's Great-Russian

chauvinism which earned him Lenin's memorable warning in 1922? Lenin feared, you will remember, that the Constitution of the Union would not protect the non-Russians 'from invasion of their rights by this typical Russian man, the chauvinist, whose basic nature is that of a scoundrel and repressor, the classical type of Russian bureaucrat. . . .'

ZINOVIEV: In the first place, Stalin was neither Russian nor did he become 'a typical Russian man'. Secondly, Lenin was a sick man at the time and uttered much that was nonsensical. In any case, his warning had a specific meaning in the context of the early 1920s which it does not have for us. It is useless to compare like with unlike.

URBAN: What about Stalin's famous tribute, at a victory celebration on 24 May 1945, to the 'Russian people' without whose endurance the USSR might have lost the war?

ZINOVIEV: Yes, Stalin proposed that memorable toast. It was a typical instance of his inspired ideological opportunism. It was a memorable occasion for me, too, because it prompted me to write a satirical poem (now reprinted in my book *The Radiant Future*) which got me into prison. But whatever Stalin said in praise of the Russian people in 1945, it was not long before the repression of the Russian nation was resumed. Once again, the camps were filled with Russian officers, soldiers and intellectuals, and colonial status was clamped down on the Russian people.

There is a tendency, too, in the Soviet Union for the small nations and minority groups to spread the word around that they are being hard done by—that there is 'prejudice' against them because they are Georgians, or Azerbaidzhanis, or Jews. But this is a myth. Let me tell you a story.

Two Soviet Jews meet in a street in Moscow. 'Well, how's life treating you?' the first asks his friend.

'N-n-n-not . . . t-t-too . . . w-w-well,' says the second with a heavy stutter.

'But why? What's happened?'

'I . . . I . . . I've . . . app-app-applied . . . f-f-for a j-j-job . . . as TV ann-ann-announ-announcer on Sov-Sov-Soviet TV and . . . I . . . I . . . I've b-b-been . . . re-re-refused be-be-be-because I . . . am . . . a-a-a . . . J-J-Jew.'

URBAN: Are you saying that all prejudice and all anti-Semitism is of this imaginary character?

ZINOVIEV: No. The Soviet Union is a very large country. Here and there spots of prejudice exist—against Muslims, Armenians, Jews, what-have-you, but anti-Jewism (which we should keep separate from anti-Semitism) is largely a phenomenon of the last two or three decades and has grown parallel with the slow but increasing emancipation of the Russian people. As their ability to compete for jobs has grown, so has the feeling that the Jewish grip on the more worthwhile types of employment is out of proportion with the number of Soviet Jews. Before the Second World War, Jews were privileged people in our country, and they are in some respects still privileged people today: they can emigrate if they want to badly enough, whereas a Russian or Tadzhik cannot.

URBAN: Surely I don't have to remind you of the history of Russian pogroms; Stalin's anti-Semitism; the 'Doctors' Plot'; the real thrust of the 'Anti-Zionist' campaigns, the penalties of Jewish emigration, and the discrimination and personal animus the ordinary Soviet Jew has to pocket from the ordinary Russian or Ukrainian every day of his life. The mere fact that his internal passport classifies him as a Jew by 'nationality' tells much of the story.

ZINOVIEV: The Russian people have never been anti-Semitic. In fact, in many ways they always preferred Jewish people to their own kind. Whenever Russians had a chance to elect a man as a leader of some group or director of some enterprise and had a choice between a Russian and a Jew, they would elect a Jew. This was an old Russian tradition, the reason being that the Russian people *were not much inclined to rule*. The Jews were, and they were very good at it because they were competent, had will-power and brains. Since the Second World War the emancipation of Russians has advanced apace, and the predominance of Jews has come to be resented. Hence the talk about Russian anti-Semitism. But, as I say, before the War virtually all the professorial chairs in Moscow, Leningrad, and the major provincial cities were held by Jewish scholars, and the Academy too was an almost exclusively Jewish preserve. In those days, however, the number of worthwhile academic appointments ran to no more than a few dozen, whereas today these and the parallel posts in industrial research and development are counted in their tens of thousand. There just aren't enough qualified Jews to compete with 100 million Russians.

URBAN: Do you, then, clearly ascribe anti-Semitism to this growing competition for well-endowed appointments and prestige?

ZINOVIEV: No. This is not only a Jewish question. The 'Mafias' come into it, for the Russian people are faced with a number of what one might call 'mafias' which they naturally dislike. The Armenians have a mafia-like group-loyalty wherever they may live; so have the Tatars; so have the Georgians; and so have the Jews. The October Revolution in a sense legitimised these with its emphasis on the equality of all peoples and cultures. The only nation which was not allowed to proclaim its special cohesion and individuality was the Russian people. As soon as the Russian nation tried to speak with its own distinctive voice, up went the cry of 'nationalism', 'chauvinism', even 'fascism'. Part of today's anti-Semitism in the Soviet Union is due to the mafia-like character of the special cohesion and transnational ties of the Soviet Jews. They, like the Armenians and other minority nationalities, enjoy special privileges which are denied to Russians. This breeds anti-Jewish feeling, which I personally abominate.

URBAN: Would you say that the US emphasis on Jewish emigration as an element of American economic policy has helped or harmed Soviet Jewry?

ZINOVIEV: It has added to anti-Semitism and, one must say, made things more difficult for that great majority of Jews who cannot, or do not want to, emigrate. If the Americans, and American Jewish interests, supported the claims of dissident Tatars, Armenians, Ukrainians and Russians with a fraction of the urgency with which they have supported Jewish emigration, the situation of Soviet Jews might be very different.

URBAN: Do you think the Soviet leaders would quietly allow Soviet Jews to leave if no American pressure were applied? Wouldn't they be losing a convenient domestic psychological scapegoat as well as a useful bargaining counter *vis-à-vis* the USA?

ZINOVIEV: I cannot confidently answer that question. What I can say is that our Jews should be allowed to emigrate if they want to, if only because the great usefulness of Soviet Jews as carriers of learning, culture, and expertise is now exhausted. The Soviet Union has enough doctors, scientists, and teachers to be able to do without the specifically Jewish contribution. But if emigration were not to prove possible, perhaps our Jews ought to be given a chance to relocate themselves more evenly throughout the Soviet Union and cease to form compact minorities. This would perhaps ameliorate the odious phenomenon of anti-Semitism.

URBAN: 'Full assimilation' ... despite the German experience?

ZINOVIEV: That is a difficult subject on which I'm not competent to talk. Suffice it to say that, in the Soviet Union, the importance of national exclusiveness is happily on the decline. I call myself a Russian, and I am—as you have noticed—deeply concerned with the well-being and culture of the Russian people, because it has been for centuries a badly underprivileged people. But at the same time I am equally conscious that I have, as a 'Russian', not a drop of Slavic blood in my veins. So I cannot be a Russian racialist. My ancestors came to Russia from Sweden and Finland, adopted Russian as their language, and were Christianised as 'Russians'. I do not, therefore, hold that the perpetuation of nationally or racially pure groups, whether Jewish or Swedish or whatever, is a great moral imperative, or for that matter historically possible or desirable. Many of our Jews regard themselves as more Russian than the Russians. I have no quarrel with that sentiment.

URBAN: One of Marx's more spectacular failures was the failure to foresee the significance of race and nationalism. Aren't you committing, as one nurtured on Marxism, the same 'ethnic' error? Aren't you, in fact, contradicting yourself, arguing as you are for the emancipation of the Russian nation while at the same time downplaying the importance of national homogeneity?

ZINOVIEV: No. There is no contradiction. I do not seek

national homogeneity. My preoccupation with the future of the Russian nation is a profound concern for the welfare and culture of the Russian people as human beings who entered the 20th century with a specific background and history. It is not racial. Think of that perhaps greatest of names in Russian literature, Pushkin, who came on his maternal side from Abyssinian stock and was so dark-skinned that he could be taken for an African. Or think of Dostoevsky, with his Polish ancestry. There are no pure races today in the civilised world—nor, I would suggest, should there be any. My suggestion, therefore, that our own Jewish population, having brilliantly performed its cultural mission, may now usefully dilute its identity by voluntary emigration and assimilation is no more anti-Semitic than my concern for a racially mixed Russian nation is anti-Russian.

Child of the Revolution

URBAN: All in all—to return to our main theme—you regard the Russian people as the victims rather than the beneficiaries of the Soviet system?

ZINOVIEV: Not in every respect, and not throughout the régime's 67 years of history. Before the Revolution 80 per cent, if not 90 per cent, of the Russian population were peasants living at subsistence level at the bottom of the social pyramid. They lived miserable lives, only an iota above the level of serfs. The Revolution did produce changes. Take my own family, who were peasants. As a result of the collectivisation of agriculture my parents lost everything they had. But my elder brother eventually rose to be a factory manager; the next one to him in age made it to the rank of colonel; three of my other brothers qualified as engineers; and I became a professor at Moscow University. At the same time millions of Russian peasants were given a formal education and some became professional men and women.

URBAN: But surely you moved to these positions over the dead bodies of those many millions of peasants who had been systematically starved in the 1929–32 period?

ZINOVIEV: Yes, if you want to put it that way. I would

simply say that the collectivisation of agriculture created many new opportunities. The whole life of the country was radically changed.

URBAN: But that is not very different from saying that the gassing of Jews and gypsies in Auschwitz was a radical piece of social engineering which 'created many new opportunities'. . . .

ZINOVIEV: The collectivisation of agriculture was an essential phase of the Bolshevik Revolution. Without it our country would have disintegrated. The Russian revolution began in 1861 and climaxed in 1917. It *happened*; and its only possible aftermath was collectivisation.

URBAN: So even now, speaking as a dissident on West European soil, you approve of the collectivisation with its fifteen million victims?

ZINOVIEV: Of course I do. I approve of it completely.

URBAN: Despite the awesome sacrifices?

ZINOVIEV: Despite the sacrifices. Collectivisation gave industry many millions of workers. And industry meant opportunity.

URBAN: Is 'gave' the right verb, I wonder? Weren't they being starved into leaving their villages or made to do so by brute force?

ZINOVIEV: They were not 'forced' to go into industry. Of course, the kulaks were liquidated. But it was quite possible for ordinary peasants to stay on the land. Life in the big cities, however, offered irresistible temptations. Country life was primitive and boring. My family lived on the land. We had a large and comfortable house. In Moscow the ten of us had to make do with a single room of ten square metres—one square metre per head. Can you imagine? Yet, we *preferred* life in Moscow.

URBAN: But surely, if your parents' land had not been taken away from them they would not have left your village. Their move was a response to an act of arbitrary expropriation.

ZINOVIEV: I don't know. It was certainly not any lack of food that made them leave. They moved because better opportunities beckoned in Moscow. Historians now tell us that the exodus from the villages was due to starvation and other pressures. Some may have left for those reasons, but the majority left in search of a better life—a collective life within Soviet institutions.

URBAN: But collective life, if that is what they were after, could be had on the land too. Some of us in the West have been under the impression that it was collective life they were *running away from*.

ZINOVIEV: Ah, but at that time collective life had not been properly organised in the countryside. *Now* it is—but in the 1920s and early 1930s agricultural collectivisation was a halfway house between the old system and the new. But, quite apart from that, in the towns people could visit libraries, go to cinemas, learn languages, meet one another. There was variety, entertainment, and culture to be had— and better wages. Don't forget that the Revolution was a great cultural revolution too. The enormous tragedies you have mentioned were accompanied by improved life-chances.

URBAN: All in all, you seem to be approving of Lenin's dictum that a generation had to be sacrificed. . . .

ZINOVIEV: I don't approve or disapprove. I take a scientific position which is neutral. What happened, happened. My job is to deal with consequential reality as it is now, not to pass judgment.

URBAN: But you *are* passing judgment, for when you say that the Soviet system would have disintegrated if collec-tivisation had not been set in train, you are in fact upholding 'the Soviet system' as worth saving even at the cost of fifteen million lives.

ZINOVIEV: Every bit of progress exacts a price and carries certain consequences. Some of these are positive, others negative. I was, as you know, an anti-Stalinist. I was arrested and imprisoned under Stalin because of my oppo-sition to Stalin. Yet, as a scientist I can, and do, make a point of explaining why the Russian people supported Stalin. I was an anti-Stalinist; yet I must tell you that it was in Stalin's prison that I had a bed of my own for the first time in my life, three meals a day, and decent clothing. Before that I was permanently hungry. After my release I was hungry again.

Think of the dreadful paradox: an anti-Stalinist who must nevertheless insist that Stalin's time was a great epoch in human history! And I was not alone in feeling that. My mother, who hated Stalin and all his works, kept a picture of Stalin in her Bible right up to her death. Millions of Russians did likewise.

URBAN: A hangover from Czarist times . . . Stalin replacing The-Little-Father-of-all-Russians?

ZINOVIEV: I don't know about that. Stalin represented the dynamism of life. He stood for the ordinary people's power. When he died, the people's power died with him. Without the Revolution my own family would have stayed stuck in the village as peasants. As it was, they had the chance to participate in the people's power.

URBAN: Would you consider your officer's commission in the Air Force another beneficial aspect of the 'dynamism of life' under Stalin?

ZINOVIEV: Yes, I would. Stalin purged the Red Army. Whatever the rights and wrongs of the trials of Tukhachevsky and his colleagues (and Tukhachevsky himself was certainly a very able soldier), the purge did away with the old class of ill-educated and undermotivated officers and made way for a completely new intake. I was one of the latter—a young lieutenant infinitely (I can assure you) more competent than the officer I replaced when he was arrested.

URBAN: Military historians tell us that if Tukhachevsky and the other generals had not been shot, Stalin's 1940 Winter Campaign against Finland wouldn't have fared so miserably.

ZINOVIEV: That is nonsense. I can tell you something else: if Stalin had *not* purged the Red Army, the Soviet Union would have suffered defeat in its war with Hitler. Our country was saved by the Red Army's new and superior leadership and the spirit and competence of the new officer class.

URBAN: 'Life has become better, life has become gayer.' Who would ever have thought one would meet, fifty years on, a Soviet dissident ready to support Stalin's famous boast?

ZINOVIEV: Well, life was extraordinarily fascinating, even if it was hard. I knew many people who realised that they were about to be shot—yet they praised Stalin. Stalin was a symbol of hope and vigour. A relative of mine, who knew that he was due to start a long prison sentence in a year's time, was (as people often were under Stalin) suddenly appointed to run a large factory. He grabbed the opportunity because, for him, the challenge of that single glorious year was worth more than a thousand years spent in uneventful living. 'I know they will kill me—but this year is going to be *my* year,' he said. He was filled with the consciousness of making history.

URBAN: Would you have felt the same, and acted as he did?

ZINOVIEV: Oh yes, and I still feel the same today. Forty years now separate me from my wartime experiences as an officer of the Soviet Air Force. I would willingly exchange those forty years for one week of my earlier life as a fighter-pilot.

I am a child of the Revolution—you must always remember that—I'm a product of the Revolution. I went to school in the 1930s and I was brought up on the romanticism of the Revolution. For me the Revolution and everything that went with it make up the whole sense of life. This does not mean, however, that I support the present Soviet régime. No: I'm a man of the 1920s and 1930s.

URBAN: You are, Professor Zinoviev, a typical Soviet Man, even though you are a dissident—*Homo Sovieticus*, to quote the title of your recent book. . . .

ZINOVIEV: Absolutely. I am a Soviet Man. I spent 60-odd years of my life in Soviet society, and always did my best to serve it: I was, I believe, a good soldier, a good Air Force officer, a good professor, and a good and hard-working member of my collective. From that point of view I am Soviet Man *par excellence*.

URBAN: Yet your merciless exposure of the psychology of Soviet Man and Soviet society earned you your expulsion. I must, therefore, assume that in some important respects you are not Soviet Man after all.

ZINOVIEV: Oh, but I am. That does not mean that I do not criticise the system. Throughout the Soviet Union the system is always being criticised at all levels—but these criticisms come from within the system. They do not question its legitimacy.

People in the West tend to think that Soviet society is, in effect, a vast concentration camp. That just isn't true. Some of my satirical writings were first given in Russia as public lectures. For example, I delivered a chapter from *The Yawning Heights*—on leadership, of all things—as a lecture at the Military Academy. I had 200 generals in the audience, and they applauded. You can't do that in a concentration camp.

I regard the existence of the Soviet system as a natural fact. My problem is how to live within that given society.

URBAN: Suppose your post as a professor at Moscow University were made available to you again, and your unorthodoxies were quietly forgiven. Would you return to the Soviet Union?

ZINOVIEV: I'd return at once. But please understand: I was (as I've now repeatedly said) bitterly opposed to Stalin and Stalinism; yet that environment was my whole life. I fought for the Soviet society of which Stalin was the leader and I fought for it willingly. At the same time I was so thoroughly alienated from Stalin himself that I was planning to assassinate him.

URBAN: You were?

ZINOVIEV: Oh, yes. Yet, whenever I was ordered by my superiors to put my life on the line for Stalin, I did so without hesitation.

URBAN: Suppose you did go back to the USSR to rejoin your 'collective', but fell foul of the system again and were confined to a psychiatric institution. Would you consider yourself to be a psychologically normal person wrongly declared to be abnormal or insane?

ZINOVIEV: No, I would not. I *would be* abnormal.

URBAN: Ah, but we must not be caught again on the horns of the 'normality' dilemma. You could be considered to be 'abnormal' only in the sense in which anyone who wants to reform Soviet society is declared to be 'abnormal' by the Soviet authorities. But surely *you* would not accept that standard. You would feel that *you* were perfectly normal and it was the *system* that was abnormal, would you not?

ZINOVIEV: But don't you see: I *would be* abnormal in a system in which the norm is to accept the system as it is. I'd be deviant from it.

URBAN: But would *you*, in your heart of hearts, regard yourself as psychologically ill?

ZINOVIEV: I would recognise the fact that from the system's point of view I was abnormal. And as there can be no other point of view *within* the Soviet system, I would accept and live with the fact that I was deviant.

URBAN: You are echoing Nikita Khrushchev. 'A crime,' Khrushchev said, 'is a deviation from generally recognised standards of behaviour, frequently called mental disorder. The mental state of people who start calling for opposition to Communism is clearly not normal.' I hate to labour this point, but for us it is the 'abnormality' which made you write *Yawning Heights* and your other famous satires of Soviet society that guarantees your normality. We admire your wit and courage, because you wrote these satires despite the pressures of the Soviet environment and it is that environment we regard as sick. Can I induce you to say, in plain language, that you really feel the same as we do? For otherwise I'd have to assume that you cannot differentiate between yourself and the subject of your study.

ZINOVIEV: Soviet society is both the subject of my study and my natural habitat. My books and their author are abnormal phenomena in the context of Soviet life.

URBAN: But would you regard yourself as ill, and therefore rightly confined?

ZINOVIEV: In the given and only possible context, yes, I would.

URBAN: But we are now talking in the West, in Scotland, a long way away from that context. You are here precisely because you rejected that context.

ZINOVIEV: Your question has no meaning outside the

context of Soviet society—therefore I cannot give you an answer outside the context of the Soviet system. Scotland is not the Soviet Union.

URBAN: An independent morality—one outside the system—does not, then, exist for you?

ZINOVIEV: It does not once you find yourself living in the system. 'Morality' depends on the total impact of your environment. The poor cannot be very 'moral'. Nor can Soviet Man, in your sense of the word.

URBAN: A time-honoured Leninist principle?

ZINOVIEV: Simply a description of Soviet reality which is an immoral reality when seen from outside. Western morality does not belong to the Soviet system.

URBAN: I'm beginning to wilt under the pressure of your dialectic. You hated Stalin, yet you loved him. You were ready to kill him, yet you were also ready to die for him. Andrei Amalrik once said to me that the whole of Soviet society is psychologically diseased.[1] I can see what he meant.

ZINOVIEV: I'm describing a very normal *Soviet* phenomenon. I fought for Stalin when my duties as an officer so demanded. I was ready to sacrifice my life for Stalin, for my military superiors and my comrades. When you have the privilege of being an officer in the Air Force, you want to be a good officer.

URBAN: There is, I suppose, a sense in which a young man—keen, vigorous and anxious to take on whatever may come his way—enjoys being a good soldier no matter what political leadership he may serve under. To be fully stretched in a fine corps of young men is an ambition we have all probably had. I suppose it was that sort of ambition that motivated you under Stalin.

ZINOVIEV: Yes, it was.

URBAN: Did you ever ask yourself whether it was Russia you were fighting for, or Communism as represented by Stalin?

ZINOVIEV: No. It was my duty to do as I was being ordered.

The Germans were my enemies. It was my job to fight them, and I enjoyed fighting them.

URBAN: Would you agree that you have, in that case, no moral grounds for condemning the great majority of *German* soldiers who fought for Hitler arguing exactly what you have just put to me: that in war you obey orders, and you obey them willingly because your first duty is to your country, your superiors, and your comrades—no matter whether you approve or disapprove of your leaders?

ZINOVIEV: The two are not comparable. In any case, as soon as the War was over I began to criticise the Soviet system, and developed the sharpest criticism yet seen in the Soviet Union.

But you must understand that my strictures came from within the system. The Soviet system was my home; my family; my life. Good or bad, I was part of it. It was beyond my power to change it. I have a daughter. She may be good or bad, brilliant or stupid—but do I love her less if she *is* stupid or disappoints my expectations? Of course I don't.

URBAN: Clearly, then, you don't want to see the Soviet system overthrown.

ZINOVIEV: That is not my concern. At the same time, I can see the grave danger that the Soviet system represents for the Western world, and I want to help in averting that danger. I am a Russian first and foremost, and I want to see the Russian people happy and prosperous. That requires the disintegration of the Soviet *empire*. I know that.

URBAN: You want to see the *empire* destroyed but not the Communist system.

ZINOVIEV: As I want the Russian people to attain independence as a sovereign state, I must logically hope for the destruction of the Soviet empire. The Communist system is another matter.

URBAN: Would your Russia incorporate the Ukraine?

ZINOVIEV: No, I would allow the Ukrainians to take care of their own problems in whatever framework they wished.

My sole concern is the future of the Russian people. I write my books as a Russian writer for Russian readers. I should like my contemporaries to read my books. I want the Russian people to be educated, cultured, and self-confident so that they can share the treasures of world culture and contribute to them. I want to lift the Russians out of their centuries-old backwardness and subjection. It is impossible for the Russian people to attain any of these things within the Soviet empire.

URBAN: You said 'the system is another matter'. Are you suggesting that the Communist system would survive even if the Soviet empire were destroyed or fell apart for internal reasons?

ZINOVIEV: Yes, my forecast is that the system would survive. I am sure that the Communist system has a future. More than that, I feel confident that the Communist system will eventually embrace the whole of mankind. But the Soviet empire will perish.

URBAN: Would you, in fact, want to see the Soviet empire defeated in war as a step towards the liberation of the Russian people and an independent Russian nation-state?

ZINOVIEV: It is not a matter of what I would want to happen. But I am as certain as anyone can be that in a Third World War both the Soviet Union and the USA would, in their different ways, suffer defeat. The Soviet Union would inevitably fall apart into a number of small and medium-size states; and I am convinced that this would be beneficial not only to the peoples concerned, but to the rest of mankind.

The Soviet empire in its present form is highly dangerous to the West. I keep coming back to this theme because the Western countries seem to underestimate the staying power of the Soviet system. As a war-making machine, the USSR compares very favourably with the Western world, because it is an empire in a state of permanent mobilisation. It can destroy Western Europe. It can destroy the USA—even though it, too, will be destroyed in the process.

URBAN: You seem to be talking as though a Third World War were inevitable.

ZINOVIEV: I'm sure that it is inevitable.

URBAN: Within a time-frame of, shall we say, ten years?

ZINOVIEV: I cannot predict the time-frame, but one thing I *can* say: the Soviet Union will be the initiator of any future

World War. I use the word 'initiator' advisedly. I'm not saying the USSR will *start* the war 'cold', as it were—but it will cause it to happen by stirring up trouble in one place, supporting anti-Western resentment in another, and so on. The policies the Soviet Union has been pursuing in Angola, Ethiopia, Afghanistan, and more recently in Central America, are stations on the road to war. At the time of the Iranian crisis the Kremlin had an incomparable chance to hammer the West from a position of strength. It missed that chance.

Now it will need at least five years to concentrate its various advantages over the West at a point of maximum Western vulnerability. The rapid rearmament of the USA and the growing Western consciousness of the reality of the Soviet threat may, of course, throw the Kremlin's calculations out of gear. But let me at once tell you: the Soviet government can wait. If the correlation of forces does not suit the Soviet book in, let us say, five years from now, the Soviet leaders will bide their time until some crisis in the Western world provides the necessary opening. The Soviet empire is not an *ad hoc* aggressor. Its expansionism springs from the nature of its philosophy and is not susceptible to change—tactical delays, yes; permanent change, no.

At War with the World

URBAN: You have spoken of 'the correlation of forces.' In the most popularly held Western view, we are ill-equipped and ill-prepared for any serious confrontation with the Soviet Union. Is that your view, too?

ZINOVIEV: Yes and no. Every system has its characteristic strengths and weaknesses. The Western world consists of individual states, each with its own interests and traditions. They are to some extent held together by NATO, but their military cooperation is clearly not comparable with the highly centralised, totalitarian structure of the Soviet Union.

At the same time the West is more flexible, more adaptable, and more inventive. My five years in Western Europe have increasingly convinced me that the Western nations have so much resilience and such colossal reserves of creative thinking, in the military as well as in the economic and cultural spheres, that the Western way of life will survive anything that may befall it—even a possible Soviet occupation after a lost war. When I lived in Russia I was convinced that we were generally better prepared for war than our opponents. I am no longer certain that is true. West European civilisation is a living organism. It can resist hard times, recover from illnesses, and develop in a great number of new directions. Even Communism would assume civilised, liberal forms if it ever reached Western Europe.

URBAN: Are you implying that 'the Western way of life' would survive a lost war but our West European social order might not?

ZINOVIEV: I believe the Western type of liberal democracy will not survive for very much longer with or without war; but I do think that the Western forms of Socialism and Communism will be different in kind from what we have in the USSR. You cannot force Frenchmen or Italians or Americans to live like Russians: to tolerate the camps, forced labour, censorship, miserably low living standards, ideological conditioning, and the rest. They just will not have it.

URBAN: You talk like a 'Euro-Communist'. , , ,

ZINOVIEV: No, I'm simply answering your questions.

URBAN: You have given me a fairly optimistic picture of the strengths and resilience of Western society. What about the USSR? You have repeatedly said that it is a menace to the Western world.

ZINOVIEV: There again we must weigh up the system's typical strengths and weaknesses. The Soviet Union is strong because it is in a state of permanent mobilisation; it is a military camp. Every able-bodied Soviet man and woman has a warlike role as a trained reservist in the armed forces. Upon mobilisation he need not be told where to go and what to do: he *knows* because he has had years of discipline and training.

URBAN: I have just been reading General Ogarkov's booklet calling on the Soviet people to prepare themselves physically and psychologically for total war. . . .

ZINOVIEV: Yes—but you don't even have to do that,

because everyday life in the Soviet Union is a life of regimentation, ideological conditioning, paramilitary training and the like. The Soviet régime is, and always has been, at war with the non-Soviet world. That is its defining characteristic.

URBAN: All of which testifies to the great military strength of the Soviet system. . . .

ZINOVIEV: Yes, but that strength is not durable, and it does not translate into successful expansionism. Let me start with the second point.

When Western Sovietologists examine the military potential of the Soviet Union they take no account of one all-important human factor: the character of the Russian people. A country set upon world conquest needs people who have it in them to be world-conquerors. They need a people who (rightly or wrongly) feel superior to the rest of mankind, and have the will and the organisational ability to run their imperial dependencies. The British and (in their different ways) the Germans and the French have all had these qualities.

The Russian people haven't got them. They are not a master race. Their history has turned them into underdogs. They are not fired by an imperial mission; nor do they feel, as the French did, that they have a right to impress their culture on less fortunate races. But your Western students of Soviet affairs, with all their fine tables, models and statistics, do not understand this decisive characteristic of Russian history and the Russian psyche.

URBAN: I've been wondering how familiar you are with what Western scholars *did* say on this subject. George Kennan, for example, in our conversation in 1975,[2] recorded an opinion which is almost identical with the one you have just expressed:

> I don't attribute to the Russians the political and ideological capability of controlling hundreds of millions of West Europeans. They would find West Europeans, by virtue of their numbers, background and sophistication, much harder to regiment and control than they did the people of Eastern Europe. . . .
> The Germans . . . had much more effective people, more capable administrators, and greater self-confidence than the Russians had ever

had. When they overran a country, they had the men who spoke the language, could take charge of the railways and the telephone system, and were not only competent to perform a great many other tasks, but were also endowed with enough self-confidence to win, to some extent, the respect of the local people. The Russians would not be able to do any of these things.

One could quote parallel examples from other Western historians.

ZINOVIEV: Well, if Kennan said these things independently from my observations, so much the better. The fact to remember is that the Russians are not a master-race.

URBAN: But wouldn't you agree that your 19th-century Slavophiles thought otherwise, that their entire philosophy sprang from the conviction that the Russian people *did* have a mission, a Messianic mission, in the world?

ZINOVIEV: This is what they said—but it was, and is, a preposterous idea. A mission like that presupposes cultural superiority, and that is precisely what the Russian people have never had. Without cultural superiority and the conviction that it is your right and duty to assert it, any missionary imperialism is a fantasy. The Russian people are generally indolent, ill-organised, and lacking in any sense of discipline and self-discipline. Their will to control other nations and 'lead' the world is conspicuous by its absence. They may be strong enough to prevent the Americans from drawing the entire world under their hegemony; but they haven't the power to do it themselves.

URBAN: This is a point Zbigniew Brzezinski has repeatedly made both in office and out of office,[3] adding for the benefit of American neo-isolationists that there is, in fact, no alternative to American world leadership.

ZINOVIEV: The Russian inability and even unwillingness to assert leadership has to be experienced to be believed. I remember from my own wartime military career that I was incapable of imposing my will on my own subordinates. Now, you might think that I had a whole air armada under my command. Not at all. I had three—*three!*—men on my staff; but I couldn't tell these three miserable subordinates what to do. They each went their own way. Later on, in Moscow, I was for a short time chairman of my University collective but gave it up as something utterly uncongenial.

URBAN: Uncongenial in what sense?

ZINOVIEV: In the sense that I could not control the people in it. More important, I did not *want* to control them. You see, I'm a typical Russian—I had absolutely no wish to push these people around. I could see that they all had different inclinations and psychological needs. Why should I put them into harness? Now this, I'm sure you will agree, is not an attitude that makes for Imperial Expansion and Happy Imperialists.

URBAN: Nevertheless, at the end of the War, when the Red Army was sweeping westwards, there was a great deal of talk at all levels of the Soviet forces of not stopping at the Anglo-American lines but 'driving to the Atlantic'. Wasn't that a popular expression of an imperial ambition?

ZINOVIEV: Two points. The 'drive to the Atlantic' may have been a slogan current in the *Soviet* Army; but we are now discussing the character of the *Russian* people. Not all Soviet troops are Russian, and the leadership of the Soviet forces now is not even predominantly Russian—it is predominantly Ukrainian. Second, the slogan originated from Stalin—and he was a Georgian. So you cannot say that driving to the Atlantic expressed a *Russian* imperial aspiration. In any case, the whole idea was grotesque, because world conquest was not part of the psychological training of the Red Army. The war was a defensive war. We were not prepared for overrunning Western Europe.

URBAN: What if another iron-willed leader, somewhat in the mould of Stalin, came to power in the Kremlin under warlike conditions? Could he not lead a willing Empire and a willing Red Army (motivated by the sort of sentiments that inspired you when you were fighting Hitler) into imperial expansionism under defensive slogans? And wouldn't that automatically constitute a predominantly *Russian* expansionism too?

ZINOVIEV: A Stalin-like figure could never again rise in the USSR. Stalin was a unique phenomenon. He was a child of the Revolution: he represented the youth of Communist society; and he was, for us, undoubtedly the greatest man of the 20th century. Lenin gave birth to the Revolution; but it was under Stalin that this newborn phenomenon began to grow and experience the joy of being alive and trying to reach for the sort of often impossible targets young men and women like to reach for in all ages and all civilisations.

URBAN: Aren't you really saying that Stalinism may have been beastly for those who got caught up in it, but *I* was eighteen, had a little money jingling in my pocket, the sun was shining and the girls were pretty?

ZINOVIEV: Your imagination is more fertile than my dialectic.

URBAN: You said a moment ago that Soviet strength is not 'durable'.

ZINOVIEV: Yes. I was making the point that whereas Western society is best compared to a healthy organism with full powers of recovery, the Soviet system is sick and easily pushed into terminal illness because it has cancer, a social cancer, at its very centre. It is an uncreative, arrested, moribund society.

URBAN: Once again, I cannot keep up with your dialectic. You have been saying repeatedly in this conversation (and, of course, over and over again in your books) that the Soviet system is extremely strong, that its military potential is gravely underestimated in the West and, generally speaking, that it is symbolic of the sort of society that will eventually embrace all mankind. *Now* you are saying that the Soviet system is cancerous. Can you help me to understand your reasoning? If the Soviet system is so weak—why is it so strong?

ZINOVIEV: This is too large a topic. The nature and future of Soviet society will have to be the subject of another conversation.

The Lie as a Way of Life

URBAN: Suppose this were February 1917 and you had foreknowledge of the sacrifices the October Revolution would bring in its wake: Civil War, the slaughters of the Collectivisation Campaign and the Great Terror, the Gulag Archipelago, Hitler's rise to power through Stalin's misjudgment of the state of the Weimar Republic, and the rest. Would you still wish the October Revolution to happen? This is a question you have yourself asked in your book *The Radiant Future*, but answered ambiguously.

ZINOVIEV: Yes, I would fight for the Revolution—today, or tomorrow. I have written a whole book about my opposition to Stalinism (which appeared in Russian in the summer of 1983). But if I were to choose between living in the truly terrible epoch of Stalin and a blander and more comfortable age, I would, without hesitation, choose Stalin's.

I don't want to repeat myself too much. Let me just say again that Stalin's was a time of idealism, dedication, and even heroism. We had an aim in life and fought for it. It is not often in history that one can do that.

URBAN: But can you envisage, can you re-enact for yourself, the screams of the tortured and dying, the hangings and shootings which (as you have said) decimated your own people under Stalin and Lenin, causing many more deaths than Hitler managed to chalk up in all his concentration camps—and still say that the Bolshevik Revolution is something you'd fight for all over again?

ZINOVIEV: The things you describe were tragic but not criminal. The Revolution brought education, health, upward social mobility, and a new beginning. We have discussed all this before. Some people perished; others made good. If you made a count of the number of people for whom the Revolution meant a great new opportunity and those for whom it involved a tragedy, you'd be surprised to find by what a colossal margin the beneficiaries of the Revolution exceeded those who lost out by it.

URBAN: Then the human sacrifice was—on balance—amply justified?

ZINOVIEV: 'Human sacrifice' is a morally loaded notion. It is inadmissible when talking about history. Morality does not enter the picture. History happened as it happened. My job is to take account of it and analyse its consequences. . . .

URBAN: As a Soviet Man. . . .

ZINOVIEV: . . . as one who was born into Soviet society and knows that it cannot be destroyed in a thousand years. We have to accept it as it is, and try to improve it, and live with it as best we may. That alone is my concern and the concern of the Soviet people.

URBAN: You have, it would seem to me, a double—an emotional and intellectual—investment in the Soviet system; and you seem to be, therefore, almost mesmerised by it as by some unbending, elemental fact. But can *our* understanding of the Soviet Union be helped by one so thoroughly committed; or is it perhaps, paradoxically, being helped *because* you are so committed? It is, after all, not an everyday occurrence that a distinguished dissident reminds us of the alleged strengths and virtues of a system which expelled him. That, if I may say so, is the piquancy of your position and indeed your special claim to fame. Are you conscious of this role? Have you, perhaps, deliberately designed it as something that will set you apart from other Soviet exiles and thus capture the headlines?

ZINOVIEV: I'm a Soviet Man and a scientist, and I flatter myself that I know what I'm talking about. Whether this helps your understanding, either because of *what* I'm saying or because *I* am saying it, is not for me to judge.

The facts are quite simple. We can assume for all practical purposes that the Soviet system is here for the rest of human history. The question I then have to ask myself is not: how do I get rid of this system?—because I know perfectly well that I can't—but, rather: how do I induce the system to give me better housing, more food, better drainage in my town, and so on? That is the meaningful line of questioning. The State? The Party? You might as well be upset about the depth of the sea or human mortality.

URBAN: But whatever has happened to Russian idealism? The history of your country in the 19th century and Russian literature of the 19th century are one long saga of young men and women burning with a selfless (and often entirely impractical) desire to salve their consciences by saving the Russian people and all of humanity. Your 'October Revolution' would be unthinkable without them. Yet here is a distinguished Russian mathematician and philosopher, who has made his name in the world with his satires of Soviet society, telling us that any notion of change in the Soviet system must be limited to a better drainage system! Imagine what a Vera Zasulich would think of that!

ZINOVIEV: Oh, many things that were possible before the Revolution aren't possible now. You can't be idealistic in front of a 50-ton truck bearing down on you on the highway. For us, the material factor you have mentioned with some disdain is not trivial. When your principal problem in life is an extra five square metres of living space, or access to some store that can feed you, or some medicine without which your child's life may be lost, things that seem trivial to the Western eye assume egregious importance.

URBAN: The system is, then, achieving its purpose—security of survival—simply by keeping the population in poverty.

Now, one set of sociologists tells us that poverty makes for unrest and revolution; another that it paralyses the will and makes for acquiescence. The Soviet case, as you've presented it, seems to endorse the latter. If so, nibbling away at the edges of the system will not help. Only whole-sale change will, or might. . . .

ZINOVIEV: That, as I've said, we must rule out for all prac-tical purposes, even as a result of war. Poverty in the Soviet Union is great, and the supply of food and other essentials worse than it has been at any time since World War II. It is hard to imagine how it could deteriorate any further. All this does, of course, confine people's zeal for reform to the satisfaction of their immediate needs. The will for greater things *is* paralysed, and that, together with the all-pervasive nature of the Communist state, also means the paralysis of any idealism and salvationism of the kind we saw in the 19th century.

Imagine for a moment how the average Soviet student or teacher goes about improving his situation—getting accepted for a postgraduate course or promoted to be a '*docent*'.

Well, he will not want to challenge the university system as such, much less the Soviet system. For him, as a matter of fact, both are quite congenial. What, then, will he do? He will take small and cunning steps within the system. He will act in such a way as to convince his superiors that he is the right man to be given promotion. And how will he do that? He will do it by offering 'presents' or straightforward bribes to the right people, and even by writing denunciations.

I have written extensively about denunciations in *Homo Sovieticus*. Let me just say that denunciations are an accepted practice in Soviet society. They are a way of life and quite natural. In a tough struggle for survival, you help yourself as best you can. For the average Soviet citizen, whether young or old, the things that matter are food, housing, clothing, footwear, health, and promotion. There is just no room or surplus energy left over for the sort of idealism that motivated young Russians in the 19th century.

URBAN: But what about the traditional Russian preoccupation with 'the truth', the refusal to accept the lie promoted by the authorities?

ZINOVIEV: Well, if a student voiced his opinion that the Soviet system or the Party was based on lies, he would at once be expelled from the Communist Youth Organisation. His prospects of employment would be seriously jeopardised. This course, therefore, is just not open to him. In any case, most young people fully accept the system, including official lying, even though, as young people always tend to be, they may be critical of this or that aspect of it.

URBAN: Alexander Solzhenitsyn placed 'the need to stop lying' at the very head of his priorities. Wouldn't you agree with that?

ZINOVIEV: It is a ridiculous demand. In the Soviet system it is impossible to live without lying. But we have to take a good look at the word 'lying' and see what it really means. In Western usage 'a lie' is something clearly reprehensible, for it stands for the negation of truth. Not so in the USSR. There are some 50,000 writers in the Soviet Union. They cannot write 'the truth' in the Western sense, but what they do commit to paper is not 'lies' either. Soviet ideology and mores define the parameters within which a writer has to work. He has to express himself within the given verbal orthodoxy. But the key to that orthodoxy is well known to his audience. They can read the writer's meaning even though it might seem to the Western observer that what the writer has given the reader is 'lies'. Solzhenitsyn makes it all sound far too simple.

URBAN: You said a minute ago that for you the Soviet system is a 'natural fact' which you don't question. It now seems to me that it is a little more than that: a natural fact which you appear to support with (if I may say so) unnatural zeal for one who has been so shabbily treated by the Soviet régime.

ZINOVIEV: The fact that I have been so treated cannot alter my basic judgment of the system. I have, as you well know, never been slow to subject various aspects of the system to very sharp criticism. I castigated it for its food shortages, for its appalling housing record, and a whole lot of other shortcomings.

I now live in Western Europe. I have plenty to eat, I have a decent apartment and possess three suits—but, believe me, I would give all that, and more, if I could once again be part of a Soviet collective.

URBAN: What, precisely, is the magnetism of the Soviet 'collective' for you?

ZINOVIEV: Soviet life is imbued with a sense of common purpose, which imparts a firm orientation and a new and rich consciousness. It makes you feel that, despite all the failures, you are going somewhere. No one in the West can experience that sort of feeling.

URBAN: A feeling of mission, perhaps even fanaticism?

ZINOVIEV: It is just a whole way of life—collective life. *Homo Sovieticus* is not an individualist, and perhaps not even an individual. Any definition of him must start with the observation that he is a member of a group and cannot be thought of away from this group. That, incidentally, is also my own tragedy in the West. I have no group. I am a fish out of water, and so are all Soviet men and women— even the most embittered exiled dissidents. Whether they live in Paris or in London, they carry the Soviet system around with them.

URBAN: You write in *Homo Sovieticus* that the Soviet collective is 'the most just system on earth'. That isn't our normal image of a Soviet *kolkhoz* or a Stakhanovite factory unit. Indeed, we tend to think that the Soviet collective is one of the most *unjust* systems in modern history because it means regimentation, thought-control, and depersonalisation, as well as very poor living standards. Are we in error?

ZINOVIEV: We are up against the problem of non-comprehension once again. Members of some primitive tribe in Polynesia or Africa owe their happiness to their total integration in the culture of the tribal community. They are not 'individuals'. The notion of individualism would strike them as meaningless. For the Soviet people, too, the Western idea of 'the individual' as an entity that has rights and deserves respect independently from the social context which sustains him is simply incomprehensible.

URBAN: Is this, in part, because Christianity does seem to have been received late, and (especially) badly, in the Russian lands?

ZINOVIEV: Whether it was or was not is not my problem at the moment. Certainly, the concept of the individual as a child of God and the vessel of an all-important conscience has totally disappeared from Soviet thinking. Soviet people are trained from childhood to look upon themselves as members of a group; and they can, by now, think and feel in no other way. To be 'a personality' or 'an individual' carries associations of eccentricity, irresponsibility, and disdain for your neighbour. Take my own example. In my Institute at Moscow University, I knew a great many people. I was aware of their attitudes to me—favourable and unfavourable—and they were aware of my attitude to them. We were accustomed to one another. We were a group. I would have sacrificed my life for any of them.

Consider the contrast with my life in Western Europe. I now give lectures in many Western countries, publish books and articles, and appear on television. People write about me: 'Zinoviev is a wise man', 'Zinoviev is a great satirist', and so on. I even get fan-mail. But does any of this mean very much to me? Not at all. It means nothing, because I live in intellectual segregation, as most Frenchmen and Americans and Germans do too . . . each in his overheated, overfurnished, personal ghetto . . . each fighting the depressions and despair that come from satiety, isolation, and the lack of a higher collective purpose.

But if someone from the Soviet Writers' Union let it be known that *he* thought I was a good writer—now *that* I would consider to be extremely important!

URBAN: But surely the Soviet Writers' Union are the very people who ejected you from Soviet society and imposed on you the indignity of having to live in the West. How, then, can you recognise their authority to judge whether you had written a good or bad book?

ZINOVIEV: Fish can live only in water, birds only in the sky. I'm a fish, and I belong to the Soviet pool. I cannot be a bird, try as I might. You may use all your power of persuasion telling me: 'Fly with us! Look at these wonderful skies, enjoy the sunshine!' I could not do it because I'm not a bird. Hence my argument that praise from the Soviet Writers' Union is still the one thing that matters to me. I am a Soviet Man.

URBAN: It is certainly very odd that, having been expelled from the Soviet Union for anti-Soviet behaviour, you should still seek ideological recognition from the same people who caused your 'downfall'. Thomas Mann did not seek Dr Goebbels' approval for the books he wrote in the USA. He would have been highly embarrassed if National-Socialist scholars or journalists had lavished praise on him.

ZINOVIEV: Soviet people cannot shed their identity. They may be dissidents, they may live abroad, they may be anti-Soviet from top-to-toe: their character as Soviet men will still stand out in everything they write and do. Even the most outspoken anti-Soviet literature is written in step with Soviet ideology—in negative step with it.

URBAN: What you are saying is that the regimentation and psychological conditioning of Soviet society have been more successful—now that the system has lasted 67 years—than most of us would readily admit. George Orwell has, after all, been proved right.

ZINOVIEV: Yes, whatever the reason—once a Soviet Man, always a Soviet Man.

URBAN: You are rather scathing about the 'isolation' of Western man in his 'ghetto'. When I think of all those millions of Soviet citizens whose one—most unattainable— ambition in life is to achieve a modicum of isolation in the form of an apartment, a few rooms of their own that they don't have to share with others, your condemnation of us does not sound quite convincing. I can think of no social situation to which Jean-Paul Sartre's 'Hell is other people' would apply more appropriately than the Soviet collective.

ZINOVIEV: I don't agree. But you are right in suspecting one thing: the longer I live in the West and the more my life in the Soviet Union recedes into the background, the rosier becomes my image of the Soviet collective. I acknowledge this as an inevitable influence on my current thinking: the tendency to forget the unpleasant side of collective life.

Who Fights for Peace, or Freedom, or Country?

URBAN: How would the East European 'allied' forces behave, in your opinion, if the Soviet Union found itself at war? Would they add to, or take away from, Soviet power?

ZINOVIEV: They would definitely boost the strength of the USSR.

URBAN: Are you saying that the Hungarian, Czech, and Polish troops would willingly put their lives on the line to aid their oppressors?

ZINOVIEV: Ah, but it doesn't work like that. Take Poland. A considerable section of the Polish people may well feel unhappy with the Socialist régime as it is at the moment; but the vast majority of Poles nevertheless accept the system. Otherwise the system would have been swept away by now.

URBAN: You talk as though Hungary in 1956 and Czechoslovakia in 1968 had never happened, as if Poland had never had martial law and self-Occupation imposed on it. Surely the East European régimes owe their survival to the USSR, and to no other factor.

ZINOVIEV: You underestimate the power of habit and vested

interests. The social *status quo* in Eastern Europe is linked to the well-being of a great many key people: the bureaucracy, the officer class, the state-employed professional élites are all its beneficiaries. This oligarchy will certainly go along with the Soviet Union as long as they are persuaded that the Soviet Union is on a winning ticket.

URBAN: Here, too, your assessment is at variance with informed Western opinion. I remember talking to Dean Rusk, the former US Secretary of State, about this problem. He was firmly of the opinion that the satellite countries would greatly weaken the war-making potential of the Soviet Union by sabotaging Soviet lines of communication, pinning down Soviet divisions, and so on.[4]

ZINOVIEV: It would be impossible to do any of that. Sabotage—well, every soldier in the Soviet armed forces 'sabotages' his unit every day of the week. This is quite normal in the USSR—yet the system survives.

URBAN: Petty theft, neglect of duty, insubordination in peace-time are one thing. Organised sabotage of the Red Army on a nationwide scale in war is, I would have thought, quite another. The Red Army's vital lines of communication run through Poland, Czechoslovakia, and East Germany. A restive Polish or Czech population, to say nothing of a disaffected Polish or Czech Army, could present the Soviet leaders with formidable problems. This, among other things, is what Dean Rusk had in mind.

ZINOVIEV: Your scenario sounds logical enough in the abstract, but on closer inspection it turns out to be absurd. The generals of the Red Army aren't complete fools, you know. The Polish, Czech and East German units are so closely tied in with the Soviet divisions that any independent move on their part is virtually impossible. They rely on the Soviet forces for their supplies of ammunition, replacement and repair facilities, food and reconnaissance. Above all, they are part of an order of battle and a command structure which rule out any large-scale insubordination, let alone any uprising on a national scale.

Remember that at the time of the Soviet invasion of Czechoslovakia in 1968, the Czechoslovak forces, which were substantial and well-equipped, were helpless bystanders because under the Warsaw Pact's integrated

order of battle they were facing westward. In any case, the
'allied' troops are most unlikely to be given sensitive front-
line duties. Their task will be to follow up the Soviet
advance, consolidate the gains, mop up resistance, and
provide the occupation forces. Such activities are easily
controlled.

URBAN: But what about the Poles? Wouldn't *they* be a
mortal threat to the Soviet lines of communication?

ZINOVIEV: No—the East European forces, including the
Polish ones, are too thoroughly integrated by now to do any
such thing. It is too late, far too late, for these hopes to be
realistic.

Of course, if the Soviet empire began to fall apart, either
as a consequence of military setbacks or internal disintegration, or a combination of the two, the East Europeans
would reassert their national independence and add their
bit to the fall of the empire. It is *then* that all the factors
you have listed might come into their own—but not, as I
believe, before. Eastern Europe would regain its independence as a *result* of the Soviet Empire expiring—not as one
of the principal causes.

Your questions turn on the problem of 'sufficiency'. How
much loyalty and subordination on the part of the East
European forces is enough to ensure the smooth functioning
of the Soviet military machine in the early phases of a war?

Take my own military career as an example. I was, as
I've said, bitterly opposed to Stalin both during the War
and after. Yet I fought for him, as we all did, because I was
an officer of the Red Air Force—and I fought for him to
the best of my ability and with complete dedication. Now,
in Poland we can see a somewhat analogous situation: the
Poles serving in the Polish forces may dislike the Russians,
the Polish régime, the suppression of *Solidarity*, whatever.
But they are *cemented* into the Warsaw Pact. The system
has a stranglehold on them, and that stranglehold ensures
sufficiency. The Kremlin may not be able to inspire the
satellite forces to be *enthusiastic* defenders of the USSR,
but *unenthusiastic* cooperation is enough.

URBAN: Sticking to the Polish example—it has even been
argued that since the Polish armed forces, and especially
the ZOMO riot police, have not hesitated to use force

against their own brothers and sisters, they would scarcely hesitate to turn their guns on Germans!

ZINOVIEV: You are right.

URBAN: The testimony of history would seem to suggest that in a warlike emergency the Western Alliance would want to see to it that Eastern Europe weakened the military power of the USSR, not at an advanced stage of Soviet disintegration but early in the game. Do you think this could be achieved by telling, for example, the Romanians and Hungarians that whichever turned its face against the Soviet Union first would have a privileged claim on some disputed territory?

ZINOVIEV: No—all East European claims would have to wait until the fate of the Soviet empire was settled or close to being settled. Until that happens, no propaganda can be effective.

URBAN: Let us look at the chances of weakening the Soviet system in peaceable ways. The Kremlin has, as we all know, a considerable hand in supporting the so-called Western 'peace movements', even though it has not created them.

ZINOVIEV: Yes, when all is said and done, the 'peace movement' is a Soviet weapon, no matter how indirectly the Soviets may be wielding it, and no matter how much genuine good faith may be the ruling motive of the Western peace protesters.

URBAN: Why are you so emphatic in saying that it is 'a Soviet weapon'?

ZINOVIEV: Because it is a training-ground for designing and running mass protest movements. Once the machinery is set up and the people are trained for one kind of protest, they can be used for another. The Soviet system works in cells and cadres. The Kremlin is extremely conscious of the need to create a basic network of like-minded people who can be used to pursue Soviet objectives. The 'peace movement' performs that role. It is a Trojan horse against which the Western democracies can do very little. Nobody is against 'peace', any more than they are against motherhood.

URBAN: Don't you think we could export, or re-export, this propagandistic obsession with 'peace' to the Soviet Union and its client states in Eastern Europe? Couldn't we tell the Ukrainians, for example, that the deployment of so many Russian missiles on their soil would do nothing for their survival in a nuclear war exactly as the Soviet Marshals are telling West Germany? Can you envisage Ukrainian 'peace'-marchers parading in the streets of Kiev under posters reading 'Ukrainian mothers will not allow their sons to die for Andropov's war', or 'KGB cooks books to exaggerate US nuclear arsenal', and the like?

ZINOVIEV: Absolutely impossible. You must understand that no internal force can be strong enough to weaken the Kremlin's obsession with military power. If the Soviet economy could afford it, the Soviet Marshals would fill every peasant barn with tanks and self-propelled guns. For a régime that is still uncertain of its legitimacy, both internally and in the world at large, it is an article of faith that military power has to be maximised at whatever cost. Domestic protest, if that could be imagined under Soviet conditions, wouldn't have the slightest impact. Soviet power and the consciousness of power can only be stopped by countervailing power of equal or superior strength. If the Soviet move into Afghanistan had met Western resistance—*that* might have stopped Soviet expansionism. But 'peace marches'?

I said '*if* domestic protest could be imagined'—well, it cannot be imagined. You don't seem to be able to comprehend to what extent Soviet society is passive and regimented. If the government orders people to demonstrate for 'peace'—they will come out on the streets, carry the prescribed 'peace' banners, and demonstrate for 'peace'. But if the Soviet government orders a demonstration for *war*, the *same* people will march and demonstrate for war. Our people are resigned. They are indifferent. They do not believe that they can have a will of their own, or that they could assert it if they had one.

URBAN: But . . . given the Ukrainians' strong feeling of a separate national identity and their second-class citizenship (as many of them see it) under Russian domination . . . couldn't we gently remind them through our information services: 'You may find yourselves in extreme danger if a nuclear war should break out, because so many Russian missiles are deployed on your territory. Show your national independence by demanding the removal of foreign rockets—and stay alive'?

ZINOVIEV: It would be senseless and useless to say any such thing.

URBAN: Why?

ZINOVIEV: Because you must put yourself in the shoes of a typical Ukrainian. His first reaction may very well be positive. He may very well say—Yes, we must get rid of these rockets. But after a moment's consideration he will find that he is helpless. He is part of a Russian group at his workplace and in his living quarters. He will lose his job if he steps out of line, and disqualify himself for any other employment. There will be a black mark on his record, if indeed he does not find himself in prison. Whereas if he obeys the orders of higher authority, demonstrating as he is ordered for peace *or* war—he is left alone to the extent that anyone is left alone in a totalitarian system.

URBAN: You are painting a picture of an absolutely seamless tyranny in which individual protest is not only impossible but also unthinkable. One wonders how the East German, Czech, Hungarian, and Polish reform movements ever came about.

ZINOVIEV: That is another matter. But let me go on about the Ukrainians. The fact is that the Ukrainian people know all about the missiles deployed on their territory and are conscious of the danger they represent. How do they know about them? Because the Ukrainians are great walkers, and you cannot go on a walking tour in the Ukraine without seeing these missiles all over the place. And then, we all have relatives in the Red Army. Our boys come home for leave and tell us how and where these weapons are deployed and of the targets they provide. So if you tell the Ukrainian people in your propaganda that they are under constant threat because they have all these missiles on Ukrainian soil, you're not telling them anything that they haven't themselves known for a long time.

But that's not the whole story. Most Ukrainians, while

recognising the danger, will tell you in the same breath: 'Ah, but we have to defend ourselves against American and British and French nuclear blackmail. Without these missiles, the Americans might destroy us.'

URBAN: Aren't you saying that the Ukrainians tend to be schizophrenic: that they are anti-Russian with one half of their minds but believe Soviet propaganda with the other?

ZINOVIEV: No, that's not it. Like all Soviet people, Ukrainians are very skilled in social adaptation. In a totalitarian system rationalisation is the condition of psychological survival. The Ukrainians will rationalise what they feel they cannot change in any case, and say: 'Yes, we'd be much better off without these Russian missiles—but we must do *something* about the American threat.'

And this rationalisation is a psychological lifebelt. What do you say to yourself and your family if there is no meat to be had in the shops? You cannot blame the whole system, or the Government. These are given. You cannot argue with them. You might as well blame 'God' or 'human nature'. Therefore you justify the situation in terms of Soviet ideology: you blame the meat shortage on ungrateful Poles and Czechs who have repaid your wartime sacrifices with rank ingratitude. Or you blame the Americans, whose nuclear threats have forced the Soviet Government to stockpile food for a rainy day.

URBAN: We are once again touching on the essential differences between your attitude and ours in the West. You say of the Soviet system and Government that these are 'given', as though they had been imposed on the Soviet peoples by some impersonal force which no human agency can change. We in the West do not believe that political systems come into being and survive under impersonal conditions. We believe (and I personally believe) that the Soviet system exists because the Soviet peoples tolerate it, and if they tolerate it they have to bear some responsibility for their own misfortunes as well as for the misfortunes the system imposes on others.

ZINOVIEV: The truth is that Western historians just cannot identify with Soviet mentality. They seem to think that categories that apply under Western conditions have a corresponding relevance to those obtaining in Soviet society. They believe that the notions of 'truth', 'freedom', 'democracy', 'human dignity', 'individual rights' carry the same urgency and associations of meaning in Soviet society as they do in parliamentary democracies. They do not.

You cannot transplant the Western 'peace movement' to the Soviet Union, because the context is wholly different. I can understand your desire to demoralise Soviet society, but in order to do that you have to concentrate your fire on areas that are truly vulnerable: food-shortages; bad housing; the scarcity and poor quality of clothing; the non-availability of certain medicines; privilege and corruption in the educational system, and the like. These are the things Soviet people worry about. These are the exposed nerves of Soviet society. But to tell the Ukrainians that they are not 'free' enough, or to hold up the example of *Solidarity* as something Russian trade-unionists ought to follow, betrays a non-comprehension of Soviet reality.

URBAN: We have been caught in a circular argument. We started this long colloquy with the observation that Western scholars, diplomats and journalists are, in your view, incapable of understanding the Soviet system; and we are ending it on the same note.

Have we, then, been wasting each other's time? I don't think so. You have, with your forthright explanations, greatly added to my own knowledge of Soviet Man—and especially one Soviet Man—even though I am just as puzzled and bewildered by him as I was many hours and many arguments ago. Perhaps it is the relentless statement of paradoxes that, in the end, illuminates reality. Perhaps there is by now an unbridgeable gulf between the values inculcated by the Soviet system and those we in the Western world hold to be essential to a free and dignified human existence. Lenin's notion that 'freedom is necessity understood' seems to underlie much of what you have been telling me in this conversation. If there is one idea the free democratic world rejects, and has to reject on pain of being untrue to its own essence, it is this Leninist denial of human freedom in the name of human freedom.

Personally, I am enough of an historical optimist to

believe that Soviet Man is a temporary phenomenon—that the quest for liberty is so original a requirement of human life that it stubbornly survives even where the experience of liberty is inhibited and its outward models are destroyed. But that would take us into another conversation.

Postscript

My conversation with George Urban has been interpreted by many people quite differently from how I would have wished, and indeed has been quite misunderstood. Of course part of the blame for this rests with me, inasmuch as I was unable to express my ideas sufficiently exactly in a language that was not my own, as well as with the conditions of the conversation and the method of publication. However, a significant part of the responsibility for this lies also with readers whose attitude towards what I said was biased, who interpreted my statements tendentiously and who saw in them what was not in fact there. One of the reasons for this lies in readers confusing my personal attitude towards various aspects of life with my comments as a detached observer of the same. This confusion is particularly apparent in V. Bukovsky's response to my comment that, given a free choice, the vast majority of the Soviet population would prefer Brezhnev to Solzhenitsyn. He took this to mean that I prefer Brezhnev to Solzhenitsyn. And this from a man who knows perfectly well that Brezhnev is the object of the sharpest satire in my books.

Here I wish to raise only two of the questions discussed in my conversation with George Urban: my view of collectivisation and of Stalin. From childhood I hated and despised everything connected with Stalin. In 1939 I was arrested for openly speaking out against the cult of Stalin. Thereafter, right up to the Khrushchev 'coup', criticism of Stalin and illegal anti-Stalin activities were at the centre of my life. But the Stalin era has now passed into history. Everyone, including former Stalinists, has started tearing his reputation to shreds. It has become quite safe, even profitable, to criticise Stalin. As for me, I gave up my anti-Stalin activity because it had lost all meaning for me. My personal attitude to Stalin and Stalinism did not change, but the angle from which I viewed this historical phenomenon did change. I began to analyse it as a sociologist. And, naturally, I had to deal with it objectively, I had to look for explanations of its causes, essence and historical role. But explanation is not justification. If I maintain that Stalinism arose not out of the evil intentions of Stalin and his henchmen, but as a result of a particular historical conjuncture, I am in no way maintaining that Stalinism was justified or that it was a blessing. Some of my readers, however, incapable of distinguishing between analysis and justification, have imputed to me the desire to justify, even make an apology for Stalinism. This applies particularly to my book about Stalinism 'Nashei yunosti polet' (*The Flight of Our Youth*).

Similar problems arise with collectivisation. Our family suffered dreadfully during collectivisation. We, and those near to us, experienced all its horrors. One of the reasons I was expelled from the Komsomol and from the institute where I was studying, and subsequently arrested, was my speaking out against collectivisation and the policy towards collective farms. That is one side of the case. But there is another: the consequences of collectivisation for society. As a result of collectivisation millions of Russian peasants were freed from the conditions of life in the country, fled to the towns and participated in the culture of the towns. Their children were educated, and many were much more successful in life than they would have been had they stayed in the country. Our family was typical in this respect. We endured the nightmare years of collectivisation, but in the end we began to live very much better than in the country. And if millions of former peasants had been given the chance of returning to peasant toil they would have refused.

This does not mean that collectivisation was a blessing; it was an appalling tragedy. But those who survived the tragedy had no desire to go back. There are other aspects of collectivisation which are outside the usual framework of notions about it in the West, and which cannot be understood simply in terms of good and evil. Some of my readers, however, who were unable or unwilling to distinguish a personal attitude to events from a historical analysis of those same events, and who confused the moralising and sociological approaches, ascribed to me personal approval of collectivisation and its nightmare results. That is at the very least dishonest.

A similar situation obtains with the other problems discussed in my conversation with George Urban. He has suggested that I make some corrections. But when I looked through the text I decided to leave it as it was when it first appeared in print and confine myself to these comments. Perhaps its very weaknesses will act as a spur to examine certain events in Soviet history that have so far reached Western readers in terms of clichés.

August 1988   Alexander Zinoviev

Notes

1. See, *Eurocommunism* (G. R. Urban ed.), London 1978.
2. George F. Kennan and George Urban, 'From Containment to Self-Containment', *Encounter*, September 1976, and *Stalinism* (G. R. Urban, ed.), London 1982.
3. See, in *Encounter*, Zbigniew Brzezinski and George Urban, 'The Perils of Foreign Policy' (May 1981), and Zbigniew Brzezinski, 'Tragic Dilemmas of Soviet World Power' (December 1983).
4. See, *Détente* (G. R. Urban ed.), London 1976.

3. GALINA VISHNEVSKAYA
Out of tune with Soviet society

Eastern Europe: The View from Moscow

URBAN: I am curious to know what you and your friends in Moscow knew and thought about the 1956 Hungarian Revolution. You depict in your memoirs the shock and silence with which Khrushchev's revelations at the 20th Party Congress were received in the Soviet Union. The truth, you say, had been known—what amazed the people was that, for the first time in Soviet history, the truth could be spoken from the platform of the Party.

GALINA: What really disgusted me was that Khrushchev and his friends spoke of the crimes committed by Stalin as though these had happened on another planet. Khrushchev said that Stalin was a maniac, a hangman, a coward—but who had created the cult of the personality? Khrushchev and his like were members of the Central Committee or even the Politburo when these shameful things happened. They had been the first to glorify Stalin and satisfy his every whim and fancy. When Stalin told Khrushchev to dance the *gopak*, dance it he did. Now he was denouncing his former master but still insisting that the Party must not wash its dirty linen in public. There was no self-examination or any sharing of responsibility.

URBAN: But surely you and your friends must have experienced relief that so large a part of official Soviet mendacity was being exposed. Stalin's despotism had covered well over half of Soviet history and accounted for the greatest carnage in the history of the Russian, Ukrainian, and other peoples.

Wasn't Khrushchev's speech a decisive step in the direction
of some sanity?

GALINA: Khrushchev was a cunning peasant. Although he
said his speech must remain secret, he saw to it that it was
widely distributed. This was a shrewdly calculated move.
Before the speech reached the public, the ordinary Russian
could say to himself that he knew nothing about Stalin's
crimes; he could protest his ignorance. But with the speech
in his pocket he could no longer. He was forced to do one
of two things: either show his indignation by trying to settle
accounts with the entire system that had made Stalinism
possible, or keep quiet and thus become an accomplice.
Settling accounts with the system was impossible, and in
any case, the Russian people had no stomach for it. What,
therefore, happened was tacit accompliceship. Much against
their will but due to their passivity, the people became
tacitly responsible for the crimes of Stalin and had every
inducement to go on keeping silent about them.

URBAN: At the recent Bern conference of the Helsinki
Process (April–May 1986) Ambassador Michael Novak, the
US Chief Delegate, made one mention of the Gulag in a
long and extremely restrained speech. The Russians were
annoyed. 'How can you be so tactless?', they complained
privately. 'How can you drag such a word into an international conference that sets out to improve cooperation
between our countries . . ?' Thirty years on, the sense of
complicity that you observed in 1956 is obviously still inhi-
biting the Soviets at both official and unofficial levels.

GALINA: I don't want you to think that the Russian people
are cowards. Far from it. During the War they distinguished
themselves defending their country against hopeless odds in
innumerable ways. But it is one thing to die a hero's death
in defence of your loved ones, and quite another to die
anonymously, in some cellar, after your own countrymen
had starved and tortured you. Die for what? There is no
heroism in fighting the faceless Moloch of the Soviet System.
But you are quite right in suspecting that in 1956 I was
greatly disturbed. 'What kind of people are we that Stalin
could have treated us with so much contempt and in the
face of so little protest?'

URBAN: Did you realise that the Hungarians had risen

against the same evil of Stalinism; that you and people of your way of thinking had allies in those young men in the streets of Budapest who were trying to throw out the Communist system?

GALINA: No, I certainly knew very little about Budapest. The picture we had was very similar to the one the Russian people are now being given of Afghanistan: 'gangs of counter-revolutionaries and bandits subverting the power of the people and of a fraternal government.' To be frank with you, the revelations of Khrushchev's speech about our own past kept us so busy that we had little time to think of much else.

URBAN: But was the official account of what the Hungarians were doing widely believed?

GALINA: To the extent that anyone paid any attention, yes, it was. But the shock-waves of Stalin's death and of Khrushchev's speech concentrated our minds with so much force on our own past that we were not interested in what was going on in Poland or Hungary. People were beginning to return from the camps. The human drama was right there, in the streets of Moscow. This is what I saw and what most gripped me.

Also, we believed that people in the 'fraternal' countries had it so much better than we had: that they had more food, better clothing, better housing. So why should they rebel at a time when we didn't and couldn't?

I was in Prague in 1955. It was my first trip abroad. I was astounded by all the things people could buy in the shops and the air of general well-being. As to the 'freedom' the Czechs were saying they had lost—I just didn't understand what they were talking about. What was the freedom they had lost when their shops were full? 1968 was a very different matter. My husband and I travelled through Czechoslovakia again and we found the country was dead. In 1955 the Czechs had been extremely friendly to Russians. Now we could not open our mouths in Russian, for the Czechs would not answer. We spoke German. We were driving through Czechoslovakia on our way back from England. We were terrified. I felt that if we were recognised as Soviets we might get killed, and this was, mind you, *before* the suppression of the Prague experiment.

URBAN: Is the impression that the East European nations are much better off than people in the Soviet Union still prevalent in Russia?

GALINA: Very much so—and with reason, because they are, on the whole, better off It is the theory behind this feeling that is so curious and wrong. When your Russian tourist visits Hungary or East Germany—what does he see? He sees meat and eggs and fresh vegetables and good shoes in the shops, and no lines of people waiting to buy them. He is at once reminded of the misery of shopping in the Soviet Union almost 70 years after the Revolution and 40 years of 'peaceful construction'. He asks himself, 'How can this be?' And he hits upon the easy answer: 'The East Europeans have all these things because *we* haven't. We have been depriving ourselves so that these people can make a good life for themselves—and what do we get? Rank ingratitude.'

URBAN: 'Colonial ingratitude', as the phrase went in the final days of the British Empire. . . .

GALINA: There was also a feeling that Russian soldiers had shed their blood to liberate these countries from Nazism. The least we could expect from them was loyalty in the face of imperialism. Yet here were these Czechoslovaks plotting to hand their country over to the West Germans! This story was widely rumoured.

URBAN: It was, as we know, an exercise in crude propaganda with no basis in reality. But how widely was it thought to be true?

GALINA: That small minority of people who were in the habit of listening to foreign radio stations were better informed and did not believe it, but the majority did. They accepted what they were told by the Soviet media.

URBAN: There is a curious phenomenon here. Many accounts of Soviet attitudes—and all accounts of attitudes in Central and Eastern Europe—tell us that the public tend to believe precisely the opposite of what the government wants them to believe. So much for the success of 'Agit-prop'. Yet you are saying that the Russian public was putty in the hands of the authorities. I would have thought that in the case of Czechoslovakia in 1968—and also of Hungary in 1956—Russian feeling and Soviet interest happened to coincide: hence the widely-shared hostility to Moscow's recalcitrant 'allies'.

GALINA: Yes, but there is also another factor we daren't neglect: the sheer exhaustion of the Russian people by the superhuman effort of trying to keep their heads above water. They had no time or energy to be exercised by the precise nature of the 1956 Polish or Hungarian or, later, the Czechoslovak upheavals. They were, therefore, easy targets for Soviet propaganda which knew how to appeal to Russian feelings while serving Soviet interests.

URBAN: Your book is one long testimony to the basic amorality and treacherousness of Soviet life. We had many accounts of this in earlier works, but I, for one, have seldom seen it articulated with so much pungency. I will not attempt to go down the list of duplicity, double-crossing, and beastliness that run through your pages with the incandescence of a tale yet to be told in its own right. Let me, however, ask you: Is this an entirely new, *Soviet* phenomenon, or does it stem from pre-Soviet or non-Soviet sources?

GALINA: This is a difficult one to answer. There is, of course, a group of people in the Soviet Union who take the trouble to inform themselves and have managed to keep their integrity intact. But the broad masses have been corrupted by Soviet ideology. I would go further: even the élite—people who are by no means stupid, people who travel and read Western books—follow the dictates of a consummate opportunism. They have formed themselves into a tightly-knit upper class with the preservation of their power and privileges uppermost in their minds. This requires them to be base and treacherous. Evtushenko is a good example. He will write verses to order; he is one of the Soviet Union's many literary lackeys. The sad thing is that the Soviet system encourages and rewards the prostitution of character.

URBAN: There is a lapidary passage in your book in which you tell us how you gave Evtushenko a resounding dressing-down after he had written some anti-American verses. You reproached him for having a bleeding heart for Cubans, Chileans, Cambodians, Vietnamese, and the American unemployed—but not noticing the murderous living conditions under which ordinary Russian men and women had to exist. I don't suppose anyone had ever given him so merciless a scolding, or ever will. How did he react?

GALINA: He gave me a sarcastic smile and said I sounded 'like a *Boyarynya Morozova*'—one of those 17th-century schismatic women who crossed themselves with two fingers instead of three, and were exiled for their pains.

URBAN: Did you find that offensive?

GALINA: On the contrary. I gave him the sign of the cross with two fingers extended, and said: 'I agree, I am a *Boyarynya Morozova*—and like her I won't abandon my belief in truth, in God, for the things of this world.'

URBAN: A righteous (not to say self-righteous) woman of your outspoken character seems to be able to get away with things in the Soviet Union that astonish me. I am not now thinking so much of your quarrel with Evtushenko as those stormy encounters you had with Soviet leaders and important men and women in the higher flights of the Government. If so much criticism and opposition was (privately, at least) tolerated, isn't there hope that the Soviet system may yet reform itself?

GALINA: Ah, but you must not draw unwarranted conclusions. Rostropovich and I were famous artists. We were in great demand at home and abroad. The Soviet state liked to parade us as typical products of the system. We had a certain licence in talking to the *apparat*, and the *apparat* showed a kind of special indulgence for a great prima donna who was vocationally temperamental and a bit uncontrollable. But the kind of no-nonsense criticism they pocketed from me they would never put up with from the ordinary citizen. I don't want you to think that, behind the scenes, the Soviet system is replete with courageous critics and bureaucrats willing to take their criticism. Cowardice and treachery are the real names of the game.

URBAN: In what way, to be more precise, does the system encourage these?

GALINA: Oh, for the average mortal sometimes in ridiculously small ways:·a 50 or 100 rouble monthly pay rise; the

promise of an extra few square metres of living accommodation; some advantage in your children's schooling and, in
special cases, the promise of foreign travel. In the Soviet
Union, where human happiness is measured by the
spoonful, these little extras carry enormous importance. In
order to gain them, most people are willing to prostitute
themselves. It's a jungle. I often ask myself: What has
Russia turned into? The idea of decency, honour,
conscience, duty has long ceased to have any meaning in
our country.

URBAN: You quote Alexander Tvardovsky telling your
husband: 'Decent people are almost extinct in Russia. . . .'
But Tvardovsky was the famous Soviet editor of 'Novy Mir'
who had launched Solzhenitsyn on his career. Rostropovich
is a distinguished Soviet musician, and you are a famous
Soviet singer: four people who saw what was wrong with
the system, and had the courage to say so and do something
about it. One assumes, indeed one knows, that there are
others. Don't these small but important pockets of insight
and courage entitle us to think that the reverse side of Soviet
baseness is an exceptionally deep yearning for truth and a
selfless determination to act on it? Isn't the presence of 'ten
righteous men' enough to make a difference, as in the story
of Sodom in 'Genesis'?

GALINA: In Biblical times 'ten righteous men' may well
have been enough to make a difference, as it is also enough
today in some free countries to make up a balanced jury.
But in Biblical times you had the Law which was universally
respected. Even under the Czars there was law and due
process. The Bolshevik revolutionaries, along with everyone
else in the realm, were protected by that legality and
survived to make a revolution and destroy the old order.
  But with the old order they destroyed the Law too. The
Soviet Union is a lawless country or, to put it more precisely,
the law is what the ruling class says it is. Russia today is
run by one vast Mafia. Its tentacles reach into every nook
and cranny of the land. The resistance of heroic individuals
cannot chop them off. You may well be right in saying that
battling against so great an evil brings out the best in those

who have undertaken to battle it; but, in the end, the individuals go under while the faceless monster goes on.

Look at the four people you mentioned: Solzhenitsyn is in exile; Rostropovich is in exile; I am in exile; Tvardovsky lost *Novy Mir* and died a much disillusioned man. A system that treats its thinking élite like that is a disaster for the people who are forced to live under it and for the rest of the world which is exposed to its influence.

Could Artists Leaven Soviet Society?

URBAN: Your views strike me as being close to those of Alexander Zinoviev. He, too, believes that the Soviet system is wicked, but he also believes that it works, that it is a seamless thing which cannot be destroyed by courageous individuals and is therefore here to stay.

GALINA: I have great respect for Zinoviev and agree with many of his ideas. He has been much maligned by the recent Soviet emigration because he has the guts to speak the truth both about the Soviet system and about the Russian and non-Russian peoples' complex involvement with it.

Ideology is the root of the problem, as both Zinoviev and Solzhenitsyn rightly say. Soviet ideology has had an appalling impact on all aspects of our lives. It's like a weed one cannot dig up: the more you pull at it the more it seems to grow. To grow a worthwhile tree takes a careful gardener and a long time, but a weed comes up in a week; it is unstoppable.

URBAN: Human nature being what it is, I can see that a convenient lie has something to commend it, but an inconvenient one? Surely an ideology that landed your father or sister in the 'Gulag' and required you to praise the system for having sent them there is not only abhorrent by any standards I can think of, but a little inconvenient too.

GALINA: It may be inconvenient but it is inescapable. It is required of Soviet people to lie in public places throughout their lives: they do it at school, at the *Komsomol*, at their workplaces, at public meetings, in letters they are told to sign, and so on. Privately, however, they know that a lie is a lie, but they have nowhere to go to say so. This doublethink deforms everyone's character and is the root cause of the corruptibility of Soviet man and Soviet institutions.

URBAN: Leszek Kolakowski puts a slightly different gloss on the same phenomenon. He says, like you, that the habit of public lying and the knowledge that a lie is a lie deforms the character. But he adds rather significantly that, having gone along with public lying for so long and so consistently, one ends up making subtle excuses for the lie, even in private life, because one cannot face up to the fact that one is a spineless and worthless human being. One has, as it were, invested in a lie and cannot now disinvest for fear of losing one's entire capital.

GALINA: I completely agree. The coexistence of these two perspectives has done great damage to everyone's sanity in the Soviet Union.

URBAN: Shostakovich, describing Stalin's persecution of Akhmatova and Zoschenko (in Solomon Volkov's *Testimony*), puts the phenomenon we are discussing in this way:

> If you are smeared with mud from head to toe on the orders of the leader and teacher, don't even think of wiping it off. You bow and say thanks. . . . No one will come to your defence and . . . you won't be able to let off steam among friends, because there are no friends in these pitiable circumstances.

GALINA: Well, I have no doubt that Shostakovich expressed thoughts of that kind, but I have a problem with the authenticity of Volkov's book. What Shostakovich, whom I knew well, is represented as saying is entirely in line with the sentiments I heard him express. These were public knowledge in Moscow. I should think Volkov collected Shostakovich's views and stories between two covers, attributing them directly to him as though they had been spoken to Volkov. I just do not believe that a conversation of that kind ever took place. That does not, however, mean that the passage you quoted is inauthentic. It is certainly a truthful description of the self-abasement of the Soviet intelligentsia under Stalin and Zhdanov.

URBAN: So what we have in the Soviet Union is a form of collective schizophrenia? Andrei Amalrik once said to me that no one who has been through the Soviet experience can call himself quite normal.

GALINA: I agree. In the West people do not, alas, understand to what extent Soviet society is also a dangerous
society to do business with. First, in a general sense, it is
impossible to predict what will come out of Soviet society,
precisely because it has a split mind. A sick person is unpredictable, and unpredictability is a destabilising factor.

But Soviet society is also dangerous in another and, paradoxically, predictable sense. If tomorrow young members
of this society were told, 'You are going to fight', they would
go and fight without asking questions. There would be no
need to persuade them to volunteer or to worry about the
effects of peace propaganda as there is in some Western
countries. They would be told: 'The Capitalists over there
have everything you haven't got: they've been stealing
things that rightfully belong to you—go and get them, go
and fight for the Fatherland', and off they would go to get
them and fight for the 'Fatherland'.

URBAN: A powerful combination of patriotism and envy.
But there is another theory which holds that Soviet
aggression and the average citizen's willingness to fight are
due to domestic frustration. As there is nothing you can
seemingly do about an unjust, oppressive system, you
fashion your indignation and pugnacity into feelings directed
against outside enemies—capitalists, imperialists, people
who allegedly threaten your survival, and so on. The Soviet
leaders are said to be aware of this frustration and route it
in the direction in which it is, in any case, only too willing
to go. Writing about his impressions of Czarist Russia in
1839, the Marquis de Custine presciently observed:

> This essentially conquering nation, greedy as a result of its hardships,
> atones in advance for the hope of exercising tyranny abroad by a
> degrading submission at home. . . .

GALINA: I believe this is part of the motivation. Our people
are driven by envy, but they are also driven by a terrible
urge to let off steam and destroy anything that may stand
in their way. And remember, the Soviet Union has a population of 270 million. The guidable aggression of so many
people is a danger the outside world is not quite aware of.

URBAN: You said that Soviet minds worked on two levels,

and that the people were, therefore, in many ways unpredictable. Aren't they unpredictable to their leaders too? Shouldn't the leaders worry that there is no telling how the sick man might behave under the pressure of this or that event? The spectacular slowness with which the Soviet authorities reacted to the Chernobyl disaster seems to indicate that their anxiety to avoid panic was greater than their sense of danger from the radioactive fall-out. They seemed to fear the Russian and Ukrainian people more than the atom.

GALINA: The Soviet leaders have always been wary of uncontrolled popular reactions. But they are no fools; they understand their own people and society and have both well in hand. How do they do that? By running, as I have said before, a Mafia-type of ruling class on a nation-wide scale. It has every feature of the real thing, including 'godfathers'. There is no evading the hand of the conspiracy. If anyone steps out of line he is destroyed. That spectacle keeps the people in their places.

URBAN: Students of the Russian historical scene often describe the Russian people as a 'dark', turbulent, unpredictable force. Professor Eduard Goldstücker, one of the Czech intellectual leaders of the 1968 'Prague Spring', once observed that the Russian people is

> an enigmatic and dangerous dragon: it is in chains, it has been in chains for centuries, and when it breaks its chains it threatens to spread chaos and disaster.

But Goldstücker felt that it was not only the Soviet leaders who were afraid of the Russian people, but the Soviet dissidents feared them too:

> Their image of the people was (and is) that of some dark, anarchic, uncontrollable mass—*tyomni narod*—a kind of lava that engulfs and drowns you if you don't put up barriers against it.

Is this overstated?

GALINA: Under the Czars the people may well have been a fearsome force because, despite all the rigours of Czarist rule, the monarch's powers were restricted. There was no totalitarian state, there were no state-controlled media, society had not been brainwashed and atomised. When the *muzhiks* were on the march (which was not too often) there was indeed something awe-inspiring and unpredictable about them. But that freedom from oppression is gone and the people are no longer free enough to be anarchistic and uncontrollable. Soviet law is made by the Mafia; the courts are controlled by the Mafia; thought is controlled by the Mafia. Any idea of rebellion is strangled at birth.

I often marvel at the naivety of Western politicians and journalists when they express disappointment that the Soviet '*nomenklatura*' fails to observe some provision or other of an international agreement or indeed Soviet 'law'. Will they ever understand that Soviet thinking is guided by the laws of expediency and nothing else—that is is useless to talk about 'treaty violations' because, to the Soviet mind, an agreement is there to be exploited, not respected? My short answer, then, to your question is: the 'dark masses' are completely under the control of a parasitic ruling class.

In the summer of 1962 there was major unrest in Novo-cherkassk and the surrounding industrial areas. The militia and security police went in, guns were used, and many people were killed before order could be restored. The strikes and clashes which had been sparked off by the simultaneous rise of food prices and reduction in wages went on for a period of weeks. I had to come to *England* to learn, more than ten years later, what had happened. Doesn't that tell you reams about the state of freedom in the Soviet Union?

At the time of the Novocherkassk unrest I lived in Moscow and moved in what you might call the highest circles—among Party and Government leaders and the cream of the intelligentsia. But not once did anyone so much as mention Novocherkassk to me and, for all I know, not many were allowed to know that it had happened. In a country where so terrible an event can be permanently withheld from the public there is very little chance that the people might get out of hand. Novocherkassk and its surroundings have a population of several hundred thousand; yet that large population, too, was keeping mum. It was party to the Soviet conspiracy of silence.

URBAN: This tells us something not only about the system but also about the success of popular intimidation and, perhaps, the docility of the citizen. The totalitarian system seems to work—it has managed to seal itself off from the outside world. Varlam Shalamov's stories about the horrors of Kolyma took decades to come out, and there the victims were counted in their tens of thousands. Marshall McLuhan's 'global village' remains fiction.

GALINA: It *is* a most sinister phenomenon, but there is a simple explanation. In a one-party state no one has the possibility of questioning the government; in a one-party state all means of communication are controlled by the authorities; in a one-party state the citizens of Novocherkassk wouldn't dare to tell what they saw because there is no legitimate organisation that would come to their support. In other words, the 'global village' only exists where democracy exists. The silence of Soviet society does not mean that everyone in the Soviet Union has been beaten into submission, but that the tyranny is merciless and all-pervasive.

URBAN: But even much closer to the heart of Europe, in the Turkish-inhabited areas of Bulgaria, atrocities were committed by the Communist authorities in 1984–85 that took more than a year to travel west and are still not fully known to us. Recently, one Bulgarian diplomat said to my face that no such atrocities had occurred—but an hour earlier I had met some of the victims. The Amnesty International report was shoved aside by him as 'hearsay' based on 'false evidence'. In any case, said the Bulgarian, the Turks had done much worse to the Bulgarian-speaking minority in Turkey!

GALINA: If the Bulgarians or Soviets had had a party or parties in opposition it would have been impossible to maintain the cover-up. A one-party state is a corrupt state, and a danger both to its own people and to its neighbours.

URBAN: The globe has become too small to permit the survival of ideological dictatorships?

GALINA: It has—

URBAN: —and this is especially true in the light of Chernobyl?

GALINA: Yes, Chernobyl has once again demonstrated that the Soviet system is not only a politically dangerous dictatorship but a technologically backward one at that. It has shown no sense of responsibility for the Russian people or the rest of Europe. One wonders whether the civilised world can afford to have such a neighbour.

URBAN: Generalisations about national character are always facile and dangerous. It is therefore with some reluctance that I put to you one stereotypical judgment about the Russian people which holds that the Russians get landed with tyrannical régimes of one kind of another because they lack civic courage. This is a variant of 'nations get the government they deserve.' Do you feel it is true?

GALINA: What in particular do you have in mind?

URBAN: There are many instances in Russian memoirs, yours and others, where ordinary people behave with great callousness towards the victims of persecution. When the NKVD's van arrives to collect some family for deportation, the neighbours look on and nod in approval. Pasternak, on receiving the Nobel Prize, is reviled and condemned by the authorities, but the Moscow writers at once follow suit, denouncing him as a 'Judas', a 'mercenary scribbler', 'an enemy and betrayer of his own people', and the like. Your own father, having served ten years in Stalin's camps under Article 58, comes out and promptly denounces you at the Bolshoi for having failed to report that you knew why he had been arrested. As you write in your memoirs:

> Of course he hoped that I would be kicked out of the Bolshoi. But Papa had miscalculated: times had changed. He died of lung cancer two years later, one more moral monster spawned by the Soviet régime.

Reading your accounts of Soviet indifference, I was chillingly reminded of Pastor Martin Niemöller's account of public indifference under another dictatorship:

> When they came for the Jews, I was not a Jew,
> so I did not protest;
> When they came for the Communists, I was not a Communist,
> so I did not protest;
> When they came for the trade unionists, I·was not a trade unionist,
> so I did not protest;
> When they came for me, there was nobody left to protest.

GALINA: It is not exactly that most people approved of what was going on under Stalin, but they were malicious and indifferent. They saw what was happening and said: 'Well, that's how things are—I'm having a bad time, why shouldn't *you* have a bad time too?' It's terrible.

Let me tell you a story which has done the rounds in Russia.

An Italian, an Englishman, a Frenchman and a Russian are summoned by God.

'You may pronounce one wish for your people and it will be fulfilled,' God says.

The Italian says: 'My wish is that the Italians should be the best singers in the world.'

The Englishman says: 'I want my people to be the best horsemen in the world.'

The Frenchman says: 'I want my nation to have the most beautiful women in the world.'

'And what about you?,' God says to the Russian.

'I want my neighbour Vasily's mare to drop dead.'

That encapsulates it to perfection.

URBAN: Is this appalling attitude an expression of straightforward envy inspired by poverty and deprivation (as Leftwing sociologists tend to believe) or is it part of the culture—perhaps both?

GALINA: Well, Russian serfdom is only 120-odd years behind us, and the habits of serfdom seem to die hard. This is, I must confess, not a very satisfactory explanation because in the USA slavery ended later than serfdom did in Russia, and yet in America you have a flourishing democracy, with the black community not a bit behind the whites in their demands for a fuller and more and more egalitarian democracy. But I feel this attitude of malicious envy *is* rooted in serfdom which has now been reinforced by Communist ideology. Life in a Communist society, with its permanent restrictions, deprivations and frustrations, is a rat-race.

URBAN: Hasn't this gross form of envy and jealousy also something to do with the materialistic message of Marxism-Leninism and the dwindling impact of Christianity? Where materialism shapes the governing principle of society, and the Church has become an adjunct of the State, perhaps we should not be surprised to find that a grabbing and 'something-for-nothing' type of attitude defines the ethos of society. One is, of course, aware that the tone of society in the so-called capitalist countries can be ugly and mercenary too. But there a higher standard-of-living and the presence of countervailing influences of a non-materialistic and anti-materialistic nature usually prevent the cruder types of acquisitiveness from becoming the arbiters of taste and ethos. In much of Western Europe it is a mark of bad breeding to be seen to be preoccupied with income and material possessions. If that is hypocrisy, surely one would like to see more of it.

GALINA: Certainly Christianity and the Orthodox Church as balancing influences can hardly be said to exist in the Soviet Union. I have no doubt that a basic variant of the Christian teaching is still deeply embedded in the hearts of many Russians; but this has perhaps more to do with the Russian tradition of seeking a kind of all-consoling spiritual order, especially at times of hardship, than with the policies currently espoused by Orthodoxy.

The Church is now an obedient tool of the Communist state. It has compromised itself in the eyes of the faithful. Its priests cannot appear before their congregations and give witness of their faith because they have to answer for their sermons.

URBAN: So Christianity as a leavening influence, in the sense of Matthew 13:11,[1] is not on its way back, as some observers have suggested?

GALINA: I hope that it is, but I wonder.

URBAN: Isn't it true, though, that when one form of spirituality is suppressed it surfaces in other forms and in surprising places? In Solomon Volkov's book *Testimony*, for example, Shostakovich and some of his friends are described as 'holy fools', *yurodivy* composers and artists. This is a phenomenon we are familiar with in Russian literature: men and women who play the fool as court jesters once did, exposing evil and the abuse of power. They have visions, flout conventions, break the moral law, are irreverent to authority and enjoy a certain licence.

In one spectacular instance Shostakovich himself mentions the pianist Maria Yudina as a 'holy fool', and tells us how Yudina once received an envelope from Stalin containing 20,000 roubles as a token of his appreciation of her musicianship. Whereupon Yudina wrote the following letter to Stalin:

> I thank you, Iosif Vissarionovich, for your aid. I will pray for you day and night and ask the Lord to forgive your great sins before the people and the country. The Lord is merciful and He'll forgive you. I gave the money to the church that I attend. . . .

The holy fool's immunity worked. Nothing happened to Yudina, and Shostakovich relates that Yudina's recording of a Mozart piano concerto (No. 23) was said to have been on the record-player when Stalin was found dead in his dacha. It was the last thing he is said to have heard.

I mention these anecdotes (and I could quote others) because I wonder whether courageous people of that sort aren't to be thought of as unconventional representatives of the same spiritual estate that used to make itself heard through the Church but can do so no longer.

GALINA: I would not agree that Shostakovich belonged to the category of holy fools. That is Volkov's view, and I feel it is unwarranted and would be so judged by Shostakovich. Shostakovich did sustain what you might call certain profoundly religious sentiments and was much preoccupied with death, but there was nothing in his character that would remotely fit your description of a holy fool.

Now there are, of course, people in the Soviet Union who rave and rage and talk in symbols and evoke the kingdom to come—but they have been put behind bars or sent to psychiatric institutions. Soviet society will not tolerate them.

URBAN: What about those popular bards who appealed with so much force to the Soviet Union's post-Gulag mood of degradation and agony? You give us a fine sketch of the impact of one of them, Vladimir Vysotsky. He 'became an idol of the people, who sank with him into the depths of drunkenness and degradation. . . . Weeping drunken tears, they wail along with him', and so on.

In pre-Communist days people of this kind sought consolation in Christianity or some revolutionary brotherhood. In an un-Christian environment they resort to such relief as they can find, and if the name of that relief is a wailing Vysotsky, so be it. Wouldn't you say that the men who offer such relief perform, in a sense, a priestly (albeit pervertedly priestly) function?

GALINA: Vysotsky was an ordinary talented song-writer who was disciplined enough not to say everything he felt could be said. He was, therefore, not a holy fool. He was more of a Villonesque character than a half-baked prophet or de-frocked priest. Certainly he offered consolation and solidarity.

URBAN: The question I'm getting at is: does Soviet society provide or tolerate outlets for the spiritual needs of the citizen apart from romanticising 'socialist construction' which is bogus, or elevating (as under Stalin) the leader to the status of a demi-god?

Let me put it to you that the vessels of spiritual escape in Soviet society—the holy fools of our day—may very well be people like yourself: artists, especially musicians, who can say things through their pianos and singing and painting that no one else can. The wordless media have a great advantage here over books and poems. Their 'message' is more difficult to identify and it is, therefore, harder to dictate to their authors.

One excellent example of this is mentioned in your book: the Soviet government's hesitation to allow Shostakovich's Fifth Symphony to be performed. The Leningrad Party 'aktiv' which scrutinised the symphony for ideological rectitude first felt that the symphony was 'pessimistic' and 'un-Soviet'. They lectured Shostakovich on how to write music. But Shostakovich had to save his symphony. As you tell us,

> He tried to deceive them in the most rudimentary way, and succeeded! All he had to do was use other words to describe the huge complex of human passions and suffering that is so apparent in his music—he described his music to the Party as *joyous* and *optimistic*—and the entire pack dashed off, satisfied.

What I am suggesting is that in a totalitarian society it is people like yourself who are most likely to be the symbols of dissent from orthodoxy—'holy fools', if you like: 'liberation musicians'.

GALINA: Here I agree with you entirely. I felt to be that symbol with great intensity when I sang Leonora in Beethoven's *Fidelio*—the very first time it was put on the stage in the Soviet Union. I wasn't at first quite conscious of that symbol in the sense in which you have just expressed it, but as the rehearsals went on I realised more and more distinctly that this was a 'liberation-opera' and it was really about *us* in Soviet society.

Of course, I knew from the beginning that *Fidelio* was about freedom, honour and love, but it grew on me only gradually that the words I was singing about freedom, the conquest of injustice and oppression were directly addressed to my audiences, and that *I* was the person entrusted by the music to impart them. My God, it was an unforgettable experience.

There I was, like Jeanne d'Arc, standing on the stage of the world, calling on the people to release those unjustly imprisoned and punish the wicked. It was a moment that changed my life.

Fidelio *under Soviet Skies*

URBAN: There is that memorable scene in the first Act of *Fidelio* where Rocco, at Leonora's urging, allows the prisoners to come out of their dungeon. Emaciated and in rags, and blinded by the sun to which their eyes had become unaccustomed, they stumble out and sing Beethoven's famous prayer to light and liberty '*O welche Lust in freier Luft*'. What did you feel when you saw them approaching?

GALINA: I had my back turned to the audience even though I had an aria coming, but I simply could not take my eyes off this devastating spectacle of human suffering. I felt that it was I personally who had brought them out from prison and was leading them and the public on to liberty. I was overwhelmed.

URBAN: This was in March 1954, a year after the death of Stalin—after the death of the man about whom the Soviet people had been made to sing:

> O Great Stalin, O leader of the peoples,
> Thou who brought man to birth, . . .

Thou who makes the spring to bloom,
Thou who makes vibrate the chords of music.[2]

Did the Soviet audiences realise that 'Fidelio' was about *their* fate—about the fate of their brothers and sisters who had been in the camps by the million and were just beginning to be released if they were lucky enough to have survived?

GALINA: No, they did not. Shostakovich and his friends, of course, did; but the public just didn't get the message. Why didn't they get it? Well, in Moscow the sort of people who go to the Bolshoi are not your men and women of culture. They tended to be people who had business in Moscow and felt it was good form to be seen at the Bolshoi, or men and women who were given tickets *ex officio* and were more or less *sent* to the opera. They went for the ambience and the spectacle, or out of a sense of duty, but were often quite irritated by the music which they didn't understand.

URBAN: I find it a little hard to believe that the public could have been so insensitive. Didn't they know what was happening around them? Could they have missed the meaning of your aria: '*Zur Freiheit, zur Freiheit ins himmlische Reich*'?

GALINA: They didn't make the connection. Some felt such things happened in Spain or in Germany, not in the Soviet Union. They didn't identify with Leonora or Florestan.

URBAN: In 1978, under the late Karl Boehm, I saw one of the great performances of *Fidelio* at the Munich opera. Boehm appended this observation to the programme:

Und mit dem *Fidelio* hat er [Beethoven] nicht für irgendeine Freiheit, sondern für die persönliche Freiheit des Menschen gekämpft.
(With *Fidelio* Beethoven fought not for any kind of freedom, but for man's personal freedom.)

I fail to see how this could have been lost on your average Soviet audience. If they missed that, what *did* they understand?

GALINA: Quite. As you say, in 1954 there was hardly a Soviet family that had not lost one or several of its members in the Gulag. And yet our audiences did not make the connection. But it wasn't only the people who didn't feel *Fidelio*'s sharp relevance to the state of society in Stalin's Russia, but the Party and the Government didn't either.

Throughout the long period of preparation and rehearsal the authorities never showed the slightest sign of realising that we were about to stage an opera deeply subversive of the Soviet system. In Russia operatic productions go through various stages of censorship. At each stage the message, the décor, the diction, and so on are examined for political suitability. *Fidelio* passed every stage of censorship. No one felt that Beethoven was addressing the oppressed masses of the Soviet Union.

URBAN: But, surely, you did?

GALINA: I first felt the message to be coming out of the music only. I didn't take in the plot or relate it to Stalin's Russia. But the music spoke for itself. That started me on my journey. The relevance of the libretto to our situation emerged as we went on rehearsing.

URBAN: Did the other singers and musicians feel that they were performing 'dissident' music?

GALINA: By the time it came to the first night, most of them felt that this was a daring enterprise. After all, *Fidelio* had never been performed in Russia or the Soviet Union, and here we were, one year after the great leader's death, putting it on the stage with our best talents. But they didn't think we were in danger, and we weren't, because the people's finer senses had been too dulled and they were too downtrodden to pick up what Beethoven was saying.

URBAN: You will recall how Wilhelm Furtwängler attracted some formidable criticism because he conducted *Fidelio* in Hitler's Berlin during World War II and sometimes in the presence of Nazi dignitaries. It was said that he and his musicians were mocking Beethoven's music by the sheer act of performing it in that environment. After 1945 Furtwängler and his friends defended themselves by saying that it was precisely in that environment that *Fidelio* had to be performed—those who could hear understood the message. What I'm saying is that *Fidelio* was a litmus-test for many Germans, especially in the German emigration. It does not seem to have been one in the Soviet Union, or in the Russian emigration.

GALINA: No, it wasn't. But there was another and quite mundane factor which accounts for the indifference. The Soviet audiences did not, as I say, much like the music— they found it heavy going. They were used to Moscow's staple fare: *Aida, Rigoletto, La Traviata, Boris Godunov, Eugene Onegin, Pique Dame.* Even Mozart was a stranger. *Fidelio* bored them. It's all very sad.

URBAN: The Moscow correspondent of the *Neue Zürcher Zeitung* reported recently (20 June 1986) that the death of individual Soviet soldiers in Afghanistan, though keenly felt by their families, was causing no national unrest and was not even registering in the minds of people as an 'issue'.

> There is in Russia no social fabric, no collective consciousness that would create spontaneous reactions of the kind the leadership would have to fear. The ability to abstract from individual suffering and to ascribe it to overall causes is just not there.

Isn't this inability to abstract from individual misfortune our best clue to your audiences' failure to react to *Fidelio?*

GALINA: I would agree. Individual people in Russia do react, and react very strongly, to their losses in Afghanistan, but you are right in saying they regard them as an act of God and will leave it at that.

URBAN: But there is another slight puzzle. You started rehearsing *Fidelio* while Stalin was still alive. Clearly, the authorities did not expect that it would attract his displeasure. Why didn't they? As we know from Shostakovich and others, Stalin was extremely suspicious of *Hamlet* and *Macbeth*. 'Stalin could stand neither of these plays', Shostakovich observed. '. . . A criminal ruler—what could attract the leader and teacher in that theme?'

Didn't considerations of this kind enter the minds of the cultural *apparat* when the decision to mount *Fidelio* was made?

GALINA: There was a report in Moscow that Stalin admired Beethoven the way he admired everything spectacular and exalted. That may have given encouragement to the cultural *apparat*. But I don't believe the rumour was true. Stalin was too much of a primitive. My personal feeling is that he could tell what a straight *play* was about—a dithering prince of Denmark or a tearful King Lear were clearly not to his taste—but he was less sure about music.

But one can think of another explanation. A believing Communist audience could have persuaded itself that *Fidelio* was about the Liberation of Man as envisaged by Lenin. By the same token, your fascist audiences in Berlin during the War could easily have thought that *Fidelio* was about the liberation of, shall we say, Europe from Bolshevik or plutocratic oppression—and *wept*. Either must have been pretty difficult to believe, but there is no limit to the perversion of the human mind and to wishful thinking.

URBAN: To what extent does the ordinary Soviet citizen really believe that his Party and Government stand for freedom, seeing that there is unfreedom around him wherever he looks?

GALINA: The ordinary citizen in the Soviet Union does not know what freedom is. Having grown up in unfreedom he is not in a position to recognise freedom, much less to criticise unfreedom. Until I came to the West, I didn't understand what freedom was either. I was not manacled— and I could walk—therefore I imagined I was free. It was only abroad that I began to have some inkling of the real meaning of liberty.

URBAN: In other words, the Soviet authorities know what they are doing when they keep the Soviet population sealed off from the outside world?

GALINA: Oh yes, from the Mafia's point of view it's a faultless policy.

URBAN: I can, just, understand that people are not familiar with the meaning of freedom (one is reminded of the Grand Inquisitor chapter in Dostoevsky's *The Brothers Karamazov*). But wouldn't you say everyone can recognise unfreedom, repression, serfdom?

GALINA: No. If you are born in the Soviet Union under conditions of unfreedom you don't realise there is an alternative way of living.[3] You don't understand the concept of unfreedom because you don't know what freedom is. Put a free animal in a cage: it will at once grasp the meaning of unfreedom and rage against it; but an animal that has never had the liberty to roam the forests because it was born in a zoo will probably not feel so deprived.

Tourists visiting the Soviet Union tend to misread the Soviet system. Even if they feel they have been shown everything there is to see in Russia, they will not grasp Russia's essential unfreedom because they are on a visit and thus always at liberty to go back home. But if you haven't got that liberty—if, every minute of your life, every choice you make or cannot make depends on the system down to the smallest detail—then you know in your bones that your physical and mental autonomy is destroyed. You are an object in the hands of forces you cannot control; you are *nothing* and *count* for nothing. You're not only unfree but you don't even realise that you are—which is the ultimate unfreedom.

URBAN: You relate in your memoirs that at one stage in your early life at the Bolshoi the KGB tried to enlist you as an informer. You went along to the extent of not rejecting the KGB outright, but when the first opportunity of freeing yourself from this connection came up in the shape of an admiring Marshal Bulganin, you grabbed it and sent the KGB men packing.

GALINA: I did.

URBAN: In so doing you must have realised that accepting the KGB connection would have been an unbearable limitation on your freedom. You were a child of Soviet society and had no model of freedom you could emulate; yet you had an instinctive understanding of what was right and what was wrong, what was freedom and what was unfreedom.

GALINA: Not quite. I could recognise *treachery*. I knew that it was wrong to spy on my fellow musicians (because that is what the KGB wanted me to do). You can be an unfree person and yet recognise treachery.

URBAN: Whether you can or cannot is a moot point; I will not press you. But surely when you asked Bulganin to stop the KGB you must have responded to the voice of some moral indignation in your soul for which there were no models in Soviet society? Indeed, it was Communist Party policy 'that every citizen of the USSR be an NKVD agent', as Mikoyan put it in 1937, commemorating the 20th anniversary of the *Cheka* secret police.

GALINA: Yes, I was led by moral revulsion. To resist treachery, baseness, duplicity—these are God's instructions. You don't have to learn them.

URBAN: But doesn't your yearning for freedom also come self-evidently from the inner recesses of your mind—without models and without 'instruction'?

GALINA: I don't think so. The Ten Commandments are one thing; freedom is another. Freedom can be negative.

URBAN: Perhaps we should think of two different kinds of freedom: freedom *from* and freedom *to*. The first is, I think, easy to recognise: 'I am free from imprisonment.' The second is more tricky: 'I am free to emigrate to Australia. . . . I am free to reject my heritage; I am free to support *Solidarity*, and so on.

GALINA: I accept that. It is the second that was beyond my understanding while I lived in the Soviet Union. I have had to live in England, France, and the US for twelve years to comprehend the meaning of real freedom—the freedom of choice. That is perhaps why I have now lost every vestige of homesickness. In Russia my 'free' life was limited to life on the stage of the theatre. Real life began when my cue came up and I began to sing. Off-stage I was *playing* at life, not living it. Here in the West I can live a rounded life as a free person, on-stage, off-stage.

URBAN: You said your realisation of the meaning of freedom was gradual.

GALINA: Yes, we first left the USSR with the intention of staying abroad for three years, perhaps four or five. Rostropovich and I felt that the Kremlin let us go because we had become a nuisance on account of the Solzhenitsyn affair. We thought that during the years of our absence something might change in the Soviet government's attitude to us; but we had every intention of going back. We lived, therefore, in the consciousness that we would return—which kept me worried. The prospect of re-entering the Soviet system was paralysing.

In 1978, however, we were deprived of our citizenship. A terrible weight I had carried all my life was suddenly lifted. I felt I was being born again. The Moloch had released me. At last I was free!

A Double Life at Home and Abroad

URBAN: You said the operatic stage was your real life, your life of freedom—off-stage you were just going through the motions of living. Did audiences matter—whether you were singing in the Bolshoi or in the touring operetta company of Mark Ruben?

GALINA: Not at all. Once I was on the stage the public became unimportant to me. I lived in a self-contained world. Everything I had thought and felt suddenly found their appointed places in the imaginative world I was creating. Everything that had been locked up in my sham existence broke through into the real life of music. It was a matter of indifference to me who was sitting in the auditorium. The stage was my pulpit. I felt I was addressing the world.

URBAN: Wasn't so much 'voluntarism' something that would worry the authorities—the 'holy fool' syndrome again?

GALINA: Our repertoire was, of course, strictly controlled. Frequently I had to sing parts I hated and despised.

URBAN: Did you apply the same professional skills and enthusiasms to these unwanted parts as you did to *Fidelio* or *Aida*?

GALINA: This might surprise you: yes, I did. Often I had to appear in some ghastly Soviet opera—Muradeli's *October* or Dzerzhinsky's *The Fate of Man*—where the music was poor and the propaganda worse. But I was forced to sing or else I would not be allowed to appear in the parts I loved, or to go abroad. But once on stage, artistic pride and perfectionism took over, and I sang the propagandistic roles with the same care and conviction as I sang the roles I respected and loved and had myself chosen.

This can, of course, be very confusing for the listener and indeed for the artist because, let's face it, singing in a 'Soviet

opera' means working for the Soviet state and selling yourself as a musician.

URBAN: Was there any way of avoiding such appearances?

GALINA: No, there was nothing we could do. Suppose you
were told to sing in some cantata dedicated to Stalin. Well,
once you accepted the fact that you had to sing it, you
couldn't do it *badly*. Certainly *I* couldn't. I put everything
I had into the part, trying to turn bad music into something
acceptable to the listener. Rostropovich, too, had this
problem. He had to perform a lot of rubbish for the greater
glory of the Soviet system. So had Oistrakh. They hated it
but did it, and did it with the artistry unique to their genius.
They couldn't give less than their best.

URBAN: I understand the dilemma. Yet, with all due
respect, wasn't it a little difficult for an artist of your
temperament to praise, for example, the humanity of Stalin
when your father was doing ten years in Siberia under
Article 58?

GALINA: Of course it was. It was awful. I tried to get out
of these commitments whenever I could, but frequently I
was compelled to go along. Muradeli's *October* is one good
example. The principal character in this opera is Lenin,
and *October* was to be staged to mark some anniversary.
Ekaterina Furtseva herself came along to persuade me.
'Galina, I implore you, please cooperate. You'll only have
to appear in the first two or three performances, then we'll
give the part to an understudy. . . .'
   I knew they wouldn't put me in prison if I refused but I
also knew that I would never be able to go abroad again.
So in 1964 I sang Marina in Muradeli's opera. The words I
was made to sing made me quite sick. Those were the most
shameful hours of my career. I did only a few performances,
but they marked me for life.

URBAN: What did you say to your husband after such
performances?

GALINA: I was emptied of feeling, but I knew I had to do
what I did; this was our life—Soviet life.

URBAN: It must have been equally difficult for you to
represent 'Soviet' music in the Western world, as you often

had to. Western critics frequently praised the great 'Soviet' singer in you and, by implication, the society that had nurtured your art. How did you feel about such praise?

GALINA: I ascribed it to the insensitivity of some of these critics or their political bias. Of course, as I said, you can never do less than give your best. Whether you appear to the outside world as 'Soviet' or Russian makes no difference. In any case, we had been trained to go to these foreign countries the way soldiers are trained to go to war and conquer. We were told we were entering a hostile, capitalist environment—our job was to resist the allurements of the enemy and bring honour to the USSR. We also brought in a lot of hard currency.

URBAN: Did you feel on these occasions that you were a Soviet, a Russian, or a Soviet-Russian singer?

GALINA: I never felt for a moment that I was representing Soviet culture. It was *Russian* culture I was representing. My country is *Russia*, not the Soviet Union. I do not agree with those émigrés who insist that Russia is one thing, the Soviet Union another. Where has Russia gone? Has it evaporated? All we can say is: what we now have in that part of the world is 'Russia under Soviet rule', but the essential Russianness of the people is untouched. It was Russia under the Mongol yoke and it is Russia today.

URBAN: Do you recognise the legitimacy of the phrase 'Soviet people'?

GALINA: No, I don't. People who live in Russia are Russian people. There are no 'Soviet people' to be found anywhere, except in the pages of 'Soviet literature'.

URBAN: Your life as an artist abroad was difficult enough. But it must have been even more difficult for someone like Shostakovich who had to represent, under Stalin's personal orders, Soviet culture at the 'Cultural and Scientific Congress for World Peace' in New York, because it was required of him not only to conduct his music but to make statements and give interviews on behalf of the Soviet Union.

GALINA: Shostakovich was aware that he was doing a

distasteful thing. But Stalin promised that Prokofieff's, Khachaturian's, Shebalin's music (as well as Shostakovich's own) would be performed again if Shostakovich agreed. These had been proscribed as 'formalist' by the censors—and Shostakovich gave in. In any case, he had to leave his wife behind as a hostage. We all had to leave hostages behind when we travelled abroad.

URBAN: You relate in your book a particularly telling incident—Rostropovich's appearance in the Royal Albert Hall in London on 21 August 1968, the day Soviet troops occupied Czechoslovakia and suppressed the Prague reform movement. This must have made a terrible demand on his, and your, sense of belonging. . . .

GALINA: It did! Especially as Rostropovich was playing Dvořák's Cello Concerto, of all things, in the framework of a Festival of *Soviet* Art! There could not have been a more ironic coincidence. There were demonstrations against the Soviet invasion outside the Albert Hall before the concert began and more was to come when the Soviet symphony orchestra entered the hall. There was whistling, shouting, stamping of feet. Some cried 'Fascists, go home'. You can imagine how we both felt. We were appalled by what our government had done, but at the same time Rostropovich had to give his best before a foreign audience. It was a terrible trial.

URBAN: I was moved by this passage in your book:

> Slava was pale, and stood as if on an executioner's block, taking on himself the shame of his government. . . . Dvořák's music poured forth like a requiem for the Czech people. . . . Rapt, the audience listened to the confession of that great artist as he merged himself through Dvořák's music with the very soul of the Czech people, suffering with them, playing for them, asking their forgiveness.

It takes a sensitive man and a sensitive woman to feel the need to do penance through their art for a government they detest.

GALINA: What took great courage was for Slava to go through with the performance. As soon as the last sounds died away I rushed backstage. I found him waiting for me, trembling, with tears in his eyes. We left at once. Outside the crowd silently parted to allow us to pass. Without looking left or right, we went to our car. Somehow we felt we were criminals ourselves.

URBAN: Were there also voices of sympathy for the plight some of your London audience must have suspected Rostropovich was undergoing?

GALINA: Yes, a few individuals—not too many—shouted that the artists were not to blame for the suppression of Czechoslovakia.

But there was one man who got up before the cello concerto could begin and held up proceedings by repeatedly declaiming '*Long Live Casals!*' and then walked out. At the time neither Rostropovich nor I understood the point he was trying to make. But some ten years later, after we had lost our Soviet citizenship, we received a letter from the same man and that explained it. The point he had tried to make in the Albert Hall in London was that if Casals had the courage to emigrate from Franco's Spain because he would not subject his art to the glorification of fascism— so should Rostropovich dissociate himself from the Soviet system of oppression. In the meantime he would not listen to Rostropovich's playing.

URBAN: What did he actually say in his letter?

GALINA: He wrote that he understood the great difficulties Soviet artists had to face when playing abroad, but now that Slava was happily released from the bondage of the Soviet state, he would like to welcome him in the West and apologised for the disturbance.

URBAN: An instructive episode. . . .

GALINA: The sort of thing you expect to happen to artists from totalitarian societies.

URBAN: I suppose we should be careful in passing moral judgment on artists who cooperate with totalitarian governments. It is probably right to demand that outstanding people like Casals and Rostropovich should stand up and be counted because they are symbols to their nations. A Thomas Mann who would betray European humanism by underwriting Hitler's *Reich* would be (if any such thing could be imagined) a traitor of a particularly reprehensible sort. But can we demand so heroic a stance from the average musician or poet—people who represent nothing to the outside world and whose defection would therefore go unnoticed in Paris, London, or New York?

GALINA: A certain conformism under the Soviet régime is inevitable for almost everyone in that society, including the most powerful. The sheer struggle for material survival demands that, in public at least, Soviet taboos and shibboleths must be respected.

The real problem is the one we have already touched on: unfreedom breeds unfreedom. Somewhere the vicious circle has to be broken, and that can only be done by breaking down the intellectual barriers of the Soviet system and offering the people the whole panorama of truthful information. Those of us who could travel abroad soon became conscious of alternative ways of seeing the world and alternative ways of living. That seems to me to be the key to freedom in the Soviet Union, and that is where Western broadcasts can play a decisive part provided they put the emphasis on Soviet *domestic* matters, for that is where we are most deprived.

Of course we cannot ask that the ordinary man or woman should display great feats of heroism. But we can and must expect decency and civility from everyone, and especially from artists, because their claim to public respect derives from their uncommon sensitivity. And what kind of an uncommon sensitivity is it that does not recognise injustice and brutality when these stare them in the face?

The 'Ideology' of Britten's War Requiem

URBAN: It is probably as interesting to look at the types of music you were not allowed to sing as those you were made to.

Benjamin Britten wrote his *War Requiem* specifically with yourself in mind for the soprano part. He had heard you sing and was persuaded that yours was the kind of tone and musical commitment he was looking for. Yet, when the *War Requiem* was finished and the rehearsals began, you were not allowed to leave the Soviet Union to sing the part. Britten pleaded with the Soviet authorities, but to no avail.[4]

The *War Requiem* was a plea for reconciliation and peace. Britten had written it in memory of the dead of the First World War. He combined in his text words of the traditional requiem mass with the poetry of Wilfred Owen:

> My subject is War, and the Pity of War.
> The poetry is in the pity.
> All a poet can do today is warn.

Why did a government that was dedicating the whole machinery of its international propaganda to 'Peace' not allow you to sing in Britten's *Requiem*?

GALINA: I tell the story in my memoirs, but let me briefly recount it all the same.

The Soviet Government is for peace, but not for any kind of peace. It is for *Soviet* peace. I will not explain what sort of peace that is because we are all familiar with its meaning. You see, Britten's *Requiem* was going to be given its first performance at the ceremonial consecration of Coventry Cathedral. And *there* was the rub! Coventry had been destroyed by the *Luftwaffe* and was later rebuilt with West German money. Our leaders didn't like that. When I went to see Ekaterina Furtseva, our corrupt Minister of Culture, she explained to me that the ruined Cathedral ought to have been left to stand as 'a monument to the horrors of fascism' so that people the world over would remember.

My own attitude must have struck Furtseva as very naive and undialectical because I said: if the Germans had offered to pay for the reconstruction of a cathedral they had destroyed, that seemed to me very sensible, for they were trying to undo a great wrong. How could that be used to justify the Soviet Government's refusal to permit me to sing in Coventry? Weren't we on the side of peace and international brotherhood?

URBAN: Did she reply?

GALINA: No. I thought she either did not have a convincing answer or was too ashamed to give it to me. In any case, she seemed to be under orders that no Soviet singer was to appear at the Coventry performance of Britten's *Requiem*. And none did.

URBAN: What is your own explanation of the ban?

GALINA: Britten's *Requiem* is a profound and moving warning against the futility of war—any war. The Soviet régime is not against *every* kind of war. It supports what it is pleased to call 'wars of national liberation', 'just' wars, wars to defeat imperialism, and the like. It supports wars of its own choosing, but no others. Britten's *Requiem* did not fit in with the Soviet concepts of war and peace.

Worse, the reconsecration of the Cathedral was threatening to undo some of the bitterness between the German and British peoples, and that could not be to the Communist advantage. The Soviet ambition was to keep the British and Germans hating one another. How could that be achieved with Galina Vishnevskaya of the Bolshoi Theatre praying for 'rest eternal' and 'light eternal' to 'shine upon the souls'[5] of all the fallen, fascists and anti-fascists alike? It was not to be.

Then there was another ideological snag. The Soviet Government keeps the public in a state of permanent mobilisation. 'Peace' is a Soviet prerogative—'war' threatens to come from the Western side only. The spectacle of the British and Germans making it up under the sign of the cross *with Soviet support* would have run against the spirit of the Soviet siege mentality and morally disarmed all those millions of young Soviet men and women who are being daily indoctrinated that they must always be prepared to go to war. In any case, anti-war propaganda is, in the Soviet view, a Soviet monopoly. Coventry was threatening to break it.

URBAN: One is constantly surprised by the lack of sophistication of Soviet propaganda. A Soviet presence in Coventry in the shape of so splendid an artist as yourself would have been of much greater benefit to the Soviet 'peace image' in Western society than Moscow's petulant refusal to let you sing. Luckily for us, the constraints of Soviet ideology make much of Soviet efforts in 'public diplomacy' stillborn or limping.

GALINA: There is only so much you can do with Soviet propaganda. The idea of forgiveness, for example, is outside the Soviet frame of thinking. The system is still run on Lenin's despicable principle '*Who/Whom*': either you vanquish your enemies or you're vanquished by them. Social tranquillity is a deception—lasting peace between antagonistic societies is a mirage—and so on. Now, Britten's *Requiem* is an act of forgiveness, an act of turning the other cheek, an act of loving your enemies. It is a Christian mass interlaced with the agonised poetry of Wilfred Owen. It just wasn't in line with Soviet hate-mongering.

URBAN: Are we in the West doing enough to make the world aware that the Soviet leadership needs this hate-filled atmosphere as the precondition of its own and the system's survival?

GALINA: No, you are not. Most people in the West do not realise that this is the basic motivation of the Soviet state and Soviet society. How this can be, 69 years after the Bolshevik revolution, after Lenin, Stalin, the Gulag and Solzhenitsyn—I cannot quite understand.

URBAN: Shostakovich makes some bitter comments about those misguided 'great humanists' (André Malraux, George Bernard Shaw, Lion Feuchtwanger, Paul Robeson) who went to look at Stalin's Russia and came back to the West with praise on their lips for the new civilisation: 'I've seen the future and it works.'

GALINA: There aren't too many of those left nowadays because the Soviet system is just too repulsive, but the media are doing their bit—whether out of bias or sheer ignorance, I cannot tell. The results are not dissimilar.

URBAN: About 18 months ago I was asked after a lecture whether I thought Ronald Reagan had grossly overstated his case when he called the Soviet Union a 'focus of evil'. I said: 'Not really. . . . The Soviet system is built on the idea of the class struggle and class hatred. When you appoint envy and hatred as the governing principles of your society, you appoint a great evil as your taskmaster.' Would you agree?

GALINA: I would say this: if a shared Christianity was not enough to stop monarchs from doing very unchristian things to one another through the centuries, we can imagine— indeed, we can see—what the principle of hatred, elevated to the governing creed of one of the world's most powerful countries, will do to the lives of all of us.

URBAN: And yet, by a strange perversion of values, the Soviets have tried to fashion Lenin and the institutionalised hatreds he spread around him into an object of love. Whether this is a hangover from Czarism need not concern us here, but what is remarkable is that it exists and plays a practical part in Soviet life. Towards the end of your memoirs you tell us that on a trip to Austria you and Rostropovich had a long conversation with Vladimir Semyonov, an educated 'liberal' who was then the head of the Soviet delegation to the Arms Control conference in Vienna.

GALINA: Yes, a man of books, some learning, and sophisticated tastes.

URBAN: You wanted to intervene on behalf of Solzhenitsyn. You wanted to have the hounding of Solzhenitsyn stopped. After *One Day in the Life of Ivan Denisovich* and some short stories, the censors had banned everything Solzhenitsyn had written. He was being slandered in the press and was unable to defend himself. Could Semyonov help? But Semyonov, far from being helpful, surprised you with a pointed question: 'But does he love Lenin?' As you write in your memoirs:

> Had I heard right? I had been prepared to expect almost anything from him, but not such an idiotic question.
> 'What?' I asked.
> 'Does he love Lenin?'
> I went numb. And as in a dream, I heard the drone of that self-righteous voice continue: 'S-o-o-o! You're not saying anything! That's it then! He doesn't love Lenin. . . .'

GALINA: Can you imagine? Semyonov expecting Solzhenitsyn to 'love' Lenin after Solzhenitsyn had spent ten years in the Gulag!

URBAN: I share your indignation, but personally I would have been less shocked than you were, for I suspect all the poor Ambassador was trying to convey to you was: 'But are you sure Solzhenitsyn is one of us?'
What I do find a little surprising is that a relatively enlightened man of the Soviet Establishment should have used the word 'love' in talking about Lenin to other members of the Establishment, because that is what you were in those days. He could have said: 'But are you persuaded that Solzhen-

itsyn is not hostile to the whole Soviet system?' or 'Are you sure he is not going to pull the rug from under all of us?'— or words to that effect. But he didn't. Even in the intimacy of the Vienna hotel bar where you were talking to him, he stuck to the devotional incantation 'But does he love Lenin?' It is this mantra that fascinates, because it shows that the Soviet leaders themselves do not quite know how to handle Lenin's principle of hatred without, that is, giving it another name.

And I can see their problem.

In the 1970s this was not a very usable quotation. Vladimir Semyonov could hardly have asked: 'But does Solzhenitsyn agree with Lenin's principle of universal hatred on which our title to rule rests?' He simply asked: 'But does he love Lenin?'—Lenin the founding father, Lenin the seer, Lenin the demi-god.

GALINA: What shocked us in Semyonov was that all of his civility and sophistication was a veneer. When put to the test it peeled off, and you were left face to face with a Party functionary. I did not examine his reaction as carefully as you have just done, and you may well be right. My reaction was one of fury that a man we suspected to be more open-minded than most should, after our cautious and confidential approach to him, come out with an expression of crude and indeed childish propaganda. I came to the conclusion that his real self *was* the self he displayed to us as an *apparatchik*. Or else he was so frightened of doing anything on behalf of Solzhenitsyn (because he must have been aware of some decision higher up in Moscow) that he fell back on a cliché as a device for protecting himself against us. Whichever it was, he gave us a useful lesson in what we could expect, even from 'liberals' in the Moscow Establishment.

'Western politicians should keep Lenin at their bedside'

URBAN: We know that you, Rostropovich, and other leading members of the Soviet artistic and intellectual world were extremely frank in dealing with the authorities, including the highest. You criticised, harangued, reprimanded Ministers, members of the Central Committee, Ambassadors, et al. You even gave Bulganin a good telling-off.

GALINA: Let me just put it on record: Rostropovich is a gentle soul. His pleas and protests were always dignified. It was *I* who opened my mouth, and often gave them a piece of my mind.

URBAN: But why was it that these on the whole intelligent and constructive forms of criticism didn't cohere into a movement? Why was it that you and your like-minded colleagues did not get together to protect Solzhenitsyn, or Sakharov, or Orlov? I ask these questions not because I'm unaware of the difficulties in the way of any such concerted action, but rather because we know from the 1956 Hungarian and 1968 Czechoslovak experience (and to a lesser extent from Poland too) that reforms in a Communist régime can come only from those within the Party or the ruling establishment. It was your opposite numbers in Budapest and Prague—Hungarian and Czech writers, journalists, scholars, poets—who started the ball rolling. Why was it not happening, and why *is* it not happening, in the USSR?

GALINA: Soviet artists are not 'joiners'. Each fights his own little corner according to the requirements of the moment. They are too idiosyncratic, too quarrelsome, and too 'difficult' to unite in a common enterprise. And there is too much treachery and jealousy among them for anything to emerge that could call itself a movement or even a pressure group. Then, Soviet society (if you can call it that, for it isn't a 'society' in the Western sense) is atomised. There is no aqueduct between those little oases of intellectual and artistic independence that manage from time to time to survive for a while in the great desert of popular indifference and often outright hostility. There is a writer here, a physicist there; but the link between them is common suspicion as much as common purpose.

Musicians, on the whole, have it a bit easier than the verbalising artists because their stuff is open to interpretation. The composer writes his music; then the musicologists of the system come along and build a whole ideological platform underneath it. They will tell you that the music is about Lenin in October or the Colorado beetles the Americans have dropped on Korea or Czechoslovakia, that it's about the glory of Soviet power or *Sputnik*, or whatever. The composer, if he is wise, will say nothing because he knows that his music will exist and give pleasure long after this ideological garbage has been blown away.

But for a writer, or for a painter, life is more difficult. His language is more immediately representational, and he is therefore more exposed to the whims of the censor. So, for that reason, too, the various groups of artists and intellectuals don't easily recognise their common interests and work together.

URBAN: Before we lose the point: you said Soviet society isn't a 'society' in the Western sense. Alexander Zinoviev made a similar observation to me about 'politics' in the Soviet Union. What precisely is your meaning?

GALINA: Simply that in the Western countries society seems to mean that whole collectivity of people who live together, take part in local life, run voluntary societies, argue about the kind of schools and power stations that should be built in the neighbourhood, elect governments, criticise the local Bishop and librarian, and so on. This concept of society is wholly foreign to the Soviet Union. Our people take no part in any of these activities. Soviet life is run to the exclusion of the public. It is run, as I've said, by a Mafia. I was going to say that Russia has reverted to serfdom, but on second thought that would be too kind because it is worse than serfdom. Under serfdom the serf knew his master; he had a one-to-one relationship with him. One master might be more permissive than another. There was human contact. Under the Soviet system every man and woman is the property of the state. . . .

URBAN: The patrimonial heritage survives. . . .

GALINA: It does, except that the present variety is more soul-destroying. Now you have no one to turn to to express your anxiety. There is no human cushion; there is no tangible safety-net. If you express your dissatisfaction, the ruling Mafia will at once take it as a sign of rebellion and crush you. As long as the members of the Mafia do not have to stand in line for meat and potatoes, nothing will change in the Soviet system. And they have no intention òf doing so. In other words: Soviet society consists of a privileged few lording it over millions of underdogs who have no say and no stake in the conduct of the nation's affairs.

URBAN: The sort of thing the Bolsheviks said they were going to overthrow in 1917. . . .

GALINA: And overthrow it they did, but then they brought it back with a vengeance.

URBAN: You have not quite finished telling me why Soviet artists and intellectuals are unable to coordinate their discontent and turn it into something resembling meaningful reform. You spoke of small oases in a desert of indifference. May I say that you and Slava Rostropovich were such an oasis and perhaps the most memorable, because you offered refuge to Alexander Solzhenitsyn at great risk to your peace of mind and your careers. You put the world in your debt as much as Solzhenitsyn.

GALINA: We did nothing we didn't feel we had to do. Solzhenitsyn was homeless. He needed some peace and quiet for his writing. Mind you, when we first took him in, he wasn't anathema in the eyes of the authorities. He was still a member of the Writers' Union; he had even been proposed for the Lenin Prize. It was while he was living with us that his harassment began. He was first expelled from the Writers' Union, and then Slava and I were told that we were to throw him out. When we refused, the militia threatened to take our *dacha* away. We stuck to Solzhenitsyn, but in the end we couldn't protect him any more than we could protect ourselves. I needn't rehearse the rest of the story.

URBAN: I still feel that you and your husband showed great and untypical courage. Oistrakh, who had been through the Great Terror, warned you of the risks; and so did others. Yet you want ahead.

GALINA: We felt: here was a human being in trouble. He was no criminal, he hadn't killed or cheated anyone, why should we throw him out of our house? Solzhenitsyn was taking the Communists at their word: 'Reveal the truth about society', as Marxism-Leninism calls for in its credo. Solzhenitsyn was doing just that: revealing the truth about the state of his people and the Soviet system.

URBAN: Did you take him in because you felt here was a man of great talent with a message to your country and the world? Because he was a famous writer?

GALINA: No, we took him in because he was a human being who needed help. That was all. I had read his books; I knew he had been in prison for all those years and had been sick. I had read *One Day in the Life of Ivan Denisovich* and found it devastating, and when I saw Solzhenitsyn I opened my house to him with all my heart. So did Rostropovich.

URBAN: So you took in a man rather than a book?

GALINA: Absolutely.

URBAN: Would you have done the same if Solzhenitsyn had written about Hinduism or a great train robbery?

GALINA: Clearly, Solzhenitsyn's leitmotif had a special relevance to me because he was passionately concerned with the Russia of our own time and experience. But the essential thing about him was that he had been sorely and unjustly tried, and needed help.

URBAN: Now that you have been cruelly punished for your courage—you lost the stage that had made you, Rostropovich lost his Russian platform, you have both lost your country—have you any regrets that you did what you did?

GALINA: None whatever. If I could live my life over again I would do exactly what I did then.

URBAN: Did you expect gratitude from Solzhenitsyn?

GALINA: None. Why should I? Slava and I acted the way we did because we heard an inner voice telling us that we had to help. It was a matter of conscience and quite simple.

URBAN: You acted, in fact, like a free man and a free woman.

GALINA: Yes, I think we did.

URBAN: But could you have done so if you had not belonged to the Soviet aristocracy—if you had been a washerwoman on a collective farm? Wouldn't you have ended up in prison before you could speak two critical sentences about the Gulag?

GALINA: If I had been a washerwoman I would probably had had a different character to start with. I can't make a comparison. Certainly our prominent position in society made us act in accordance with that prominent position—openly. We didn't think we were slaves. Looking back on our lives in the Soviet Union it is quite clear to me that everyone in the Soviet system *is* a slave; and we were slaves too, otherwise we wouldn't have been forced to leave. But at the time we didn't realise that we were. Artists and certain intellectuals are permitted a semblance of freedom while they are at the top of their fame; but when it comes to harnessing that freedom to a serious purpose, that's the end of it.

URBAN: I'm still slightly puzzled why those various 'semblances' of freedom that you and many other artists, scholars and scientists enjoyed could not be organised to some purpose. Isn't it true that people who believe they are free in a certain area tend to act as free people, and eventually acquire some of the real thing if they are persistent and lucky enough?

András Hegedüs, the former Hungarian Communist Prime Minister, now a measured critic of the Communist system, talks in his autobiography (*In the Shadow of an Idea*) about the 'autonomy' certain prominent individuals have been able to carve out for themselves under Communist rule. These autonomies, he says, are the achievements of the individual and tend to be respected, within limits, by the Communist authorities. His own is, perhaps, the best example.[6] He negotiated his freedom of action with the Hungarian authorities as though he were a government bargaining with another government. I suppose what goes for Hungary does not go for the USSR?

GALINA: No, it doesn't. The 'autonomies' you mention cannot be brought together under Soviet conditions. First, you would need big, courageous, shrewd and consistent personalities. There are very few of those. Second, you would have to have the freedom to organise, which you haven't either. I grant you, if Solzhenitsyn, Rostropovich, Shostakovich, Richter, Gilels and others had been able to get together to present some petition or other to the Central Committee about, say, a composer or a musician who had been banned from the concert-halls, the Central Committee would have been obliged to take note and do something about it. But prominent people in the Soviet Union just aren't capable of cooperating like that. One is afraid, another is sick (or says he is), a third cannot agree with the language of the enterprise, and so on. There is no solidarity in our ranks.

Those of our artists and intellectuals who did manage to obtain a certain 'autonomy' can now enjoy their autonomy in exile: Solzhenitsyn, Sinyavsky, Maximov, Zinoviev, Vladimov, Voinovich, Bikovsky, Rostropovich, myself, and others. It's a bitter story.

URBAN: Bitter and sad. Those critics of the Soviet system who believe that in the nuclear age some *modus vivendi* must be found between the West and the Soviet Union still feel that the absolute precondition of a more trusting relationship is the reform of the Soviet system, and by 'reform' they mean first and foremost a decent respect for human rights and the observation of the Helsinki Accords. Going by what you have just said, the prospects of so thoroughgoing a reform of the system are remote, because the only people who could push for them with some hope of success are unable or unwilling to do so.

GALINA: The system has been with us for the best part of seven decades. It has not changed and I don't believe it *can* change. It is rotten from the ground up. You pull out a single brick and the whole building collapses. There is therefore no room for reform or experiments. The ruling Mafia know this and won't jeopardise the system and their own power by allowing a single brick to be removed. The system is as good as it ever will be, and that is saying something profoundly depressing not only about Soviet Communism but about the human condition too.

URBAN: So what are we to tell those Western hopefuls who seem to detect a turn to liberalism, legality, 'thaw', a willingness to rein in the arms race every time there is a change of guard in Moscow? Malenkov, Khrushchev, Kosygin, Brezhnev, Andropov, now Gorbachov, and even Stalin were, at the beginning of their incumbency, all celebrated as harbingers of a modern and enlightened type of Communism. And we were asked not to make life more difficult for them because they were busy fighting off the influnce of hard conservatives in the Politburo.

GALINA: Such observers are to be pitied, because they are either genuinely ignorant or so blinded by their hatred of the society they live in that they are forever hopeful that some utopian solutions will yet come out of the Soviet dictatorship. My advice, for what it is worth, is very simple: You can only hope to live in peace with the Soviet type of tyranny on your borders if you are strong and let the Kremlin know that you are. Western politicians and opinion-makers should keep Lenin by their bedside, for he set the rules that still run Russia today.

Marshal Bulganin Falls in Love

URBAN: You had, as you tell us in your book, a curious contretemps with one of Lenin's heirs, Nikolai Alexandrovich Bulganin, Marshal of the Soviet Union and Prime Minister at the time. He was, not to put too fine a point on it, strongly attracted by your charm and your singing and tried to win your favours. Unfortunately for the Prime Minister, you had just married Slava Rostropovich. His advances did not make very good progress, yet neither you nor Rostropovich could afford to be discourteous or uncooperative. This is not the place to reveal the whole story; I am interested in the 'patrimonial' side of Bulganin's courting you.

GALINA: Bulganin was very upset because I had just been snatched from under his nose by an unknown cellist, a man much younger than himself. His courting was crude and passionate. He would send me his adjutants with carloads of flowers. The invitations to dine with him privately would pour in; he would telephone to urge me to sing at some reception or other, or would get the Minister of Culture to persuade me if he couldn't.

URBAN: How did you meet the Chairman of the Council of Ministers?

GALINA: I met Bulganin in Belgrade when he, Khrushchev, Mikoyan and others made their 'trip of Canossa' to pacify Tito. It is the custom of the Soviet leadership to add some attractive singers, actresses, or dancers to their own dour company. So I was summoned to join the party and asked to dine with Tito, his wife (whom I was made to toast), and the entire Soviet delegation. That's where I met Bulganin. He was a portly man with an avuncular air and a ready smile about him, looking like everyone's idea of a great Czarist general (which he imagined himself to be). The very next day the first flowers arrived, and I knew I would have to do some clever manoeuvring to avoid trouble.

URBAN: You were becoming a member of a charmed circle and stayed there throughout your Soviet career. Was the circle charming, too?

GALINA: I had known these men only from the posters we had to carry, from the press and television where they had been displayed as supermen. Wisdom, virtue, foresight, a caring concern for the good of the people, revolutionary vigilance and suchlike were riveted to their names in the popular imagination. In reality I found them to be a closely-knit circle of ordinary power-conscious men of crude manners and sparse education, with a worm's-eye view of the larger world, and unspeakable conceit. They were at the apex of the Mafia and they didn't make much of an attempt to conceal it. Also, most of them (and their wives) were very ugly to look at.

To answer your question: their charm was not immediately obvious, but their power was, and so was their addiction to alcohol. The number of times I had to sing to the chomping jaws of our drunken leaders is too many to remember. When I finally refused to comply with any more of Bulganin's invitations, I told him quite openly that I was tired of the gossip, that buffooning before his inebriated chums disgusted me, and that I found the whole experience humiliating. But that, of course, didn't put off the Prime Minister.

URBAN: What fascinates me most in your story is that Bulganin tried to treat you as part of his baronial estate. He was the great feudal lord who retained a kind of *ius primae noctis*, a right of the first night, *vis-à-vis* the women of his choosing. Wasn't this Imperial Russia all over again?

GALINA: Had Bulganin's passion for me arisen a few years earlier, neither Rostropovich nor I would have escaped.

Without Stalin at the helm things were made a little more difficult for him. But Nikolai Alexandrovich was openly hankering after the days when men like Beria could hunt down the women they wanted and have them delivered by the security police. In his many alcoholic stupors Bulganin related to us with relish and a good deal of envy Beria's amorous adventures. I think he did look upon me as his property—one that had been temporarily rented but would be available again. Could he evict the tenant?

URBAN: Did it occur to you that he might have really loved you?

GALINA: It did, and I think he might have. Certainly the scenes that occurred between Bulganin and Rostropovich on the theme of who-loved-me-more and who-should-have-me belonged to a comedy; but Bulganin's feelings may well have been genuine.

URBAN: I don't think we can improve on the description that you've given us in your memoirs of how these extraordinary threesomes actually happened.

> N.A. drank a lot, and he made Slava drink. But Slava didn't need to be persuaded; he drank out of sheer wrath.
> When they would both get tipsy, the old man would stare at me like a bull and start in on Slava.
> 'Yes, you beat me to it.'
> 'It looks that way.'
> 'And do you love her?'
> 'Very much, Nikolai Aleksandrovich.'
> 'No. Tell me, *how* can you love her? You're just a boy! Can you really understand what love is? Now, *I* love her. She's my swan song. But, all right, all right! Let's wait. I know how to wait—I've had my training.'
> I would sit there between them and listen. He didn't acknowledge that Slava had any right to me. Every drinking bout ended with an explanation to my husband of how much he loved me and that anything I asked for I could have.

URBAN: In a totalitarian system it is no small thing to be so passionately courted by a power-holder. Had you not been just married, might you have succumbed to Bulganin?

GALINA: Perhaps I might. As I say in my book, the temptation to be a Czarina to the Communist Czar would not have been all that easy to resist. I must be entirely honest: I'm not going to say, 'Oh, it couldn't possibly have happened', because it might have. . . .

URBAN: Did you find Bulganin attractive?

GALINA: Czars are never unattractive. If you look at a portrait of the Sun King, Louis XIV, he was an absolute nightmare. Nevertheless he had great success with women. Power is a magnet.

URBAN: Didn't Bulganin's declarations of love give you some small satisfaction—one of the Olympians, a Communist Prime Minister, prostrating himself at your feet?

GALINA: Let me put it this way: Bulganin's fervour did not in any way offend me.

URBAN: Nikolai Alexandrovich had the reputation of being an intellectual sort of Marshal. Was he?

GALINA: In comparison with his cronies in the Party and Government he wasn't quite so barbaric. He had slightly better manners and a slightly more lucid mind.

URBAN: Soviet society takes great pride in 'Communist morality', which is Victorian and rather prissy by our standards. I find it surprising that the man who was Prime Minister in that society should have pressed his case quite so blatantly in front of your husband.

GALINA: Ah, but he was the Chairman of the Council of Ministers! He was our master and the rest of us were serfs. That was his basic attitude to Slava and myself. We were, in fact, lucky that we didn't live in Stalin's time. Beria used to have his girls' hands tied behind their backs—and on to the bed. Without any question: under Stalin my husband would have been sent to the Gulag or handed to the executioner.

URBAN: Was Khrushchev aware of Bulganin's infatuation?

GALINA: Of course.

URBAN: What was his attitude to it all?

GALINA: Khrushchev was a cunning and vulgar peasant. He would smirk and enjoy the story.

URBAN: He didn't come up to you and say: 'Galina Pavlovna, you have a duty to Socialism'?

GALINA: No, he didn't. I saw Khrushchev only very occasionally.

URBAN: You said the leadership were very close-knit and power-conscious. . . .

GALINA: That is putting it mildly. They were drunk on power and highly arrogant about it.

URBAN: No revolutionary 'humility' in the style of Lenin?

GALINA: None, if indeed Lenin himself ever had such humility.

A few years ago I was attending a concert in the Kennedy Center in Washington with Rostropovich conducting. In the foyer in the interval I saw Zbigniew Brzezinski, whom I had met a year earlier when Carter was President and Brzezinski his personal National Security Adviser. I walked past Brzezinski but didn't go up to him because I thought I had really nothing to say to him. Then suddenly I heard Brzezinski call out: 'Hello, Galina! How are you? Don't you remember me?'

I was thunderstruck. Did *I* remember one of the most powerful men in the United States of America? And how could this still powerful man be so informal as to call out to me in a public foyer within the earshot of all and sundry: 'Don't you remember me?'

This was as though, shall we say, Marshal Ogarkov or Mikhail Suslov had had the humility to think that he was an ordinary mortal whose image was not graven in perpetuity on the minds of all who had ever seen him. It just could not have happened in Moscow. Our leaders took it for granted that anyone who had ever had the honour of meeting them would remember them all their lives and do obeisance to them if they were fortunate enough to see them again.

URBAN: Stalin once made the famous remark that Communists were 'special people', but probably he didn't quite mean it in the sense in which you have depicted the Soviet ruling class.

GALINA: They are indeed 'special people'. Seventy years

ago they occupied our land and have kept electing and re-electing themselves ever since. Their images are our new icons, their wishes our commands. They are 'special' in the way all history's tyrants were special to the people who were unlucky enough to fall into their hands.

In the Silence

URBAN: Anyone who has read your memoirs is, I think, tempted to agree with Virginia Woolf that it is hard for a West European reader to identify with Russian life and the Russian character. She observed in one of her finest essays, 'The Russian Point of View',[7] that there is 'a cloud which broods above the whole of Russian literature.' In Chekhov, there is too much bewildering inactivity, in Dostoevsky too much 'soul', with its 'violent diseases and raging fevers', and in Tolstoy too much questioning of the meaning of 'life'. 'We find [she writes about Tolstoy] always at the centre of all the brilliant and flashing petals of the flower this scorpion "why live?" . . .' We are both enthralled and repelled; the landscape is breathtaking but alien to us.

Your book struck me with a similar force of enthralling strangeness. Yours is no fiction, and one should, I know, apply a different yardstick to it. But the common reader cannot quite do that. He reads you as a testimony to the most cruel period in Russian history, but also as history that might have taken a different turn had Russian 'soul' and 'life' not stamped it with their signatures. Your characters suffer from appalling luck; when they go down they die miserably of alcoholism or starvation; an air of doom envelops them and their families the moment they appear in our sights, and we pray that they be spared the tragedies we witnessed on earlier pages.

And where the air is less heavily laden, we marvel at strange and scandalous happenings. Who is that woman accepting a $400 bribe from the hands of Galina Vishnevskaya? Why, it is the Minister of Culture of the Soviet Union. Who is that man dropping dead at the rehearsal of Shostakovich's symphony dedicated to the theme of death? Why, it is Pavel Ivanovich Apostolov, Shostakovich's ideological watchdog and tormentor. Who is in that strange collection of singers who denounce Vishnevskaya and

Rostropovich to the Central Committee for betraying the trust of the Soviet state and people? Why, they are Galina's favourite protégée Elena Obraztsova, and her Bolshoi friends, Atlantov and Nestorenko. . . . One could go on. Such amazing images flit past our mental screen in bewildering succession and we are left wondering: Are they real? Are they the portents of yet stranger things to follow?

GALINA: Your gentle mockery is well taken. I have no objection to your parallel with Dostoevsky and Tolstoy; if you accuse me of having written about the same country and the same people Dostoevsky and Tolstoy had written about—to that I plead guilty. But my story is sadly real, and very different from the sort of reality that inspired 19th-century fiction. Life under the Czars may have been hard and even beastly, but no one expected Tchaikovsky to write cantatas to glorify the deeds of the Czar and no one told him to make public denunciations of his fellow composers on pain of losing his livelihood. *Absolutism* is one thing, *totalitarianism* another—and that is my theme. The figures alone show the difference. According to respectable calculations, between the 1917 Revolution and the death of Stalin the Soviet authorities slaughtered, starved, beat or tortured to death or otherwise killed some 40 million of our own people. This is more than twice Russia's losses in the Second World War. Nothing like that happened in the 19th century.

Now, when your whole country is one festering wound, your individual men and women will bleed from a thousand wounds too. They will die of starvation, they will eat the flesh of fellow prisoners, they will betray their kith and kin for three square metres of living space; they will even write film music to the glory of Stalin (as Shostakovich had to).

And don't forget another thing: the Soviet Union is an enormous empire. It is the stage on which hundreds of nations, languages and civilisations clash and mingle. The conflicts in culture and perception are legion and the nervous energy they generate stupendous. Therefore it isn't (as you suggest) that the Russian people are unduly sensitive and metaphysical—although, for all I know, they may be that too—but that Soviet activism, superimposed on the permanent drama of the conflict of nations and civilisations, leaves the ordinary man in a state of breathless bewilderment.

Imagine the whole of Europe run by a single government, from a single centre, under a single ideology. Imagine the problems you would have to deal with as between Frenchmen and Serbs, or Englishmen and Spaniards, between Mediterranean and Germanic attitudes to work and time-keeping. That's the kind of permanent turmoil you have in the Soviet Union.

Let me, therefore, say that your slight incredulity is a sign that even sophisticated people in the West are not quite able to make the imaginative leap to understand what goes on under Soviet rule.

URBAN: Don't misunderstand me. Personally I find the Russian inclination to use almost any human problem as a departure for profound questioning most congenial. It betrays a serious bent of mind, and the courage to face that great emptiness which is often the result of our quest for final answers.

GALINA: This was more true of our writers and thinkers in the last century than it is today. Our 'talking classes' today have more pressing preoccupations, such as finding a decent roof above their heads.

URBAN: Nor did I seriously think for a moment that Soviet life wasn't exactly as you painted it. Indeed, I believe it is paradoxically the intolerance of the Soviet system that has caused an important spiritual element to be injected into Western thinking, for which we must, by way of *felix culpa*, be grateful to both Russia and Communism.

Pope John Paul II is said to have remarked not so long ago that the Church does not need intellectuals but witnesses, and to the extent that it does need intellectuals it needs them only as witnesses. It is, I would suggest, the great merit of many of those Russian writers and artists who fled or were expelled from the Soviet Union that they are such witnesses—whether they are Christians, Jews, Muslims, or agnostics. They have brought back to us the authentic voice of suffering and the cry for deliverance at a time when our own culture raises them only hesitantly (or not at all). When Solzhenitsyn arrived in Western Europe he was first celebrated not only as a great writer but as a seer and a prophet.

GALINA: I hope you are right, but I am not absolutely convinced. The truth about the Soviet system had been told in volume after volume by the most authentic witnesses long before Solzhenitsyn. There has *never* been any excuse for a lack of knowledge. The question has always been whether people in the Western countries were ready to take in the truth that was reaching them from the East, and to do something about it. And there you may be right in hinting that Solzhenitsyn may have played a vital part, because he is not only an inspired chronicler of the history of Communism in the Soviet Union, but also a tormentor of the Western conscience for having done so little to oppose Communism as a menace to mankind.

I regard my own small role in the same sort of light. Now that I live in the West I feel it to be my duty to tell people what is really happening under Soviet rule. Anyone who has read my book cannot possibly say 'I didn't know', or 'I don't believe it'. All Russians in the West have that duty, and I go on telling the truth about Communism to whoever happens to come my way: friends, the bus-conductor, the girl who serves me in the grocer's shop, my gardener. Let them all know—there must be no excuse left for anyone saying, 'We weren't told. . . .' That much we certainly ought to have learned from the silence which surrounded Hitler's extermination of the Jews.

URBAN: Talking about silence, there is a scene in your book which left me with a lasting impression.

Solzhenitsyn's wife, Alya, came to say goodbye as she was about to join her husband in Switzerland. More than a month had passed since Solzhenitsyn had been deported by the KGB. Alya Solzhenitsyn had assumed that your house was bugged, so she brought a blackboard and you proceeded to talk to one another by writing questions and answers on it, erasing the words as soon as they had been put down.

GALINA: Alya wanted to know whether we too were planning to go West—and at the time we were not. Little did we suspect that Solzhenitsyn's deportation and his reception in the West would soon make it impossible for us too to go on living in Russia.

URBAN: But wasn't this a scene of pungent symbolism—you, Rostropovich, Alya, and through her Alexander Solzhenitsyn, trying to communicate with one another on a black-board, in silence? I was reminded of Beethoven's deafness—and I could not help remembering your vibrant interpretation of Leonora, in *Fidelio*.

GALINA: Yes, we were all of us what you might call people of 'the word' and 'the voice'. Sound was our medium. Yet there we were, sitting in complete silence, like conspirators, trying to make ourselves understood in sign-language, and through chalk-marks on a blackboard.

Our voices had been strangled, first in public and finally in the privacy of my kitchen, too. If I were to make a film about our lives in the Soviet Union, this would be its final scene.

1986

Notes

1. 'The Kingdom of Heaven is like unto leaven, which a woman took, and hid in the measures of meal, till the whole was leavened.' Matthew 13:11.
2. 'Hymn to Stalin', published in *Pravda*, 28 August 1938.
3. In a debate reproduced by the Moscow journal *Ogonyok* (14 April 1988) L. Y. Gozman, of Moscow State University, observed:

   'It is postulated, for example, that man wants to be free. And since the reforms will produce more freedom, this means that the reforms are clearly beneficial in psychological terms. But this is not so! No, it is not. Freedom means responsibility, freedom means lack of rigid definitions. Life in conditions of freedom demands efforts and certain aspects of personality which have not been very actively nurtured hitherto. On the contrary, there was acclamation for subordination to the majority opinion, to the collective, which at times meant the suppression of individuality . . .

   Where will people acquire the skill to live in conditions of freedom given that, psychologically, we were a society without alternatives for so many years? . . .

   People are unaccustomed to feeling masters of their own fate. Until such time as this feeling of being master (which, incidentally, includes strictly moral aspects like, for example, a sense of one's own dignity) is restored, I don't think we can talk about adequate guarantees.

   Freedom, just like submissiveness of spirit, takes a long time to learn.'
4. Galina Vishnevskaya was eventually allowed to appear in a performance of the *War Requiem* in the Royal Albert Hall in London, with Benjamin Britten conducting and Dietrich Fischer-Dieskau and Peter

Pears in the baritone and tenor parts. A recording was subsequently made (Decca, set 252–3).

5. '*Requiem eternam dona eis, Domine: et lux perpetua luceat eis. . . .*'
6. On Hegedüs's memoirs, see, in *Encounter* (September–October 1985), 'The People are Coming!'.
7. Virginia Woolf, 'The Russian Point of View', in *The Common Reader* (First Series, London 1925), pp. 219–231.

4.   ALAIN BESANÇON
Breaking the spell

Make-Believe

URBAN: My theme is the role of mendacity in totalitarian
thinking. Dr Goebbels boasted that 'the bigger the lie the
more likely it is to be believed. . . .' Solzhenitsyn reminds
us that the only means of redeeming the individual from
the embrace of the Soviet system is to ask him to 'stop
lying'. One of the slogans most prominently heard on 23
October 1956 in the streets of Budapest was a protest against
the mendacity of the official radio station: 'the Radio is
telling lies (*hazudik a rádió*).' One might, in a sense,
describe the Hungarian Revolution as a nationwide protest
against the prostitution of the meaning of words and the
destruction of the 'mental hygiene' of an old European
nation.

There are many examples in Hungarian life and letters of
the good-natured liar lost in the mists of remembrance
(János Háry) and of the excusability of poetic licence as a
trick no writer dare miss (Arany's 'Ars Poetica'). But this
roguishness running through some celebrated pages in
Hungarian literature has never been the defining characteristic of the temper of Hungarian life. Rather have a search
for truth and a consummate sense of honour. Stalinism and
the institutionalised Lie that came with it in 1947–48 had,
therefore, a hard row to hoe.

The question that interests me most apropos the recent
30th anniversary of the Hungarian Revolution has to do
with deception and self-deception in totalitarian societies.
Is Soviet ideology a 'falsification' of the real world to fit the
power-holders' interests? Or is it another sort of reality

which we do not quite understand, even after seven decades of Communism? And, whether it is one or the other, at what point is the official ideology most likely to come unstuck as it did, within a single week, so spectacularly in Hungary?

BESANÇON: The lie as the essential element of totalitarian control has by now a formidable literature. Boris Souvarine made a famous statement about it as early as 1937, insisting that the lie was the very core of the Soviet system. In a world in which lying is standard behaviour, he said, the lie itself becomes lied about.

> The USSR is the country of the lie, the absolute lie, the integral lie. Stalin and his subjects are always lying, at every moment, under every circumstance, and by dint of lying they no longer even realise that they are lying. Where everything lies, nothing lies. The USSR is nothing but a lie based on fact. In the four words those initials stand for, there are no fewer than four lies. . . .

And so on, and so on.

In the early 1920s, long before Souvarine, Evgeny Zamyatin, a former Bolshevik, depicted in his novel *We* a horrendous utopia in which a cosmic 'Well-Doer' subordinates mankind, and society is run on the lines of a vast railway timetable. Then we have Bulgakov, Solzhenitsyn, and Alexander Zinoviev in our own time. They have all exposed official mendacity as the heart of the system. So did, before them, the Croatian writer Anton Ciliga who wrote *The Country of the Disconcerting Lie* and *The Country of the Great Lie*—both were based on his experiences in the Soviet Union before the Second World War. I need hardly mention George Orwell, who coined 'Doublethink', 'Newspeak', 'Oldthink', 'Crimethought', 'Bellyfeel', and so on—words which, as he explained, 'not only had in every case a political implication, but were intended to impose a desirable mental attitude upon the person using them.' We are walking on well-trodden ground.

URBAN: It is a nice question whether the Lie, or that intricate network of lies that makes up Soviet ideology is *sui generis*, or whether it has roots in the Russian past. I am struck by a passage in your book *The Rise of the Gulag*[1] in which you show that 19th-century Slavophilism was, in reality, an unacknowledged import from Germany and France. The Slavophiles, you argue, imported the concept of Nationalism, 'removing any labels indicating country of origin'. They then proceeded to build a Slavophile 'ideology' and turned it against Europe.

> They were thus led to construct a fictional reality, a fictional history, a fictional religion and fictional politics in every field.

Wasn't this vast tampering-with-reality a precursor of what would happen under the Bolsheviks a hundred years on?

BESANÇON: Certainly the element of make-believe was common to both, and so was their broad public acceptance. But the Slavophiles were simple falsifiers and plagiarists. They would publish some theological document claiming that it was an old unpublished Orthodox manuscript, whereas in fact the document would be copied from the work of some Tübingen theologian. Their 'naturalisation' of German Idealism was a manifest travesty.

In talking about Soviet ideology, however, we face a very different phenomenon. The real question is whether the word 'lie' is well chosen to identify what Souvarine, Solzhenitsyn, Zinoviev and others describe as 'lies'.

'Lie' in its habitual meaning stands for conscious departure from a known reality; it means that the liar is familiar with the truth, and when he departs from it to tell a lie he knows that he is rendering a distorted version of the truth. In ideology you have a different process. You no longer entertain reality against unreality, truth against untruth, but you witness a curious splitting or decomposition of reality itself. You are dealing with two divergent realities—a reality and a pseudo-reality: a reality that you can see and hear and touch, and another that exists purely in your articulations, in language, in propaganda.

To put it quite simply: 'socialism' claims to be 'scientific'. It claims to be able to predict and engineer the future. With the 1917 Revolution socialism was put in power; and it was expected by Lenin and his successors that the theory of socialism would be translated into the reality of socialism precisely because socialism was scientific and all the right conditions had been created for socialism to take off and fly. But socialism refused to happen; it remained a theory in the minds of the Bolsheviks. So how were they to proceed, given the fact that their power was based on the scientific character of socialism—on their alleged ability to monitor the design of history and help it along by putting themselves in phase with its rhythm?

They could only proceed by acting *as if* socialism had really happened. The whole unreality of Soviet ideology is based on the rulers' need to pretend that things exist that do not. Soviet statistics are a fake; the results of the Five-Year Plans are a sham; a Soviet 'parliament' never existed; 'elections' have never been elections; 'the spontaneity of the masses' is the result of meticulous organisation; the tractor girls' 'happy life' is a mournful farce; the new 'Soviet man' is the old Adam; and so on. Ideology put a smoothing cover over these unpleasant facts. It demanded that people see what wasn't there, and speak as though it existed.

URBAN: After the suppression of the Hungarian Revolution Ignazio Silone noted how the Soviet ideological vocabulary had stood reality on its head. His argument of December 1956 is germane to the point you are making.

> The worst tyranny of all is that of words. In order to start learning to think honestly once again, we must first tidy up our language. Believe me, that's not easy. For example, why the devil do we keep referring to the Russian army as the 'Soviet' army? In reality, the Soviets disappeared from Russia as early as 1920, and the only soviets that exist in the world at present are precisely the Hungarian revolutionary committees! And they are soviets in the most genuine sense of the word, open, elementary and improvised forms of the people's power in a country where autocracy has prevented the organising of political parties. . . .
>
> Nevertheless, in order to be understood by everybody, we too are forced to abide by the current and distorted meaning of words; for example, we have to write: 'the Soviet troops against the Hungarian insurgents', whereas the simplest respect for accuracy would oblige us to write, 'the Russian imperialist troops against the soviets of Hungary'. That's how things stand: *Nomina perdidimus rerum*—we have lost the names of things. . . .

BESANÇON: Yes, the best way to describe the unreal language generated by Soviet ideology might be to liken it to a spell or bewitchment. It is an aura and a state of mind as well as a vocabulary. It envelops the whole being of those who are captured by it. It is something akin to what we read in medieval literature about Merlin the Sorcerer; or in the legend of Ariosto's *Orlando Furioso* about some dark forest from which there is no exit; or some fairy princess imprisoned in a magic castle. But then suddenly the spell is lifted and your heroes emerge unscathed.[2]

Communist ideology is like that. It is ephemeral. The bewitchment dissolves; and *hey presto!* you are free, awakened to reality as though you were coming out of a coma or shedding a nightmare. And that is exactly what the people of Hungary experienced in October 1956, the Czechoslovaks in 1968, and the Poles in 1981. They dropped their chains, found their sense of reality unimpaired, and filled the gap between reality and the unreal world in which they had been forced to live without difficulty.

URBAN: But if ideology is so fragile, why is it so robust? For there can be no doubt that while the bewitchment lasts it has an all-encompassing fascination even for those who resist it. I heard a blistering attack on 'Sovietism' by a distinguished German professor at a recent conference. The point that registered with me in his lecture was the extraordinary gusto with which he outlined the post-War successes of Soviet ideology and expansionism before shooting them down as a menace to democracy. He depicted the advantages of having a simple political faith and determined leadership with so much enjoyment that he was in fact paying a backhanded compliment to the ideology he was repudiating.

BESANÇON: Ideology appeals to some of the ingrained, Manichean, black-and-white predilections of human nature. Soviet ideology shows the world split between good and evil—between the virtues of the coming classless society and the sins of the outgoing capitalist society. You had a parallel dichotomy in Nazism where the conflict was between Jewish 'guilt' and Aryan 'virtue'. For Hitler, the Jew was the fount of all evil, while for the Marxist-Leninist it is 'bourgeois' or 'capitalist' society. The attribution of guilt for all the world's sins to a single source is as old as the human race itself. Hence its easy penetration even of the minds of men who ought to be immune to it.

In a book I once wrote about this kind of problem (*The Falsification of the Good*) I make the point that all ideological theory is about the identification of evil: what is 'the Jew' or what is 'capitalism', and how do you locate and eradicate either? Ideology offers a ready recipe. But then a strange thing happens. In trying to eradicate evil you discuss and parade it on the stage of the world, and by so doing you make it look immensely powerful and ubiquitous. Never has evil looked so strong and even attractive as in the act of being struck down. This may explain your professor's eloquence.

But, to come back to the credibility of ideology, so long as ideology is not in power, it is only the ideological theoreticians who live under its spell. It is only they who have to accept unreality as though it were real. But when Communist ideology attains power, ideology has to be checked against reality in very practical ways. At that point the challenge to the Communist power-holders is to persuade the people not that 'socialism' is a good thing, but that socialism *exists*. The people must be able to digest the fact that they are prisoners in the sorcerer's castle from which there is no escape.

URBAN: Can you see a way in which the ordinary man—a man who neither has religion to back him nor wants to be a hero or a martyr—can exempt himself from the impact of ideology? Can he withdraw into his inner shell and live 'away' from society? Can he construct for himself a world of readings, friendships, art and life-styles that would protect him? We have heard of such cases, but can we offer something like a practical formula for those who want to live at arm's length from official society but don't quite know how?

BESANÇON: That is a difficult one. The moment the individual accepts the language of the ideology, he allows his mental world and his sense of self-respect to be hijacked along with the language. No matter how inadvertently he may have stumbled into the use of the official vocabulary, he is now part of the ideology and has, in a manner of speaking, entered into a pact with the devil.

Why do I use such strong words? Because frequently the individual stoops to using the hijacked language only for 'official' purposes, the better (as he thinks) to be able to safeguard his private integrity. But this does not work. He soon discovers that, having made one concession in public, he is filled with a sense of shame in private and develops a growing interest in obliterating the duplicity and adopting the language of the ideology in *all* his articulations.

The 'internal emigration' that you have mentioned as an alternative to all this is not easy to attain. I suppose it could be done *if* you stopped having any communication and transaction with the State and official society; *if* you were unmarried and had no children, and *if* you were strong enough to live in poverty and become a hermit. And that is what some Soviet individuals have envisaged as an ideal, and have from time to time been able to realise.

But, on the whole, this can be a remedy only for the most exceptional and heroic people—those of unbreakable convictions or a saintly nature.

URBAN: Doesn't religion help as a counter-force? We have much evidence to show that, for example, Baptists and Pentecostalists survived the Gulag in a much better state of mind than the average political convict. Also, I would have thought the force of Polish Catholicism explains a great deal about the ordinary Pole's immunity to the ideology, even though the Church in Poland stands for a much wider area of loyalties than those we conveniently list under 'religion'.

BESANÇON: Well, religious convictions undoubtedly help, but I wouldn't want you to think that I look upon religion as a 'counter-ideology'. Religion is something you 'have' and 'believe in'. Faith is an act of spiritual loyalty at the deepest level. Communist ideology is different. It does not—or should not—exact an act of faith, because it is supposedly scientific and thus open to demonstration. You do not 'believe' in ideology—you accept it (if you do) with your rational self as *true*. I would, therefore, not endorse your implication that religion is a counter-force to ideology—a kind of thinking that could, shall we say, invalidate ideology.

The morality that helps us to oppose Communist ideology springs from the very nature of man. The world did not wait for religion to come along to equip us with a moral dimension. It has always been there. Honesty, truthfulness, loyalty are given us with human nature. What I'm saying is that you can (if you can at all) protect your integrity in a Communist system by virtue of your strength of character and natural morality. You don't *have* to be a man of religion.

Let me, however, say in the same breath that a concern with the life of the spirit is one way of building a wall of decency around you and detaching yourself from ideology. Some (a few, I should think) have managed it. For example: a French engineer friend of mine was sent to the Urals to assist in the erection of some factory we had 'sold' to the Soviet Union—naturally on French credit. He was forced to live in a human environment that he found so debased and debasing that he could hardly find words to describe it. But one day he met a couple of Jews in this incredible filthy small industrial town in the Urals who observed the Torah, literally from dawn-to-dusk every day of the week—and he found them to be human beings who were untouched by the foulness, the sham, the poverty, and the hijacked language. He could talk to them—they understood each other. But, as I say, you don't have to live the life of a hermit to be able to do that. It is enough to be a decent human being.

URBAN: In a seamless Orwellian state, I rather suspect, decency would not be enough, because decency has to be supported by some familiarity with the past, the assimilation of certain books, music, and other components of a received culture. In an Orwellian state such as the Chinese during Mao's Cultural Revolution or Cambodia under Pol Pot, the past is abolished and the books are destroyed. In a world of that sort, wouldn't 'decency' alone prove too weak a reed to uphold the values of liberal civilisation? Fortunately, the perfect Orwellian society has so far failed to materialise on Western soil; but Stalin had a frighteningly effective shot at it and Hoxha's Albania went one better.

BESANÇON: The Soviet leaders have, as you say, never quite managed to create a perfect totalitarian society. They always needed some contact with the past—whether because they needed educated people to carry on the business of government or because they were anxious to endorse their legitimacy by allying themselves with national consciousness.

But of course the Soviets realised the dangers of not going flat out for a totalitarian order, and were often torn between using and obliterating the past. One day Dostoevsky was available; then unobtainable; then again available on Soviet bookshelves. The same was true for Pushkin and other classics, both Russian and foreign.

In China under the 'Cultural Revolution' and in Pol Pot's
Cambodia such considerations were not allowed to interfere
with the serious business of 'true revolution'. Mao's young
thugs and the Cambodian bully-boys put the destruction
of private libraries high on their list of priorities. They
demolished culture and all symbols and artefacts of the
'bourgeois' past. The Soviets never quite managed to do
that—much less, of course, the régimes in Eastern Europe.

URBAN: There was in Eastern Europe a great deal of 'Russification' under Stalin; but nowadays the East European
régimes are just as keen on underpinning their legitimacy
by reinterpreting the national past and harnessing it to
Communist ends as is the Soviet government. In East
Germany, Martin Luther, Frederick the Great, Bismarck,
and now even German Expressionism of the early years
of this century have been marshalled among the natural
forebears of Marxism-Leninism. It cannot be long before
'primitive Christianity' and 'the egalitarian Christ' are
deployed to the same ends. Indeed, before the 1968 Prague
Spring, some Czech Marxist theologians began to pave the
way for that kind of reinterpretation in their dialogue with
Western Catholics.

BESANÇON: The moment you suspend deletion of the past
and begin building on it in the hope of imposing a forged
version on the public, you are letting yourself in for trouble.
Because in so doing you have to preserve the books and
look after your churches and monasteries. No matter how
heavily footnoted your Tolstoy may then be, the text is
there to tell its own story, and the deletion of culture just
cannot happen. Rebuilding the royal castles in Warsaw and
Buda is a double-edged weapon for the régimes. It could
easily boomerang on them; and it most probably will.

Integrity in a Corrupt Environment

URBAN: Let me take you back to the question: how does
the ordinary man evade the encroachments of ideology if
he has neither religion nor the courage of heroism to support
him? We have partly answered it by saying that his access
to the past, his reading, and his inborn sense of decency

might help. These are no doubt some of the necessary conditions of his sanity—but are they sufficient?

BESANÇON: No, they are not. You have to have contact with people in practical life where common sense prevails—entering into contractual obligations, talking, negotiating, buying and selling, and so on. The logic of these activities is wholesome because they are difficult to ideologise. Then you should have like-minded people around you, friends and acquaintances with whom you can discuss your family problems, your housing, the difficulties of shopping and the like, because in talking about these matters you cannot use the wooden language of ideology. The normal morality that goes with this kind of intercourse is a haven of sanity in an ideologised society.

Even foreigners living in the Soviet Union can establish a network of friends and acquaintances of this kind, although they frequently have reason to suspect that their friends are corrupt and inform on them. When I lived in Russia I had quite a few friends whom I cherished; but I knew that some had an obligation to write reports about me for the security authorities. I could, nevertheless, have decent relations with them in various fields of life. In other words, you can protect your integrity by concentrating on the ordinary business of living and having friends and being a friend to others.

URBAN: But what about people who feel they are gifted in, shall we say, the craft of journalism or managing a bureaucracy? If they were to be true to their principles they would have to forgo using their talents because in a Communist society there are no newspapers and no bureaucracies completely outside the control of the state and its ideology. Should they, then, resist making a career in Communist society even though they are unlikely to make one in any other?

BESANÇON: It very much depends on what kind of a career you envisage for yourself. Clearly, journalism and management are areas where the official ideology is firmly in control. A man anxious to protect his integrity would not, in my view, go in for those careers unless he were prepared to take the consequences for the rest of his life. That is why survival as a decent human being has become a whole art in Communist societies. For example, if you are an historian you will avoid specialising in anything after the middle of the 19th century—you will concentrate your erudition on Byzantine texts and the like, where you are less vulnerable. You are also safe if you are a mathematician—hence the extraordinary number of mathematicians we hear about in the Soviet Union—because figures and theorems are difficult to ideologise. But for a sociologist or psychologist life becomes extremely difficult, and for a philosopher or economist utterly impossible.

URBAN: Here again, mightn't the Russian past help us to see things in perspective? After Czar Nicholas I had suppressed the 1848–49 Hungarian Revolution, his fear that the European ferment might reach Russia was such that philosophy was banned from the university curriculum, and letters signed with the words 'all my love' were censored because they implied the denial of proper affection for God and the Czar.

BESANÇON: Yes, philosophers are, as the word makes clear, 'lovers of wisdom', and that is dangerous for despotisms of every kind. *Thinking* is dangerous because you can never tell where it will take you. . . .

URBAN: What you are saying is that in Soviet society you are more likely to survive in value-free occupations—if, that is, there are any. . . .

BESANÇON: Yes, but even a mathematician works for the state, and there is no telling what the state may demand from him. Suppose he were asked to step down from his ivory tower and make calculations about nuclear fission, or the number of 'labourers' it would take to build a canal or reverse some river—he would then suddenly find himself in the embrace of tyranny, even though he might find a hundred ways of convincing himself that he was not.

URBAN: The cases we have mentioned are somewhat untypical. The majority of people in Communist society are neither historians nor mathematicians. How does the ordinary family man—a man of lazy habits, fond of his drink, not particularly concerned with the state of the world, with a wife and children to support, and exposed to daily propaganda in the official press and television—how does he manage to keep his head above the murky waters of ideology?

BESANÇON: It would be presumptuous for me to offer a patent remedy, but having seen Soviet society from the inside, let me just say that a man of ordinary decency can do, or avoid doing, several things in order to save his soul from 'damnation'. He cannot avoid being a member of the Pioneers, or even the *Komsomol* when he is young, but he is relatively free not to join the Party. There is no automatic escalator from the *Komsomol* to the Party. You have to perform certain duties and attract the attention of the right people in order to be considered eligible for Party member-ship. If you do decide to join, this is an expression of your free will. If you don't, that, too, is something you have freely chosen. No one forces you to become a Party member.

URBAN: So not to become a Party member is a kind of automatic barrier against the grosser forms of ideological pollution?

BESANÇON: Yes, it is. You are in no way predestined to join the Party. If you don't, you simply join that nine-tenths of the Soviet population who are not Party members. You don't *have* to support dictatorship. But, as you rightly hinted, for a man with ambition in his belly it is not always easy to stick to high moral principles. What is it he should avoid doing, in addition to not becoming a Party member?
   He should avoid any form of social ambition, because that would attract the attention of the Party and his advancement would become dependent on Party membership. He should avoid asking anything from the State; he should not try to live in Moscow if he is not automatically entitled to it; he should avoid asking for a better apartment, a more inter-esting job, privileged holidays, a better deal for his children at school, and so on. It's a tall order—too tall for the majority of ordinary people. The traps are many; and I should not want to throw stones at people who have fallen into some of them. You need extraordinary strength of character to avoid them, hence you cannot always criticise Soviet dissidents for not being completely 'clean'. You don't have to befriend them and you don't have to employ them,

but you cannot condemn them without investigating the circumstances.

URBAN: A principle we would, no doubt, want to apply to the members of all totalitarian parties, whether of the Left or the Right?

BESANÇON: Yes, I'm sure neither of us would want to subscribe to any notion of 'collective guilt'; but as in the Soviet case Party membership is largely a matter of choice, former Party members cannot ask us to extend to them the presumption of innocence without showing us why and how they came to join the Party—if, that is, they want to have credibility in the West.

URBAN: What you are saying, and what many Soviet observers such as Amalrik and Zinoviev have been saying for a long time, is that all 'Soviet Men' are to some degree infected.

BESANÇON: Yes, and I can give you a telling example. Jewish people in the Soviet Union form something of an élite, and among them there is an élite within the élite: Jewish scientists, doctors, writers, *et al*. Now, within this élite of the élite there is a *super*-élite: people who are determined enough to face years of harassment, discrimination, and unemployment in order to obtain their exit permits to emigrate to Israel. But once they have arrived there, they frequently cannot find jobs commensurate with their qualifications. Doctors may have to serve as nurses or medical orderlies; physicists may have to teach mathematics in elementary school; and so on. This is, understandably, unpopular. But what my friends in Israel tell me is that this Soviet Jewish super-élite has brought with it all the characteristics of 'Soviet Man': they are rude to those serving under them and servile to their superiors. They are demanding and take their new lot without dignity. In brief, they are unable to deport themselves according to the standards and mores of Occidental Man. Now, this is the cream of the élite of Soviet society. What can you expect from the ordinary citizen?

URBAN: The strange thing is that Czechs and Poles and the Chinese do not behave like that in emigration. Soviet Man does. Are we prejudiced in seeing him in this light?

BESANÇON: I don't think we are. Take the most ideologised and fanatical section of Chinese Communist society—the 'Red Guards' who wreaked such terrible havoc during the Cultural Revolution. Many of these young brutes found their way, for one reason or another, to Hong Kong. And how do we find them occupying themselves there? Within weeks they took jobs; they married; sent their wives to work in factories; adjusted to local 'capitalist' conditions; and eventually became successful businessmen. Not for them the heritage of ideology, or brooding over the glory that was Mao's China.

Soviet émigrés, by contrast, are mostly misfits throughout their emigration. They live in a state of self-imposed isolation and refuse to learn our language. They fret and storm about in the Western world, letting everyone know who is prepared to listen that Soviet society may be awful but the West is pretty hopeless, too, even though for a different set of reasons.

URBAN: Is this an entirely 'Soviet' phenomenon? Some of the 19th-century Russian émigrés behaved in a very similar manner. Herzen's strictures on the inadequacies of the West were no less pointed than are those of Solzhenitsyn. And Alexander Herzen was a 'Westerniser' whereas Solzhenitsyn is not.

BESANÇON: Yes (*pace* Solzhenitsyn), there is a heavy admixture of the Russian heritage in the behaviour of Soviet Man as an émigré. He has brought with him the late 19th-century tradition of *duhovnost* (spirituality), which in the particular context of Russian culture means a salvationist feeling of Orthodoxy, mixed with Russian nationalism. This imbues him with a sense of resignation because his 'spirituality' could not and cannot be satisfied. It colours and deepens the malaise he carries with him as Soviet Man.

URBAN: The differences from the Chinese are truly astonishing: like the dutiful children of Confucius, the Chinese seek to make good in this world through application and intelligence, while ex-Soviet Man burns the midnight oil in his Parisian attic thinking delightfully hopeless thoughts about the deliverance of his Nation and the ingratitude of the World. I must confess to you that I have a good deal of (perhaps misplaced) admiration for men so passionately given to lost causes, and only one cheer for the practical Chinese.

BESANÇON: I won't quarrel with you on that score; but let me just note in passing that this Russian predilection to despise and evade practical action and, in a sense, all 'modernity', and to fret and brood when the workaday world gets in the way of Utopia is, again, very much *pre*-Soviet. It predates *duhovnost* and has to do with Russian religious education in the early decades of the 19th century.

Of course, all 19th-century Russian education was religious, but the Russian education of the time took its special cue from German Idealistic philosophy (Illuminism), adding to it a good dose of thinly disguised Russian nationalism. It taught the young to despise the world of law, the world of money, commerce, industry, and financial self-improvement. Indeed it was hostile to the whole of West European 'bourgeois' civilisation. Europe was corrupt, it held, because Europe had given way to the spirit of the Enlightenment and Science, and the United States was a caricature of Europe. It taught that Divine Providence had saved Russia from the destructive impact of both Catholicism and Protestantism, and that it was for the Russian Church to promote the spiritual revival of Europe.

Now, the Soviet intelligentsia, whether in Russia or in emigration, has inherited some of the spirit of 19th-century Russian education. Its contempt for the modern world helps us to understand why the most brilliant and sensitive Russians tend to suffer from a sense of alienation, and why some of them find it so difficult to shed the integument of ideology.

URBAN: There is supposed to be a sense in which the Russian people 'enjoy' suffering because suffering seems to equip them with a passport to higher insight and self-respect. Some have asserted this is because the Russians are the world's natural Christians, others because they are natural 'slaves'.   .

BESANÇON: It was the mid-19th-century satirical writer Mikhail Saltykov who (writing home from a visit to France) made the remarkable observation: 'In Russia things are worse than they are here in France, but, in fact, they are

better because we Russians suffer more. . . .' Perhaps they
do enjoy hardship.

URBAN: Mightn't there be yet another, or an additional
explanation? In your book *The Rise of the Gulag* you tell
us apropos your analysis of Nechayev's *The Catechism of
the Revolutionary* that there is in the Russian radical
tradition not only a communion of saints but also a
communion of sinners:

> Russian religiosity is ready to believe that there is a community in evil
> as well as in good, a communion of sinners, just as there is a
> communion of saints. Which provides a major temptation for
> adolescent souls.

I would have thought the 'misunderstood Russian', the
'Russian isolated in emigration', the 'Russian rejected by
the world and nursing his *Weltschmerz* would belong to your
'communion of sinners'—people who feel elevated by their
defection and the challenge they offer to any society. Aren't
there in the Soviet emigration as well as in the Soviet Union
itself a great many people whom one could describe as
'outcasts by choice'—men who thrive on the freedoms of
the intellectual *franc tireur* and think of themselves as saintly
sinners?

BESANÇON: There is in the Russian philosophical tradition
a certain disregard for law, jurisdiction, and even the
commonly accepted ethics of society. The 19th-century
Russian intellectuals in particular assumed that there was
something sublime about challenging and negating the
moral code of society. Dostoevsky put the malicious Stav-
rogin on the fringes of sainthood. The Russian revolutionary
atheist was a believer with his faith turned upside down. He
belonged, by temperament and language, to the monastic
orders.

Now, this was *not* a typically Russian attitude. It
stemmed, like so much else in 19th-century Russia, from
Germany, but was turned into a provincial caricature under
Russian skies. The abstract reflections of Fichte and Schel-
ling became fiery do-it-yourself tracts and pamphlets in the
hands of Bakunin, Chernyshevsky, and Nechayev. The
Russian Social Democracy and then Communism partook

of this tradition. The early Bolsheviks did think of themselves (even if they did not often say so) as a communion of saintly sinners. Today, your displaced dissident, the Soviet intellectual hankering after his 'collective' on the Left Bank of Paris, or the Soviet writer living in a state of permanent ennui on the shores of the Starnbergersee does, in a sense, inhabit a psychological world close to the one that bred the Bolsheviks.

URBAN: But to come back to the Hungarian Revolution—can we identify the point in the life of the Soviet type of ideology where disenchantment sets in and the unreality of the whole construct hits you in the eye? At what stage does it start dawning on the objects of ideology that the whole thing is a sham?

BESANÇON: Limiting ourselves to Soviet (as distinct from satellite) ideology, we must always bear in mind that, as in judo, our normal reflexes do not apply and we must re-educate them to get the hang of Soviet thinking. If your question means: do the Soviet people believe in ideology, or do the Soviet leaders believe in ideology, or does even Gorbachov himself believe in ideology—then I would have to say this is not a meaningful question. The question in the USSR is not belief but, rather: do they conform with the demands of ideology? do they speak within the framework of the official vocabulary? And my answer to those questions is an unhesitating: Yes, they do, without exception.

That said, one has to ask what precisely is the meaning of that enormous energy expended every day in television, radio, the printed media, schools, factories, offices and so on, by millions of propagandists after almost seven decades of 'Socialism'? Why does the régime expect 250 million Soviet citizens to listen to the Party line in which nobody believes? Is it a rational enterprise from the Communist point of view? What does it prove?

Soviet propaganda proves the presence of power. As long as the ordinary man and woman submit to this ritual, they recognise their slavish condition. As long as they do not cry out in anger, 'All this is nothing but a vast pack of lies', as long as they obediently mouth the phrases read to them from *Pravda*, they render proof, not only to the régime but to themselves too, that they have been subdued.

URBAN: Again—isn't this a Russian phenomenon? Wouldn't Communism of the Soviet inspiration take a different form in France, for example? When 'Eurocommunism' had its heyday in the mid-1970s it was widely believed by Western socialists that in Italian or Spanish (or even French) hands, Marxism-Leninism would turn out to be a more civilised, more democratic and pluralistic affair than it did under Russian auspices. The Italian Eurocommunists even began to talk about a '*K* factor', meaning the bad odour Italian Communism had acquired from its Russian connection in the perception of Italy's electorate.

BESANÇON: I don't believe in this theory (and having seen your book on *Eurocommunism* I know that you don't either). Communism in France would be exactly the same as it is in the Soviet Union. As long as there is a French Communist Party waiting to climb to power, all you can expect in France is Soviet-style Communism. Look at the objectives depicted in any local Communist bulletin in the provinces—they are in no way different from the objectives and the language used in Communist bulletins in Kabul or Viet Nam. Basically, the same language and the same intellectual-political programmes prevail throughout the Communist world.

URBAN: You don't think French national traditions, history, and culture would have a decisive impact?

BESANÇON: An impact, yes; a decisive impact, no. One of the characteristics of Communism-in-power is its ability to pick up those traditions in a country's history which are useful to its purpose and which it can parade as having prepared the way for the nation's historical consummation in Communism. In Russia the Bolsheviks could build, as they did, on the Czarist traditions. In China Mao's people used the Imperial heritage. In East Germany Communism exploits the Prussian tradition, and in France—well, there would be a whole big reservoir of happy forerunners from Philip the Fair to the Jacobins and the Napoleonic Prefects.

One of our most sinister pieces of evidence of the uniformity of Communism is the language used in private conversation by Communist leaders of different nations. A

French Gaullist and a German Social Democrat in after-dinner conversation would use the ordinary no-nonsense type of down-to-earth vocabulary that they'd use in talking to their car-insurance agent or their tennis partner. Not so the Communist leaders. They use the same wooden language in private conversation as they do in their public articulations. This is, to my mind, a powerful clue to what we can expect from Communist rule in any country.

URBAN: There is a mass of evidence to endorse your obser-vation—my favourite one being Veljko Mićunović's Diary of his years in Moscow where he was Yugoslav Ambassador from 1956 to 1958. Much of his story revolves on the 1956 Hungarian Revolution and the execution of Imre Nagy and his associates. Mićunović makes a point of showing how the 'unorthodox' Khrushchev insisted on using, in their confi-dential conversations, the standard vocabulary of Soviet propaganda: 'socialist camp', 'peace offensive', 'imperi-alism', 'socialist legality', and the rest were all deployed by Khrushchev in exactly the same manner as he habitually used from the public platform. Mićunović, to show his disagreement, put all such phrases between quotations marks.

BESANÇON: We should certainly not be astonished. In what other tongue *can* you communicate if you are a Soviet ruler? You are, indeed, selected to be a Soviet ruler *because* that is the language you speak. The language is your sole justifi-cation; you couldn't choose another without jeopardising your position.

Four different languages are in use in Soviet society. One is the 'wooden' language of ideology which is the prescribed means of public communication. This we have dealt with. At the other end of the spectrum you have the 'natural' language of personal communication—the mother's language with her child; the language of lovers; a friend talking to a friend. Between these come two pseudo-langu-ages: the 'pseudo-wooden', which is much used when you want to create the impression that you share the make-believe of the wooden vocabulary but do not make it quite convincing; and the 'pseudo-natural', which the Soviet rulers use under certain circumstances to create the impression that they are 'like everybody else'. Khrushchev was a master of the pseudo-natural. It is also the language Soviet diplomats use when talking to Western diplomats, their objective being to let it be known that they are, really, just like Western officials and can be dealt with on the same assumptions as one Western country uses in its dealings with another. These four languages constitute, to my mind, the linguistic universe of Communism.

URBAN: Let me try and test these linguistic groups a little. Clearly, the preservation of your 'natural' language is most important. My impression is that as long as people spend most of their time making statements like 'I want a loaf of bread' or 'I love my husband' or 'That roof needs mending', they maintain, as you say, a natural barrier against ideological pollution. But the Communists are not unintelligent. When they demanded from the public that they say 'I love Comrade Stalin' or 'We love Comrade Rákosi', they were transposing ideology into the kind of natural language the ordinary man could comprehend even though he loathed what he had to say.

So my question is: could the régime corrupt and even eliminate natural language, too? The ideal thing from a Communist point of view would be to induce people to say (and to feel), 'I love dialectical materialism'—and we know that Mao, for example, hated the personalisation of 'socialism' and looked upon his own cult as a concession to the standards of a 'backward' peasantry.

George Orwell tells us in *1984* that the one thing ideology could not touch was the private thinking and private loyalties of individuals. That is the meaning of love between Winston and Julia. But, Orwell asks, would Winston betray Julia if he were put to torture, would Julia betray Winston? Yes, they might. They might be forced to confess. But, 'Confession is not betrayal,' Julia says. 'If they could make me stop loving you—that would be the real betrayal.'

'They can make you say anything—*anything*—but they can't make you believe it. They can't get inside you.'
'No,' he said a little more hopefully, 'no; that's quite true. They can't get inside you, if you *feel* that staying human is worth while, even when it can't have any result whatever, you've beaten them.'

Could this kind of loyalty and the natural language expressing it be eliminated by a Mao or a Pol Pot?

BESANÇON: I don't think it could, and Orwell does not think so either. By suppressing it the system would be suppressing that part of reality on which it must rely for survival. Soviet society is a parasite on reality and, like all parasites, it needs a body to feed on. It needs people in a certain state of health, in a certain state of education, with a certain intelligence capable of planning and working. To destroy these, too, would be to destroy its very basis of power.

URBAN: Can you envisage some psychological manipulation whereby a man could be induced to think and to say 'I love Comrade Stalin' and yet be rendered incapable of saying 'I love Julia'?

BESANÇON: Saying 'Yes', thinking 'No'. 'Loving Stalin' was the régime's concession to natural feeling and natural language. The statement 'I love Julia' can go together with 'I love Comrade Stalin', but it cannot go together with 'I love Communism'. Stalin was, after all, a real person, a real *Vozdh*. You could 'love' him the way people loved the Czar or the Great Khan. But I can see no way in which a man could say he loved Stalin but could somehow be so manipulated that he could not feel love for Julia.

URBAN: So the régime's demand that the ordinary man should mouth the phrase 'I love Comrade Stalin', or 'Death to the traitor Trotsky', is the régime's concession to the ordinary man's humanity, the régime's admission that it has failed to adulterate human nature?

BESANÇON: Paradoxically, yes. Such, you might say, are the ways of the dialectic.

Can Alternative Cultures Survive?

URBAN: There is, of course, a monastic conception of Communism which frowns upon private feelings and loyalties because they distract from 'revolution'. This 'kill-joy' Communism was much in evidence during the Cultural Revolution in China; but in the Soviet Union, too, it permeated for a long time the moral code of the Party. Much has been written about the fierce but chaste *apparatchik*, not least by Milovan Djilas. The Party's objective was to breed a kind of human being who could say with sincerity: 'I love dialectical materialism'. . . .

BESANÇON: That was the utopian purpose, but it never worked. It is true that Russian Communism in its puristic forms is an austere creed; it is against pleasure; it frowns upon desire; it thinks highly of martyrdom and suffering. Here, too, we have a link with the kind of feeling expressed by Saltykov in the 19th century.

Chernyshevsky's hero Rakhmetov (in his novel of 1883, *What's to be Done?*) is perhaps our best example of that 19th-century socialist/scientific asceticism which Plekhanov and then Lenin and the Bolsheviks took for their model; and this too is where the Communist idea of the 'New Man' had its beginnings (Chernyshevsky's book carried the subtitle *A Tale of the New Men*).

Rakhmetov finds himself (accidentally) falling in love. This could not be allowed: 'I must curb this love: it will tie my hands. They are already tied and they will not easily be undone. But I will manage it. I must not love. . . .' Rakhmetov loves humanity; what he cannot stand is people.

> I do not touch a drop of wine. I never touch a woman. . . . It must be so. We are asking for a total enjoyment of life for men, and our lives must bear witness that we do not ask it to gratify our own private desires, that it is not for us, but for men in general.

In other words, the repudiation of personal relations and natural language is to some extent rooted in Russia's intellectual past.

URBAN: In distancing themselves from that heritage some East European dissidents have chosen the indirect approach. They remain vaguely within the Marxist—though not the Leninist—universe and use its language. They seem to think that their only chance of reforming the system is from within, much in the same way as the early Humanists went on using the vocabulary of the medieval Church while expressing ideas that were more and more hostile to the tenets of orthodoxy. Can you see the categories and language of Marxism so employed as to lead to a serious critique and then, perhaps, to the withering away of the system? Marxism being destroyed by the weapons of Marxism? Something of that sort did happen in Hungary in 1956 and Prague in 1968.

BESANÇON: That would be choosing the difficult path with uncertain results, though it may, under certain conditions, be the only one available. The clean way is to turn one's back on the whole corrupting climate of ideology.

That is why I admire Vladimir Bukovsky. He took the conscious decision that it was not enough to be a dissident and an émigré. He took up biology as a hard science because he knew that the habit of mind that goes with scientific enquiry would immunise him against ideology more effectively than any 'counter-ideology'. Marxism as a 'science' is bogus; biology is not. To become a biologist you have to study the books, learn to respect evidence, subject your thinking to a rigorous logic, and so on. You cannot make deductions from a 'general system', as you do in Marxism, without making yourself the laughing-stock of your peers.

Bukovsky's way is the honourable way and the only one that can be really effective. The Poles under *Solidarity* acted in the same manner. They did not attempt to harness the Party or the ideology to their own ends (although they exploited the weaknesses of both) but decided to renounce the ideology and articulate an alternative system of values and culture.

URBAN: The idea that the Central and East European nations can live outside the grip of ideology while accepting the system as an evil they are powerless to destroy, is now prevalent not only in Poland but also in Hungary, and to a smaller extent East Germany and Czechoslovakia too. This is a remarkable development in that it is based on the premise that Soviet ideology has totally failed to penetrate the consciousness of the people. In Hungary, for example, writers like István Csurka and Sándor Csoóri advocate a state of affairs in which the nation would raise, out of its own and uncontaminated resources, a parallel culture, a parallel system of education, a parallel code of values, and so on. These would not directly challenge the official ideology but rather lead a life of their own outside the reach of the ideology. Can this opting out of the system succeed?

BESANÇON: The premise of an alternative society and an alternative culture is no longer a premise—it is a fact. I never cease making the point that there is no such thing as 'socialist' society or 'Soviet' society. What you have is 'the Communist domination of the remnants of normal society'. 'Socialist' society is a projection of ideology.

The pressures of Communist domination can, and often do, reduce the remains of normal society to the individual; but this individual can retain his identity, his human decency, and even regain some ground if the circumstances are right. In Poland and Hungary some of the circumstances are right at the moment. Hence I regard the notion of an alternative society and culture as right and realistic *within* certain strictly circumscribed limits to which I will come in a moment.

But there are differences even between Poland and Hungary. In Poland there is a deep gap between real society and the Communist world. The two are hardly in contact. Poland is, in fact, a country under the occupation of its own Communist Party. In Hungary the gap between society and government is not quite so wide. Hungarian society is more corrupt than the Polish; at the same time the Hungarian Communist Party is less hidebound than the one in Poland. But, as I say, the conditions for an alternative society and culture exist in both.

What are these conditions? In Poland a strong Church, independent farming and a wholly Western cultural tradition have supplied the basic requirements for a self-contained national society and culture. In Hungary the opportunities are more restricted. The Church, with the Primate of Esztergom at its head, does not enjoy the same prestige or independence as the Polish Church. The non-conformist Catholic 'Basis Communities' under Father Bulányi have a wide following, and the lure of cultural cooperation with the régime has been stronger than in Poland. At the same time, the Party has shown a greater readiness for compromise and made the ideology perform some spectacular somersaults, not least in the economy. 'Privatisation' and running a stock exchange in a 'socialist' country do not immediately come to mind as inevitable parts of the programme of Marxism-Leninism.

URBAN: You said an alternative society and culture are realistic things to aim for within limits. Before asking you to say how you see those limits, let me quote a passage from one of Csurka's speeches in which he sets out the rationale for an alternative Hungarian culture.

> Recognising that the Hungarian people, relying on its own strength, is unable to change the world's power-relationships, Hungary's geographical position or even the domestic facts of power, we must work out a life-strategy for Man grown independent from the world of politics. We must work out the principles of conduct for that industrious, malleable, reliable citizen who does not question power and authority and does not, consequently, induce the authorities to take nervous and fear-inspired actions of violence, but does, rather, define entirely by himself his inner autonomy, his life-style and the scope of his individual existence. His resistance to pressures threatening him from all sides will not emphasise the act of resistance but rather the fact that he will simply live his own, autonomous, self-constructive life to the extent this is possible in the given framework. . . . This self-constructive programme has to be emphatically Hungarian . . . it has to be permeated by love. . . .

Does this strike you as practicable under Soviet rule?

BESANÇON: Well, it is a curious declaration. It's a very Lutheran type of declaration, leaving the business of the world to the Prince of the secular world while relegating everything else to the private conscience of the individual. It is a highly apolitical declaration, too, in trying to build a society without its political dimension. It would strike a Plato or an Aristotle as an impossible undertaking; and I think it *is* impossible.

Of course, we must not dismiss it as meaningless, for it *is* a programme of escape from ideology. But the idea of leaving the city of the world to the Prince of the world—so that you can save your soul by building a decent, clean, and free inner world—is sheer escapism. The Poles under *Solidarity* tried a similar formula—a self-liberated, autonomous, clean Polish society was somehow to live side by side with a political régime that was neither free, nor autonomous, nor Polish. It cannot be done. Society is a whole thing. You cannot excise the political dimension and still say it is an autonomous and decent society.

URBAN: But aren't Poles and Hungarians past masters at doing just that? Their experiences from the last century are not so difficult to transfer to this one, even though all the conditions are outwardly different. The Hungarians, for example, had to learn the art of supporting a 'parallel culture', writing in Aesopian language, etc., between the defeat of the 1848–49 Revolution and the 1867 Compromise. They learnt how to ignore, tame, and then absorb the forces of oppression. It may well be that those who advocate a parallel society in Hungary today have, subconsciously perhaps, Ferenc Deák and the 1867 model in mind. Revolution has been tried—absorption remains to be tested.

BESANÇON: I am sure you are not serious about the parallel. Austrian oppression was a veritable delight in comparison with the Soviet type of controls that have kept Hungary in place for four decades. It left the structure of society and the minds of individuals untouched. The *ancien régime* was built on the theory that State and Society were separate. The State took care only of those problems which Society itself could not take care of: defence, jurisdiction, law and order and the like. But the Habsburgs would have been horrified if anyone had suggested that they install a totalitarian order in Hungary. They would not have understood what you were talking about.

URBAN: You don't seem to believe that the Polish-Hungarian 'programme' for an alternative society has a future.

BESANÇON: It will be a close thing. No matter how modestly you define the area in which individual men and women preserve their autonomy, the clash with the surrounding 'Soviet reality' will be inevitable and continuous. At every turn there will be conflicts; compromises will have to be struck, and these will undermine much of the essence of the desired alternatives.

URBAN: One curious feature of the Soviet type of oppression is the enthusiasm which not only its servants and administrators, but its victims, too, are expected to show for it. You lose your freedom as a practising Christian or Uzbek patriot, but you are expected to enjoy and celebrate your new status because it represents, according to the

ideology, a higher form of liberty. 'Freedom is Slavery'—
as George Orwell puts it in *1984*.

That kind of mentality would not, as you rightly imply,
tolerate alternative cultures and societies; and it may well
be that it is premature to draw conclusions from the incipient
Polish and Hungarian models.

BESANÇON: I think it is, even though both are most desirable. Soviet ideology absolutely demands that the citizen
should go beyond the correct use of language and celebrate
the triumph of the system with street dancing, bands,
choruses and other manifestations of officially engineered
euphoria. It is expected of him to show that the pseudo-
reality which surrounds him *is* reality.

An historian friend of mine remarked to me the other
day that he could not understand certain things about the
Soviet annexation of Estonia. He said: once the invasion of
Estonia had been completed, the oppression of the country
was wicked but understandable, the faked plebiscite was
wicked but understandable. But why the happy gatherings
to celebrate all these terrible events? Why the music and
the girls in folk costume?

This is, of course, where ideology comes in. Soviet policy
is a totalitarian policy; it cannot allow reality to intrude. If
the Soviets said the Estonians had been liberated and joined
the USSR of their own free will, then the Estonians had to
show that this is exactly what they had done, never mind
the truth. The Soviets need the Estonian dancers to prove
Soviet legitimacy. That is why I do not believe that alternative societies and cultures have much of a future under
Soviet suzerainty. I hope events will prove me wrong; but
if so, something fundamental will have happened to the
Soviet system.

URBAN: When President Reagan pointed to the Soviet
system as the 'focus of evil' in the world, was he, in your
opinion, thinking of this massive cultivation of the Lie as
the principal element of 'evil'? And why was it that the
Soviets got so upset by what amounted to a fairly harmless
quip in an old polemic?

BESANÇON: I was present when the President made that
remark, and I was struck by the truth it expressed and the

simple way in which the President put it. Reagan has been mocked and abused for his formula but I believe his statement went to the heart of Communist rule. No one has yet given us a more graphic, stripped-down definition of what the Soviet system is about. 'Focus of evil' is a philosophically perfect formulation.

URBAN: I was once asked after a lecture what I thought about the President's remark, and I said it expressed a profound truth in the sense that all Communist doctrine was based on the idea of the class-struggle and that that involved the institutionalisation of hatred. There could hardly be a greater evil, I observed, than the elevation of hatred as the governing principle of society.

BESANÇON: I would go even further. It is certainly true that Soviet ideology converts a vice—hatred—into a virtue, and celebrates it. This is bad enough, for it has been used to justify the killing of millions of peasants in the Ukraine in the early 1930s, Stalin's Great Terror, and all the other horrors in Moscow's genocidal history.

But the core of the evil Reagan spoke about goes deeper because it amounts to the reversal of our entire sense of values and the demolition of reality itself. It is a general attack on everything civilised man has been brought up to believe was of good report and decent intention.

You've asked: Why did the Soviets get so upset about Reagan's 'harmless quip'? This is the reason. For the Soviet leaders, 'focus of evil' wasn't a harmless quip at all. It meant unmasking the lie about Soviet rule in three simple words with the authority of the President of the United States of America. Mr Reagan touched the exposed nerve of Soviet reality.

A Socialism that Never Was

URBAN: Hopeful students of Soviet society have forecast the impending arrival of another alternative culture, too, one based on the culture of science. It has been said, for example, that scientists who deal with sophisticated intellectual problems in Novosibirsk will just not tolerate the blinkers imposed on them by a dated and primitive ideology. How can you work in research and high technology (it has been asked), and parrot at the same time the May Day slogans of the Communist Party? But in the real world of the Soviets the two do seem to be going together happily enough.

The successful coexistence of ideology and the exact sciences is not a good omen, and defies much we have been led to believe about human rationality since the Enlightenment. Do you feel an alternative culture based on science is any more likely to emerge than one based on the ordinary man's moral withdrawal from the contaminated world of 'socialism'?

BESANÇON: No, I don't. The scientists and economists in Novosibirsk build excellent computers and think up bright new models for the Soviet economy. But the sophistication and scientific rigour needed in the pursuit of these activities have not affected their thinking to an extent that would have led them to repudiate the ideology. Certainly, they don't much like the gibberish they are asked to live by; certainly they don't enjoy the wooden language; but they realise that they have a *political* as well as a scientific career to make and cannot abstract themselves from ideology. Hence they toe the line. Solzhenitsyn felt the indignity of it all more than anyone else. In his letter to the Soviet leaders he pleaded: 'Rule us despotically if you must, but please deliver us from ideology.' As long as the Soviet system is what it is, Solzhenitsyn is asking for the impossible.

URBAN: All of which takes us back to an earlier question: at what point is the ideology most likely to crumble? You have poured cold water on my hope that we could draw up a set of conditions, the meeting of which would make it at least more likely that the ideology would collapse. Going by the 1956 Hungarian example, I would still maintain that the demise of ideology precedes the collapse of power. I regard it as pretty well proven that in Hungary the ideology expired the moment the infallibility of the Communist Party was publicly called in question. And it was called in question by at least three factors: Khrushchev's revelations of the 'mistakes' of Stalin; the rehabilitation and reburial of László Rajk; and the Soviet acceptance of Gomulka. The Emperor stood naked, and everyone was saying so.

BESANÇON: I don't quite see it like that. Ideology collapses when Communist power collapses. Power and language are, to my mind, the same thing. When Rajk was reburied the régime was rehabilitating history; it was giving the lie to a whole vast fabric of misrepresentations (that Rajk has been Tito's agent, a spy, a stooge of imperialism, etc.). That fabric had been its title to power. When that was surrendered, and when Khrushchev surrendered to the truth at the Twentieth Party Congress, Communist power, Soviet-style, was given up *together* with the language. Or, if you like, ideology and language collapsed together with the legitimacy of Communist rule. The language of Communism *is* the power of Communism.

URBAN: But, to take the 1968 Czechoslovak example, there, too, the rebellion of Communist journalists and writers who made the Prague Spring was the cause of the collapse of Communist power, not its consequence. These writers were (if my interpretation is right) ahead of the rest of society; they were, literally, talking the Party out of power.

BESANÇON: I would say that the same men who had coined and used the official jargon began to sense the coming end of Communist power and adjusted their language accordingly. They began to speak with their own natural voices because power was collapsing around them. They were like Ulysses's companions (whom Circe's potions had changed into swine) shedding Circe's enchantment and changing back from their piggish bodies into human beings. I don't think we have to look further. The collapse of power is the necessary and sufficient condition of the collapse of ideology. The two are the same thing.

URBAN: Is it your view that in Poland, too, in the heyday of 'Solidarity', the Party and the official ideology crumbled as two aspects of the same phenomenon?

BESANÇON: No, it is not. Members of the Party, whether 'convinced' Communists or just opportunists and *apparatchiks*, knew that they had to hang together if they were not to hang separately. They had nowhere else to go. Equally important, *Solidarity*'s ideological stance was weak from the beginning. It could never find the courage to denounce the official lie totally and formally. It never dared to denounce 'socialism' as such. *Solidarity*'s argument for not denouncing it was that it would have been 'bad tactics' to do so under Soviet suzereinty, that nobody believed in 'socialism' anyway, and that repudiating it would, therefore, have been of no importance

This was a serious error. It disarmed some of the leaders of *Solidarity*, confused the issues, and disoriented the people.

The Church was in the unhappy position of trying to maintain a false symmetry between 'Capitalism' and 'Socialism'. This too had a disorienting influence on *Solidarity*. The Church had, in fact, entered into a compromise with the régime from the very beginning; it did not repudiate that compromise during the *Solidarity* period but simply tried to make it more effective. For all these reasons the collapse of Communist power and ideology in Poland did *not* take place as it had done in Hungary or even Czechoslovakia in 1968—

URBAN: —But could have done and was pretty close to doing so. . . .

BESANÇON: Yes, and that is why it is an absolutely vital interest for any Communist system in power not to permit *any* loss of power, any 'restoration of capitalism'. For it is not the restoration of *capitalism* that the power-holders really fear, but the sudden discovery that socialism never existed—that the 'building of socialism' had been a gigantic fraud all along.

URBAN: You seem to have left out of your calculations the strength of the Communist 'Establishment'—people who have by now a vested interest in the régime and tend, therefore, to deceive themselves into believing that what they and the system are doing is morally right.

BESANÇON: The question of numbers and 'believing in Communism' does not enter the picture. In the existing tradition, a Communist is he who is a member of the Communist Party—there is no other definition. And when that Party crumbles or collapses, as it did in Prague and Budapest, there is suddenly nothing left of Communism, whatever the interests and beliefs of the Establishment. And the Communist Party, any Communist Party of the Soviet type in Eastern Europe, can collapse at any time because it is built on sand.

I will not give hostages to fortune by speculating how and why Communist Parties might collapse in the future, and whether the coordination of their collapse in several countries is something Western governments ought to support. Let me just say that the Communist Parties' continuing battle to sustain their isolation from real society is encouraging. The Party knows and real society knows that one has nothing to do with the other.

URBAN: One of the most startling aspects of the Hungarian, Czechoslovak and Polish upheavals has been their almost complete lack of impact on the nations of the USSR. (Courageous individuals did, of course, respond and had to pay a price for it.) The Russian nation's reaction was, if anything, directly hostile to the aspirations of the Magyars, Czechs, Slovaks and Poles, while the minority nations were—with the exception of the untypical Balts—quiescent, or sufficiently so as to make no difference. We have recently gone over the grounds for this through the perceptive eyes of Galina Vishnevskaya and came to the conclusion that the ordinary Soviet person's reaction was simply: 'If we can't have a better life, neither should they. . . .' Have you a more convincing explanation?

BESANÇON: Well, again *pace* Solzhenitsyn, the explanation lies, alas, in Russian tradition. About 150 years ago the Marquis de Custine observed on his trip to Czarist Russia that the reverse side of the ordinary Russian's obedience at home was his aggressive imperialism abroad. 'The kneeling slave', he wrote, 'dreams of the domination of the world.'

This is as true today as it was in the 1830s. The sad thing is that the ideological submission which the totalitarian system requires from you results in disgust with yourself. You despise yourself as a human being because you have not had the guts to say '*No*' to the system. And you revel in your own dishonour: 'If I'm a son-of-a-bitch, well, then let me behave like a son-of-a-bitch!'—and you do!

URBAN: I observe, like you, the continuity of the illiberal tradition in Russian-Soviet affairs. The most terrifying thing about the fate of the Russian dissidents is not their arrest and humiliation by the authorities (one expects that in the Soviet Union), but their almost total lack of support by the people. Men like Yuri Orlov were reviled and maltreated by their fellow-prisoners (as well as their official tormentors) for no reason other than the 'outlandishness' of their human rights' protest. And we now know from people close to Gorbachov in the Soviet hierarchy (Fyodor Burlatsky, for example) that under Khrushchev the run-of-the-mill Soviet citizen had no sympathy with 'de-Stalinisation'—indeed he went on supporting the ways of Stalin.

There can be no question that Custine's description of the 'kneeling slave' in 19th-century Russia was right because others made similar and even more prescient observations. Alexander Herzen wrote in 1851:

> Russia's future will be a great danger for Europe and a great misfortune for Russia if there is no emancipation of the individual. . . . I believe there is some justification for the fear of communism which the Russian government begins to feel: communism is the Russian autocracy turned upside down.

Jules Michelet, the French historian, warned in 1871 that on Germany's eastern borders the Russians were clamouring for a place under the sun as a 'young' nation whose appointment with history had now struck. With rare foresight he predicted a 'socialist tyrant', a new-fangled Czar who would become a 'Messiah of the serfs, a barbarous Messiah, terrible to Europe'. It would have been hard to forecast more accurately the fate that was to overtake Russia and much of Europe under Lenin and Stalin—

BESANÇON: . . . except by Karl Marx himself, who observed the same traits, and outbid both Custine and Michelet in his bitter condemnation of Russian despotism. In 1853 he forecast, quite accurately, the Iron Curtain that was to be imposed on Europe a hundred years later, notably the 'annexation of Hungary, Prussia, Galicia'.

But to come back to your question about the Russian people's lack of response to the Hungarian, Czech, and Polish upheavals: What can the Soviet system offer to the man-in-the-street if not a feeling that through the State and Communism he belongs to a powerful empire? This is the clue to his deafness to the call of revolution on the peripheries, and it was the clue to his support of Czarist Russian imperialism, too, about which Custine wrote.

Here we must, of course, note a fundamental difference between Soviet 'Communism' and East European 'Communism'. For an East European citizen the Communist state is 'their' state, not his. For a Russian, *faute de mieux*, the Communist state is 'his' state. That state inspires fear in foreigners, and it is always agreeable to be feared if you have no other satisfactions in life. To be feared by the rest of the world is one satisfaction the ordinary Soviet citizen shares with his rulers. It constitutes a powerful bond between them.

What is more difficult to explain is the silence of most of the non-Russian nations and nationalities. Here one would have to do a case-by-case analysis which we cannot undertake in this conversation. Let it suffice to say that some of the smaller nations, especially the Estonians, the Latvians and the Lithuanians, regard themselves as simply occupied and are awaiting a favourable moment to regain their independence. They did take note of Hungary.

The Uzbeks are a large nation and an ancient civilisation who are conscious of being both, and of having bred men of the stature of Avicenna when the Russians were, so to speak, still in the trees. Unlike some of the smaller Central Asian peoples, the Uzbeks have, therefore, no cultural complex *vis-à-vis* the Russians. They expect their old empire to re-emerge unscathed from Soviet occupation and they comply with the demands of Moscow precisely because they are confident of their future.

The Ukraine is a different matter, and it is difficult for me to tell how much of a separate Ukrainian consciousness survives to sustain a fully separate nationhood. The Ukrainians' plight is a mixture of what befell the Poles in the 19th century and the Irish in the 18th. Their language has been pushed into the background and their culture ignored or suppressed. They did, incidentally, react to the 1968 Prague events and to some extent the Polish revolution, although our evidence is patchy.

The Ukrainians' special tragedy is that the conquest of the Ukraine was the condition of Russia's emergence as a great power. Without the grain, the minerals and manpower of the Ukraine, Russia might have achieved the status of, shall we say, Canada, but would never have attained that

of a world power. This is not the place to review the ups
and downs of Soviet nationalities policy. Let me just say
that the Kremlin's political and material investment in the
Ukraine is so great that I, for one, cannot envisage the
survival of Soviet power without its Ukrainian component

URBAN: Haven't some of the Russian dissidents given us
hope that in a post-Soviet dispensation the Russian nation
would want to shed its colonial dependencies?

BESANÇON: Yes, Solzhenitsyn in particular observed that a
post-Soviet Russia would have to permit the Ukraine to
determine its own future. This is the one hopeful sign in an
otherwise bleak picture even though it is not something for
tomorrow or perhaps even for the day after. But it is something we ought to take note of because it represents a break
in Russian national thinking, and may well betoken a future
Russian national state that will be strong, at peace with
itself and the world, but will not be an empire. Whether
and how the 'kneeling slave' syndrome will be overcome to
pave the way for Solzhenitsyn's vision is one of the great
questions of our time. That the 1956 Hungarian Revolution
and the 1968 Prague events did not induce the Russian
people to overcome it does not mean that it will not be
overcome under a different constellation.

URBAN: Observers of the Soviet scene tend to make the
point that the state of the Soviet empire might be very
different today if the various upheavals in Eastern Europe
had coincided. In the last forty or so years there has been
a rebellion or defection every ten or twelve years—in Yugoslavia in 1948, Hungary and Poland in 1956, Czechoslovakia
in 1968 and Poland in 1980–82. To mark the 30th anniversary of the Hungarian Revolution (on 23 October 1986),
we did see a coordinated declaration of solidarity with the
heritage of the Hungarian Revolution by dissidents in
Poland, East Germany, Czechoslovakia, and Romania, as
well as, of course, Hungary itself. There were 125 signatories representing all shades of non-conformist opinion. Do
you see this as an early indication that, the next time round,
one explosion in the peripheries might lead to others?

BESANÇON: Naturally, it would be most desirable if a rapid

chain-reaction did set in; but I cannot quite see it happening. I do not, as a matter of fact, expect an *explosion* but rather an *implosion* in the Soviet empire, and that would happen in the country where the system is most vulnerable and absurd and invites the contempt of the people: the Soviet Union itself. It is ultimately in Moscow that the threat to the Soviet system is greatest.

The precondition for any effective change in the peripheries is an implosion in Moscow. We had a foretaste of that in 1956 when Khrushchev's destruction of the myth of Stalin resulted in the uprising in Hungary and a dramatic confrontation between the Soviet leadership and the Polish Communists in Warsaw. This sort of thing might happen again. I have no doubt that the smallest eclipse of power in the centre would lead, perhaps in one single day, to the liquidation of Communist power throughout the satellite empire.

URBAN: You don't think that, if such a situation were to arise, the Western countries would come to the rescue of the Soviets on the calculation that in a dangerous world *any* stability is better than none? In 1956 the Western nations did not even bother to recognise Hungary's declaration of neutrality; much less did they contemplate any action, apart from falling out among themselves over Suez.

BESANÇON: I share your pessimism. But that is no reason for us to ignore the troubled state of the Soviet system and the incendiary materials it has accumulated. After Chernobyl the Soviet leadership was silent for thirteen days. One can only imagine that Gorbachov and his colleagues were clueless or in a state of panic, reminding us of Stalin's long silence after Hitler had invaded his country and the panic that (as we now know) preceded his first nervous broadcast.

In 1976–77 there was a state of near-famine in the Soviet Union. The Western world and the US in particular saved the Soviet system from the consequences of its own follies, partly because American farmers needed outlets and the politicians needed votes, and partly (as people like George Kennan argued) because the food-weapon was thought to be an unethical weapon to be used against any country! Right now, a much enfeebled Soviet Union is receiving cheap grain from America—grain subsidised by the same American taxpayer who is also asked to fork out billions of dollars to counter the Soviet military threat. The simple fact is that without Western help the Soviet system would have imploded a long time ago and could do so still. It's the West that has kept the Soviet system going.

One day our governments will have to understand that it is, in the long run, not only more honourable but also safer to allow the Soviet system to collapse than to bail it out time and again in the hope that it might reform itself. The Soviet Union will never become a quiet and responsible member of the international community. It will never behave like France or Holland or Canada. That is not the mantle Mr Mikhail Gorbachov inherited from Lenin, Stalin, Khrushchev, Brezhnev and Andropov. That is not what 1917 was about.

URBAN: You said that the threat to the Soviet empire is greatest in the Soviet Union itself, because the system is absurd and corrupt and is seen to be such by the people. It seems to me that Gorbachov is well aware of the absurdity and corruption, and has set out on the hazardous journey of trying to 'restructure' the system. Leaving aside the controversial question of whether it would be in the Western interest to have an 'acceptable' type of Communism in Russia rather than the clearly unattractive kind which Gorbachov inherited, wouldn't you say that Gorbachov is now trying to kick the system into the 20th century and the Russian people into something like the Protestant work-ethic?

If so, shouldn't we extend a guarded welcome to his reforming zeal on the principle that even Khrushchev's short-lived reformism left an historic mark on the Soviet empire by taking Stalin down from his pedestal, dispersing the Gulags, causing the Poles and Hungarians to rebel, and destroying the monocentric world Communist movement? These mighty consequences of de-Stalinisation had been unforeseen by Khrushchev and the men who supported him. What started out as a drive for greater efficiency and demo-cratisation within the Party soon got out of hand and had to be throttled back to prevent an 'implosion'. But the damage was done, and the world learned a thing or two about the vulnerability of the Soviet system.

Mightn't we describe Gorbachov and his policies as cast in the mould of Khrushchev, and aren't these policies therefore 'objectively speaking' likely to be of benefit to us even though they don't (yet?) match the broad sweep of the reorganisation Khrushchev tried to set in train or the 'openness' prevailing in Hungary and Poland?

BESANÇON: I am deeply sceptical. Gorbachov does not so much remind me of Khrushchev as rather of Stalin in the early 1930s. He is conscious, as Stalin was, that the Soviet system needs to undergo radical change if the Soviet Union is not to be fatally handicapped in its bid for world domination. Now, as in the 1930s, the Soviet system is facing an international emergency. Just as 'industrialisation-at-any-cost' was thought to be Moscow's answer to the emergency under Stalin, so technological modernisation and 'restructuring' are thought to be the answers to the Soviet Union's grave structural weaknesses under Gorbachov.

For quite a few years, while he was establishing himself in power, Stalin was looked upon by Western scholars and observers as 'a pragmatist' and 'a moderate'. Emil Ludwig came away from a long interview with Stalin thinking he had met a man of sobriety and reason—the year was 1931. In the Ukraine peasants were being deported and starved by the million. The Webbs, H. G. Wells and, even much later, Churchill and de Gaulle felt Stalin was a man with whom they could do business; a believer, to be sure, but not a fanatic. Midge Decter, the perceptive American writer, recently observed:

> the Russian Revolution is seventy years old. During those seventy years the Soviet Union, not counting a couple of brief interregnums, has had seven 'leaders', four of them within the past six years. Leaving aside Lenin . . . each of them has been hailed by American journalists at one time or another as ushering in a new era.

This desperate desire to find liberalism, real reforms, even the beginnings of systemic change where (to my mind) there aren't any, is riding high again. It tells us more about the mentality of Western journalists and diplomats than the mind of Mikhail Gorbachov. Assisted by a much smarter team (Dobrynin, Yakovlev and Falin gained their spurs as Ambassadors in the US, Canada and West Germany) than were any of his predecessors, Gorbachov has learned how to appeal to the American sense of guilt and the West European sense of accommodation—how to upset Amer-

icans by pointing to shortcomings in *their* human rights
record and flatter West Europeans by appointing Russia a
place under a common European roof and a shared culture.
Above all, he has learned how to unnerve both Europeans
and Americans by playing on their fear of the nuclear factor
That he is doing so using the Chernobyl disaster for his text
shows the nerve the man has, and the perverse advantage
centralised dictatorships enjoy over us in not having to
contend with inquisitive legislatures, a critical press, and an
unpredictable public opinion. Gorbachov is harnessing his
system *and* our own to his objectives, and with considerable
sophistication.

Leninism with a Human Face

URBAN: My impression is that Gorbachov is a more radical
reformer (if that is the right word) than his activities have
so far betrayed although, since the January 1987 plenum,
the thrust of his 'restructuring' policies has been increasingly
obvious, and therefore increasingly resisted by the old establishment. He is facing a double dilemma in that he is up
against the dogmatic ways of a vast and comfortable Soviet
élite as well as the backwardness of Russian political culture.
He has to beat the potential Stalin that lurks in the soul
of every '*apparatchik*' of any power *and* the heritage of
'Oblomov'. It is a tall order, and when Gorbachov speaks
of the many years it will take to tame the two-headed
monster, he seems to be saying that he is aware of the
nature of the beast.

It is, just, possible to imagine that Gorbachov will tame
the spirit of the 'Gulags'; but can he change the spirit of
the 'Dead Souls'? Any Eurocommunist worth his salt will
tell us that it was Russian political culture that torpedoed
in 1917 the 'humanitarian vision' of Marx. Might it not do
the same to Gorbachov's '*perestroika*' in 1987, and should
we, in that case, not show Gorbachov a little more understanding than we have, on the whole, done so far if only on
the (admittedly less than self-evident) principle that a Soviet
system at peace with its own people would be less of a threat
to the outside world?

BESANÇON: What we are witnessing in the USSR today is

another power-struggle. Gorbachov has won the first rounds but he is not home-and-dry yet. How do you establish yourself as the 'new and vigorous man' in the Kremlin? You 'disclose' the facts about the bankrupt stock you have inherited—you castigate your forerunners for having left you and your nation such a forbidding legacy—and you demand change to put things right. You don't, mind you, demand change of the sort that might upset the apple-cart and fling *you*, too, out of power—no, you demand just enough change to get rid of your opponents and clear the decks for the rule of your own oligarchy. You want the intelligentsia on your side, you want 'openness', 'democratisation', and several candidates to run for local elections.

Multiple candidacy in the Party is an especially refined device, for it saddles the *apparat* with a sense of insecurity. Stalin practised it to good effect in 1934 when 'secret voting' was used by him to destabilise his opponents. What you do *not* demand is that the monopoly of the Communist Party should be broken, nor do you ask for genuinely free elections or the freedom of public opinion. Gorbachov came up in the Soviet system. He knows what is good for him.

URBAN: Gorbachov, on your showing, is a Leninist with a human face. He wants us to see the human face but not the Leninism. As the Western public knows what a human face is like but has only the haziest notion about Leninism, isn't it gratuitously playing into Gorbachov's hands?

BESANÇON: Yes, it is, and Gorbachov is making excellent use of it. One important objective of his new 'openness' and reform policies is the acquisition of Western goodwill. He needs credits, modernisation, joint ventures, and some assurance that the American investment in the Strategic Defense Initiative will not drive him into a corner, although I don't think SDI is now the real issue. It seems to me to be a lever designed to extract from the West more concessions than would otherwise be forthcoming in certain areas which the Soviet government considers to be crucial, as for example the removal of medium-range nuclear weapons from Western Europe.

What threats and bluffing could not achieve in Soviet propaganda or at the negotiating table, Gorbachov's outwardly spectacular reforms, his smiles and bonhomie might, or so he clearly hopes. Sakharov's release is a good example. Sakharov is sceptical about SDI. He is now free to say so. Gorbachov appears to have harnessed Sakharov to his anti-SDI propaganda at the cost-effective price of releasing a few hundred prisoners who should not have been put behind bars in the first place. Gorbachov can now say to Reagan: 'I agree with Sakharov—do you?' Will Reagan risk being seen to take sides against Sakharov?

URBAN: You have not dealt with the unwanted and unforeseeable consequences of Gorbachov's reforms. In Bratislava, unidentified Slovaks pinned a poster on a building in the centre of the city—'WE WANT GORBACHOV'—only to have it removed by the police. Ceausescu has been openly critical of Gorbachov's analysis of 'real existing socialism' and said the Soviet way was not for him. So, less openly, did Honecker.[3] In East Berlin, Gorbachov's long speech to the January 1987 plenum was first published only in carefully chosen extracts; in Prague not at all. *Pravda, Izvestia* and *Literaturnaya Gazeta* acquired the status of *samizdat* publications in the Czech capital and were selling at a premium! When students at the Charles University protested at a lecture that 'The Soviet Union is our model', they were told, 'One cannot automatically apply Soviet political experience to Czechoslovak conditions'. Dubček must have been rubbing his eyes.

I can foresee a number of interesting developments. The spectacle of undernourished Communist Romania being 'liberated' by Soviet tanks with popular Romanian approval is only one, if Gorbachov stays the course. But I can also foresee the forces of disaffection, especially in the peripheries of the empire, hijacking or subverting Gorbachov's programme and putting the system under great strain (with the hearty approval of the Italian Communists), as they did in 1956 and 1968. In August 1988 the pro-Gorbachov chants in Armenia gave way to a cry of 'Beria–Stalin–Ligachev', and the *Solidarity*-style V for Victory signs of the protesters were replaced by the raised clenched fist.

Isn't Soviet history suddenly a bit more open again? And shouldn't our practical politicians use the leverage that's been unexpectedly given them rather than bank on a cataclysmic turn of events?

BESANÇON: Nothing is impossible in the world of politics, but I would have thought civil society in the Soviet Union has been so thoroughly weakened that the chances of Gorbachov being overtaken by those driving in the 'liberal' lane are almost non-existent. He might, as Khrushchev was, be overtaken by nationalism and the drive for independence in Eastern Europe, the Baltic States and Central Asia, but in the Soviet Union itself his fear must be a *putsch* by 'conservative' forces on his right and the general disaffection of the *apparat*. If so, his fall would go unlamented by the people because Gorbachov is not popular. He has been challenging too many of Russia's stick-in-the-mud, lazy, egalitarian traditions. The Oblomovs are, as you say, a hardy factor.

In the final analysis, I cannot see the Soviet system reforming itself into something really different without ceasing to be the Soviet system. Once the power struggle is settled, the new masters of the state will have to enforce their rule with the same determination as had earlier ones who had also arrived with a new or revamped message but threw it away as soon as they felt themselves to be firmly in the saddle. I say 'have to enforce their rule' because there are no freely chosen democratic institutions in the Soviet Union for running the affairs of the state and society in any other way. Perhaps it is as well that the Soviet system is what it is. It is making it extremely difficult for heretics and reformers to turn it into something better and thus to deceive a gullible world.

On Gorbachov's own evidence, and all the evidence we had before Gorbachov took the lid off Soviet reality, I would say this in conclusion: there is no doubt that the Soviet system is so caught up in its mendacity, its internal contradictions and inefficiencies, that its end is now beginning to come within our vision. What will be most fascinating for an historian to observe is the speed of its demise, the manner in which it unravels, and the collateral impact these will have, not only on the world balance of power, but on that whole tradition of revolutionary utopianism of which the Soviet Union is the most lasting and devastating expression.

And if the Soviet system does not go under within the tangible future, it will be even more fascinating to see why and how it will have been saved by the 'capitalist' West—

whether the totalitarian dictatorship will have been upheld by our sense of charity, our fear of being dragged down by the Soviet colossus, or simply our decadence.

1987

Notes

1. New York, 1981; originally published as *Les origines intellectuelles du Léninisme*, Paris 1977.
2. Eighteen months after these words had been spoken the following observations by the Soviet historian Natan Eidelman appeared in *Moscow News* (no. 30, 1988).
   '. . . What was Stalin's secret? Fear, terror? These are important factors. But no tyrant could stake his claim on terror alone – and last.
   Stalin relied on his apparatus (they created each other), but it accounted for only 2 or 3 per cent of the population. More important is that the remaining 97 or 98 per cent evidently believed Stalin's claim that "life has become better, life has become gayer", when life had become sadder. It seems as if a significant part of the population in the 1930s, 40s and 50s was living under a special social hypnotic spell . . .
   While the working people were creating the country's wealth, they sincerely thought that Stalin was "the creator of all good things". "Thanks to Comrade Stalin for his fatherly concern! . . . For our happy childhood! . . . For the happy life!"
   How could "nationwide love for the Great Leader" grow stronger under conditions of mass terror? Millions watched the extermination of innocent people, but "under hypnosis" it all seemed justified – *they didn't notice* . . . Millions enthusiastically *approved* of the bloodshed . . .'
3. By the middle of April 1987, however, Kurt Hager, East Germany's chief ideologist, had made his Party's scepticism about the Gorbachov line abundantly clear. Speaking to *Stern* magazine (9 April 1987), he said: 'Would you, seeing that your neighbour was having his apartment redecorated, feel obliged to have your apartment redecorated, too?'

5. VLADIMIR BUKOVSKY
The quiet exit of Soviet Communism

Bukovsky's Castle

URBAN: A friend of mine with whom I once burnt the midnight oil puzzling over 'the meaning of life' was in the habit of saying: 'Everyone must have a "*petit château*" in his imagination where he can find shelter from the hard knocks and banalities of the human condition.' I recalled this phrase vividly when I first read your book *To Build a Castle*, for the '*château*' you were constructing for yourself during your imprisonments in the Soviet Union was (or so it seems to me) precisely that kind of refuge—a haven of hope and sanity in a world of coercion and psychiatric abuse.

BUKOVSKY: The way I came to think of the image of a castle takes me back to my childhood. I was a young teenager, thirteen or fourteen or so, when Khrushchev's impact began to be felt in the Soviet Union. Of course, at the time I did not understand half of what was going on around me; but what I did understand was that some momentous change was looming and that I did not like the world into which I had been born. I was a voracious reader but could not bring myself to read Soviet literature. It wasn't that I was consciously hostile to it. I just had an instinctive dislike of the stuff because I found it mean and drab. So I ploughed through the Russian classics and the non-Russian classics in translation; and in my Russian books—Chekhov, for example—I ran repeatedly into scenes that occurred in spacious country houses which gave the reader a feel of a rather gentle, thoughtful, reflective type of living, light-years away from Soviet reality.

I spent some of my childhood in one of the historic quarters of Moscow, the Arbat. My grandmother often took me for walks there, and it was in the Arbat that I first saw old, gracious mansions of the kind I was to encounter in the classics. In other words, by the time I came to read about the sort of life people lived in a traditional and cultivated milieu, I was already attuned to it by the fusion of a child's instinctive aspiration to a more inspiring order of things with the mysterious beauty of the mansions in the Arbat.

URBAN: You were clearly not one of the success stories of ideological conditioning by the Soviet system. . . .

BUKOVSKY: No, I wasn't, even though I came from a fairly poor family, and was in reality nothing but a street urchin when these impressions began to register.

As time went on, I developed great love for those buildings in the Arbat and, looking back on my thinking as an adolescent, I suppose it would be true to say that those mansions represented a form of mental escape for me, although I wasn't aware of it at the time.

URBAN: Your genes seem to have been stronger than the impact of your environment.

BUKOVSKY: Much stronger. What is more, style seemed to me more important than substance. The architectural grace of the buildings in the Arbat induced me to weave a whole world of values and ideas that began to sustain me spiritually.

URBAN: What you are saying is that Pol Pot and the Red Guards under Mao were, in their way, right. Your resistance to the system was greatly helped by the availability of the Russian classics and the survival of old buildings. Pol Pot took care to demolish all remnants of a 'bourgeois' past, including books and buildings, and indeed even the spectacles through which to peer at them.

BUKOVSKY: From his point of view Pol Pot *was* right. Fortunately Stalinism was slightly less thorough, and the lip-service it had to pay to the Russian past made it impossible for the Stalinists to do a demolition job on the whole of Russian culture and history. They did it on selected parts, and at times best suited to their purpose.

URBAN: So the idea of a 'castle' came naturally from your inclinations as a child and an adolescent?

BUKOVSKY: It developed from the skein of factors I have described. By the time I first went to prison, it was there.

URBAN: Perhaps it wasn't just a mental escape but a subconscious protest against your environment, against 'proletarian culture' and 'socialist realism'?

BUKOVSKY: Looking at it from today's perspective, I would say it was. Soviet reality is grey and ugly, and the artefacts of life are just tasteless and boring. I am grateful to my own choosiness as a child that I never read Soviet literature. I escaped its corruptions.

URBAN: You managed, in fact, to develop on a small and rudimentary scale something like your own sense of values and culture? A remarkable feat for a young boy.

BUKOVSKY: In a modest sense, yes. I would not go so far as to call it an 'alternative culture', for my friends and I were too young and ignorant to think in such sophisticated terms; but as far as my own aesthetic ideas and values were concerned, yes, I think I did begin to develop alternative ways of feeling and being.

URBAN: In prison, your castle was, in fact, a life-saver. In the frightening void of your solitary confinement you hung on to it the way a drowning man hangs on to a lifebelt. Or, if you like, it was a source of hope, as faith and prayer are for a believer.

BUKOVSKY: It was all those things, but the castle also performed the simple function of occupying my mind and keeping it concentrated. This was most important. I knew people who went berserk in solitary. Any systematic thinking helped—such as remembering the plot of a classic novel, or solving mathematical problems.

URBAN: There are indeed many examples. George Faludy, the distinguished Hungarian poet, committed a large number of poems to his own and his fellow inmates' memory when he was in prison in Recsk. More recently, Irina Ratushinskaya preserved her sanity by writing poems even though she had nothing to write with.

BUKOVSKY: Please, don't mention poetry to me as a means

of escape; I'm allergic to the stuff. We had a surfeit of poets
and poetry in our movement. Poetry seemed to be oozing
out of the pores of every young Russian who had a grudge
against the Soviet system. Verses, poetry readings, and
budding poets flaunting their alleged talent—I had my fill
of all that by the time I was 19!

But you are quite right: the castle was a symbolic and
real means of escape. You could hide behind its walls; it
imparted privacy and security.

URBAN: Some political prisoners in the Soviet Union
needed all the religious faith they could summon to steel
themselves for survival. You are said to be an agnostic—or
is it an atheist? I would have thought a devout Baptist, or
an Orthodox person like Solzhenitsyn, might wonder how
you did it, seeing that so much of your challenge to the
system had spiritual roots which were, nevertheless, not of
the religious kind.

BUKOVSKY: You are asking me a question I have deliberately tried not to answer, because it is probably too early
for me to answer it; but here is what occurs to me. My
generation had brought itself up to disbelieve in religion.
Our reaction was not against Christianity, but against Stalin
and the worship of Stalin. We had been raised in the
Communist religion, which we knew was nonsensical. We
felt we had been betrayed and misled by our elders. The
ceaseless and ubiquitous adoration of Stalin was a powerful
vaccination against any form of belief—so believing, for me,
became a symbol of gullibility.

URBAN: You went through the Pioneers and the usual
Soviet education. You must have been very much part and
parcel of the cult of Stalin.

BUKOVSKY: I was. I was eleven when Stalin died. As a child
I did believe in Stalin, and thought he was something very
close to being God. We sang his praise in prose, verse, and
cantatas. The older generation had a broader view because
they could remember the time before Stalin and the build-
up of Stalinism. Those who decided to go along with the
glorification of Stalin did so on rational or opportunistic
grounds. But we were *handed* the cult of Stalin as a doctrine,

and consequently rejected every type of faith as part of our opposition to the worship of Stalin. But our rejection did not end there. We hated and rejected 'socialism' and all the other *in*-words of the Communist vocabulary as well, simply because they had been rammed down our throats by the Communist Party as part of the official philosophy. Children don't discriminate. Whatever had to be done under duress we rejected.

URBAN: Did you, nevertheless, appreciate the particular tenacity of the Baptists and Pentecostalists among your fellow inmates? We have much evidence that religious believers were more successful than most in keeping their integrity and hope alive. You will remember the record of Pastor Bonhoeffer and Father Kolbe under the Nazis, and one could quote the testimony of any number of religious prisoners in Communist camps. Irina Ratushinskaya is a good recent example.

BUKOVSKY: Religious faith gave strength to some people, but on the whole it appeared to me artificial and superficial. In a prison cell you get to know your fellow inmates extremely well—too well. One is not meant to know every-thing about another human being, but when you share a prison cell, you cannot avoid it. So it was that I found out more than I would have wished about the minds of my colleagues in prison; and so it was that I came to the conclusion that religious believers made unpleasant inmates.

URBAN: Were they intolerant?

BUKOVSKY: Not really—in a cell you have to be tolerant. It was rather that their faith did not strike me as being genuine. They were trying hard to convince themselves that they believed when in fact they did not. I could not trust their sincerity. For example: I was, at the time, pretty well versed in the Bible. The reason was that I had been asked to translate certain religious texts which contained a great many biblical quotations. This made me familiarise myself with the Old and New Testaments which I got to know pretty well (I have by now forgotten much of both). Well, one of the things you do a great deal in prison is to argue. I frequently fell into argument with religious prisoners and found to my amazement that their knowledge of the Bible was very small, or nil. Their faith was a new thing, a lifebelt under adverse conditions.

I am, mind you, not belittling the importance of having a lifebelt, but the faith of these people was skin-deep. Of course, I also met prisoners with deep religious convictions whom I admired and respected. One was a Ukrainian, Levko Lukyanenko, who was serving fifteen years when I shared a cell with him, and got another fifteen years as soon as he was set free for having joined the Helsinki Monitoring Group. He was serene about his fate.

URBAN: Did many of the religious prisoners acquire their faith actually in prison, under the pressures of imprisonment?

BUKOVSKY: Quite a few did. It was remarkable that people who had arrived in prison as Marxists were the most likely to change their Marxist convictions for religious ones. I knew Marxist Ukrainians who became fervent Christians and Marxist Jews who had forgotten all about their Jewish background but developed, in prison, a fervent Orthodox Jewish identity. This tells you something about the kind of mind these people had to begin with: they needed an ideology of some sort to relieve them of uncertainty; and if Marxism-Leninism could no longer do it, some other belief had to be put in its place.

URBAN: The history of Communism in Western Europe provides similar examples—disillusioned Communists turning to Catholicism or other forms of religion to replace, as you say, the loss of an all-interpreting set of values and ideas, and, above all, to give them hope.

BUKOVSKY: But you can have hope without religion. This may, however, not be the whole truth. The man who convinced me that hope without religion may not be enough for some people was Armando Valladares, whose book I have just read and written about.[1] Here is a man who is deeply religious and, like most genuinely believing people, does not like talking about his faith—perhaps because he is conscious of Matthew 6, 5–6,[2] perhaps because his natural modesty forbids him to do so. He is in Castro's prison, as he thinks, for life: He is exposed to the daily horrors of

Cuban imprisonment—torture, humiliation, the sound of executions—and comes face to face with the fact that 'here I may have to die'. Under these terrible conditions religion gives him strength. 'My imprisonment and my death will have an ethical meaning,' he says. 'Ethical meaning'—*that* I fully understand. If your life has to be sacrificed in the struggle against a great evil, you want to feel that your sacrifice fits into a meaningful order of things.

URBAN: I am fairly sure that if one collected an anthology of the last cries of those about to be executed, your point would be borne out by the evidence. Those I have come across in my life and in Western literature stress the condemned man's loyalty to some principle that will, as he hopes, not die with him . . . to country, cause, faith, or even ideology.

But I'm not sure I would agree with your observation that the religion of those who acquire it under the pressures of hardship is necessarily less profound or less worthy of our respect than that of those who are given it at birth or acquire it under more serene conditions. I would have thought the acquisition of faith under extreme conditions is perhaps the most common and most human way of acquiring it, even though it may well be true that religion so acquired is less well informed than a man of high culture would wish. The Sermon on the Mount offers the Kingdom of Heaven to those 'which are persecuted for righteousness' sake', but does not demand that they should be well-versed in religious literature. On the contrary, it is enough to be 'pure in heart' to be admitted to the sight of God. Irina Ratushinskaya tells us: 'I had started to appeal to Him some fifteen years before I held any religious literature in my hands. . . .'

BUKOVSKY: I didn't mean to belittle the sincerity of the conversion of a person suddenly bereaved or struck down by some mindless act of man or nature. Sickness, frustration, poverty and defeat are part of the human condition, and those who cannot deal with them rationally seek a meaning and consolation in religion. This I respect. What I did not like in some of my fellow inmates was the transparent opportunism with which they changed from what they thought had been a winning horse to another which now looked more likely to be first past the post.

No amount of charity, not even the parable of the

prodigal son, can persuade me to respect the Christianity of a man whose Marxism got unstuck and who therefore decided in his cluelessness to turn to another 'divinity'. You see, sincerity of faith is also a Christian requirement.

'Not everyone who calls me "Lord, Lord" will enter the Kingdom of Heaven', Jesus says in Matthew soon after the words you have quoted, and he warns those who are insincere that they will be punished: 'Then I will tell them to their face, "I never knew you: out of my sight, you and your wicked ways!"' (Matthew 7, 21–23).

URBAN: I don't think we can take this further without starting a different discussion. But you said: one could have hope without religion. This sounds commonsensical enough, but what in particular did you have in mind in the context of resisting the pressures of imprisonment?

BUKOVSKY: You can believe in your destiny—a destiny that tells you that you must challenge the wrong and the lies that surround you. What we had in my own case and the cases of my friends was, so to speak, a conspiracy of the hopeless. We never expected to be able to achieve any of the liberties we wanted. Personally I had a persuasive feeling that there was no way out, but the same feeling told me that I must preserve my sanity and fight the ideological insanity that surrounded us; and if I was to suffer and die for doing so, I might as well die sane. That was all.

Our movement was highly impractical. We never sought to achieve anything concrete; we never had a 'programme'. In the event, we achieved, to our amazement, a hundredfold what any of us imagined could be achieved, and did so perhaps precisely because we hadn't done any planning. We were being propelled by an inner feeling of necessity. Certain challenges *had* to be met, certain lies *had* to be nailed, certain absurdities *had* to be unmasked. This was something we knew in our bones. We had to do it for self-respect, for sanity, for human dignity.

We were in the grip of an elementary revolt of the mind—but we had, as I say, no pragmatic model to guide us. We didn't want to 'change' anything. We rebelled because we had been driven to rebellion. It was a question of self-preservation.

URBAN: Those Poles, Hungarians and Czechs who talk

nowadays about an 'alternative culture' and alternative ways of being and feeling are led, I am convinced, by a similar, uncalculating, elementary sense of rebellion. All rebellions in history tend to start in that manner—the programmes and rationalisations (and frequently the admissions of *non possumus*) come later.

BUKOVSKY: Looking back on that period, I would say we shared Albert Camus's philosophy more than any other. We rebelled because Authority told us, 'You are going to be different', and we said 'We are not!' We didn't just react to specific acts of arbitrary rule. We acted from a deep-seated conviction that our inner sovereignty was under attack and that we had to stand up for it. The mental pollution had to stop.

URBAN: You have seen the record of my conversation with Alain Besançon. We talked about the unreality of Soviet reality, the deadly farce of make-believe.

BUKOVSKY: Yes. Besançon's analysis is, I feel, spot on: he is one of the sharpest observers of the Soviet system. Soviet unreality is all-pervasive even though everyone knows it to be unreal.

URBAN: Did you fall into some of those semantic traps that go with this unreal reality? Did you act as though the unreality had been real?

BUKOVSKY: I read that part of your conversation with Besançon very carefully and thought I was lucky to have been born too late to have to contend with the full force of the collective schizophrenia that gripped Russia under Stalin. By the time I was politically conscious enough to grasp what was happening around me I had developed great distaste for all things Soviet and created a private world for myself (based, as I said, on classical literature). I simply lived outside what remained of the unreality—and plenty remained and remains to this day.

My political consciousness was the result of having read Alexander Herzen: he instilled in me the language of protest. The need to seek an alternative to the Soviet system was there in my mind from the beginning. That you can't instil; you either have it or you haven't. But the cutting edge of my attitude was due to Herzen's formulations.

URBAN: Would you look upon yourself as a 'Westerniser'?

BUKOVSKY: I'm certainly not a Slavophile. I share many of Herzen's ideas but I'm a scientist by inclination and profession. I never saw much sense in making a sharp, not to say divisive, distinction between 'Slavophiles' and 'Westernisers'.

URBAN: Do you agree with Alain Besançon's characterisation of you as a man who has taken the logical step of not only rejecting Soviet unreality, but of purging his mind of the last scraps of Soviet consciousness by the simple device of having his mind reshaped by science?

> I admire Vladimir Bukovsky. He took the conscious decision that it was not enough to be a dissident and an émigré. He took up biology as a hard science because he knew that the habit of mind that goes with scientific inquiry would immunise him against ideology more effectively than any 'counter-ideology'. . . . Bukovsky's way is the honourable way, and the only one that can be really effective.

BUKOVSKY: I'm afraid Besançon may be admiring me for the wrong reasons. My interest in biology is an old thing— I had it as a child and adolescent. I did not develop it as a reaction to the semantic traps of Soviet ideology. It's true, though, that biology helped me and still helps me to keep the insanities of Sovietism at bay. It's an implied corrective to nonsense.

One also has to remember that in the Soviet Union science is the common escape of intellectuals who want to keep their integrity—science and mathematics. These disciplines are extremely difficult to politicise. They provide a safe haven for those who want to use their minds to some purpose and evade the corruptions of the system. That is why there are so many scientists in the USSR and why theoretical physics, for example, is so highly developed.

URBAN: The number of Soviet mathematicians and physicists American universities are able to absorb always struck me as just short of a miracle, especially at a time of retrenchment.

BUKOVSKY: It is, as I say, explained by the large numbers,

and the high quality that competition produces. The gifted Russian's escape from ideology ultimately benefits Western science and technology. . . .

URBAN: A short-sighted policy which Gorbachov should be anxious to correct.

BUKOVSKY: He should, but whether he can is quite another matter. But to come back to your question about semantics: my first clash with Soviet thinking came at school when I was about fourteen. Official dogma required us to believe that man's mind is shaped by economic and social forces. I revolted against this idea and did so empirically: here I was, an urchin, living with criminals under miserable housing conditions in one of the poor districts of post-War Moscow. Was I being shaped by my social environment? Not at all. I was developing ideas that were diametrically *opposed* to my environment.

Here was my great friend Kolka. He came from a large and equally poor family where the father was a drunkard, the mother a prostitute, a couple of the sons were criminals—and yet Kolka was a most decent fellow.

'How is all this possible, teacher?', I said to our schoolmaster. I just wouldn't buy his rubbish. I believed that there was something at the core of every human being that was not shaped by economics or the environment—that man was autonomous. At the time I didn't realise that I was questioning the very basis of the Marxist system. That came to me a little later, but I was glad to have done so so early in life.

URBAN: If we were to be very pedantic we might add that the Marxist canon was somewhat amended by Engels's interpretation. Writing (to J. Bloch) on 21 September 1890, he stressed that 'according to the materialistic conception of history, the production and reproduction of real life constitutes *in the last instance* the determining factor of history. Neither Marx nor I ever maintained more.'

Engels pointed out that constitutions, legal theories, political and religious conceptions and institutions all have an impact on determining the course of history, and those Marxists who thought otherwise misunderstood the theory and were turning out 'a rare kind of tommy-rot'. He added almost by way of apology that—well, to make a point is not enough. You have to drive it home by exaggerating your message and shocking the reader into agreement:

> Marx and I are partly responsible for the fact that at times our disciples have laid more weight upon the economic factor than belongs to it. We were compelled to emphasise its central character in opposition to our opponents who denied it, and there wasn't always time, place and occasion to do justice to the other factors in the reciprocal interactions of the historical process.

BUKOVSKY: At school we were, of course, not made aware of such refinements. Indeed the Soviet system is based on a very narrow interpretation of Marx, and that was the kind of Marx we had rammed down our throats.

URBAN: 'Vulgar-Marxism', as Georg Lukács was in the habit of calling it in 1945 and 1946 in his lectures at the (Bishop) Pázmány Péter University (as it then was) in Budapest—without, of course, saying whom he had in mind as the 'vulgarisers'.

BUKOVSKY: Whatever Engels may have said about applying shock tactics to beat down the opposition, the fact is that the logic of Marxism does require that the economic-social factor be recognised as the determining factor in understanding society. It was that factor (whether correctly interpreted or not) that gave the Bolshevik Revolution its legitimacy and the Soviet system its entire *raison d'être*. I happen to believe that Soviet society is a highly accurate realisation of the Marxist canons. It is, at best, a half-truth to say that Marxism degenerated in Russian hands—that it assumed the despotic characteristics of Russian history of the last 400 or so years. It is precisely because the system is so true to Marx that it is at odds with human nature. And that is why it is so repellent and ultimately untenable. I learned all this, as I say, at the tender age of fourteen in the slums of Moscow, and to this day I have had no reason to change my mind.

The Costs of Inner Freedom

URBAN: Would I be right in thinking that imprisonment for you was in some ways a refuge from the feverish life of a dissident—a place of retreat, if you like, where you could read and think and 'recharge the batteries'? Some of your observations in your memoirs lead me to that conclusion. In one place you say that you were, after your 'hectic' life outside, quite glad to be sent to the Lefortovo Prison because 'nothing depended on me any longer'. Did you gain a sense of inner freedom that had eluded you outside?

BUKOVSKY: I told you at the beginning of this conversation that our little movement was launched—launched itself, would be a better way of putting it—with a very simple moral idea. We said: 'As far as we're concerned, we are not going to be part of the machinery of official society. Leave us alone.' We weren't planning to make a revolution. We had no programme. We were just anxious to isolate ourselves from the whole polluting unreality of the Soviet system.

Little did we suspect that in a totalitarian system there is no such thing as neutrality or isolation. The moment we did what we did, we were making a highly political statement which was immediately seen as such both by the Soviet authorities and by observers abroad. But, more important, we were ourselves soon forced to see our activities in that light, too. We discovered that our 'dissent' thrust responsibility on us for all sorts of things we had never considered our responsibility: the nation, the state of society, liberty, and so on. We became the centre of social and political turmoil, and having said a we had to say b, too. We came face to face with the notion of responsibility concerning a whole range of questions which made our original wish to live away from Soviet society in calculated isolation rather Utopian.

For me, this meant a kind of enslavement. I was and I am a very private person. I am happiest when I'm left alone. I dislike all forms of social involvement, and I hate politics. You can imagine how unhappy I was to discover that my ambition to be lifted out of Soviet reality had plunged me even deeper into it.

I didn't *ask* to be imprisoned and I didn't *like* it inside, but I was quite determined to make the best of an unpleasant situation and utilise it in very practical ways. I learned English; I studied biology; I buried myself in books that one couldn't obtain outside but were readily available in the prison libraries. No one in the KGB had thought of raiding the *prison* libraries for forbidden literature! In that sense, I was freer than I had been outside.

URBAN: Some prisoners looked upon imprisonment as an occasion for introspection—or doing penance for mistaken lives, a sinful ideology, whatever. In the Great Purge of 1937–38 faithful Communists were searching their hearts in prison to discover where they had gone wrong in interpreting the sacred books—whether Stalin had been misled by dishonest courtiers and so on. Alexander Weissberg gave us one good account in his book *The Accused* (1951).

BUKOVSKY: I was totally untouched by ideology; I was a realist. What I did find prison quite useful for was the inner freedom it gave me to think for myself, to test myself, and to get to know other people. The prison cell is an incomparable laboratory for looking into the hidden recesses of the human soul, for discovering what motivates people, for analysing their fears and phobias. Prison offers you a Shakespearean panorama of human nature, and that is a great source of education.

   Another thing I discovered in prison was the scope of my own mind. I suddenly found that my head was full of ideas—ideas I had no time to concentrate on when I was outside; in prison I had the inner freedom to sort them out.

URBAN: Weren't you, then, really in retreat?

   Let me tell you about a somewhat analogous experience I underwent some twenty years ago. I was sent to hospital with mumps—I'd caught it from my children. This, for me, was 'prison'. I had a high temperature—high enough to make me see the world in its (as I thought) true dimensions. The problems I had brought in from 'outside' kept bubbling to the surface of my mind—but they seemed trivial. Did I really worry about such things 'out there'? Why—they had such simple and obvious solutions! Suddenly, right and wrong stood out with great clarity. There was a transparency on the faces of people I saw walking in the hospital gardens. They were going somewhere with a purpose. The sun shone on the late February snow with an openness that seemed to be saying: this is the way snow and sun were meant to be since the day of Creation. The world was 'transfigured' and my mind was at rest. If I didn't feel, 'God's in his Heaven, all's right with the world', I felt something pretty close to it.

Friends of mine who spent time in prison tell me that they underwent similar changes of perspective.

BUKOVSKY: That happened to me only under severe conditions—when I was put in solitary or went on hunger-strike. On such occasions, it is true, my confused ideas had simple and often beautiful solutions, and many things I could not disentangle outside fell into place. But let me tell you, as a physiologist, that the arrival of that august transparency and plasticity of things that seem unattainable outside prison is a deception. Once you are back in your normal surroundings, the complications and grey colours reassert themselves.

URBAN: Might it not be the case that high fever, solitary confinement, or simply isolation through imprisonment induce us to imagine that we are in the 'ante-chamber of death', with all the happy hallucinations that the act of dying is sometimes said to conjure up in our minds?

At the same Hungarian University where I heard Lukács lecture after the War, the philosopher Pál Harkay-Schiller ran a somewhat unconventional seminar on human behaviour in extreme situations.

'Have any of you ever been dead, ladies and gentlemen?' he asked a startled audience one fine spring morning. As many of the students had just come back from the War, from concentration camps, or Soviet captivity, the answer to that question was frequently 'Yes—in a way. . . .'

What the professor wanted us to describe was the mind of a man on the verge of death—and we had people in our seminar who had been put up against a wall but were, at the last minute, not shot for some reason; soldiers who had been abandoned for dead in the Russian winter; a girl who had been herded into a gas-chamber but came out alive because that morning the pressure was insufficient for the killings; and the like. What came out of this rather gruesome questioning was accounts of 'fear and trembling'—but of fear resolved, as the supposed moment of death moved closer, by a great calm, a sense of overpowering clarity, and a resolution of all the tangles.

BUKOVSKY: I did, to some extent, have a similar experience while I was in a punishment cell in 1974. I had been on hunger strike and was badly undernourished. I was suffering from stomach ulcers and in constant pain. My skin was peeling off. I was so weak that standing up was an effort, and when I did manage to stand up, the world was in a spin around me. I was convinced that I would die but the consciousness of death approaching didn't make me panic. I was composed, serene, stoical. 'So this is what it feels like to die', I thought to myself, as I watched my reactions with the eyes of an outsider.

Yes, I did feel a great peace descending on me, but it was the peace of helplessness and resignation rather than the kind of august clarity and disentanglement that your Hungarian veteran students seem to have experienced.

Experiences of this sort vary. I had Lithuanian partisans in my cell who had fought in the Lithuanian resistance and were barely alive when they were captured. They had hallucinations, but whether these were healing hallucinations of an all-encompassing 'transfiguration' or hallucinations inspired by animal fear, I could not tell.

URBAN: Do you miss prison?

BUKOVSKY: No, I don't.

URBAN: Did you ever miss it?

BUKOVSKY: No, I didn't, but the great advantage of living in a free society is that you can create your own seclusion, your own solitude, if that is what you need for your work or your happiness. You cannot call this house I live in 'a prison'; but very often I lock myself in, don't answer the door or the telephone, don't go out for meals, because I have something to think over or write. I need the concentration of solitude because I hate writing and find it extremely difficult.

URBAN: You create your own prison. . . .

BUKOVSKY: Yes, but you cannot equate a freely chosen seclusion with imprisonment.

URBAN: My reading of Solzhenitsyn's life-style in Vermont is that he feels deprived without the constraints and regularity of camp life and is trying to recreate them. The electric fence around his grounds and his great reluctance to see people or even pick up the telephone are telling us something.

BUKOVSKY: Only that the man is busy writing and doesn't want to be distracted or interrupted. His fence is a signal-wire to keep out the moose and elk, nothing more sinister. He has a large estate.

URBAN: Solzhenitsyn's work came out of the challenge of two concentric prisons: the general prison of Soviet society and, within it, the camp in which he was held. My impression is that he is slightly ill-at-ease in the permissive climate of American society. Hence the fence and the monastic order in his life.

BUKOVSKY: I don't know Solzhenitsyn all that well, but I do know that he is engaged in monumental labour. The sheer size of his output makes it essential for him to be functional and economical with his time and energy. Indeed, his self-imposed régime in Vermont is so rigorous that it outdoes the austerity and regularity of prisons I have known. Whether, and to what extent, he 'needs his prison' I cannot tell you, because there is, as I say, an alternative explanation. But it is possible that both explanations are in a sense true, or even that they feed on one another.

URBAN: Alexander Zinoviev once told me that he felt deprived without his Soviet 'collective'. I would have thought that, for Solzhenitsyn, Soviet camp life was the speck of sand that irritates the oyster into producing the pearl. American society is uncompetitive in that respect.

BUKOVSKY: It's possible; but we'll have to suspend judgment until Alexander Solzhenitsyn comes along to tell us. He is most unlikely to say 'I need my camp', but I doubt whether that would make you change your analysis of why he lives the way he does.

URBAN: I once had a discussion with Don Salvador de Madariaga on a similar topic, taking Arnold Toynbee's 'challenge-and-response' for our cue. We were wondering where one should draw the line between 'useful hardship' and 'hardship that kills'; for it was clear to us that a man or civilisation that has too easy a time of it, or is just treading water, is unlikely to be creative. We observed that between the unchallenged type of human life and the experiences of Auschwitz there were many gradations of hardship that put the right mixture of pressures on us to make us more 'creative' or just more 'fully rounded' and more sensitive human beings. I took the view that a good deal of historically- or socially-induced suffering was good for us. Salvador de Madariaga, on the other hand, felt that the ordinary hardships of human life—sickness, bereavement, frustration, the terrors of old age, the disloyalty of friends, and so on—were enough to equip us with the 'right' amount of suffering, and there was no need to ask a Franco or a Stalin to provide additional punishment, or to have famine or war visited upon society. He was probably right.

It seems to me that your own experiences fall into the category of profitable suffering, for imprisonment and the pressures of Soviet society in the 1960s and 1970s—though still appalling by Western standards—were no longer what they had been under Stalin.

BUKOVSKY: Freedom is an inner quality which cannot be bestowed or taken away by anyone but yourself. Using for a moment the crude terms of the market economy, I would say you can almost always have your freedom if you are willing to pay the price for it. In the Soviet system the price of freedom is exceptionally high, in the Western liberal democracies it is exceptionally low. In a Soviet prison you may decide to help a friend who has been unjustly punished, and be punished yourself for helping him. Or else you may decide, 'I'll ignore it', and escape punishment. The choice is yours; it's a question of how much you are prepared to pay for your inner freedom. I was gratified to read that Valladares in Cuba felt the same, although his imprisonment by a vindictive Castro was closer to the horrors of Stalin's camps and prisons than mine was.

It's been frequently held against me that 'Ah, but your time inside was a mild affair! You could talk back; you could demand to read the Soviet Constitution—and the prison governor himself would bring it to you so that you could write your complaints. You could lecture your interrogators. You could do many things, because the context had been changed and torture had been ruled out.

Now, in 1938! In 1938 they would have beaten you into pulp, and your friends abroad would never have heard about it.'

Well, it's perfectly true that under Stalin the price of inner freedom was exceedingly high, but even then you could attain it. Varlam Shalamov, who spent years under severe conditions in the frozen Far East in one of the worst of Stalin's camps, tells us that even there you could preserve your inner freedom. The price was high—oh, it was high!—but you could have it. In other words, so long as the system doesn't kill you, you're likely to emerge a 'better', a 'more sensitive' man.

URBAN: But what, in your judgment, would be the right mix of hardships? Poets, playwrights, philosophers have given us a great many memorable words about the creative beauty of unrequited love, the fascinations of 'Inferno' as distinct from the placid tedium of 'Paradiso', and the like. But one wonders whether people undergoing the agonies of unrequited love, or roasting in the fires of 'Inferno', would approve of their ordeal if you told them: 'Ah, but you are the anvil on which the future Dantes and Goethes will hammer out their immortal work!'

BUKOVSKY: To forge character, promote independent thinking or even to fulfil himself, man needs to run into obstacles and be constantly challenged. When I lived in the USA I noticed that most people around me in California were miserable although they lived in highly relaxed and comfortable conditions. Why? Because they lacked the challenges of hardship. They were in search, not of food or shelter, but of *themselves*. They had 'identity crises'. The Californian asked 'Who am I?', and went off to the psychiatrist to find a reassuring answer. And it wasn't only Californians, but Americans in general who seemed to suffer from the sort of self-questioning that comes from too much comfort, too much superficial living, and too little suffering.

Challenges can have degrees of usefulness. There are challenges that stimulate some people but not others. Suffering, too, has its gradations. Some lead you to a better understanding of the human condition while others send you into depression. There are anvils that temper you and anvils that kill you. Hardship may lead some people of strong character and great stamina to feats of creativity, religious insight, sacrifice and the like, but these exceptional achievements are usually attained under conditions that would simply destroy the majority of ordinary people.

So let's not rejoice too much over the achievement of those who were lucky enough to become heroes, because the peaks they represent for us are surrounded by mounds of the unsung dead. I will never subscribe to the argument that the Soviet system is good for you because its particular beastliness produces exceptional dissidents. The novelist C. P. Snow could not bring himself to criticise censorship in the USSR because he felt it showed that Russian writers were being taken seriously! . . . No, the price is too high, far too high.

URBAN: But you do agree that challenge and hardship are necessary for the good of any society; and a Christian society, which most of our societies still say they are, should, in theory at least, welcome suffering as a gift that brings members of that society closer to the sacrifice of Christ?

BUKOVSKY: Well, the British have understood in their instinctive and inarticulate way that hardship is essential to the stamina and character of society. Whether it is the Puritanical heritage or some less elevated factor (such as indifference and apathy) that has induced them to live their lives under maximum discomfort, the fact is that their lives are about as uncomfortable as it is possible to make them in the 20th century. Most of their homes are uninsulated and ill-heated. Their beds tend to be damp, too short, and too narrow. Their food is indifferently cooked and available only at highly restricted hours. Their bathrooms are cold; their trains draughty, noisy, underheated and unpunctual. Their plumbing is unique in the Western world in that it stops functioning at three degrees of frost; and so on.

Can all these be coincidences? I don't think so. There is, at the back of the minds of the British people, a subconscious assumption that too much comfort is bad for your character and that you need to be challenged.

URBAN: Your explanation has the virtue of being all of a piece, but that, I fear, does not necessarily make it true. While the tradition of self-mortification and 'doing without' has deep roots in British culture, the characteristics you describe have to do more with basic inefficiency and straightforward indolence than a by now (alas) vanished Puritanical Christian culture. Let's not, however, be tempted into a discussion of 'The English—are they human?'

BUKOVSKY: Let me add just one thing: British middle-class parents never stop telling me how much they suffered in public school and how much they hated it. But the first thing they do when their children reach school-going age is to send them to the same public schools, where conditions are not dissimilar from those one has in Vladimir Prison: harsh discipline, the tyranny of the older 'inmates', physical punishment, poor food, and so on. Parents wouldn't do this to their children if they didn't feel that those tough conditions were 'good' for them and their nation—unless, of course, there is another factor at play here: the British people's peculiar attitude to children. I was amazed to see that the British do not like children and do not treat them well. They prefer pets. Whether this has to do with self-hatred in the Puritanical sense (the child being the carrier *in nuce* of original sin, which has so powerful a hold on you as an adult) would require more profound thinking than we can give it in this conversation.

URBAN: You said a little earlier that there are, in a totalitarian society, no neutral topics. Even your attempt as a member of a group of adolescents to isolate yourself from Soviet reality became a political statement which saddled you with responsibility for things entirely outside your personal experience.

I was glad to hear you say that, because it confirms what I have been telling my friends and colleagues ('communicators') for a number of years. Communication by radio to the Soviet Union and Eastern Europe, for example, brooks neutrality as little as does Soviet society—and this is something Western politicians and communicators do not always find easy to understand.

BUKOVSKY: The Western approach to propaganda—let us be absolutely clear, at least in our own minds, that it is propaganda we are talking about—is strangely antiquated. It is an attitude that pre-dates radio, pre-dates newspapers, and belongs to the steam-age of communication. It fails to appreciate what totalitarian society is like and how it goes about conditioning the mind of the citizen. The word 'propaganda' has come to be looked upon as unclean, and in American usage the awful euphemism of 'public diplomacy' has taken its place. This prissy attitude is something to be marvelled at. It reminds me of Queen Victoria's reaction to the news brought to her by an adviser that a submarine had been successfully tested and that this offered a revolutionary addition to British naval power. 'I don't want to hear about that,' she is alleged to have said. 'It is utterly un-English for officers of the Royal Navy to fight enemy shipping without showing their colours.'

URBAN: Mrs Margaret Thatcher, the British Prime Minister, had the audacity a few years ago to compliment the BBC on its excellent track record in international 'propaganda', expressing the hope that it would do even better in the future. The BBC's indignation was boundless. The then Managing Director of the External Services protested in the 'Letters' column of *The Times* that the BBC was doing no such thing. It was providing objective news and fair comment. As a wartime listener to the BBC I can testify that propaganda is exactly what the BBC does and did, but it does it with such consummate skill and so fine a sense of hypocrisy that it manages to lure its own communicators into believing that what it does is not propaganda. Such self-deception is, surely, the hallmark of the best in propaganda.

BUKOVSKY: The ineptitude of the Americans in this area is especially surprising. It is they who invented advertising, both crude and subliminal, and yet their understanding of the Soviet attitude to propaganda is infantile and their inclination to play that particular intellectual game to good effect is small. What the Americans don't realise is that, at the turn of the 21st century, communication in the international field is one of the weapons (and, I would say, one of the vital and indispensable weapons) in the West's continuing engagement with the Soviet system. Anyone who has studied Lenin and has learned the first three lessons about the Soviet system knows the immense importance Communism attaches to 'agitation and propaganda', both in keeping the system on a steady keel and in subverting its supposed critics and adversaries abroad.

That is why there is no such thing as 'objective' broadcasting to the Soviet Union. Putting Shakespeare on the air is a most political act (need I say why?). Broadcasting jazz and rock music is a political act. Recounting the history of Kievan Russia is a political act—and *not* broadcasting the history of Kievan Russia is a political act, too. When you address yourself to a totalitarian system, whatever you say or don't say is a political statement. That American Senators and Congressmen do not grasp this is something I cannot understand, except in the rather devastating sense of the USA not considering itself to be a player in the field of world politics. If that is really so, we're all in trouble.

URBAN: You are echoing a sentiment Ambassador Jeane Kirkpatrick expressed in the melancholy sentence: 'The Soviets are playing to win, whereas we are trying to get out of the game.' She expressed it, mind you, critically—I don't believe *she* would want to get out of the game; indeed, I'm certain she would want to win it—but your description of the USA as a reluctant player is not unlike hers.

BUKOVSKY: Here is something about the character of Americans that people in the Soviet Union find hard to comprehend. A superpower given to high moral rhetoric but unable to see which side its bread is buttered! I sometimes feel that the USA is either too virtuous or too infantile to deal with the affairs of this sinful world. The two may even be connected.

URBAN: 'Irangate', it is claimed, has weakened the American Presidency—and weakened it, in the European judgment, unnecessarily. It is said to be another 'own goal' in a series in which we cannot afford too many. Will Moscow rejoice or snigger?

BUKOVSKY: It isn't as clear-cut as that. In one sense—yes, the Soviet leaders are rejoicing. The US government has lost some of its credibility; the President's authority is undermined; it doesn't now take a lot of daring to twist the lion's tail. The Soviets realise that the USA has suddenly become more vulnerable, and lost no time exploiting this weakness to improve the Soviet position in Afghanistan.

For let me assure you that it is by no means coincidental that the Soviet 'truce-offensive'—the offer to recognise

Islam as the official creed of a future Afghanistan, and the bizarre move to lure back the King—were made at a time of maximum American confusion in high places. Dobrynin knows what he is about. At any other time, Washington would have exposed such Soviet moves as propaganda, but with the Iranian scandal on their hands, the Americans were subdued and, by omission, they allowed the Soviets to score some important points in the world contest of ideas.

The Kremlin is also gratified to see the Presidency's authority generally weakened: after the revelations of Irangate, any American President will find it much harder to run undercover operations of the kind the Soviets are so adept at running against the USA. Congress has done some of the Soviets' work for them.

URBAN: Are you saying that the American Constitutional system is inadequate for dealing with totalitarian régimes?

BUKOVSKY: That is exactly what I am saying. It is antiquated. It is 200 years old. Two hundred years ago it was not unrealistic for Americans to imagine that they could keep out of 'foreign entanglements'. Even during much of the 19th century the USA could rely on the protection of the seas and the British Navy. Not today. It takes a missile fifteen minutes to cross the globe, and propaganda covers the world in a fraction of a second. The separation of powers and the Americans' proclivity to drive democracy to its grotesque extremes have made the USA a difficult country to defend.

I doubt whether American democracy could survive in the vicinity of a powerful dictatorship. Yet, because the world has shrunk, America is now a direct neighbour of the Soviet system, even though the American people have so far refused to take in this drastic change in their geography.

URBAN: It seems to me that the Soviet élite find it difficult to make realistic judgments about US motives and US intentions. They cannot make sense of that vast and alien spectrum of factors that American policy-makers have to work with and work against. I'd dearly like to know whether the Soviet oligarchs laugh at us in their lighter moments, or whether they feel that we are in the business of hatching super-clever conspiracies to wipe them off the face of the earth.

BUKOVSKY: They often laugh at the contortions and cluelessness of US policy. But they also believe that the farce has to be taken seriously because the plot has been specially laid on by the Americans to 'pull a fast one' on the Soviet leadership. The men in the Kremlin are Marxist-Leninists. They believe in conspiracies. Until quite recently, they thought that the fumblings and failures of the US authorities were deliberate shows of incompetence to confuse the world, but that behind it all was hidden a clever, no-nonsense capitalist government, a kind of Comintern-in-reverse, which was pulling the strings and controlling the players. So the Soviet leaders were never quite sure whether the laugh was on the Americans or whether it was they, the Soviets, who were being taken to the cleaners.

URBAN: Our attribution of smartness to them is matched by their attribution of fiendishly clever policies to us. . . .

BUKOVSKY: Yes, it is. The Soviet leaders have to believe that 'the capitalist enemy' is very cunning—or else, how come they haven't managed to eradicate it internally in all these years?

URBAN: It was remarkable, however, that at the time of the Watergate scandal the Kremlin showed no 'Schadenfreude' and was keeping quiet about Nixon's tribulations. Two explanations have been offered. First, that Nixon had been the architect of *détente*, which the Soviet leaders were anxious not to damage. Second, that giving a blow-by-blow account, in American fashion, of the unravelling of the President's authority and his creeping impotence as chief executive might have had a copycat effect within the Soviet system: 'Aha! So that's how one exposes a powerful man's abuses of authority. We have men infinitely more guilty than Richard Nixon!'

BUKOVSKY: I don't think our leaders held back on Watergate for that sort of reason. It was more important for them not to present the American side as weak or even weakening. In order to maintain its grip on the population, the Soviet system must show itself to be facing a powerful enemy.

If you suddenly display on the pages of *Pravda* the ineptitudes of the US government and the ignorance of American politicians—well, where is the big devil? If the Americans are so ham-fisted, why do we need all this expenditure on nuclear weapons? Why our vast standing army? Why the permanent mobilisation of Soviet society? Why the ubiquitous warning that 'the enemy is listening'—when all the enemy is doing is squabbling and shooting himself in the foot? No, that wouldn't have done; so the Watergate affair was played down.

The myth of the big devil had to be kept going.

Revolution from Above

URBAN: Soviet Man! This is a hoary topic, but for me it has a continuing fascination because it is the key to the question 'Is there such a thing as "socialism" or "communism" in the USSR?'. You have said that the concept of Soviet Man was the starting-point for all the illegalities you experienced in your country.

BUKOVSKY: The idea of Soviet Man is so diffuse that any ruler or any KGB officer can interpret it in any way that suits his purpose. Broadly speaking, it depicts a non-existent type of human being—one who 'builds Communism', endorses the policies of the Party, fights for 'Peace', and condemns the machinations of 'Imperialism'. This is the gross propaganda side of the concept. In practical life, however, more subtle use is made of it. You are blackmailed into saying whether you regard yourself as a Soviet Man; and if you don't, there's hell to pay.

URBAN: You write in your book:

> 'You are a Soviet Man,' says the KGB detective, 'and therefore obliged to help us.' And what can you say in reply? If you're not Soviet, what are you? Anti-Soviet? That alone is worth seven years in the labour camp and five in exile.

The strange thing about the idea of Soviet Man is that it is not written into the Constitution any more than the role of the Party General-Secretary. (What, one may ask, is Mikhail Gorbachov doing in the Kremlin as General-

Secretary, seeing that he is neither President nor Prime Minister?) Soviet Man is a purely ideological concept. In law you are a Soviet citizen, but you need not be a Soviet Man. One of the achievements of your Civil Rights group was to have made that distinction, and to have educated the legal sense of the citizen to a point where he would demand the enforcement of the letter of Soviet Law and the Soviet Constitution.

BUKOVSKY: Alik Volpin was the father of the idea in our circle that we should insist on a clear distinction being made between ideology and law. We said: Yes, there is such a thing, on paper at least, as a 'Soviet citizen'—but there is no such thing as 'Soviet Man'. Despite the totalitarian nature of the system, the comrades could never quite translate ideology into legislation. Hypocrisy and the needs of propaganda always demanded that the penal code and jurisdiction should reflect certain civilised standards that the rest of the world would accept, no matter how consistently they were being violated in daily practice. They *looked* good to the Webbs and to the Lion Feuchtwangers, and that was of great propaganda value to the young dictatorship.

URBAN: And the double-talk worked. Harold J. Laski wrote these lapidary words about Andrei Vishinsky, Stalin's Public Prosecutor, after a visit to the Soviet Union in 1935:

> I was disposed to think of him essentially in his capacity as prosecutor. . . . I found him a man whose passion was law reform. . . . He was doing what an ideal Minister of Justice would do if we had such a person in Great Britain. . . .[3]

What you and your group did was to turn Soviet hypocrisy to good account, demanding not only that 'sin should be paying tribute to virtue', but that some of the sinning should cease—a most daring undertaking.

BUKOVSKY: It was, and for a simple reason: if the Soviet Constitution and Soviet Law were to be strictly translated into reality, the system would collapse. Everyone knew that they were not meant to be taken seriously. Popular opinion accepted the farce and the double-think as the inescapable backdrop to the fiction of 'socialism'. We thought otherwise.

URBAN: How does a group of very young dissidents force

the mighty totalitarian empire to respect its own laws and the Constitution?

BUKOVSKY: We did it by stages and (as I said) without any planning. Of course, we could not *force* the authorities to do what they were determined not to, but bit-by-bit we insinuated our way of legal thinking until it caught on and established itself as the natural method for voicing dissent.

Don't forget that in 1917 the Bolsheviks abolished legality and independent jurisdiction, ushering in that profound sense of official lawlessness and indeed barbarism that paraded for a long time under the name of 'revolutionary justice'. They assaulted the people's sense of religion and subverted all existing norms of morality. That was the barren land we had to sow on.

I am amazed to see, 25 years after our first efforts, that those little beginnings have now become the established way of protest. Whoever has a complaint or wants things changed will refer to the existing legal instruments and beat the public drums to draw attention to his demand. In other words, we have induced the authorities at least to *talk* the language of Law, and that is the first step to making them *respect* the Law. In an ideological system that is the only way in which an essentially lawless society can be slowly transformed into something resembling a normal society.

URBAN: Isn't that slow transformation now being boosted by Gorbachov's own insistence that 'socialist legality' must be strictly observed?

BUKOVSKY: Yes it is, even though the pre-Gorbachov history of the enforcement of 'socialist legality' does not give one a lot of hope for the future. Not only that, but look at the slogans Gorbachov is now using to open up Soviet society. *Glasnost* (openness)! Why, we used to go to jail for demanding it! Our very first demonstration in Pushkin Square in 1965 had one single slogan: '*Glasnost*', and now it is the General-Secretary of the Communist Party pinning it to his mast. The reason? Gorbachov is an intelligent man; he understands what the people want and how to muster support for himself. His interpretation of 'openness' is not the one we demanded, but it is a step in the right direction.

URBAN: Western historians and students of the Soviet scene have often noted that the sense of law, and of individual rights and civic courage, is weak in Russian society. Russian history and tradition are blamed for much of this weakness. Going by the amount of persuasion you had to use on your fellow prisoners to make them understand their legal rights, and the many complaints and appeals you wrote on their behalf, it would seem that you had direct experience of both the Soviet sense of legalised lawlessness and the ordinary Russian's isolation from the law. I tend to believe that even the elementary courage of saying 'These are my rights, and I'll stick to them' will have to be implanted in the Russian people by some revolution from above, and it may well be that Gorbachov's reforms will promote that awareness as one of their perhaps unintended consequences.

BUKOVSKY: You're touching on a sore point. One question that tormented many of us in the dissident movement in the Soviet Union was the question of our national worth. Why was it that other countries were mature enough to attain and maintain democratic government and the Russians were not? Was there a consciousness of law and responsibility missing from the Russian psyche—a willingness to assert our rights as individuals? What explained our role as the greatest oppressor of nations in the world—our reputation as a universal trouble-maker?

Well, as long as I was inside the Soviet Union I found any number of cosy if self-accusatory explanations: the heritage of serfdom; the traditions of Czarism; the destruction of the law by the Bolsheviks; the mockery of jurisdiction under Stalin (the Show Trials); and so on.

But when I began to live in Western Europe and especially in the USA, my implied sense of guilt and inferiority as a Russian fell away. For what did I experience? I discovered that the ordinary Frenchman's and German's sense of law was every bit as tenuous as that of the ordinary Russian, and that in many ways the conformism of the Western citizen was more bovine and depressing than anything I experienced in the Soviet Union. I found conformism, timidity, and sheer ignorance especially sobering in the USA. Your law-conscious, individualistic, brave and upright Americans were conspicuous by their absence. Like the hedges and lawns around American homes, the average

US citizen's mind seemed to be cut to a single basic pattern; and woe betide those who failed to conform.

All this induced me to rethink some of the received readings of the Russian character and to come to the conclusion that we would be no worse as citizens of a future liberal democracy than are members of other nations. Indeed, in some respects your Russian is more individualistic because he has a stubborn strain of anarchism in his blood. He hates authority and derives great pleasure from outflanking and defeating it. I doubt whether, in any competition for individualism and non-compliance, your dutiful German or American, with his impeccable record as a taxpayer, could hold his own against a true-blooded Russian.

URBAN: Are you saying that a return to some form of Stalinism would prove impossible in the Soviet Union? If the Russians are as anarchistic as you say they are, both Lenin and Stalin might have had a piece of truth on their side when they insisted that 'barbarism could only be defeated by barbarism'. Mightn't, paradoxically, barbarism *à la* Lenin and Stalin—and, who knows, *à la* Gorbachov—be the first steps towards democracy in the unhappy context of Russian history and society?

BUKOVSKY: Absolutely not. There can be no return to Stalinism in the Soviet Union. Chekist terror is a thing of the past.

URBAN: Even though there are no institutional guarantees against either?

BUKOVSKY: Yes, despite the lack of institutional guarantees. Even totalitarian systems go through stages of natural development and decline. The Soviet system has aged; it is rapidly declining. It couldn't muster the self-righteousness and ideological drive to install another reign of terror.

The backdrop to Stalinism was Civil War, two World Wars, and the fierce commitment of a fairly large number of Communists. That combination of factors cannot be repeated. Never again will the Soviet Union have Communist leaders with so profound a sense of ideological drive that they would, or could, terrorise the vast majority of the population.

URBAN: Mightn't the exigencies of a profound economic crisis force even relatively 'liberal' leaders of the stamp of Gorbachov to impose order on the Soviet peoples—in the name of '*perestroika*' and, ironically, 'democracy'?

So far we have bailed out the Soviet system every time it found itself in deep trouble. But what if we stopped doing so and said, as we might under present conditions: 'Your economic weakness is greatly to our advantage. We'll do nothing to give you another breathing space'? Wouldn't the Soviet system have to revert to some form of Stalinism?

BUKOVSKY: First, I don't think for a moment that the West would or could exploit the economic crisis of the Soviet system in terms of a well thought-out and coordinated policy. It would probably pay 'protection money' the way innocent and frightened people often do, given a tough enough extortioner. Secondly, economic hardship would certainly not induce the Kremlin to return to Stalinism. On the contrary, it would force it to move even further and faster towards a market economy than it is already doing. The NEP (New Economic Policy) of the early 1920s was the system's typical response to the crisis of the economy. It would respond in the same way now, as it is indeed doing.

URBAN: We should, then, let the Soviets stew in their own juice and not fear the incalculable reactions of a cornered system?

BUKOVSKY: That's right. In order to hasten liberalisation in the USSR and cause the Kremlin to take up a more peaceable posture towards the outside world, the pressure has to be kept up. It is already paying dividends. Gorbachov's spectacular climb-down on INF (Intermediate Nuclear Forces) could not have happened without it.

URBAN: But to return to 'glasnost'. Could that slogan prove dangerous for the cohesion of Soviet society? Could it perhaps prove dangerous for Gorbachov himself?

BUKOVSKY: It is, in my view, dangerous for the *system*. It is my deep conviction, and that of many of my friends, that the Soviet system cannot exist as an open society. You can open it up a bit to let off steam and to assist you in installing a new leadership—but then you have to close it down again or face the consequences. That Gorbachov has hijacked the slogan of *glasnost* from the dissidents shows that he has a keen sense of what has to be said and what he has to avoid saying in the critical situation he is now facing. But he also knows that 'openness' cannot be implemented.

URBAN: Hasn't he gone beyond '*glasnost*', though—demanding, in fact, reforms and a thorough reorganisation of society . . . which amount, in the Soviet context, to revolutionary transformation? Gorbachov does use the words 'revolutionary transformation', referring not only to change in the economy but also to radical change in the behaviour of people and institutions.

BUKOVSKY: Gorbachov first spoke exclusively about revolutionary change in the *economy*. It was only after the 27th Party Congress that he began to widen the term to include other areas of Soviet life; and his emphasis continues to be on economic reconstruction. It is the Soviet Union's economic backwardness that upsets Gorbachov most, because he sees it as a great hindrance to putting the Soviet empire on the map as an all-round superpower. One has to be extremely circumspect in using the word 'revolution' in a Communist environment.

URBAN: I think Gorbachov is aware of that, yet he hasn't shied away from using the word 'revolution' on a great many occasions and in a non-economic context. Addressing the Khabarovsk Party *aktiv* on 31 July 1986, he said:

> The current restructuring embraces not only the economic but all other facets of public life: social relations, the political system, the spiritual and ideological sphere and the style and the methods of work of the Party and of all our cadres. Restructuring is a capacious word. I would equate the word restructuring with the word revolution. Our transformations, the reforms mapped out in the decisions of the plenum of the Party's Central Committee and of the 27th Party Congress, are a real revolution in the entire system of social relations, in the hearts and minds of people, in the psychology and understanding of the modern period and, first of all, of the tasks engendered by rapid scientific and technological progress.

BUKOVSKY: Taking Gorbachov's various utterances as a whole, though, I would still insist that he is principally concerned with the economy. He is hoping that the reform of the economy can somehow be accomplished without everything else being reformed too, because 'everything else' would mean unbuttoning the whole straitjacket of the Soviet system. That he does not want to do. In a subsequent passage of the speech from which you have just quoted, Gorbachov makes it very clear that the 'revolution' he advocates must happen 'not beyond the boundaries of socialism but within the framework of our system, revealing the potential of the planned economy, socialist democracy, culture and the human factor'.

URBAN: But even if Gorbachov did want to confine himself to the reform of the economy, he would still be Marxist enough to realise that you cannot do that without affecting the 'superstructure'—your political life, your arts and letters, and so on. But Gorbachov has gone far beyond the notion of just economic 'restructuring'; and even where he does not use the word 'revolution', it is quite clear from the context that radical change in the economy and *beyond* the economy is what he has in mind.

For example, talking to workers of the Gagarin Aviation Works in Komsomolsk-on-Amur on 29 July 1986, he said:

> I can see that a lot of problems have accumulated here. As I listen to you I become even more convinced that everything we have started is correct. A great deal has been piled up, a great deal, and we need a large bulldozer to sweep it away.

And later, answering complaints about enterprise management, he made some observations (to the applause of the workers) that are especially unlikely to make him popular with the 'Nomenklatura':

> It's essential that the manager does not take the view that having been appointed to his post he's now a kind of apanage prince. . . . The people must know everything and keep a check on it, because the human factor is the most important one. . . . What kind of socialism is it if things are kept from the people? Is this some private concern of entrepreneurs? . . . We've taken the country thoroughly in hand. We have strength enough; we have character enough. No one is going to knock us off the track.

These are, to my mind, pretty radical sentiments in an ossified Marxist-Leninist environment even if they don't herald the institutional reform of the system. They must be anathema to a great many people in the Establishment.

BUKOVSKY: What is so fascinating about the drama we can now observe unfolding under Gorbachov is that he and his supporters understand the crisis of the Soviet system in exclusively Marxist terms.

The Soviets have been building their society since 1917 according to the books, and the books have produced a diseased Marxist system. Now they are being forced to apply to it the critical apparatus of Marxism. This is ironic, because traditionally Marxism was harnessed to the understanding and then the destruction of slave-owning, feudal, and bourgeois societies in the hope of preparing the way for the consummation of history in a socialist and then communist world society.

Marx did not say what precisely would happen under a socialist system nor did he say whether or how his theory would apply under 'socialism'. All he said was that he was no 'Marxist' and that it would be absurd to build a political party on Marxism. The rest was left open. Now that the world's first truly 'scientific' Marxist society is in deep trouble, it remains to be seen how the tools of Marxism can help it to attain a measure of health.

URBAN: Whether Gorbachov is trying to do it exclusively by applying Marxism is not self-evident. Many would say that Gorbachov's—and Deng's—rescue-operations represent heavy borrowings from the market economy and capitalism: such as their insistence on the profitability of enterprises, competition, wage differentials, ownership by local cooperatives, and the like.

BUKOVSKY: Let's look at the way in which Gorbachov and his supporters define the crisis. They say, in true Marxist fashion, that a conflict has developed between 'social relations' and 'productive forces'.

URBAN: In plain English, that the ruling class has a vested interest in keeping things as they are because upheavals in the economy would threaten their privileges. . . .

BUKOVSKY: Yes, that's the gist of it, but they put it differently, and that's what intrigues me. Tatyana Zaslavskaya, one of Gorbachov's principal advisers and gurus, has restated and re-emphasised Marx's point that a clash between 'social relations' and 'productive forces' leads to trouble, and unless the reorganisation of the existing system of productive forces in taken in hand, Soviet society will continue on its downward slide. But, she asks, how can such a reorganisation be 'entrusted to social groups that occupy rather high positions in the system and accordingly have a vested interest in its maintenance?' Her answer is: Never mind the vested interests—do it, because if you don't, the clash will lead to social upheaval, turmoil, and even revolution.

Now, this is classical Marxism—suddenly applied to the ills of Soviet society. But she goes further and says that even a so-called 'mature' socialist society is not exempt from this rule, and here we come to what I take to be Gorbachov's so far 'hidden' agenda. Zaslavskaya asks: And what is the essence of a Marxist society? It is the public ownership of the means of production. She does not go much beyond putting the question, but I take it to be a hint heavy with meaning, for what the Gorbachov reformers are really driving at is some change in the ownership of the means of production. But that would be opening up Pandora's box, because we all know that the form of ownership established in the Soviet Union 70 years ago is 'the dictatorship of the proletariat' which in turn means the dictatorship of 'the advance-guard' of the proletariat, that is to say, of the Communist Party. Hence, in my judgment, the Gorbachov reforms point to a thorough reform of Enemy No. 1—the Communist Party bureaucracy itself; and they do so, as I say, strictly according to the letter of Marxist analysis.

URBAN: We are now talking about prediction, not about facts. . . .

BUKOVSKY: We are, but I flatter myself I can read between the lines. Now, what kind of changes in ownership do the reformers foresee? They do not, of course, suggest that they would want to return the means of production to private hands or dissolve the Party (although they may mean both in their private thoughts). They simply imply that *some* change in the Communist ownership of the means of production must be put in train.

Remember that the Marxist definition of ownership (based on Roman law) is: owning, using, and managing.

What do the reformers say? They say that Soviet society
does not require that all three functions should be united
in the hands of the Party—it is enough that the Party should
have one or two, leaving the rest in the hands of 'the public'.
This is truly amazing, for it foreshadows a wish to 'restructure' Soviet society right from the bottom. The question is:
Can an ossified, unfree society be made to be flexible and
free? According to the Marxist tenets, it can. Gorbachov's
people argue that in ancient societies slave labour was abolished when it ceased to be competitive. By a similar token,
the present methods of 'socialist' production are inefficient
and must give way to more cost-effective ways of
production. And if vested interests ('social relations') stand
in the way, it's too bad for the vested interests.

URBAN: We can see why Gorbachov is having a bumpy
ride. The question of returning state property to 'private'
hands is, in fact, now being openly raised in the Soviet
Union. The official excuse for raising it is the debate on the
new law concerning the future of State enterprises, and
more particularly the proposed issue of shares as part of the
process of conferring financial autonomy on them. In one
television discussion (Moscow TV, 10 March 1987), a
viewer's suggestion that the devolution of control should
lead to some form of private ownership was strongly
rejected by Evald Figurnov, head of one of the economic
departments of the Central Committee. But the manner in
which the question had been raised and was turned down is
intriguing because it indicates that '*glasnost*' is now inducing
people to think—and to say—the unthinkable. Figurnov
said:

> [The question] presupposes that the introduction of complete financial
> autonomy would lead to a transition from the property of the whole
> people, I should say, to that of a cooperative, or even of a private
> person, since everyone would have shares, or bonds, something that
> would represent one's personal, private property, wouldn't it? Well, I
> should like to emphasise that no such transformation of the property
> of the whole people into cooperative property, and much less into
> private property, will take place once the Law on the State Enterprise
> comes into force. Not at all. That is to say, the property of the whole
> people, in accordance with the tenets of the economic theory and
> political economy of socialism, will remain the same property of the
> whole people . . . there is not going to be private property here.

BUKOVSKY: What fascinates me is the reformers' almost comical determination to stick to the framework and language of Marxism, never mind what they might really think. The *muzhik* is being encouraged to rent cattle. *Rent* cattle! The peasant family is given the option of renting a cow. Why this particular 'reform'? Because renting a cow is not ownership; the peasant can exercise some of the ownership functions of having a cow—he can milk her and sell her products, but cannot *own* her. But even this 'radical' innovation has failed to induce enthusiasm among the farmers for better production, and the reason for that brings me to another important point: you cannot reform the Soviet economy in a political vacuum.

URBAN: Which Gorbachov seems to be aware of. None of us can teach him about public relations and propaganda.

BUKOVSKY: Personally, he may be aware of it, but the people he has to work with aren't. It is, you see, not enough to offer the *muzhik* the cow he is milking. You cannot inject elements of a market economy into a Communist economy with any hope of success if you haven't obtained public backing for what you are trying to do. In a command economy you don't need public confidence—you just command. But the moment you offer the peasant the use of a cow you are asking for his initiative, for good husbandry, efficient marketing, and the like; and these he is not going to give unless he trusts you and your reforms. Renting of cattle has been a failure.

URBAN: But private plots are now being made more easily available, and the long-term 'socialist leasing of land', as it is now euphemistically called, is about to be introduced for work-teams and even family units of not more than two or three people. If we go by the Hungarian examples, couldn't these reforms help to fill Soviet shops and markets with some of the items that are in chronically short supply?

BUKOVSKY: The Soviet peasants' mentality differs from that in Hungary. They don't take to private plots or work them the way the Hungarians do. For 70 years neither the Soviet élite nor the farming population or the working class was allowed to have any experience of running anything remotely like a market economy. No one in the USSR knows how a market economy operates. Cost-effectiveness, profitability, marketing, quality control, and the like, are ideas that will have to be acquired through trial-and-error over a long period of time. 'Profit' was a boo-word in the Communist vocabulary. Can you make it respectable overnight?

URBAN: Your diagnosis chimes in perfectly with what Gorbachov's men themselves now take to be the ills of the Soviet economy. As Academician Abel Aganbegyan (talking on Hungarian television, 4 March 1987) observed:

> You have got used [in the Soviet State Planning Committee] to issuing direct instructions to the enterprises on what they should produce and how much. This method will now disappear and it is said that you should go over to economic regulators. However, in reality you do not even know what they are, you have never come across this method. Thus you might feel that there is no longer firm ground under your feet. After all, you have worked in the accustomed way for decades. . . . They [the conservative managers] are afraid of independence, yes, they are afraid of being independent. What is more, if they are given independence, they fail to make use of it. They continue to ask permission to do this or that, even though they do not need permission any more.

What is remarkable about this statement is that Aganbegyan should have been quite so open about the exasperation which Gorbachov's policies are causing among Soviet managers, and that his critique should be quite so close to the views held by 'antagonistic' observers such as yourself. Perhaps there is, after all, life left in the Soviet economy?

BUKOVSKY: To answer that comment, let me go on telling you how unfamiliarity with the facts of life in a non-command economy, together with pussy-footing piecemeal reform, can defeat the objectives of the reformers.

In the mid-1970s Brezhnev wanted to revitalise agriculture in the non-black-soil areas of Central Russia, where production had been poor. He came up with the revolutionary idea that people would produce more if they were paid more. Great investments followed; many millions were harnessed to the hope that 'more pay will produce better results'—not in itself an irrational proposition in a market economy. But what really happened was that production actually declined in proportion to investment.

Why? Because the moment your farm worker was paid higher rates on the collective farm, he began to reduce the work he put into his private plot, on the simple principle that there was very little to buy in Soviet shops, hence you could only use a limited amount of money. Once you earned enough to buy what you needed—and what was available— you had done enough.

What I'm saying is that a basically sound economic idea can misfire if applied in an uncongenial environment. Partial reform is going to prove very difficult in the Soviet system. You'll have to open up the whole of the economy or face the prospect of repeating the Brezhnev experience and on a much larger scale.

URBAN: Mikhail Gorbachov's reformism recently involved him in some revealing articulations about the way in which he envisages 'democracy' operating in a revamped Soviet society. He suggested on more than one occasion that since the Soviet Union does not cater for 'opposition parties' (and thus for reliable feedback), the Party itself would have to provide a wide spectrum of critical opinions. For example, talking to Soviet writers (on 19 June 1986), he said that the restructuring of society was made more difficult by the absence of a loyal opposition.

> We don't have an opposition. How then can we monitor ourselves? Only through criticism and self-criticism. And most of all through *glasnost*.

This may strike us as a feeble remedy, especially as Soviet history is replete with enthusiastic calls for 'criticism and self-criticism', none of which prevented the Soviet economy and the political system from ending up in its present crisis. Nevertheless, the fact that Gorbachov has had the courage to mention the need of an 'opposition' shows that this entirely Soviet man has a realistic understanding of where the shoe pinches and what sort of footwear he would buy himself if he could start all over again.

Commenting recently to a television audience about the poor quality of Soviet industrial products, Gorbachov said:

> Only socialism could have tolerated these for so long; they would have bankrupted capitalism.

That his real meaning was 'A market economy would never have permitted the production of such shoddy goods' cannot have been lost on his listeners.

BUKOVSKY: Gorbachov has his ear to the ground and picks up a lot of popular wisdom. In the 1960s I travelled extensively in the USSR and used to run into the kind of sentiments Gorbachov is now voicing. 'We have no opposition parties and no private ownership—is it any wonder that our state-run industries are mismanaged and public property is pilfered?', I used to be told. 'Of course, under a master (*khozyain*), under a good owner, such things would not happen.'

The curious thing was that the people who talked like that had, for the most part, never set eyes on a 'master' or 'owner'. But they had had it handed down from their parents, and perhaps knew in their bones that the 'master' of a peasant household was the kind of fellow you could trust. All this is common wisdom in the Soviet Union; people will talk like that at the drop of a hat. The 'good master' is what people in the Soviet Union widely feel is lacking in Soviet society, and Gorbachov seems to be sharing that view.

URBAN: A heritage from the *ancien régime*? From the Bible?

BUKOVSKY: It may be a bit of both, but it's predominantly ordinary peasant wisdom and common sense. You have a very similar phenomenon in England. Council houses will be poorly looked after; but the same council houses sold to the tenants will at once take on a different appearance. Ownership stimulates pride; self-interest demands that you maintain and improve what you've got.

I once saw an amazing spectacle in Siberia. A gang of young fellows was planting rotten potatoes.

'What are you doing?' I asked. 'Those potatoes are dead, they will never grow.'

They laughed. 'We're not paid to grow them, we're paid to plant them.' But then they added: 'Of course, none of this would be happening under a "master"; he wouldn't allow it. But now—there is no ownership; nothing belongs to anybody. . . .'

That's the key to the malaise of the Soviet system.

The Enemy Within

URBAN: Aren't we, at this point, back to 'Soviet Man' again—a formula for irresponsibility and cynicism? You said in your book that every citizen of the USSR harbours 'a Soviet Man in his soul'. One suspects that most people hate themselves for tolerating this hidden enemy; hence much of the collective schizophrenia of Soviet life. At the same time, however, they realise that the maintenance of law and order, now that the Soviet system is an established fact, depends on the survival of this enemy within. It is not a dilemma I'd like to live with. . . .

BUKOVSKY: Again, it's not a straightforward dilemma; it's a *Soviet* dilemma.

Let me illustrate what I mean. One of the most fervently pursued aims of Soviet educational and psychological conditioning is to render the citizen helpless.

URBAN: To atomise society. . . .

BUKOVSKY: Yes, you put a man in a cell and tell him that there is no escape from it—that is the prototypical situation. In ordinary life this helplessness assumes milder forms; these can, however, be just as devastating.

Take the notion of Soviet 'elections'. My release from one of my imprisonments, I think in 1966, coincided with 'elections'. To go or not to go to the voting stations is a headache for most citizens. You will not be sent to prison if you don't, but you are made to feel that you are a bit of a fool, a fusspot, and a pedant. How is that done? Well, your local election people will come up to you and say:

'Please, comrade, come and get it over with. You really have to do it. You see, if you don't we'll be obliged to go on haranguing you until midnight. You would be punishing *us*, not the government, and why should you want to do that? These are not *our* elections; *we* haven't invented them. But we have children at home who have to be fed, and if you go on being difficult, how can we get home on time? . . .'

They will give you this cynical and maudlin stuff until you can't stand it any longer and go to the voting booths out of a sense of exasperation and pity for these wretched propagandists.

Well, in this particular case, I told my agitators that I really couldn't go and vote for the government—it was against my nature and all my convictions.

'Oh, never mind your convictions,' they assured me. 'We understand your doubts. But please, just go to the voting station and write anything you like on your ballot paper.' So, reluctantly, I went off to vote.

'And what do I do to vote *against*?' I asked one of the officials. 'Just cross out the name printed on your ballot paper', he said.

So I borrowed his pen, crossed out the name of the one and only candidate, and dropped my vote into the box. I felt that I had demonstrated my displeasure. But had I?

I shouldn't have knuckled under. I should have said, 'To hell with your faked elections'. But that is where the Soviet Man in my soul got the better of me. I accepted the situation because it seemed unalterable and I had been rendered helpless.

'What difference would it make if I refused to vote?', I thought to myself; and that is a fatal thing to feel. Multiplied by 200 million, it makes for the preservation of the Soviet system.

URBAN: Would you say Soviet Man is a specifically Soviet-Russian phenomenon, or would Soviet Man arise in any Communist country? Would a Roman or a Londoner become Soviet Man too?

BUKOVSKY: Absolutely. Soviet Man is not a product of Russian culture or the Russian race, if that's what you're driving at. It could happen anywhere, and in some countries it might happen much faster than it did in my country. It is bound up with the nature of Communism, as you and Alain Besançon have recently demonstrated.

URBAN: But many distinguished historians and observers of the Soviet Union hold the view that abject Soviet Man is, to a degree, a hangover from serfdom.

BUKOVSKY: I don't think he is. Historians are usually clever people who believe that the ordinary man is as conscious of the past as they are. He is not; he is normally ignorant and uninterested. If you were to ask a simple Russian in the Soviet Union today, 'What do you know about serfdom?', he would probably say that he had a vague recollection of what he had been taught about it at school, but that sort of knowledge would not influence his behaviour.

URBAN: But wouldn't he have inherited certain cultural attitudes? Wouldn't, for example, obedience to authority and the acceptance of paternalism be part of his heritage? We saw in Mao's China that Confucianism, with its respect for discipline and the veneration of one's forebears and elders, melted invisibly into the amalgam of 'Maoism'. Chinese Communism would be unthinkable without these influences.

BUKOVSKY: These are, to my mind, elements that can be found in any culture and can be encouraged to rise to the surface in the mind of any human being. Most of us succumb to violence or the threat of violence. Under certain conditions, most of us feel helpless or want to feel helpless. If you saw a friend of yours shot before your eyes for having done or said something that did not please the authorities, you'd think twice before repeating his offence, unless, of course, you had decided to be a kamikaze and wanted to court the risk of suicide—as we did. We did so as a matter of conscious decision, but most people don't want to take that risk. Let me assure you that any human being would become Soviet Man under Soviet conditions, and I am certain that the ordinary American would become 'Soviet Man' much faster than we did. Much faster.

URBAN: I cannot share that view, but I very much share your insistence that the only way in which the man-in-the-street can keep his integrity in tolerable order is to refuse to cooperate with the system. And we have just seen from the example you have given how very difficult that can be even for a man of your courage and intelligence.

   Bear with me if I reinforce your observations about 'helplessness' with another example that impressed me. In his introduction to the bilingual edition of the poems of Marina Tsvetaeva, Professor Robin Kemball relates the tragic story of the most gifted of 20th-century Russian poets, who, after a short and tormented life in Western Europe and the USSR, committed suicide in the town of Elabuga in the Tatar Republic in 1941.

   Alexander Gladkov, recalling a conversation he had with Pasternak a few months after Tsvetaeva's death (it took place on February 20, 1942), quotes him in his memoirs as saying: 'I am to blame for not dissuading her at the time from returning to the Soviet Union. What awaited her here? She lived like a beggar in Paris, she died like a beggar amongst us. But over here even worse was in store for her—the senseless, unspeakable tragedy of annihilation of all her dear ones, which I still can't find the courage to discuss.' When Gladkov asked who was to blame for the fact that Tsvetaeva, back in her own country, had been condemned to lead the lonely, unsheltered existence that led to the tragedy of Elabuga, Pasternak (without a moment's hesitation) is said to have replied: 'I am!'—and then added: 'We are—all of us. I, and Aseev, and Fedin, and Fadeev. And all of us. . . . We were full of good intentions, but we did nothing, consoling ourselves with the thought that we were helpless. Oh, it is so convenient sometimes to think one is helpless. The State and ourselves. It can do everything, and we—nothing. Time and again, we decided we were helpless—and went off to have a meal. For most of us, it didn't even spoil our appetite. That is our common crime, the result of our criminal egoism.

This shows your diagnosis of Sovietism as a low-intensity creeping disease to be absolutely right.

BUKOVSKY: It *is* a good example. Sloth and indifference are powerful ingredients of our nature. It's so much easier not to notice things than to notice them. The first doesn't require you to take action. The second does, and that can be uncomfortable for your conscience and take away from your prime TV time. It is, therefore, tempting to fall in with Sovietisation. It appeals to your sense of inertia and your instinct to go for the easy way out.

Perhaps the most difficult part of running against Sovietisation is the sense of ridicule to which rejecting it exposes you. You don't become, in average Soviet eyes, an heroic dissident, but a figure of fun. This can be more lethal to your morale than the fear of the KGB or Siberia.

And why do you become a figure of ridicule? Because you are thought to be tilting at windmills, resisting what is irresistible, and, not least, because you're wasting everyone's time. If you start making difficulties at meetings by speaking against some resolution that everyone knows has been handed down from above and has to be rubber-stamped, well, you are keeping busy and exhausted people from doing their shopping—and shopping in the Soviet Union is a full-time occupation. And why are you keeping them there? Because you want to satisfy some silly individual whim of yours. So, 'Don't make an ass and a nuisance of yourself', your fellow citizens will sneer at you, and that is a powerful disincentive. I always felt it to be more powerful than the threat of arrest.

Another factor that keeps many people obedient and Sovietised is the pursuit of their talent—real or imagined. How do you exercise your talent in a totalitarian system? Only by going along with the system, because it alone can provide you with a stage, a platform, a publishing house, a microphone.

Of course, the devil never asks for too much. You are, in the beginning, asked to make only very small concessions, but those are enough to align you with the system and start you on your way to complete Sovietisation. One educated fellow I met in prison said to me:

'Why do so many people feel they must become dancers, singers, writers and so on, kowtowing to the régime in the service of their alleged talent? Why can't they be satisfied with being workers on the assembly line or garbage collectors? That wouldn't involve them in betraying their conscience. . . .'

The answer is that talented people feel that bringing out whatever they have in them is more important than guarding their integrity. There's the rub.

URBAN: This does seem to me a rather Russian phenomenon. In Eastern Europe it was precisely the 'talented' people—writers, journalists, television producers—who were the first to refuse to be wrapped around by the system and started those momentous movements of dissent and resistance that eventually resulted in the Hungarian Revolution in 1956 and the Czechoslovak upheavals of 1968—and who are now leading the dissent in Yugoslavia. And, again in contrast to the Soviet Union, they are looked upon by the people not as mavericks who are making themselves ridiculous by being out-of-step with the complicity of the ordinary person, but as respected vehicles of national consciousness and democratic values.

Why is it that the majority of Russian people do not identify passionately with distinguished dissidents such as yourself, or Solzhenitsyn or Orlov or Sinyavsky or Sakharov? Is it, as Galina Vishnevskaya told us, because they are jealous of anyone wanting a better or even just a different sort of life? If so, does this betray a commendable sense of egalitarianism under conditions of general hardship, or just straightforward bloody-mindedness?

BUKOVSKY: It isn't the case that the ordinary Russian does not identify with us. The Soviet Union is a vast country. Unlike Poland or Hungary, it is heterogeneous—there are 130 nationalities on its territory with almost as many languages and customs. These nations and nationalities have their own heroes and dissidents. Like your Hungarians in 1956 and Czechoslovaks in 1968, the majority of our dissidents tend to wrap themselves in their national colours and fight the Soviet system first and foremost as oppressed nations and nationalities.

URBAN: Might they be preparing to repeat the pattern of the 1848–49 revolutions in considering their demands for national independence to be one and the same thing as their quest for democracy? Hungary in 1956 was, in the judgment of historians like Hugh Seton-Watson and Melvin J. Lasky, very much like that.

BUKOVSKY: That's what we are beginning to witness. But coming back to popular support for Russian dissent—we cannot, in the absence of figures, really tell how much support we have, or would have. Nor can we really claim that the intellectual type of dissident enjoys general support in Eastern Europe. In Yugoslavia the protestors are more concerned with national and even separatist issues than human rights, and dissenters like Milovan Djilas, though respected, carry no public influence. In Czechoslovakia, too, it would be an exaggeration to suggest that 'Charter 77' has anything like mass appeal. The tendency to lie low and conform until circumstances make it safe not to is not a peculiarly Russian trait.

But, as I say, we do have support in the Soviet Union. I can't tell you how widespread it is, and I don't know how public opinion would react if an opening occurred for radical change. But here are some impressions.

I once spent time in camp with a large number of ordinary criminals. They represented a cross-section of Russian society, and were in the majority decent people who had fallen foul of the law by stealing food for their families or helping themselves to some building materials at their work-place. There was a *muzhik* I got to know rather well who had pinched three buckets of bran for his children and got three years—a year per bucket, as his judge had tactfully told him.

Well, one day the sentence of an influential inmate was up and he was being released. He called his gang and made a little speech by way of a valedictory. He pointed to me and said: 'Whatever you do, protect this man because he's in for the common good—he speaks for all of us.' I was amazed. I never expected him to speak like that—I had had very little contact with him.

Another example. Towards the end of 1971 I was on hunger strike in the central KGB prison in Moscow. I was having a legal squabble with the authorities because they had refused to agree that I should be defended by a lawyer of my own choice. As the Governor diplomatically explained to me, anyone going on a hunger-strike was on a suicide mission—and to make that point absolutely clear, he put me in a cell where others normally awaited execution. A delicate touch, that.

My cell was a horrible, small, kennel-like establishment with all the 'furniture' screwed to the ground so that you could do no damage to yourself or the warders. I will not treat you to the details of force-feeding because this was a form of deliberate torture, and it would, I'm sure, make you sick to be told the methods the KGB thugs used on me. The idea was to make the feeding so horrifying that you'd give up any idea of staying on hunger-strike.

One night, about ten days into my strike and after a particularly gruelling session, I was in great pain and lay awake. In the small hours of the morning, I suddenly heard the trap-door open. One of the KGB guards was standing there looking concerned.

'What made you go on hunger-strike?' he asked.

I explained why I'd been arrested and how I was trying to defend myself.

'I was sure you'd done nothing', he said. He was visibly moved by my story and the pitiful figure I must have cut. He had come to express his sympathy. This, happening in the citadel of the KGB, was something new to me.

Then there was my camp in the Urals (I went through, you will notice, quite a representative sample of these institutions). We'd been brought there for complete isolation, because the ordinary camps for political prisoners had proved too leaky for the comfort of the KGB. Not only did we have a network of communications with the outside world, with the guards serving as messengers, but these communications were so sophisticated that I, for example, had whole tape-recorded CBS news-programmes smuggled in to me by courtesy of Alexander Ginsburg.

Well, the new camp was out in the wilderness. We had fresh and specially picked guards who proved resistant to our approaches. Not only that, but the prison régime was tightened up. We were desperate. When a prisoner's lifeline to the outside world is cut, half his life is cut too. The hardship and hopelessness began to take their toll; people began to die. The whole camp went on hunger-strike.

But then a miraculous transformation in our fortunes occurred. The guards began to talk to us. We were told that our hunger-strike was proof in their eyes that there could be no KGB stool-pigeons among us. (It is the standard fear of guards in the USSR that spies planted among the inmates will give them away if they show any leniency towards the prisoners.) For a stool-pigeon would not be asked and could not be persuaded to risk his life. So the guards began to cooperate. They would take messages to our friends outside, and life in the camp became bearable, as camp-life goes in the Soviet Union.

URBAN: Weren't these guards just reverting to the Russian people's basic good nature?

My father, a young conscripted lieutenant of the Austro-Hungarian Army in the First World War, spent a couple of years as a prisoner-of-war in Siberia. He used to tell me about the altogether tolerable life he and his fellow-prisoners were allowed to live in their camp near Chita. Indeed, as a child I often saw the programmes of the operettas and concerts which the prisoners-of-war mounted, the syllabus of the language courses they attended, the camp newspapers they wrote and printed, and even photographs of life in this Far Eastern Russian war prison.

In one of these my father was shown with an armed Cossack guard on each side—the picture had been duly signed by the two Cossacks. In another, enormous beer-barrels were shown in which, I was later told, Chinese ladies of less than immaculate reputation had been smuggled in (with the guards' connivance) to entertain the inmates.

My father had nothing but good words to say about the way he and the other prisoners had been treated, and especially about the common sense and humanity of the Russian private soldier—the *muzhik* in uniform. In 1917 he escaped, and he got back to Hungary a few weeks before the War ended. Throughout his long and hazardous journey he was well treated by the ordinary people; they helped him with food, clothing, transportation.

Between 1917 and 1987 many things seem to have happened to the character of the Russian people. Where have all 'the good Russians' gone?

BUKOVSKY: You cannot, under Marxism-Leninism, expect the ordinary Russian to behave as his grandparents did. In your father's day, and for centuries before that, it was the most natural thing for a Russian *muzhik* to help convicts on the run. He did it as a fellow-sufferer and Christian: 'There, but for the grace of God, go I.' Our literature is rich in examples. But when Communist ideology was injected into Russian thinking in 1917, fear and hatred were injected with it too. Helping a prisoner with so much as a piece of bread was declared to amount to complicity. The population was divided into angels (the proletariat) and devils (the class enemy), and you walked in fear of your life if anything you'd done could be interpreted as aiding 'the enemy'. So the ordinary Russian's reactions changed. He was desensitised and brutalised. The more significant, then, the awakening of his solidarity with the civil rights movement in recent years.

Solzhenitsyn describes in his great work how the principal problem inside the Gulags was the ordinary criminals' bitter hostility to the political convicts. That's now all gone. The moment you arrive in prison or camp as a 'political' you are treated with respect. The common law criminals feel that you stand for the ordinary man's rights—that you are *their* representative, too. They would not be able to explain their feelings in these terms because they are mostly simple and inarticulate fellows, but they do understand your ability to speak for them, lay out the law and write petitions on their behalf. I spent much of my time in prison answering their questions, trying to solve their personal problems and deciding their disputes as a kind of umpire. Friends of mine who left Soviet prisons quite recently tell me that the same attitudes prevail today, only on a much wider scale.

We can, I think, infer from all this with reasonable certainty that our case is now well understood by the Russian people, and that if some of the fixtures were to come loose on the deck of the Soviet ship, we would have a lot of support in chucking them altogether.

Purging the Crimes of Stalinism?

URBAN: It's reassuring to be told that some of the Russian people's collective fears are now being shed and that the popular conscience is reawakening, but when will the perpetrators come forward and say, as Pasternak did in that memorable passage about the death of Marina Tsvetaeva, 'I am to blame. We are—all of us'?

You make a profound case in *To Build a Castle* for the assumption of individual responsibility as the only means of redeeming society from collective complicity. One is surprised that in a nation traditionally preoccupied with crime and punishment no one has yet come forward to say 'I've done it—please listen to my story and judge me if you must', or sentiments to that effect.

Where have all the 'judges' gone—the people's assessors, the camp-guards, the torturers, the executioners, the men and women who meted out 'administrative justice', the informers, the denouncers, the bearers of false witness, those tens of thousands of servants of the *Cheka*, GPU, NKVD, MVD and now KGB, who created and ran the monstrous régime of the Gulags and starved the Ukraine into submission in the early 1930s? Why haven't scores of them escaped to the West to ease their conscience? Why was it left to Solzhenitsyn to assemble the evidence from the victims and survivors, but never, as far as I'm aware, from the men who waded deep in the blood of their own countrymen?[4]

There is also another and more institutional side to this Soviet version of *die unbewältigte Vergangenheit* (as the Nazi past is known in Germany). Marxism is a profoundly historical analysis of the successive activities of men. It claims that nothing in society can be understood without going back to the forces that shaped it. I fail to see how Marxism-Leninism can, in its Soviet incarnation, hope to gain a measure of health and acceptability without subjecting the Leninist-Stalinist past to a rigorous historical analysis, naming names, punishing those responsible, and publicly rehabilitating those who have been persecuted.

Khrushchev, with his speech at the 20th Party Congress, made a valiant beginning. He did half the job. Isn't it now up to Gorbachov to do the other half—to launch a series of 'Stalin-crime trials' precisely in the name of loyalty to Marxism?

I hasten to add in all fairness that Gorbachov and his supporters have themselves recently indicated that they want to see the past re-examined and accounted for. But will they do it? *Can* they do it? Going by your reading of Soviet psychology, it will prove an extremely hazardous undertaking. You speak in your book about the need to shatter 'the internal excuses with which we justified our complicity in all the crimes'. Isn't it a lot easier to change institutions than the justifications of wrong-doing in the minds of men?

BUKOVSKY: The problem of individual responsibility is encapsulated in your quotation from Pasternak. A lot of people felt and feel the way Pasternak did but very few had the courage to say so. The system makes for silence. It proffers compliance as the lesser evil. To stand up and say: 'Yes, we have known all about the executioners, the deportations. . . . Yes, we closed our eyes so that we wouldn't feel responsible', this takes an heroic person and an abnormally heightened type of consciousness. And then to be derided, to boot, for 'tilting at windmills' by the very people whose rights you are trying to protect at great risk to yourself is a little too much even for a courageous man to bear. When a policeman threatens you under investigation, 'Don't be a fool, toe the line', he may very well steel your resistance, but when the same is said to you by ordinary people you have known and liked all your life, your inclination is to give up in disgust.

If you want to induce Soviet people to allow their better selves to come forward and take responsibility, you have to change the entire context of their lives. You have to make it safe for them to speak the truth. Perhaps that context is now being slowly changed under Gorbachov. It's too early to say, but if so, I am certain that people will eventually come forward and do exactly what you have suggested is expected of them. Individual writers have already done so in the emigration. Men like Lev Kopelev have owned up—'There's blood on my hands', he says, in effect, in his autobiography.[5] They tell us how blindly they believed and cooperated, and how slow and painful it was for them to exorcise this self-delusion and regain a measure of self-respect.

But what you seem to be suggesting is something much wider. You would like the Soviet Union to cleanse itself through an act of collective repentance, and you're right. This is what Solzhenitsyn demands and what I also feel has to be done. Soviet society must go back to the 1930s, '40s and '50s, and dig up the crimes of the era of Stalin. We must re-live Stalinism if we really want to stamp on it. If we don't do it and do it quickly, Soviet-Russian society will never be able to shed the stigma of collective complicity. There are, of course, different ways of doing it. Solzhenitsyn wants to see it done on religious grounds; my own grounds are secular—but we both want the same thing.

URBAN: But you agree, don't you, that names will have to be named, trials held, and individuals as well as entire classes of people rehabilitated?

BUKOVSKY: Naturally. This is what we all expected Khrushchev to do after he had broken the ground with his speech at the 20th Party Congress. But he didn't do it. It turned out that he used de-Stalinisation merely as a tool for establishing himself in power. He didn't go to the ideological and institutional roots of Stalinism, he didn't punish the guilty (except the men around Beria, and removing them was part of the power struggle)—and, consequently, the spectre of Stalinism has never stopped haunting the USSR. What is more, once in the saddle, Khrushchev encouraged the cult of his own person to replace that of Stalin and made himself both hated and ridiculous for it. He proved the truth of Marx's observation that things tend to happen twice in history—first as tragedy and the second time as farce.

URBAN: I do not share the current Western euphoria about

Mikhail Gorbachov's reforms, but—talking as we are about digging up the crimes of the Soviet past—Gorbachov's people themselves are now pushing the reform movement in that direction and saying so quite openly in the teeth of opposition. Vitaly Korotich, editor of the Soviet journal *Ogonyok*, had this to say to the *Christian Science Monitor* on 20 February 1987:

> Up to now we've been shadow-boxing over reforms. Now it's a real fight. There are real threats. Real phone calls. People call and say 'things will go back to the way they were, and then you'll shut up'. I don't think there is any alternative to what Gorbachov is doing. I know I don't want to live the old way. . . .
>
> The opposition came from some of the editors. Of course they didn't say 'We're against *glasnost*'. They said, 'Do we really need to touch on all the painful points in our history? Our system?' Gorbachov took the opposite line. He told the meeting, if we have real democratisation, that means that everyone can be criticised, including himself. . . . Is it necessary or not to talk about 1937? I think so. Until we resolve the question of Stalin we'll never move forward. Other people object. They say: 'Do we want to create the impression that the achievements of socialism were based on a crime?' And others—very sober people—feel that, well, Stalin may have been a bandit, but he got things done.

BUKOVSKY: It is, of course, gratifying to see that people like Korotich, who didn't always talk the way he does now (and who knows how he may be talking tomorrow?), demand the resolution of 'the question of Stalin'. But I'll believe it when I see it. Khrushchev promised the same thing with much greater fanfare and in more open language, and the results were non-results.

URBAN: The point Korotich raises is an incisive one. Would the exposure of the past really repair the reputation of the Soviet system ('We had the strength to face what had been done in our name and to punish the perpetrators')? Or would it prompt the public to say: 'The Soviet system was conceived and born in crime—nothing but more wickedness is likely to come out of it'?

To put it another way—would the Soviet public think of the reforming leaders: 'Whatever your protestations, you're all tarred with the same brush'? Or would it rather say: 'It's remarkable how, behind bureaucracy's stony façade, a great deal of doubt, dissent, and even rebellion—and some honest men—appear to have survived'?

BUKOVSKY: For the intelligent and realistic Soviet observer, all the current talk means very little unless talk results in action. The Soviet public is hard-bitten—it will advance no trust to this or any leadership. If the US and West European governments want to make advance payments to the Gorbachov team in terms of Arms Control concessions and economic aid—that is their business. But I can assure you that the Soviet public will not. Remember one thing: no government and no leader in the USSR enjoys a 'presumption of innocence'. The ordinary man's attitude to authority is to say: 'Show me that you are *not* guilty', and that is as it has to be in the light of the Soviet past.

URBAN: Nevertheless, some of the pronouncements of Gorbachov's economic advisers make me think that behind their scholastic language there lurks a genuine will to break out of 'the system'. Tatyana Zaslavskaya, for example (whose vocabulary is, incidentally, by no means always scholastic), let it be known to a Yugoslav journalist: 'The top leaders should first introduce a process of freeing people from their chains and giving them their rights. . . .'

True, she spoke these remarkable words in a socio-economic context and to a Zagreb paper, but language of this kind has a way of making the rounds, turning up in unexpected places and having unforeseen results. Mightn't sentiments so unequivocally expressed induce the Soviet people to temper some of their scepticism?

BUKOVSKY: Not at all. Soviet history has always been long on declarations of libertarian intent and short on results. 'Democratisation'—'the even better enforcement of Socialist legality' (I always liked that 'even')—'the exploitation of the hidden reserves of the socialist economy'—'criticism and self-criticism'. . . . Why, hardly a year has passed since 1917 that slogans of this kind have not been hammered into the consciousness of the Soviet citizen.

But out of the slogans came poverty-as-before and national-imprisonment-as-before—first because Stalin was Stalin, then because Brezhnev was Brezhnev, and Chernenko was Chernenko. No one blamed the system; no one blames it today.

URBAN: There is an old Negro proverb which says: 'Cheat me once—shame on you. Cheat me twice—shame on me.'

BUKOVSKY: That sums it up. The Soviet people—a very patient people—will not be cheated yet again.

Accelerating Soviet Decline

URBAN: What would you want a completely enlightened Gorbachov to do? How would you define your criteria for saying whether he has, or hasn't, begun to walk down the road that leads to fundamental change in the system?

BUKOVSKY: Ah, that's a good question, because it has, or should have, an immediate relevance to Western thinking about Gorbachov's Russia. The Western public is confused—the political class is deceived or is perhaps deceiving itself in the hope that somehow or other the problem of Soviet power and the Soviet system will go away. Eventually it might, but here is what I think should be our yardstick.

First, the Soviet system has sprung from a concept. It is an ideological society. To change it you must go back to the theory. Nothing less will do or can do. Nothing in fact works in Soviet Russia unless a theoretical justification has been given or the sacred texts have been amended or repudiated. That should, ideally, mean the repudiation of Marxism as an anachronistic concept, irrelevant to our problems at the end of the 20th century.

But, for obvious reasons, we cannot expect the Soviet leadership to do that. They would be signing their death warrant. So what is it we *can* expect, and what is it the Soviet peoples should insist on?

It should be quite possible and feasible for the Gorbachov leadership to say at some point in the not too distant future that, in the post-industrial, high-technology age, the idea of 'antagonistic' contradictions between 'socialist' society and 'capitalist' society is nonsense. This would mean repudiating the class struggle and, of course, the dictatorship of the proletariat.

URBAN: Can you see the Church turning its back on the Trinity, Original Sin, and the Immaculate Conception?

BUKOVSKY: No, I can't—and neither can I see the Soviet leaders turning their backs on Marx *and saying so*. But much has been done in history in the name of an idea that has, in fact, become meaningless. I would expect that a truly reforming Soviet leader would keep the sacred names and slogans going, while marching, in reality, to a very different tune. He could learn from the Chinese.

URBAN: But aren't some of Gorbachov's covert critics even within the Party leadership doing precisely the opposite— using the language of '*glasnost*' and '*perestroika*' to promote pre-Gorbachov and indeed Stalinist types of ideas? V. V. Shcherbitskiy, for example, gave us the following interpretation of 'restructuring' at the 25th Congress of the Ukrainian *Komsomol*:

> Restructuring provides conditions and calls for the rebirth of the romanticism of intense shock work. . . . Our dynamic times call for new heroes and true champions of restructuring and acceleration. We are confident that the *Komsomol* will bring forth young heroes of our times! The creation of a museum of the Stakhanovite movement would undoubtedly facilitate the moulding of such heroes.

I thought this was a fine case of 'The voice is Jacob's voice, but the hands are the hands of Esau. . . .'

BUKOVSKY: Shcherbitskiy is undoubtedly at odds with what you and I take to be Gorbachov's message. We shall see whether he will last as a member of Gorbachov's Politburo.

But coming back to the criteria by which I would measure Gorbachov's reforms, I would say, secondly, that he and his colleagues will have to level with Soviet history. The question is: how far do we expect them to go in rehabilitating the victims of the Soviet past? There are some who say that clearing the name of Bukharin would be enough— and the least difficult because some of Gorbachov's economic policies are in fact similar to those Bukharin advocated at one stage of his life. Others say: If Bukharin, why not rehabilitate the Mensheviks? Some go further still: they feel that, with the bankruptcy of Soviet collectivised agriculture increasingly exposed and the Gorbachov team's drive for 'private' production making the headlines, the time has come to repudiate the collectivisation of agriculture in the 1929–32 period and the massive crimes associated with it, especially in the Ukraine.

URBAN: But aren't you now voicing the rather exacting demands of a small, educated élite who tend to believe that no political action can be taken without philosophical justification? Doesn't the evidence of 'life itself' (as the Communists are in the habit of saying) tell us a different story?

BUKOVSKY: Not at all. Marxism is an historical concept. The Soviet system is its direct and gravely sick offspring. But it, too, is constructed in such a way that you cannot change any part of it without offering an internally consistent set of ideological and historical reasons.

The third thing that I would insist would have to be changed is Soviet Law. Article 28 of the Constitution says that the Soviet Communist State supports revolutionary and national 'liberation' struggles throughout the world. So long as this stipulation remains one of the governing principles of the Soviet state, the Kremlin will go on having an excuse for expansionism.

This is something the rest of the world cannot tolerate and the present Soviet leadership cannot afford, if, that is, Soviet protestations of 'peace' are to have any credibility. If the Soviet leaders want peace let them show the world that they will not be going to war in the Third World or sponsoring wars by proxy and subversion. Let them change the Constitution and, for example, withdraw from Afghanistan as a first step.

There is, further, Part 3 of Article 64 of the Penal Code. This states that a civilian leaving the Soviet Union without lawful authorisation commits a crime no different from military desertion in war. What does this mean? It means that civilian citizens of the Soviet Union are 'at war' with the rest of the world—that Soviet civil society as a whole is at war with the rest of the world. How can this be made to square with Soviet peace propaganda? The Soviet Government must delete this stipulation of the Penal Code if it wants to put its relationship with the outside world—and the Soviet people—on a new footing.

Moreover: how are we to interpret the continuing existence of the International Department of the Central Committee? Surely this is the Comintern in disguise, and thus directly subversive of the stability of countries with which the Soviet Union says it wants to live in peace. If

Gorbachov and his men mean business, they must abolish the International Department as a serious stumbling-block to peaceful cooperation with the international community.

URBAN: Would you want the Soviet leadership to end the monopoly position of the Communist Party and reintroduce a multi-party system?

BUKOVSKY: I would—but we cannot expect them to go that far; and it would not be necessary.

URBAN: Meaning that the reforms you have just sketched out would be enough to dismantle the Communist system as we know it?

BUKOVSKY: Not quite. I have made a study of the medium and long-range prospects of the Soviet system, and my reading of the future, taking into account the Gorbachov-factor, is roughly as follows. The Soviet Union is in rapid decline. The decline can be slowed down in the hope that 'something will turn up' on the way, but it cannot be stopped. If radical reforms are not made, the system has about 20 years before it unravels and the empire crumbles. If Gorbachov's reforms and future reforms—including the radical ones I have just mentioned—are put in motion, then, and only then, can the Kremlin hope to buy time and postpone the day of reckoning.

URBAN: I'm a little sceptical about prognostications. Didn't Andrei Amalrik ask, in a famous tract in the 1960s, 'Will the USSR Survive Until 1984?' He thought it wouldn't, but it did.

BUKOVSKY: There is always a risk attached to forecasts, but I hold these views on the best evidence I have and the best extrapolations I am capable of making.

URBAN: I keep coming back to the point: can you ask the Soviet leadership to commit what amounts to suicide? What-ever Mikhail Gorbachov is, he is not stupid. He can, I am certain, see as clearly as either of us that repudiating the class struggle and opting out of the 'internationalist duties' of the Communist state would totally undermine the system's title to legitimacy. Once the system is open, cultur-ally liberal, free-market oriented, and non-expansionist in its international relations, it is only a matter of time before the public will say: 'Can't we have all these things more fully, more cheaply and with a greater sense of self-respect under a properly elected democratic government? What need is there for the costly pretence of "socialism"?'

BUKOVSKY: I don't think the Soviet leadership has much choice in the matter. That the threat to the system is grave and the leadership realises that it is—all this we know from Gorbachov himself. He is, in effect, asking the Western world to assist him in slowing down the decay and postponing the demise of Soviet Communism. Hence his return to the zero-option without SDI strings; hence, in large part, his cultural and economic liberalisation and much else.

URBAN: Should we go along with him?

BUKOVSKY: To a limited degree—yes. What do I mean by 'going along'? Gorbachov is now trying to decentralise some of the economy, conferring the responsibilities of management on individual enterprises. The West should not go along with that until and unless the reforms have begun to bite. But once restructuring is really under way, the West should contribute to the speed and particular character of decentralisation by offering to cooperate with these increasingly self-managed enterprises. It could hasten the liberalisation of the system from within.

In other words, the West should neither automatically go along with the reforms, nor automatically refuse all of Gorbachov's pleas for assistance. It should, under certain conditions, take part in the reform process on the assumption that, while Western help might indeed slow down the withering away of the Soviet system, it might nevertheless lead to a gradual dismantling of its totalitarian characteristics, and could do so without cataclysmic upheavals. This would seem to me to be the most painless way to go, and the most realistic.

URBAN: But wouldn't even qualified rescue operations of this kind (one-sided moratoria and the like) amount to bailing out the Soviet system and making it stronger? Wouldn't it, also, be ignoring the evidence of history to believe that so sophisticated a policy could be consistently pursued by a disunited West and a less than perfect American leadership?

As for economic cooperation: joint ventures with decen-
tralised and self-managed enterprises have been tried,
especially in Yugoslavia, and found wanting. Admittedly,
Yugoslavia is, as a result of Western cooperation, a more
pleasant and more liberal place to live in than the Soviet
Union, but it is hardly a model that either the Soviet population or Western governments would make great sacrifices
to emulate.

BUKOVSKY: For a system as hide-bound as the Soviet, the
Yugoslav model is not to be despised *as a transition*. In any
case, a beginning has to be made, and we are now in the
position of seeing a semblance of a beginning being made
by the Gorbachov leadership. The West's best policy is to
accelerate the 'acceleration', widen the 'openness', and
boost the 'restructuring'—always bearing in mind that *its*
purpose is not to help the Soviet system, but to make it
disappear without drama.

URBAN: There are, as I see it, at least two dangers in giving
Gorbachov the sort of vitamin-injection-cum-pain-killer that
you tentatively suggest. The first (to which we have already
alluded) is the danger of making the Soviet state stronger
and the Soviet empire more enduring—perhaps, as you say,
in the short term, but perhaps permanently. At present the
Soviet Union is a superpower in military terms only. In most
other respects it's closer to being a Third World country.
Mightn't your carefully timed economic assistance nevertheless make us into suppliers of the proverbial rope with which
the Soviets have always said they would one day string up
the suppliers?

BUKOVSKY: Well, as we are indulging now in a bit of crystal-
gazing, let me be slightly speculative. I don't think that
danger would arise. We are talking about retiring the Soviet
system. The moment you do that, the Soviet empire goes
with it. And once the Third World part of the empire is lost
and the East European dependencies crumble as part of
the disintegration of totalitarianism at the centre, I doubt
whether the Soviet Union itself could maintain its integrity
within its present borders. The Baltic states would be the
first candidates for independence, followed perhaps by the
Ukraine and others, mainly in Central Asia.
    What you are left with, then, is the Russian Federation,

which should be no threat to the world. Anyone who knows the state of Soviet industry, the backwardness of the Soviet exploitation of natural resources, the environmental and social problems the country faces, realises that it will take at least two generations for a reduced Russian state to attain a sense of normality, and very much longer to turn itself into any kind of 'power'. Real superpower status will be completely outside its reach.

URBAN: The second danger I can foresee is this. Coming to the temporary assistance of the Gorbachov team by helping them to bury themselves without a fuss would, in the short term, probably make the system look rather attractive in the eyes of Eurocommunists and even a great many American liberals and European social democrats. They would have some reason for saying: 'We can now see that the Soviet system *is* reformable. Excise the alien element of Stalinism, and Marxism gains a fresh relevance to the condition of man at the turn of the century. . . .' Voices of that kind can already be heard on the strength of the mere promise of the Gorbachov reforms, no matter how firmly men like Igor Ligachev and Alexander Yakovlev go on telling us that under no circumstances will 'democratisation' be allowed to lead to political pluralism, much less a multi-party system.
Ligachev said this in Saratov on 4 March 1987:

> [Western critics] still cherish the hope of weakening our system from within the path of democratisation and turning it into a channel for political pluralism. These are pipe-dreams.

Yakovlev (speaking to the Spanish press on 11 March 1987) put it even more forcefully:

> Sometimes we are told: 'You are now going towards liberalisation; you are going towards a Western type of democracy.' Nothing of the kind. We are moving away from it. We think and even hope that in certain respects you will have to follow our example.

Gorbachov wants your 'transitional' period to become permanent. He has pointed out time and again: the main *hope* of the capitalist enemy is to preserve the Soviet Union in its present backward state and to increase its difficulties through foisting on it senseless military spending. The main *fear* of the enemy is a successfully restructured, modern, competitive and attractive Soviet system.

I cannot fault Gorbachov's analysis. Wouldn't your shrewdly conceived tactical cooperation result in helping the Soviets to re-establish their reputation as a reformable system, reviving some of the ideological and political magnetism the Soviet model once had but mercifully lost over the last 30-odd years?

Summing up the results of G. P. Razumovskiy's visit to the 26th Congress of the Austrian Communist Party, a *Pravda* despatch observed (on 28 March 1987):

> It was particularly noted that the [Communist] party organisations are showing sincere interest in the restructuring which is now taking place in the Soviet Union, and this creates favourable opportunities for stepping up the activities of the Austrian Communist Party and attracting new members to its ranks.

BUKOVSKY: I don't share your concern. We are talking about a *transition*. If my analysis is correct, there will be no time for a 'social-democratic' type of USSR to put down roots and make an impact on the world. The logic of economic devolution will make for ever greater openness and *de facto* pluralism. I can foresee no stable state occurring in the gradual unravelling of the system as we have known it, and nothing for the European Left and American liberals to get too hopeful about.

Danegeld for the Russians

URBAN: I don't want to spoil your scenario, but I'm fairly certain that practical officials sitting in the State Department, for instance, or the British Foreign Office, would shake their heads and say that no government could build its foreign policy on so large and so speculative an historical forecast. They would refuse to accept that US or Western foreign policy should aim at dismantling the Soviet system (that, they would say, was a strictly internal matter); and they would be horrified by the suggestion that our policies should somehow assume or (perish the thought!) contribute to the disintegration of the Soviet state. Milder suggestions have sent American and European diplomats into paroxysms of indignation. President Reagan and Mrs Thatcher could probably tell us a tale or two about the '*déformation professionnelle*' of officials manning the State Department and the Foreign Office.

BUKOVSKY: Well, if that were to be the State Department's reaction, then the State Department would be plainly wrong. It isn't a question of *whether* the Soviet system is on the way out, but under what circumstances and at what speed it will make its exit. Gorbachov knows this as much as you and I do.

Some years ago Dr Helmut Sonnenfeldt suggested that an 'organic relationship' between the Kremlin and its client states in Eastern Europe was a desirable American objective and deplored the fact that such a relationship did not exist. This was an erroneous analysis at the time, and it would be doubly erroneous to go along with it today. If, as I am convinced, time is up for the Soviet system, then (to repeat) the only sensible thing for us to consider is how to make the Soviet decline crisis-free for the Soviet leadership. This will leave plenty for the State Department people to do. No area-specialist would have to join the dole queue.

URBAN: So what practical action do you suggest Western governments should take in the immediate future?

BUKOVSKY: So far Gorbachov and his team have only been *talking* about reforms—no real reforms have yet been instituted.

URBAN: The openness, moreover, comes from a closed circle of leaders. The freedom of discussion is decreed by fiat. Decentralisation itself is centrally directed. The 'revolution' is from above, and so far well under control.

BUKOVSKY: Yes; unless we can see early and convincing signs that reforms are really happening, the West should provide fresh incentives for the *perestroika* to take off and fly. This would have to mean stepping up pressure on the Soviet empire in terms of increased military competition including, of course, SDI, and refusing to relax pressure on the USSR's Third World components as well as Eastern Europe. Western governments should be especially careful not to give massive economic assistance or offer technological cooperation at the present juncture. This would kill the reforms and jeopardise Mikhail Gorbachov's plans for a generally reorganised Soviet system.

URBAN: Your scenario assumes that Gorbachov will remain at the helm and that the cohesion of his team and their reforming zeal will remain intact for the foreseeable future. I wonder, and so do others. Galina Vishnevskaya, for example, believes that Gorbachov is cast in the mould of Khrushchev—an iconoclast and impatient reformer while fighting to establish himself in power, but a conservative once he is safely home and dry, and has spawned his own mafia.

BUKOVSKY: Gorbachov's power appears to be safe at the moment. It is true that he is facing opposition in many quarters, but this opposition is neither strong enough nor smart enough to threaten him.

What does leave the new team's power base open to doubt is the safety of the socialist empire itself, because that is endangered by the poor performance of the Soviet economy. Gorbachov is not much worried about the working man's standard of living in Voronezh, though he would clearly like to push it up. What does worry him is the inability of the Soviet system to sustain the burdens which Cuba, Ethiopia, Yemen, Afghanistan, Nicaragua and the East-Central European states have placed on it. His empire is built on quicksand.

URBAN: Old-fashioned imperialism used to draw economic benefits from the colonies. The Soviet variety exports the command-economy to the new dependencies as part and parcel of the export of 'socialism' and makes them just as bankrupt as the mother country itself. Famine in Ethiopia, the upheavals in the Yemen, food-rationing in Cuba and Nicaragua give us some measure of the effects of 'socialist internationalism'. Moscow's imperialism is certainly unselfish in a grotesque sense of the word. . . .

BUKOVSKY: Blind and dogmatic would be a better way to describe it—and someone has to pay the bills. The urgency behind the present reform movement comes from Gorbachov's realisation that the Soviet economy will simply not be able to carry 'world socialism' on its back and compete, at the same time, with the US in the arms race. Who, then, will be footing the bills? Who, in fact is footing them now? Naturally, the hated and derided capitalist system.

The next question a reasonable man must ask is why is the West so obliging? My answer is that the Soviet Union, seeing itself as the hub of 'world socialism', has been conducting, as its *raison d'être* demands, a non-shooting war against the rest of the world over the last seven decades. Since Watergate and the US débâcle in Viet Nam, Soviet expansionism and the Soviet nuclear build-up have accelerated, and after a careful weighing of 'the correlation of forces' the Soviets seem to have come to the conclusion that they could now undermine the US as a world power by making trouble for it in its soft underbelly in Central America.

Through Cuba and Nicaragua they could reach Mexico, and if Mexico could be manipulated to turn itself into another Viet Nam or Nicaragua, American arms and attention would be so fully occupied on America's long southern border that NATO would become an orphan and the Soviets would come a mighty step closer to achieving the main objective of their entire post-War policy—that of detaching the US from Western Europe and becoming the dominant power on the Euro-Asian landmass. The 'Finlandisation'—and worse—of Western Europe would then be a heartbeat away.

URBAN: An outflanking movement on the grand scale. . . .

BUKOVSKY: Yes. The Soviets' earlier attempt to outflank Western Europe via the oil factor and Arab unrest in the Mediterranean failed; it is now the turn of Central America and with a much better prospect of success.

All these are, in effect, warlike actions. Western Europe and the US are under duress. The public can feel this; they can feel it but cannot deal with it. Their and their governments' reaction has been to put off the moment of truth by paying Danegeld to the Soviet Union.

Let's call a spade a spade: those American computers which have recently converted the antiquated machinery of the Romanian police-state into one of efficient oppression, and those West German steel-rolling mills which now augment Soviet military production (for example, the automated works in Lipetsk), are sophisticated bribes the West is paying to keep the Communists at bay—in addition to being lucrative business for short-sighted bankers and industrialists.

URBAN: What you're saying is that we are being 'held to ransom'.

BUKOVSKY: That is exactly what is happening. The Soviets are drawing a regular supplement to their budget from the Western taxpayer. He is now obliged to support not only his own country's military expenditure to protect him against the Soviet threat, but also the Soviet military budget, which makes that protection more and more difficult, and more and more expensive.

URBAN: But mightn't a hardbitten Western citizen argue that it is better to bribe the enemy and keep him quiet than to fight him? What's wrong (in an imperfect world) with appeasing a murderer if that stops him committing murder? When people like Genscher and Giscard say that we should somehow or other 'help the Soviet Union', and especially assist it in making a success of its new course under Gorbachov, that is what they really mean, although they aren't in a position to phrase it quite so candidly.

BUKOVSKY: Being held to Soviet ransom is not only dishonourable but also counter-productive. You will remember Lenin's phrase about 'useful idiots'—and the old Communist practice of passing the beggar's hat around when you are in difficulty, but punishing your benefactor as soon as you are out of it. The overall curve of Soviet policy since 1917 *vis-à-vis* the rest of the world shows rapid expansionism—I will not go into the details; the facts are well known. Bribes and appeasement have never stopped the Soviets from spreading their power across the world, using Marxism-Leninism as their passport, and periods of internal reform both under the Czars and under Soviet rule have been especially notorious for their expansionism.

Right now, under Gorbachov, the October Revolution is being remembered in these words on its 70th anniversary.

We live in a world which has changed profoundly under the influence of our Revolution. More than one-third of mankind has already cast off the fetters of capitalist exploitation. Socialism exists, it is developing, it is growing stronger as a world system. There are no more colonial empires—there are dozens of young sovereign states.

The forces of the international proletariat have multiplied and their interests are expressed by Marxist-Leninist communist and workers' parties. Mass, democratic, anti-imperialistic and anti-war movements are developing. The general crisis of capitalism is deepening.[6]

Such ideas are unlikely to be put in cold storage in response to aid-and-trade by the United States or West Germany.

URBAN: You mentioned 'the correlation of forces'—the Soviet term for 'linkage'. The USSR is a totalitarian country in a state of permanent mobilisation and with a message to the world. Linkage for a state of that sort is a natural policy and one relatively easy to put into practice. Not so for the Western world. I can foresee no set of circumstances— short of a 'shooting war'—under which any Western country would agree to put itself on a war footing. Nor can I foresee the West following a grand conceptual design to counter that of the Soviet Union, much less any willingness to link one issue to another or even to pursue a common economic policy. We will probably go on supplementing the Soviet military budget in the name of peace, and eliminate our own INF forces on the reasoning that the ramshackle Soviet system has ceased to be a threat.

BUKOVSKY: The ultimate cause of Western clay-footedness is twofold. First, the Western, and especially the American, inability to comprehend the conceptual character of the Soviet system and the ideological roots of Soviet policies. Second, the inability to come up with a conceptually-based policy of the West's own making, and the will to apply it consistently over a long period of time. Apart from Dr Henry Kissinger (who is intellectually a European), American politicians just do not think in conceptual terms, and have neither the sophistication nor the patience to challenge the Soviet leaders on their own ground. They could take a lesson or two from Gorbachov.

For all these reasons, my hope for a free world is not anchored in 'the free world'. It is anchored in the fallibility of the Soviet system, which has a fine record of having repeatedly saved the West from its own follies, and will no doubt do so again. I am just a little saddened to see that the world's most advanced nations should be so barren of ideas and deficient in will-power when offered an opportunity to take a hand in shaping the demise of Communism and the decline of the Soviet empire.

Notes

1. *Against All Hope: The Prison Memoirs of Armando Valladares*, (Hamish Hamilton, London 1986).
2. 'Again, when you pray, do not be like the hypocrites; they love to say their prayers standing up in synagogue and at the street-corners, for everyone to see them. I tell you this: they have their reward already. But when you pray, go into a room by yourself, shut the door, and pray to your Father who is there in the secret place; and your Father who sees what is secret will reward you.'
3. Harold J. Laski, *Law and Politics in Soviet Russia* (London 1935), p.21.
4. 'Each of us, if he honestly reviews the life he has led, without special pleading and concealment, will recall more than one occasion on which he pretended not to hear a cry for help, averted his indifferent eyes from an imploring gaze, burned letters and photographs which it was his duty to keep, forgot someone's name or dropped certain widows, turned his back on prisoners under escort, and—but of course—always voted, rose to his feet and applauded obscenities . . .

   Need I mention the common or garden informers, traitors and sadists of whom there must surely have been more than one million, or how could such an Archipelago have been managed?

   And if we now long . . . to go forward at last into a just, clean, honest society—how else can we do so except by shedding the burden of the past, except by repentance, for we are all guilty, all besmirched? We cannot convert the kingdom of universal falsehood into a kingdom of universal truth by even the cleverest and most skillfully contrived economic and social reforms: these are the wrong building bricks.'
   Alexander Solzhenitsyn, 'Repentance and Self-Limitation in the Life of Nations', in *From Under the Rubble* (Little, Brown and Co., Boston 1975, p. 118)
5. Lev Kopelev, *No Jail for Thought* (Secker & Warburg, London 1977), *Education of a True Believer* (Wildwood House, London 1981).
6. Address by the Central Committee (14 March 1987).

6. GIORGIO NAPOLITANO
Gorbachov and the Italian model

How much Political Pluralism?

URBAN: Italian Communism appears to be coming up for
yet another time of stock-taking and self-examination. Over
the past fifteen years or so, your Party saw the Soviet
Communist Party and the Soviet super-power as profound
threats to liberal democracy and the unconventional
character of Italian Communism. If the Soviet system overwhelmed Western Europe (so it was argued) all genuine
democracy there would perish, but it was especially feared—
and on good evidence—that a particularly unpleasant fate
would await the heretical Eurocommunists in Rome and
elsewhere. The annihilation of the Mensheviks and Social
Revolutionaries under Lenin and Stalin were your early
warnings, but the sailors of Kronstadt, the Central European Social Democrats, Imre Nagy and Alexander Dubček
fared no better. The only safe environment for Communism
to develop seemed to be Capitalism. Do these factors still
hold under Gorbachov?

NAPOLITANO: We believe that a difference certainly exists
between the foreign policy pursued by the Soviet Union
under Brezhnev and the one that is now unfolding before
our eyes under Gorbachov. It would, however, be an over-
hasty conclusion to say that the West can now do without
a defence and security policy or that the Warsaw Pact and
NATO will disappear by a process of natural attrition. We
are convinced that the West European countries and the
US must maintain the defensive North Atlantic Treaty
Organization and ensure that there is a military balance

with the Soviet-led alliance. At the same time, we believe that the West should seize every opportunity to reach agreement with Moscow on arms reduction and control, a safer military environment and mutual security accompanied by confidence-building measures.

In the 1970s, in the wake of the American defeat in Viet Nam, the Soviet Union took advantage of American demoralization and made heavy inroads in the Third World. It set in train a remarkable military build-up which culminated in the Soviet invasion of Afghanistan. But since the death of Brezhnev and the demise of the principal protagonists of his expansionist policies, a serious rethinking of the whole range of domestic and international policies has been going on in the Soviet Union under Gorbachov's leadership. Undeniably, the new Soviet leadership is more open to compromise than were its recent predecessors, and if we include, as we must, the psychological factor as one factor in international relations, then we are entitled to say that something has already changed for the better in the international climate.

URBAN: What you are saying is almost identical with the line taken by Conservative governments such as the British, German and French. That would seem to mean that you have, as a Communist Party, come to consider yourselves and your interests as indistinguishable from the old-fashioned notion of 'the national interest'.

NAPOLITANO: We want to promote a more propitious environment in international relations without jeopardising the independence and democratic values of the West European countries. By doing so, we stand for the Italian national interest too.

URBAN: You described the Soviet moves into the Third World in the 1970s as 'expansionism'. I am slightly surprised. I would have thought that even a reformist Communist Party such as yours would nevertheless stick to the convention that when Soviet power and influence are projected into new areas, those areas are drawn into the historically inevitable and 'progressive' domain of 'socialism' with all the improvements socialism is supposed to bring with it in terms of more human freedom, a juster economy, a more profound culture, international solidarity and the like. You do not seem to subscribe to that idea—

NAPOLITANO: No, we do not and have not done so for the last ten years, although earlier in our Party's history, we did use that kind of language. I would put it like this: in a different world-situation and at a different stage of our evolution as a Communist Party in Western Europe, we identified Moscow's international policies with the cause of peace, with the cause of socialism and with the cause of helping the national liberation movements in the Third World. We still think that up to the final defeat of colonialism the Soviet Union played a positive role in promoting the liberation struggle of the colonial peoples—

URBAN: —in cooperation, I think we should add, with the Americans who were, as the original de-colonisers, just as anxious to reduce the British, French, Dutch and Portuguese empires—

NAPOLITANO: Yes, in many respects, for a few years during and after the war, the two converged.

For a long time we found it difficult to see that the power-interests of the Soviet Union and those of the world socialist movement were different. We believed that Soviet foreign policy was so designed that it simultaneously served both the security interests of the Soviet state and the world-wide struggle for national liberation and socialism. But gradually we began to realise (and Enrico Berlinguer's courageous analysis helped us in this realisation) that the Soviet Union had become a super-power which saw itself involved in a global confrontation with another super-power and was trying to maximise its influence in the world. We began to see that the conflict of interests between the US and the USSR had its own logic which had less and less to do with socialism. The Soviet endeavour of trying to export the Soviet model of socialism and implant it in inhospitable conditions appeared to us absurd and self-defeating.

URBAN: So the equation mark between the Soviet model of socialism and genuine socialism is null and void for you?

NAPOLITANO: We reject that equation. At the same time we say that certain proposals put forward by the Soviet Union in the international area are useful and conducive to *détente* and a more peaceful environment. The 1987 US–Soviet negotiations about eliminating intermediate range missiles were one such development. Whether the proposal for a zero option was originally an American proposal is less important for us than the fact that it resulted in an arms reduction treaty.

URBAN: Signor Natta and his colleagues have been to Moscow to see Mr Gorbachov. How did and how do the Soviet leaders now react to your decision to stop identifying genuine socialism with the Soviet model of socialism?

NAPOLITANO: Oh, for a very long time they didn't like it. It is only since Gorbachov consolidated his position that our relations with the Soviet Party are less conflict-ridden. In the second half of the 1970s and the first of the 1980s the Soviet Party was ideologically hostile to us. We were regularly attacked in the press and relations between our two parties were practically frozen. The thaw was due to Gorbachov's initiative and is based on the premiss that each Communist Party is entitled to its own view as to what socialism is about and what strategy it should pursue. The Italian Communist Party no longer considers itself to be part of the international Communist movement because we do not recognise that any such movement exists. But we do say: let us, nevertheless, consider, in an atmosphere of mutual respect, concrete political issues and see whether there is room for agreement.

URBAN: After the 27th Soviet Party Congress in March 1987, the Italian Communist journalist Alberto Jacoviello observed in the pages of the newspaper *La Repubblica* that your Party was giving full backing to the Gorbachov line and resuming close relations with the CPSU—but with a difference. 'While in the past,' he wrote, 'our close relations were with the entire CPSU, whatever its position might be, now a distinction is made between the policy charted by the General Secretary and those forces within the CPSU that seem to resist this policy.' Does this accurately reflect the Party's view?

NAPOLITANO: Yes, it does. We are an independent Party. It is a happy occurrence for us if and when any political Party, whether in Italy or elsewhere, shares some of our convictions. To the extent that much of the leadership of the

CPSU is now recognizing the crisis of the old Soviet model of socialism and is pursuing radical reforms, we support that leadership. But we are not issuing a blank cheque to the CPSU or any part of it.

URBAN: Paolo Spriano, the Italian Communist historian, observed shortly before the 27th Party Congress (*l'Unità*, 16th January 1987) that there was a fundamental link, in the view of your Party, between the lack of freedom and democracy in the Soviet system, and economic waste, bureaucracy, stagnation and corruption 'that are today being bluntly described by Gorbachov and the ruling group gathered (at least so one hopes) around him . . .'

> We must openly say [he continued] that only through the affirmation of forms of true political democracy in the USSR (and this argument is, moreover, valid for all countries and societies of the East, from Czechoslovakia to China) will there be a qualitative leap, a historic innovation, an expansion of socialism.

I take it this expresses the views of the leadership of your Party?

NAPOLITANO: Spriano is a member of our Central Committee. That would by no means make all his views representative of Party policy, but it so happens that the passages you quoted express the views of our Party and of myself personally.

URBAN: A little later in the same article Spriano says, 'the system of the single party, and of a party that experienced the forms of repression and even degeneration to which Togliatti drew our attention more than 30 years ago, is a major obstacle to democratization.'

This would seem to mean that your Party is opposed to the single-party system in the Soviet Union. Is it?

NAPOLITANO: We are in favour of pluralism, both in the Soviet Union and in Eastern Europe. What form that pluralism should take is not for us to say. The Gorbachov leadership has come to realise that political pluralism has to be part and parcel of their reforms. In the first reform period Gorbachov more or less restricted himself to demanding economic change, but it didn't take him long to see that even economic reforms cannot be had if one does not recognise the existence of different social interests in

Soviet society and does not give them the freedom to express themselves. Soviet society is not a homogeneous society. It is made up of different social strata which want to be identified and see their interests institutionally protected—

URBAN. Which runs counter to the Communist claim that 70 years after the Revolution such conflicts no longer exist. Tatyana Zaslavskaya said in the US the other day (27th August 1987) that in her search for 'socio-national' interest groups she and her collaborators identified 75! Soviet reality seems to have given the lie to one of the most cherished official predictions.

NAPOLITANO: That is so. It is difficult to say when and how the Soviet Communists will embrace genuine political pluralism but they are, as I say, increasingly aware of a certain de facto pluralism in society and culture—and that is progress.

URBAN: Some of them, such as Fyodor Burlatsky who is known to be one of Gorbachov's close advisers, do call for 'social pluralism', but this can hardly mean more than tolerance for a greater variety of opinions *within* the Communist Party.

NAPOLITANO: The resistance to political change and fundamental economic reform is great, and the opponents of such change do not just come from the bureaucracy with its deeply rooted vested interests in the status quo, but also from many sections of the labour force who have got so used to secure jobs, poor productivity, minimal quality control, low discipline and non-legal perquisites that they look upon *perestroika* with suspicion. There is a national investment in inertia and apathy.

URBAN: The Soviet people's social contract with the State is said to be: 'You pay us little—we work little. You pay us badly—we work badly. As long as our jobs are secure—so is your power.'

NAPOLITANO: It is that contract Gorbachov is trying to end. The Soviet policy of egalitarianism adds to the troubles of the system because it prevents the economy from offering proper rewards to those highly skilled and dedicated to their work.

URBAN: —a malaise the 1968 Prague Spring was anxious to remove from 'socialist' societies of the Soviet type—

NAPOLITANO: Yes, and it is a bitter reflection that in 1968 Czechoslovakia suffered an invasion, and some of its socialist leaders and thinkers were sent to prison for having pioneered something very similar to what is now official Soviet policy. It is a terrible blot on the Soviet record. No wonder that Alexander Dubček chose Gorbachov's (Spring 1987) visit to Czechoslovakia, and then the 70th anniversary of the October Revolution to remind the Kremlin of the great injustice that had been done to the Prague reformers, and has now (10th January 1988) also voiced his complaint openly in the pages of *l'Unità*.

URBAN: Do you as a Party advocate complete political freedom as a desirable goal for Eastern Europe even if you do not think it is within the realm of the possible for the Soviet Union? Talking to a correspondent of *l'Espresso* you said recently that the success of the Gorbachov reforms would make it easier for the Soviet Union to have flexible relations with the East European 'socialist' countries because it would remove the 'fear of disruptive effects with regard to the balance between the two blocs'. What exactly did you mean?

NAPOLITANO: My meaning was simple: a new *détente* between the East and the West would favour more autonomy in the domestic and international policies of the East European countries and would make such autonomous policies more acceptable to Moscow. But after 40 years of socialism in Eastern Europe it is difficult to imagine that a multi-party system could be suddenly re-introduced there.

URBAN: But would it be, in your opinion, *desirable* to have several genuinely independent political parties? Gorbachov, for all we know, may be toying with certain ideas here that he cannot state publicly. Addressing representatives of the fraternal parties on 4th November 1987, he spoke of 'the arrogance of a belief in one's omniscience', and in his book[1] he admits (with, I think, bogus objectivity) that after the war 'serious problems arose' in Eastern Europe: 'Drawing on Soviet experience, some of these countries failed to consider their own specific history.'

NAPOLITANO: You ask: would we consider it desirable for Eastern Europe to return to a multi-party system? I do not exclude the possibility.

URBAN: Talking to Lucio Lombardo Radice, a member of the Central Committee of your Party in 1977, I raised a similar question. I wondered whether complete individual liberty (which Lombardo Radice strongly advocated) wouldn't necessarily imply 'the legitimacy of a variety of political programmes, including that of saying "no" to Socialism'? And this is what he said: 'I don't believe any such thing would happen. Would any part of the population want to see a regression from Socialism, a retreat from a higher form of society to a lower?' He said I was putting forward 'an impossible hypothesis'.[2]

NAPOLITANO: Well, those were Lombardo Radice's views in 1977. We believe in an open society and the rule of the ballot box. In Italy we are striving to be elected to power by scrupulously democratic means and would relinquish power if defeated. But when it comes to the East European states, you must remember several complicating factors. First, as I have said, 40 years represent almost two political generations. People who have never seen a multi-party system in action might find it difficult or even undesirable to try to work one. Second, we know very well, and so do the West European and US governments, that a drastic reversal of the regimes in Eastern Europe or a direct challenge to the equilibria between the East European regimes and the Soviet Union would lead to a dangerous destabilisation first in Europe and then possibly on a world scale.

URBAN: There are respectable arguments for saying that it is precisely the current state of relations between the Kremlin and its East European dependencies that is the cause of instability in Europe. As Czechs, Poles and Hungarians are, on the evidence of history, most unlikely to reconcile themselves to the perpetuation of their colonial status, stability can only come from a sea-change in Soviet attitudes. Gorbachov's declarations in his book *Perestroika* may be a token of such a change if we take his words at face value.

NAPOLITANO: Let me just say that the monolithic structures are already on the way out in some of the East and Central

European countries. In Poland, for example, power is, in fact, shared between the Party and the Church; and with the revitalisation of the Sejm and the introduction of various other policies of a more liberal nature the Government has taken certain steps on the road to pluralism even though that pluralism is as yet not wide enough. Hungary has cautiously broken with the single-candidate elections though not with the Party-approved nomination system. It allows a good deal of cultural freedom and foreign travel. The Churches, including the Jewish community, enjoy considerable liberty and there is good hope that the current economic difficulties will lead to further reforms, more political pluralism and a certain separation of Party and State. With the Gorbachov policies making rapid headway in the USSR, I have no doubt that in the other Central and East European countries, too, there will be growing pressures for change.

Revision of Old Dogmas

URBAN: Yet, the key words about Eastern Europe in Gorbachov's book *Perestroika*, do not go beyond Lombardo Radice's observations in 1977. While insisting that relations 'between socialist countries must be based on absolute independence', Gorbachov nevertheless observes that the 'problems' that arose in Hungary in 1956, Czechoslovakia in 1968 and in Poland both in 1956 and in the early 1980s were resolved 'differently' (a royal euphemism, that), noting with satisfaction that 'a return to the old order did not occur anywhere'. So crude a misrepresentation of history hardly needs comment, but what is implied here with great clarity is that while 'democratization' and other changes within 'socialism' will be encouraged or tolerated, a change from the 'socialist' system to some other system will not.

In other words, Gorbachov's statement can only be interpreted as meaning that the Brezhnev doctrine would be put into action again if, say, the Poles threatened to break away from the 'socialist' community. To make things absolutely clear, Gorbachov talks about the independence of each Communist *Party* and 'its right to decide the issues facing it in a sovereign way', but not about the independence of the nations themselves. His message is that the East

Europeans can have any kind of democracy as long as it is 'socialism'.

NAPOLITANO: Gorbachov's statement is, nevertheless, a tremendous advance on all previous Soviet positions. The very fact that he has publicly stated that relations between Moscow and the other socialist states have been most unsatisfactory and that he is urging immediate change in the direction of sovereignty and independence for Eastern Europe, is highly significant. He must realise that any talk of independence, sovereignty and national accountability— even if these are limited to the Party—offers hostages to fortune and may lead to renewed trouble in Eastern Europe. That he has, nevertheless, opened up this extremely delicate subject even though (as you say) he economised with the truth in telling the story of 1956 and 1968, earns my respect. Gorbachov has strong opposition. This is probably as far as he could safely go under present conditions.

URBAN: 'Finlandisation' comes to mind as an alternative that the peoples of Central and Eastern Europe would, in my judgement, be happy to accept. Might Gorbachov's thinking be heading that way?

NAPOLITANO: I don't know, but thinking as we must in power-political terms, I would doubt it. Perhaps in 1956 Moscow should have reacted to the Hungarian upheavals less violently. Perhaps Hungary's membership of the Warsaw Pact could have been replaced with a bilateral Soviet-Hungarian security treaty that would have satisfied both sides. But the Soviets acted otherwise. Finland has never been part of any power-bloc and has its own security relationship with the USSR which works well. Other countries could follow the Finnish example, enjoying complete domestic liberty while being reliable security partners of the Soviet state. But if this were to happen, the Soviet Union might perhaps see itself as having agreed to the retreat of socialism—or so a Finlandisation of Eastern Europe might be interpreted. I do not think this is on the cards. At the same time, please note that the ties between Moscow and the East European capitals are changing. It is clear from Gorbachov's articulations that each Communist Party in Eastern Europe is now responsible to its own nation and no one else.

URBAN: When an imperial power loses its will to rule and begins to take democracy seriously, the Empire tends to disintegrate. This is how the British and French empires came apart. Will the Soviet empire follow suit? I cannot see how a Polish or Hungarian Communist Party, once it is made accountable solely to the people and not to its sponsors in the Kremlin, could stay within the Warsaw Pact or even in power. Mightn't Gorbachov's 'new thinking' lead many people to think what has so far been unthinkable?

NAPOLITANO: I cannot agree with that. Many of the developments in Eastern Europe today are due to the interplay of purely domestic forces. The Hungarians began their cultural and economic reforms well before anyone else did and took them to exceptional lengths by Brezhnevite standards. The Romanians, on the other hand, have apparently acquiesced in a form of Stalinism without any sort of interference from Moscow. The Czechs, while paying lip service to the Soviet type of reforms, have decided to move slowly or not to move at all, but no one can say that the Soviets are interfering with the domestic affairs of Czechoslovakia in order to nudge them to fall into line.

URBAN: But should Gorbachov's 'new thinking' take root in all of Eastern Europe, wouldn't we be facing an entirely new ball-game—the abrogation of the 'divine right of the Party' and the arrival of 'constitutional Communism'.

NAPOLITANO: We would, and socialism would be none the worse for it. It would mean a return to the democratic and humanitarian essence of Marxism.

URBAN: You would not, as Italian Communists, be worried that so radically a different ball-game might lead to the evaporation of 'socialism' in Central and Eastern Europe?

NAPOLITANO: No, we would not.

URBAN: But in Soviet thinking—and, as I have just said, probably even in Gorbachov's 'new thinking'—a 'socialist' gain can never be surrendered.

NAPOLITANO: We do not share that view—we do not share it outside the borders of Italy any more than we do in Italy. Don't forget that in Marxist theory the dictatorship of the proletariat has always been conceived as a short *transition* to the final victory of the revolution. Once the revolution is firmly established, the dictatorship falls away. In the Soviet Union this transitional period has, for a variety of reasons, become a long one, but there is no reason why it should not now come to an end. It is, of course, very difficult to see how the rigid forms of 70 years of dictatorship can be made to dissolve, and Gorbachov could probably tell us more about those difficulties than anyone else. But *perestroika* is a valiant beginning which we hope will succeed.

URBAN: But there is a stumbling block in Communist theory that bothers me. It is an article of faith with Leninists that the Party and the Party alone is the repository of the *real* interests of the people. Free elections might reflect the will of the *majority*, but not what is *right*. You have already told me that you do not share that view, but do you think Gorbachov does?

NAPOLITANO: I cannot speak for him, but my guess would be that he does not share it either.

URBAN: But at the moment you accept single-party rule in the Soviet Union, don't you?

NAPOLITANO: We realistically say that this rule will continue.

URBAN: But do you think Gorbachov would be prepared to face free elections when the 'transition' has run its course?

NAPOLITANO: Yes, I do. Gorbachov's dilemma (if that is what it is) is less real than you might think. He is probably convinced that in the Soviet Union there would be a popular consensus for the rule of a democratised Communist Party if freer elections were held—

URBAN: A recent poll of Muscovites found strong disapproval of freeing political prisoners. That tells us something. Andrei Sakharov said the poll was most depressing. It is.

NAPOLITANO: Well, you must remember the historical context. Russian political culture and traditions are very different from, say, Czech political culture and traditions. The Russian people are almost wholly unversed in the intricacies of a multi-party system. Whether you and I like it or not, single-party rule is probably acceptable to most Russians. It is a rational hypothesis that genuinely free elections would confirm a reformed Communist Party in power. This would perhaps not be the case in the other socialist countries, but it might in the USSR. Another reason why Gorbachov might eventually go for freer elections is simply this: 70 years after the October Revolution the Party cannot possibly say that free elections are a risk and a luxury it cannot afford! It cannot possibly go on insisting three generations on that the Party is right, no matter what the Soviet people might think. Gorbachov himself is in no way deceiving himself that the Soviet people or, for that matter, he personally has learned all there is to know about democracy. With admirable humility he goes on telling us that not only the organisation of the economy and society, but the mental attitudes of the population and the Party too will have to be revolutionised and made ripe for democracy. A reader's letter in the now very open *Moscow News* asked the other day: 'How is it possible that 70 years after freedom and democracy are said to have been ushered in in our country we have to go to infant school to find out about democracy?' (or words to that effect). To which the editor said in reply: 'Yes, we have to educate ourselves in the ways of democracy.' I found this a courageous point to make.

URBAN: If one can extrapolate from the present curve of developments in the Soviet Union, won't a point soon be reached where the Gorbachov leadership will have to revise some of the most cherished tenets in Marxist-Leninist theory? Gorbachov's 'new thinking' points to such a revisionism *au fond*—indeed a number of important pronouncements in Gorbachov's speeches and in his book already display a good deal of commendable innovation, not to say heresy. Isn't it time for all Communist parties to sit down together and purge the theory of everything that has proven to be false prediction or unworkable?

NAPOLITANO: We in the Italian Party have long thought this was overdue and did so at our last two or three Party conferences. That is why we were in a great many ways at odds with the pre-Gorbachov Communist Party of the Soviet Union. Now the Soviet Party is well on its way to subjecting some old myths to realistic examination. Gorbachov and the Party have ceased to talk about a struggle to the end between socialism and capitalism. For example, in his book he specifically draws our attention to the fact that

Marxist-Leninists *used* to believe that the logic of imperialism would inevitably generate armed confrontations as well as revolutions in the capitalist countries. He tells us that Marxist-Leninists, therefore, *used to* forecast a third world war and the world-wide defeat of the capitalist system. But, he says, they do so no longer. The nuclear factor has rendered our planet too dangerous a place for such confrontations.

> We have now clearly 'divorced' the revolution and war themes, excluding from the new edition of the Party Programme the following phrase: 'Should the imperialist aggressors nevertheless venture to start a new world war, the peoples will no longer tolerate a system which drags them into devastating wars. They will sweep imperialism away and bury it.' This provision admitting the possibility of a new world war was withdrawn as not corresponding to the realities of the nuclear era.

Well, you can hardly ask for a more radical change—

URBAN: —heavily prepared for him by similar articulations by Khrushchev and Brezhnev—

NAPOLITANO: Yes, but Gorbachov seems to be making peaceful competition, and in many ways global cooperation between the two systems, a cardinal point in his 'new thinking'. He goes to the length of saying that Khrushchev's famous phrase 'We will bury you' did not mean what most people in the West thought it did.

But he goes even further than that. He tells us that there have emerged risks and problems in the world—the environmental crisis, nuclear energy, uncontrolled regional conflicts, famine, food production, the indebtedness of the third world—which cannot be resolved without global cooperation. Add to these the dangers of high technology, population growth, religious fanaticism especially in the Muslim world, and you have a vast panorama of urgent problems facing you which fifty years ago one could hardly imagine, much less offer cures for.

URBAN: Why not call a grand international conference—an epoch-making synod as the Church does from time to time—to read everything false and dated out of the movement and put it on a more realistic footing? I would have thought the Italian Communists would be best suited to do so because as a non-ruling Party they would have the kind of freedom the ruling parties do not have. In the light of all the things you have just said it would probably not be too difficult for you to make a simple but resounding declaration: 'At the end of the 20th century we are no longer a millenarian movement; we no longer preach violence; we do not believe there is a single set of answers to all the world's problems; we do not believe in proletarian internationalism; we do not believe in the socialisation of property; we do not believe the working class is getting poorer under capitalism—we are one of several democratic parties of the Left which speak for the underdog and have a humanitarian national programme.' That sort of thing.

NAPOLITANO: It is difficult to call a universal conference. Even the Socialist International which embraces many parties of the European Left and faces a similar assortment of problems has found it a quite formidable task to arrive at theoretically formulated conclusions that would be acceptable to all. But the Italian Communist Party does, both at its Congresses and at various cultural and theoretical forums, deal with these questions. For example, our position on private property is, and has been for a long time, that the nationalisation of all means of production is not only an insufficient condition for creating a progressive society but is unnecessary and undesirable. We repudiate the old model which looked upon industrial growth as an end in itself. It used to be believed by Communists that once the working class had seized power and the means of production had been collectivised and put in the hands of the State, the class struggle would end and social conflicts would disappear. Today it is widely realised that that analysis was false. Antagonisms of various kinds continue to exist in the USSR and Eastern Europe even though the adjective of 'class' is not appended to them. So we repudiate that theory too. I could go down a list of faulty assumptions and hopes, much longer than the one you have just given, to show you that in Western Europe at least a complete theoretical revision of some old dogmas is now well under way.

URBAN: Can you see the Soviet Communists doing likewise in the admittedly very different context in which they have to operate? The pronouncements of people like Aganbegyan, Shmelev, Zaslavskaya and others seem to indicate that we may be on the eve of a thoroughgoing *perestroika* in Soviet Communist theory as well. Above all, Gorbachov's own formulations lead me to suspect that for him *perestroika* is not just a matter of 'mending and making do' but one of drawing from his vision of 'new thinking' certain lessons that would apply to all the ills of the modern world. That this is, for a man hard put to it to rescue the 'socialist' system from the consequences of its own follies, an egregious conceit, goes without saying. But Gorbachov appears to be all set to pursue it. The very title of his book is an indication: *Perestroika: New Thinking for our Country and our World*; and in his speech to the festive session of the Central Committee and the Supreme Soviet on 2nd November 1987 he said: 'The new thinking, with its criteria which are those of the whole of mankind and its orientation upon reason and openness, has started to make its way in world affairs.' Utopia dies hard in Communist thinking.

NAPOLITANO: I don't believe that conditions in the USSR are ripe enough for the creation of an entirely new official Soviet platform. Gorbachov warned the Party recently that a 'sclerosis in the theoretical field' going back 50 years (not just to the Brezhnev era but to the 1930s) was hampering the work of *perestroika*, and we in the Italian Communist Party sincerely hope that the sclerosis will be removed. In the meantime we will just keep our eyes open for a Soviet re-examination of the entire Stalin period. Without it there can be no real regeneration. Gorbachov's speech at the 70th anniversary celebrations of the Revolution went only part of the way.

We shall now have to treat Gorbachov's policies pragmatically. There are still some dark spots in his vision. We'll have to test his propositions empirically and test them again and again. In the international field, the West should neither reject his initiatives as propaganda nor accept them at face value. In the meantime, we Italian Communists appreciate the important steps he has already taken in releasing dissidents, liberalising the media, generating what looks increasingly like public opinion, and creating possibilities for future pressures and much wider reforms. We are convinced that the changes he is now setting in motion will be very difficult to stop.

URBAN: But you would agree, wouldn't you, that in his

speech to the leaders of 'fraternal' parties (4th November 1987) Gorbachov already moved pretty close to what used to be thought of as heretical Italian Communist positions, and forecast precisely the sort of wholesale revision of Communist theory your Party has been pressing for? For example:

> Just as not all propositions of Marx and Engels could be dogmatically extrapolated to the imperialist epoch at the beginning of the century, so too the postulates of the 50s and 60s are of no use in assessing the world today . . .
> A new reading is needed of the theoretical legacy of our predecessors in the name of man's social emancipation . . .

To make things even more explicit, Gorbachov then invited all 'socialists and social democrats', and indeed 'all those who cherish the gains of the human spirit . . . to cooperate and join in the search'.

Couldn't these words have been spoken from an Italian Communist platform in 1987?

NAPOLITANO: Yes, they could. Gorbachov's speed is as impressive as the boldness (for Soviet conditions) of some of his pronouncements.

No Privileged Relations with Moscow

URBAN: When Vadim Zagladin of the CPSU was interviewed by *La Repubblica* (12th April 1986) about certain theoretical formulations that had been adopted by your 1986 Congress, he made a number of observations that put me on my guard. For example, he was asked what he thought about your Party's stand that it now considered itself to be an integral part of the European Left and no longer of the international Communist movement. Zagladin answered:

> this does not disturb us at all. There is the Communist movement; there is the Socialist International—in short, there is in Europe a Left that is not homogeneous . . . From this point of view we Soviets also consider ourselves an integral part of the European Left.

Would you accept that definition of the role of the Soviet Party?

NAPOLITANO: I most definitely would not. This is a malicious self-definition of the position of the Soviet Party. Zagladin was present at our 1986 Congress in Florence. He must have realised that when we re-defined our position as an integral part of the European left we meant—and we were absolutely clear on this point—the *West* European Left and *not* a European Left that would include Central and Eastern Europe. The Italian Communists and Socialists, and indeed most West European Communist and Socialist Parties, while wanting to have good relations with the ruling Communist Parties in Central and Eastern Europe, share a common attitude to democracy and civic freedoms which they definitely do not share with the ruling Communist Parties on the Soviet side of Europe. There is a set of fundamental historical and theoretical differences that separate our vision from that held by the Communist Parties in Eastern Europe. We in the West have developed our strategies in the framework of capitalist societies and liberal parliamentary democracies. Some of us—not all—support the Western military alliance as a defensive shield in a divided Europe. In other words: the profound differences that separate the West European Parties of the Left from the Communist Parties in Eastern Europe cannot be ignored. We are not parties of the same nature. We reject the implications of Zagladin's interpretation.

URBAN: I would have thought Zagladin's words could be given a different interpretation. 'If the Italian Communists say they are of the European Left—so are we. If they are accepted as reliable partners for cooperation by the European Social Democrats—so should we be accepted. Indeed, the Italian Communists might form a bridgehead for our acceptance as bona fide partners'—this is the sort of reasoning I seemed to detect behind Zagladin's thinking. It would be consistent with Gorbachov's calls for broad cooperation among all forces of the Left in pursuance of a global *perestroika*—a kind of 'popular front' for the nuclear age.

NAPOLITANO: I don't think the Soviet leadership needs a bridgehead in Western Europe. It has direct and very open relations with many Socialist and Social Democratic parties. We have absolutely no role to play in this and we would certainly not agree to serve as intermediaries.

A popular front? I don't think that is on the cards. The Soviet leaders are realistic enough to be aware that in Western Europe the parties most representative of the working class are the Socialist and Social Democratic parties. With the sole exception of the Italian CP the Communist parties have a limited influence. In other words, the basic ingredients for popular fronts of the 1930s type do not exist. There can be and has been cooperation between Communists and Socialists as, for instance, recently in France where the Socialists had much the better of the deal. In Italy? I can see no prospect for a popular front. Our Party occupies a unique position. It is large, wields great popular influence and has a completely different theoretical and practical programme from that of any other Communist Party. We may go in for alliances with the Socialists and minor progressive parties as the situation requires, but no popular fronts.

URBAN: You may have taken my hint about popular fronts too literally. My meaning was: the Soviet Union has a very real interest in creating mistrust between the US and Western Europe. With or without Gorbachov, decoupling one from the other continues to be a Soviet objective. In Western Europe some of the principal agents of mistrust of the US and often direct anti-Americanism are the sort of groups that tend to look to what you have called the progressive parties for leadership, such as your Party. Ethnic minorities, homosexuals, 'autonomous' organisations of various colours, 'peace-fighters', extra-parliamentary oppositions, some trade unions, liberation theologians and the like have come to wield a lot of influence in our media; their diffuse protest is much more likely to be given a meaningful political purpose by your leadership than by any other force in Western society. I would, therefore, infer that the Soviet leaders might be interested in using the Italian Communist Party as an agent of influence in the Western camp. They might hope to fan the flames of anti-Americanism by agreeing to see the Italian Communists have a foot in both camps. They would be of the European Left for West European consumption, but also 'one of us' because they are, after all, Communists.

NAPOLITANO: First, if the Soviet Communists really sought to pursue such objectives they would get nowhere. We are not available to be used by anyone. We have our own identity, our own ideas and our own political strategy, and that is enough. Second, the Soviets would be knocking on the wrong door because we are not an anti-American party. For example, in the very serious discussions leading up to our 1986 Congress and at the Congress itself we made ourselves crystal clear on this point. We said: We understand the feelings and concerns that inspire the peace movements of Western Europe; we recognise the fact that there is genuine fear of a nuclear confrontation on European soil, but we do not always identify our position with those of the peace movements, and that for two reasons. First, because we are not unilateralist disarmers on behalf of Italy or Western Europe—on the contrary, we believe in a balanced and controlled process of arms control. Second, because we harbour no anti-American ideology. Indeed, we want to develop close relations with all democratic and progressive forces in America and especially within the US Congress.

But there is another fact here we must discuss. If there existed, in the early 1980s, a certain feeling in Western Europe against the US and NATO, responsibility for that lay with the policies of the current US Administration. The Reagan Administration adopted policies on a number of vital issues—not only in the military field—that were so high-handed and unilateral that they provoked bitter responses in many places in Europe. There was the high interest rates' policy which sucked enormous amounts of European capital to America, the handling of the dollar, now the vast budget and trade deficits, and so on. Some of the anti-Americanism one may experience in Western Europe is, therefore, self-inflicted.

URBAN: You don't think West European anti-Americanism is also due to the fact that many West Europeans have, especially since the elevation of Gorbachov, 'gone soft' on the Soviet threat and are opposed to what remains of President Reagan's conservative foreign policy?

NAPOLITANO: I would say this: it is perhaps more broadly realised in Western Europe than in the US that the Soviet Union is in trouble on almost every front—its technology is backward, the economy is in dire straits, the level of military expenditure is unsustainable, the wound in Afghanistan is wide open and even the Party is involved in a profound self-questioning. The Europeans, being closer to the USSR and perhaps more experienced, can sense that what the Soviet Union now needs and needs badly is a long breathing space.

URBAN: Should we give the Soviets that breathing space? Should we help Gorbachov to get his country out of trouble even if a rejuvenated Soviet system may one day be a greater threat to us than is the faltering empire?

NAPOLITANO: 'Should we help him?' is not the right way of approaching the question. International relations are about mutual advantage, not charity. Agreements between nations always involve give-and-take. It is not only a Soviet but also a Western interest to cut military expenditure and reduce the level of military confrontation. Mutual security can be had at a lower level of preparedness in both the nuclear and conventional fields than exists at present. 'Sufficiency' is the code word and we support it. Arms control is of special concern to the European Left. We cannot pursue our political and moral obligations to the under-privileged and disadvantaged in our own societies and to the Third World as long as vast resources are pumped year after year into the world's various war-machines. We are, therefore, especially committed to disarmament, *détente* and peace. So it is not a question of 'helping' or not helping the USSR but seizing the opportunities that now exist for a more humane and intelligent global policy.

URBAN: The opponents of this process offer a cogent argument. *Perestroika* and the person of Gorbachov (they say) are a dangerous mixture. They will improve the performance of the Soviet economy, de-emphasise military expenditure, increase, up to a point, Soviet living standards and create a modest sense of cultural and personal liberty. These will make the Soviet threat *greater* not smaller, because they will create the impression that the Soviet system has undergone fundamental change whereas, in reality, it will remain the same unpleasant system but one that can fill the bellies of the population and elicit genuine loyalty. Gorbachov and his supporters (so runs the argument) do not want a different system—they want a more acceptable and therefore stronger Soviet system. That cannot be in our interest any more than a Nazi Germany that had given up

Belsen and replaced Hitler with a more civilised leader would have been in 1944. Can you fault that argument?

NAPOLITANO: Well, at meetings I have recently had with distinguished Americans I heard the opposite story, namely that a swiftly reforming USSR would represent a diminishing threat because beyond a certain point of restructuring the Soviet system would cease to be the Soviet system.

But to deal with your point that the Gorbachov reforms might make the Soviet system deceptively attractive—I don't think this is something for the near future. At the same time, important changes are occurring, as we have both said in this conversation, and I would warn against making too fine a distinction between 'fundamental' changes and 'formal' changes, because the 'formal' reforms can cumulatively amount to fundamental ones, and even small and piecemeal improvements can transform the character of the system from one of monolithic rigidity into something we can live with.

In the real world, such gradations are important. More freedom of information is better than no freedom of information. Some dissidents released from prison is better than no dissidents released from prison. No jamming of the majority of Western broadcasts is better than the almost universal jamming of Western broadcasts. Life is being made easier and more just for the man in the street in the Soviet Union. We cannot disapprove of that.

URBAN: Would you care to live under Soviet conditions as reformed by Gorbachov?

NAPOLITANO: No, I would find them unacceptable, but my starting point was the lamentable state of Soviet society *before* Gorbachov and the expectations of the *Soviet*, not the Italian, citizen. Seen from that point of view, there has been progress.

URBAN: Your Party was perhaps the first to diagnose the crisis of Communism world-wide. From China to Angola, there isn't a single Communist government that does not find itself in trouble, and I think the sources of trouble can be reduced (at any rate, for the purposes of this discussion) to two main factors: (1) the violence and coercion with which power has been acquired and practised, and (2) the rigid dogmatism of economic management. Whether we think of Deng's reforms in China, Gorbachov's in the USSR, the various Yugoslav and Hungarian attempts to defy the heritage of centralisation and party control—the whole body of Communist doctrine is now threatened. It is not only that Communism is poorly applied, but that Marxism and, *a fortiori*, Leninism do not seem to be applicable to human affairs on the eve of the 21st century. Gorbachov's great virtue is that he can sense this even though he cannot always say so. Are the present troubles the birthpangs of a new and sturdier Communist alternative?

NAPOLITANO: In their critique of the Soviet system, the leaders of our Party have often stated that the inspiration of the October Revolution has been exhausted. The thinking and practices of the ruling Communist Parties have become anachronistic. A completely new inspiration is required. The Chinese have done the necessary stocktaking and, with minor setbacks, changed course. It seems to us that Gorbachov is doing likewise. We hope that these trends will prove irreversible because their negation would have serious consequences.

URBAN: I notice that Alessandro Natta's and Gian Carlo Pajetta's visit to the Soviet Union for bilateral talks with the Soviet leaders (February 1986) produced a lively controversy on two theoretical points: whether 'proletarian internationalism' should be read out of the movement in favour of the non-belligerent Italian conception of a 'new internationalism', and the 'vanguard' role of Communist parties in the international workers' movement. It seems that— verbally, at least—Moscow conceded the first point, but I am not quite clear how the concept of the 'vanguard' was settled. According to an interview in *l'Unità* (9th February 1986) Natta objected to the Soviet insistence that the Communist Parties should call themselves 'vanguard' on the argument that in many countries they were clearly nothing of the sort.

NAPOLITANO: The 'vanguard role' of the Communist Party is a traditional and by now dated expression in the vocabulary of what used to be the world Communist movement. It denoted the hegemonistic leadership of the Communist Party within the working class movement. It claimed for the

Party some privileged right to leadership because it was allegedly equipped with an unerring and winning ideology.

We Italian Communists reject all that. We say more modestly that we are an important force of the West European Left. Of course, we compete with other parties of the Left and we hope to garner votes by the force of our arguments and our record, but we also cooperate with other parties of the Left because we are anxious to promote the solution of common problems. We have absolutely no desire to *lead* our partners of the Left as a Party of some unfailing Truth or Historical Necessity.

URBAN: But if you haven't the wind of history in your sails and have given up proletarian internationalism—what makes you different from any of the European Socialist parties? Isn't a large chunk of idealism, indeed utopia, the distinguishing mark of Communism and the secret of its (chequered) success? If I were a sensitive young Italian, I would not vote for you because you were promising better hospitals and a higher standard of living (any party can do that), but I might if you were saying 'fiat justitia et pereat mundus' (let justice be done, though the world perish). The Communist movement, it seems to me, is a secular religion or it is nothing.

NAPOLITANO: 'Utopia' is perhaps putting it too strongly— but I agree with you that we, as all parties of the Left, need idealistic long-term objectives. These must, however, be completely different from those that guided the thoughts of our political parents and grandparents. We see the survival of mankind endangered by a whole spectrum of cross-national and cross-ideological problems that require global planning and cooperation: the abuse of the biosphere, the husbandry of our non-replenishable resources, the poverty-gap between the Northern and Southern hemispheres, the problems of the depersonalisation of the individual in technological society, the coexistence of political and religious systems of different provenance and ideology, and so on.

URBAN: But there is surely nothing specifically 'Communist' about that programme. The Catholic Church would not have put it very differently. Gorbachov, who embraced in his 70th anniversary speech much of the 'Italian' agenda, nevertheless insisted that the solution of these transnational problems would by no means do away with competition between 'socialism' and 'capitalism'. You seem to have written it off, if I understand you correctly.

NAPOLITANO: You are right in saying that our programme is no different from that of all progressive forces and indeed some of the Catholic world. Our idiomatic way of putting it is: we are anxious to cooperate 'with progressive people both lay and Catholic'. Cooperation amongst us is not something for the future—it already exists in our day-to-day commitment to joint objectives.

URBAN: Suppose the Communist Party of the Soviet Union managed to reform itself to Italian standards—can you envisage a set of circumstances in which the Italian Communist Party would, once again, look to the Soviet Party for inspiration and support—as your leading pro-Soviet figure, Armando Cossutta, has suggested?

NAPOLITANO: Whatever Cossutta may have said, under no circumstances would we return to taking the Soviet Party for our model, or having privileged relations with it. Even if Gorbachov's reforms succeeded, we would maintain our complete ideological and political sovereignty. Our relations would remain strictly secular and bilateral—away from any ideological framework and away from any kind of common international organisation. The Soviet Party is one of many political parties for us with which we maintain cordial relations.

URBAN: In the 1970s your Party was anxious for a 'historic compromise' with the Christian Democrats in order to gain access to power. It didn't make it because the crisis of Christian Democracy was never deep enough, your popular vote never strong enough and the reputation of your Party for independence never credible enough to make *compromisso storico* a practical proposition. Do you think the Gorbachov reforms and the changing image of the Soviet system will make you more acceptable to the Italian political class and the electorate, if only because the Party would be relieved of the damaging 'K-factor'—the burden of long and slavish association with the Soviet system?

NAPOLITANO: I like to think that our eligibility for office will always be considered on the merit of our current programme and our recent record and not somebody else's. That the Soviet system is beginning to move closer to what we have long been saying and practising can certainly do us no harm. But we are not a function of Soviet politics. We do not march and we don't want to be seen to be marching in step with Soviet policies.

1988

Notes

1. *Perestroika*, (London, 1987).
2. See *Eurocommunism*, pp. 32–57.

7. MILOVAN DJILAS
New Utopias for old

Yugoslavia—Model or Anti-Model?

URBAN: A 'revolution within the revolution' is taking place in the Soviet Union—so we are told by the General Secretary of the Soviet Communist Party in his speech at Murmansk (10 October 1987)—'a revolution without shots, but a deep and serious one. . . .'[1] This is an astonishing claim. Gorbachov's language alone should give us pause, for there is nothing in the Marxist canons that would suggest that the revolution of the proletariat could be anything but the final consummation of History, from which a new order of man would arise 'free from taint of present vice and past depravity'.

How then, can the leader of the Party of the victorious proletariat talk about 'revolution' 70 years after the October Revolution? Was 'Great October' not that universal re-ordering of human affairs that Lenin, Stalin, Khrushchev and Brezhnev said it was? Was it flawed in some essential respects we have not been told about? Did it go wrong, and if it did, who or what group of individuals was strong enough to thwart the will of History? Such are some of the questions the Soviet citizen is bound to ask without expecting to receive proper answers.

'Can the dictatorship of the proletariat be revamped into anything approaching a free and democratic society?'—this is the question Gorbachov's *perestroika* raises for a disinterested historian, although it is not the one he is, on the face of it, asking of history. Whatever his rhetoric, Gorbachov appears to be content to pursue limited objectives. At home he seeks economic reconstruction and consumer satisfaction, and, abroad, strength based on an economically

and militarily powerful and well-respected Soviet system.
All this within a selectively applied Marxist-Leninist
ideology and under the rule of a single, albeit reformed
Party. These are, nevertheless, towering ambitions. The
General Secretary himself may well be wondering whether
the existing Soviet order is resilient enough to accommodate
them.

Two related questions come to mind. Can the Soviet
system reform itself to an extent that would cause an independent observer to say: 'The tyranny has gone—the system
remains—but men of compromise can now live with it
because it is, strictly speaking, no longer the Soviet system'?
Second, can the Yugoslav example of devolution from
totalitarianism to self-management and decentralisation
serve as a model for Mikhail Gorbachov and his supporters?

Djilas: The essence of any Communist system is the
monopolistic rule of society by the Communist Party.
Communism is about the possession of power. It is, moreover, about the possession of totalitarian power, because
Communism looks upon itself as fully entitled by the design
of history to change and to control *not only* man's
allegiances and behaviour as a political being, but also his
readings, his tastes, his leisure time and, indeed, the whole
of his private universe. Communism cannot, therefore,
transform itself into a free society. That would be squaring
the circle. What it can perhaps do, and what is now being
attempted in the Soviet Union, is to make improvements in
various economic and cultural areas, keeping them,
however, ostensibly at least, within the framework of the
existing ideology.

But let us be quite clear about one thing: the Soviet
leaders' attempt to reform the system is not inspired by
some noble realisation that the system is unjust or poorly
regarded abroad, but by hard necessity. They have come
to realise what other Communists in Yugoslavia, Poland,
Hungary, Czechoslovakia and China realised much earlier—
namely that Communism doesn't work. It works neither at
the economic level nor at the level of satisfying essential
human needs and liberties. Put all these factors side by side
with the rapid technological advance of the Western and
Far Eastern worlds and you cannot help realising that

Communism is a 19th-century relic and a prescription for disaster.

The Soviet leaders are now trying to draw level with the modern world. Like politicians everywhere and at all times, they want to save their bacon; and they have come to see that they cannot save it without making concessions to reality. But it is only the *methods* of Communist rule that are now being challenged, not the rationale and character of the rule itself.

URBAN: The crisis of Communism is, as you have hinted, worldwide, but what is, ideologically speaking, so interesting (though historically much to be expected) is the variety of forms dissent and rebellion have taken in a once uniform and centrally inspired World Communist movement. I can detect two very important, common characteristics: the flight from any central model or authority, and the grudging admission that the command economies have failed because economic planning and human nature are on a collision course.

All the other centrifugal characteristics we now see coming into play have to do with national identity, culture, religion and group interests. Kazakhs want to be Kazakhs; Armenians to be Armenians; and Estonians to be Estonians; and so on. The national—and racial—factor, long denied, derided or swept under the carpet by Marxist-Leninists, has reasserted itself. It will, I suspect, assert itself even more forcefully as Gorbachov's drive for economic decentralisation and autonomous management gathers disciples in unexpected places.

DJILAS: The crisis from Belgrade to Peking is continuous. Every Communist country suffers from the inbuilt inadequacies of the system. Most are now trying to put things right through piecemeal economic and social engineering. Those who offered more drastic remedies—the Hungarians in 1956 and the Czechoslovaks in 1968—were ruthlessly suppressed. (And I am, incidentally, not putting an equation mark between the two because they were differently inspired.) What we now have in the world is a kaleidoscope of Communist societies, each struggling to keep its head above water, each still militant in its rhetoric but straining to go its own way, even though some are not free to do so.

International Communism no longer exists as an organised force. What Communists still have in common is a joint vocabulary and the will to monopolistic power. That is a lot, but not enough. Moscow as the seat of the Communist papacy is gone. Stalin as the grand vizier is gone too. Any analysis of the roots of Communism in the world today has to be specific to the circumstances of each country. Few generalisations are possible except one—that Communism of the Soviet type is and will always remain totalitarian. The totalitarian character of the system may be more predominant, or less, depending on local conditions. But it is one of the iron laws of Soviet-style Communism that the moment there is a crisis and the survival of the system is threatened, the totalitarian component takes over.

URBAN: Would you say, in that case, that the Gorbachov initiatives are untypical? or will not prove to be lasting? After all, we are told by the General Secretary himself that the USSR is in a pre-crisis situation (even if not in a fully fledged one). If so, it is the old totalitarians who should be calling the shots if your reading of the system is correct, and not new-fangled reformers like Gorbachov.

DJILAS: The jury is still out on that question. The Soviet system is in an economic crisis, not (or not yet) in a general crisis of the sort that threatened Hungary's régime, for example, in the 1955–56 period. We shall have to wait and see how the Soviet economic crisis develops and how the totalitarians react to Gorbachov's rescue operation. The Ligachevs and Chebrikovs make no secret of their fears that the Gorbachov reforms may explode in their faces—as they may well do.

URBAN: Instinctive return to a protective old orthodoxy is a standard reaction in every human crisis, whether collective or individual. 'Hold on to nurse for fear of worse.'

The Communists, too, behave like that, only more so because they are nature's zealots. Your study of Tito provides a telling illustration of the flight to orthodoxy in Communist thinking. I have in mind the passage where you and Tito discuss the kind of political freedom Yugoslavia should be given after the triumph of Communism.

DJILAS: I suggested to Tito that we should allow for an opposition—and free elections. Tito said that we should phrase the laws in such a way that free elections were on the statute books but the Communists would, nevertheless, always retain the monopoly of power. It was, he argued, unacceptable for Communists to suppose that they could be ejected from power by the whims of an electorate once they had been installed in power by the will of history (or words to that effect). He reacted as a typical Communist.

URBAN: I find the Communists' contempt for the will of the majority and their parallel insistence on the 'democratic' character of their system endlessly fascinating. 'Democracy is not identical with majority rule . . . Democracy is . . . an organization for the systematic use of violence by one class against another', Lenin observed in *The State and Revolution*. And, quite recently, Teresa Toranska, in her compelling interviews with some of the Stalinist Polish old-guard[2] elicited these words from Poland's once powerful Jakub Berman:

> . . . in an election, we can't go by the criterion of the majority, because there isn't any one we can hand over power to . . . Well, whom would you have had us hand over power to? To Mikolajczyk, perhaps? . . . You'll be telling me in a moment it would have been democratic if we had. So what? Who needs that kind of democracy? And we can have no more free elections now than we could ten or twenty years ago, even less so, because we'd lose. There is no doubt about that. So what's the point of such an election?

DJILAS: A typical ultra-conservative attitude. Yet we must not allow it to colour all our judgements about the renewability of Communism. The arrival of Mikhail Gorbachov demonstrates what some of us have long suspected—that certain indigenous Communist parties, notably the Yugoslav and the Soviet, have sufficient inner resources left in them to shed the Stalinist incrustations and make a fresh start. The Soviet Party did have democratic features in its early history. Gorbachov is trying to water that desiccated plant and revive it. It is not an easy task because, even under Lenin, Soviet democracy was a highly limited affair— nothing a man sitting in Westminster or in the *Bundestag* would recognise as democracy.

URBAN: Would Gorbachov be aided by the Yugoslav

model? Until Tito's death that model attracted many admirers and emulators in some of the East European Communist parties. More recently, however, Yugoslavia itself has fallen on hard times. The economy is in dire straits, corruption is rife, and the Republics are drawing apart.

DJILAS: Yugoslavia is both an example and a counter-example. It is an example in the sense that it demonstrates the reality of the conflict between the totalitarian and reformist wings of any Communist Party and the possibility of the defeat of the totalitarians. It is a counter-example in the sense that a speedy devolution of power from the centre to the autonomous constituent Republics can lead to chaos.

I take the positive model first. Yugoslavia has become a kind of laboratory for the destiny of Communism world-wide. The show (even if not the reality) of self-management, cultural liberalisation, local autonomy, economic partnership with the West, has marked her out as a front runner. But, more important, the Party is also vaguely groping for a re-conceptualisation of the whole Communist experiment. The conservative old-guard has not been finally defeated, but it is in a minority and probably in permanent opposition. At the same time, the 'reformers' cannot be said to be in power either. The majority of Yugoslav Communists are in a state of alienation and grave disaffection, and so is the majority of the population outside the Party. Between them they keep the Stalinist hardliners at bay and the leadership under pressure—without quite knowing how precisely to set about reforming the system and attracting public support.

Local autonomy has led to great variations in the hard-line/softline spectrum. Semi-independent fiefdoms have developed—some hardline such as the Republic of Bosnia, and some liberal such as Slovenia. Centrifugal nationalistic interests are frequently intertwined with vested personal and institutional interests. If Yugoslavia is a positive model, it is easier to *feel* than to describe what it is; and that may not be too helpful to Gorbachov.

URBAN: Then, in the final analysis, Yugoslavia demonstrates a reckoning with paleo-Communism of whatever provenance, and probably a recognition that the whole idea of putting Leninism into practice is absurd.

DJILAS: It does both, but let me add a note of caution. As

paleo-Communism is now a relic, so the language of old-fashioned anti-Communism should be. There is a kind of gutter-critique of Communist thinking that was probably justified by its effects during the Cold War but is now wholly counter-productive. It is puerile to say that 'all Communists are tarred with the same brush' or 'once a Communist always a Communist'. That sort of rhetoric, quite apart from being false, now plays directly into the hands of the old guard. I am, of course, not saying that we should soften our critique of Communism as a flawed or even impossible social system. But we should address the system with the serious-ness and intellectual discernment it deserves. Millions of people have, willy nilly, come to live under Communism. We owe it to them to offer an intellectually respectable, well-argued, and realistic alternative. The Hollywood-type of anti-Communism will not do. We have seen too much sloganeering, and too little mature assimilation of the social and intellectual history of Marxism and Leninism.

URBAN: But isn't it possible that too much study of the history and of the rationale of Communism tends to make us subliminally accept the Marxist-Leninists' terms of refer-ence? Hasn't it happened in many foreign ministries and research establishments? And doesn't this approach under-mine our ability to think about Communism with complete freedom? American conservatives of the country club type tend to say: 'Don't plague us with the "theology". We know perfectly well what's wrong with Communism without having to bother our heads about its indigestible literature. We can tell an evil system when we see one. . . .' That sort of approach was President Reagan's great strength early in his Presidency, and it put the Kremlin on the defensive.

DJILAS: There is no case for that approach now. Are you suggesting that a judge who is sophisticated enough to study the jargon of the thieves who will come before him becomes their accomplice? Of course he doesn't. But he has to under-stand, when considering the case, what the defendants are talking about.

URBAN: The moment we adopt words such as *glasnost* and *perestroika* in English, French, German or Italian we buy a good deal of Mikhail Gorbachov's thinking with them. He is aware of this and is proud of it. Isn't that a warning that the 'crude' American conservatives may have a better instinctive understanding of what the Communist system is about than trendy journalists and policy-pundits?

DJILAS: No. The answer to a foggy understanding of the Soviet system is a clear understanding of the Soviet system. The answer to subliminal propaganda is reason and the knowledge of history. You can't cut corners in the study of human affairs.

URBAN: I would have thought Gorbachov would do well to extract at least one practical lesson from recent developments in Yugoslavia—the rising vulnerability of the 'dominant' nation in a multi-racial state, once decentralisation has taken effect. I am thinking of a by now famous 'unfinished memorandum' of the Serbian Academy of September 1986.

DJILAS: Well, this remarkable document did indeed give an important warning. It claimed that the largest nation in Yugoslavia has been reduced to unequal status, not least because the Serbs (unlike their neighbours in Croatia and Slovenia) have not been allowed to create their own state, or to use their own language or alphabet. The academicians said that this inferiority of the Serbs *vis-à-vis* the other nations of Yugoslavia was due largely to the 1974 Constitution which had turned the country's Federal system into a loose Confederation. Individual republics had acquired the right to veto the will of the majority, and the Serbs came to be looked upon as 'hegemonists', 'centralisers' and 'policemen'.

URBAN: Wouldn't all this have a familiar ring to people like Alexander Zinoviev, Vladimir Maximov and Alexander Solzhenitsyn? They would argue (as, in fact, they have done) that in the Soviet Union, too, it is the dominant nation that is now the underdog. It is the Russian heritage, they would claim, that has been distorted by an imported ideology. It is Russian living standards that are way below those of the Baltic republics, Armenia and Georgia. Disproportionate numbers of the most influential jobs are being held down by non-Russians in the *apparat*, in the armed forces and in culture. Russia is being de-Russified, they argue, and deprived of its character. These have become favourite Russian themes in the Soviet Union; and they have their followers within and outside the Party.

I would have thought Gorbachov would be well advised *not* to follow the Yugoslav example if the status of the Russian nation within the Union is dear to him. The question is: Can he sustain democratisation and openness as his key policies without giving fresh relevance to the right of national self-determination as guaranteed in Article 70 of the current Soviet Constitution? What would there be to prevent Armenians, Uzbeks, Kazakhs, Latvians and Ukrainians from saying: 'Democracy must surely begin at home— we want our own form of government and our independence'?

In a remarkable appeal to the 19th All-Union Party Conference, the Plenum of the boards of the Estonian 'Creative Unions' has already said so, and has had its message printed in the official press:[3]

> It is relations between the Republics and the Union bodies, joined voluntarily to form the Soviet Union, which are at issue here. It is the need to re-establish the Leninist principles of sovereignty and equal rights.

And if this were not explicit enough, Heinz Valk, a rank and file member, reminded the Plenum:

> Nigol Andresen [one of the first Estonian People's Commissars] said on 22 July 1940: 'The joining of the Socialist People's Union as a nation, as a formerly separate state, should not be understood by others, who are evil-minded thinkers, as the abolition of our independence. . . .' At the same time, however, a man who is well known to us was twirling his moustache in the Kremlin and thought of the matter quite differently . . . according to Article 60 of the Estonian SSR Constitution, Estonia is indeed a sovereign state. . . . Why is it that a sovereign state, which can decide its affairs independently, must ask Moscow even for permission to publish a newspaper?[4]

DJILAS: The analogy between Serbs and Russians is tempting but not quite right. The Serbs are not a hegemonistic nation in Yugoslavia; the Russians are *very* much a hegemonistic people in the Soviet Union (whatever Solzhenitsyn, Maximov, Zinoviev and their followers may be saying to the contrary). True, Great Russian nationalism is, officially at least, not much in evidence *qua* nationalism; but the elder-brother role of the Russian nation through the

Communist Party of the Soviet Union and the imperial bureaucracy is crystal clear and openly cultivated. For example, until not so many years ago, the national anthem of the Azerbaidzhan Republic contained these words: 'The mighty Russian brother is bringing to the land the triumph of freedom and with our blood we have strengthened our friendship and our kinship with him. . . .'

URBAN: Even today, the Uzbeks start their anthem with the phrase: 'Hail, Russian brother, great is your people!'

DJILAS: In other words, the Czarist legacy is alive and well. Centralisation, linguistic imperialism, the denationalisation of ethnic cultures of large parts of the Soviet Union, notably of the Ukraine and Byelorussia, are long-standing features of Soviet life. They have grown out of Russian history which is a history of centralisation and of expansion.[5]

Russia did not follow the European path from nationhood to statehood. Muscovy came first—the Russian sense of nationhood came later. Hence the Russian people's obsessive fear that the state may disintegrate; that if the state loses its grip, the Russian nation may fall to be gravely weakened. That the Communist system, too, promotes centralisation for its own reasons is a bonus and a happy coincidence.

None of this is true for the Serbs. The erosion of Serb standing among the nations of Yugoslavia cannot, therefore, be quoted as a warning to Gorbachov without a great many qualifications.

But you are right in saying that 'openness', 'democratisation', and 'restructuring' give hostages to fortune in their own right. One cannot, as Gorbachov and his friends do, preach the freedom of the spirit, democratic participation and individual initiative without encouraging the Ukrainian citizen to ask: 'And why should I be taught in the Russian language when my language is Ukrainian?'. Or Estonians to protest: 'We don't want to be swamped by Russians in our cities—put a limit on Russian immigration'. Or Armenians—including Armenian Communists—to demand the revision of their Republic's frontiers, as they have, in fact, done in the case of Nagorno-Karabakh?

Gorbachov and his friends preach to the Soviet people every day of the week about the 'truth' which, they say, can at long last be openly spoken in Soviet society. After 50 years of suppressing the truth, Viktor Yakovlev reported in Kaluga Oblast (14 July 1987), 'our collective return to the truth'. If this is so, I can hardly imagine how the truth of national self-determination or the 'truth that socialism may not be everyone's choice of an ideal society' can be barred from open discussion, or divorced from the process of democratic 'restructuring'. For many people *glasnost* and *perestroika* may mean precisely non-socialism and independence.

URBAN: Such claims, still scored in the approved key, are already being widely heard, and Gorbachov does not like them. At his meeting with representatives of the Soviet media (in July 1987) the following exchange was recorded (*Pravda*, 14 July 1987):

> A. A. Belyayev (Editor-in-Chief of *Sovietskaya Kultura*): The awareness of the international essence of Soviet socialist culture is disappearing from the speeches of certain personalities in the arts who advocate the originality and purity of national cultures.
> M. S. Gorbachov: Every people has its language, its history, it wants to understand its roots. Can that be contrary to socialism? Of course not. But on the other hand, if someone retires into himself, struts about and starts passing this off as an absolute value—that is unacceptable.

Echoing Gorbachov but speaking more openly in Hungary, Alexander Yakovlev put the Soviet fears bluntly (Hungarian TV, 30 July 1987).

> Nationality policy requires special tact and extreme sensitivity. When any kind of friction starts to develop regarding the nationalities, this can swell into an avalanche irrespective of the endeavours or wishes of this or that person.

DJILAS: The Armenian–Azerbaidzhani conflict has proved Alexander Yakovlev only too right. On 9 July 1988, in Vilnius, a large gathering of more than 100,000 people, representing the three Baltic Republics and a pro-*perestroika* group from Byelorussia, heard calls supporting the Armenian plea for the self-determination of Nagorno-Karabakh. The call of nationalism travels with great speed.

The Soviet leaders *are* worried, and with good reason. Shortly after Gorbachov's visit to Yugoslavia, Fyodor Burlatsky warned: 'Yugoslavia shows us the limits of decentralisation. . . . We have to lessen central power, but not go as far as Yugoslavia. . . .'

But let me add, before we lose the point, that there is, of course, a small element of truth in the Solzhenitsyn–Zinoviev–Maximov type of argument about the 'unequal' state of the Russian nation. It is true that the ordinary Russian bears the main burden of empire, without sharing its blessings. But the fact is: almost every Russian, lowly or elevated, embraces with enthusiasm the idea of Russian aggrandisement and takes it for granted that he has to make sacrifices for it. He compensates for these sacrifices by the conscious enjoyment of Russian hegemony—a hegemony which is now donning the mantle of 'socialism'.

Lenin who was, by Russian standards, tolerant towards the non-Russian nations of the empire and was hard on 'Great Russian chauvinism'[6] nevertheless reconquered almost all those bits of the Czarist Empire that had taken pre-1917 Bolshevik propaganda seriously and seceded from the new Communist state. He quashed Ukrainian independence; retook Georgia after the Georgians had been solemnly assured (in the Treaty of 7 May 1920) that their independence would be respected; invaded Khiva and Bukhara; and so on. By the end of the Civil War all parts of the far-flung Czarist Empire were back under Bolshevik Russian rule with the exception of Finland, Poland, and the Baltic states (which had become independent under international recognition) and Bessarabia (which had been annexed by Romania).

URBAN: What you are saying is that even a reforming and apparently tolerant Gorbachov, with *glasnost* and democratisation on his lips, would not permit his ideas to be translated into independent national, much less separatist, policies, no matter what the Soviet Constitution may be saying about 'self-determination' and, indeed (under Article 72) about the right of every Republic 'freely to secede from the USSR'?

DJILAS: That is what I believe to be the case. In Communist theory 'socialism' is a superior form of social organisation for nations which are supposed to be transitional ('consciousness lagging behind life'). This is, clearly, rubbish. But it has always given the Soviet leaders an excellent excuse for denying restive Uzbeks and Tatars self-determination and their right to independence.

Mind you, my impression is that Gorbachov will have to

go a long way towards meeting national and ethnic demands, even if he does not underwrite the independence of his colonial territories. The logic of his own propaganda will confront him, in Hegelian fashion, with some highly unexpected and unpleasant consequences. This may not be a bad time for the Baltic nations, the Ukrainians, the Uzbeks and others to come forward with their demands— as the Armenians have already done, and the Estonians and Latvians are in the process of doing. For a start, the Soviet leadership would have to agree to respect the Soviet Constitution and to live up to their commitments under principle VIII of the Helsinki Accords which spells out every nation's right to self-determination. The resolution of the All-Union 19th Party Conference on the 'relations between nationalities' has fudged the issue.

URBAN: The problem (as Moscow would see it) with the Armenian demand for the re-incorporation of Nagorno-Karabakh in the Armenian Republic was that it had, originally, no anti-Russian or anti-'socialist' edge. It fed on the ancient Armenian conflict with Islam and the injustices of Stalin's nationality policy. It was, therefore, difficult— though not impossible—to brand it as 'nationalism' and 'extremism'.

Doesn't the ethnic distribution of Armenian Christians inside Azerbaidzhan and of Muslim Azeris in Armenia— and the current tension between the two nations—remind you of the terrible things that happened to Serbs living in Croatia and Croats living in Serbia during World War II?

DJILAS: Yes, it does; but there is an important difference. In pre-Communist Yugoslavia, no one imagined that the state, or its governing philosophy, offered a magical cure for the elimination of national conflicts. Communism does make such a claim. Consequently, the Armenian upheavals strike at the very heart of the contention ('myth' would be a more appropriate word) that proletarian consciousness, Soviet rule and 'internationalism' automatically heal the feuds and absorb the conflicts among nations. Of the many misconceptions underlying Communist rule, this may turn out to be the most lethal.

URBAN: Article 78 of the present Constitution says that the boundaries of the USSR's Republics may be changed only by the agreement of the Republics concerned and with Moscow's approval.

DJILAS: This will make Gorbachov's job even more difficult, for I cannot see the Azeris agreeing to surrender Nagorno-Karabakh, or how Moscow could overrule them—assuming that it wished to, which it does not. It has, in fact, decided to suppress the Armenian protest.

The 23 March 1988 resolution of the Praesidium of the USSR makes the point that giving way to the Armenian demand would spell the end of the 'friendship of the peoples of the USSR as an integral, federal, multinational state'. It would lead to 'unpredictable consequences'. And so it might! Yet, on 12 July 1988, the Governing Council (Soviet) of Nagorno-Karabakh announced its secession from Azerbaidzhan and declared itself an autonomous region of Armenia under the ancient Armenian name of Artsakh—which the Azerbaidzhani Supreme Council immediately rejected.

Remember Gorbachov's words in his 70th anniversary oration. In 1917, he said, 'mankind crossed the threshold of real history . . . we departed the old world and irreversibly rejected it.' Well, Nagorno-Karabakh demonstrates that, stripped of the Utopian rhetoric, Soviet reality bears an uncanny resemblance to the 'old world' which has after all, not been so 'irreversibly' rejected.

'The New Class' As Early Warning

URBAN: As long as the Russian element, both inside and outside the Communist establishment, persists in believing that it has a right to rule, one cannot see how regional bids for independence, or even 'sovereignty', Soviet-style, can be successful. And there are no signs that the Russian nation would allow its estate to shrink. In the matter of 'Empire', the Party and the Russian nation seem to speak with one voice. The loss of a Union Republic would be a blow to Russian hegemony and it would probably spell the end of the Soviet Union as well as Gorbachov himself. Aren't we, therefore, unduly optimistic in expecting that Gorbachov will live up to his words on the peripheries of the Empire—or else admit that the 'truth' that is relevant to economic *perestroika* does not apply to 'the colonies'?

DJILAS: The Soviet Communists have never shrunk from locking up loquacious mullahs and suppressing 'bourgeois nationalism'. Of course, Gorbachov and his men do not relish the prospect of Muslim fundamentalism reaching their own Muslim territories from Iran, for example. But they can deal with it so long as the disease stays outside the Party and the *apparat*. They are experts at suppressing nationalism and organised religion. What they must be worried about is the penetration of the *Party* and the *bureaucracy* by nationalism and religion. When the local Party, too, wants to pull away from the Centre because it is closer to the nation it rules than to the power-holders in Moscow—that is when the alarm bells should start ringing in the Kremlin. And this is what appears to have happened in Alma Ata and is now happening, on a much larger scale, in Nagorno-Karabakh and in the Baltic republics. In Kazakhstan, Gorbachov used the whip hand because he would take no risks with the Empire. He then packed the Kazakh leadership with Russians and had the ringleaders punished. He behaved very much like a competent Czar.

URBAN: The 'indigenisation' of Bolshevism has produced some unexpected consequences. It was Stalin's fervent ambition that 'indigenisation' would deepen the roots of Soviet rule in the peripheral national communities. And so it did, under Stalin. Under Gorbachov, however, it seems to be promoting the 'nationalisation' of the local Party and the *apparat*, with the results we now witness with increasing frequency. In Armenia and Nagorno-Karabakh, the administrative apparatus as well as the Armenian Church under Vazgen I, the Supreme Patriarch, came out openly (26 February 1988) in support of attaching Nagorno-Karabakh to Soviet Armenia. Some of the first calls for the rehabilitation of the victims of Stalin came from within the Latvian and Estonian Communist establishments.

But coming back to Yugoslavia: in the matter of regional independence the Yugoslav model must surely strike Gorbachov as, literally, counter-productive. Liberalisation of the Federal structure has turned Yugoslavia into so many ministates: each with its opinionated and often recalcitrant local leadership, and each conceiving of itself as a self-contained oligarchy (tempered, though, by degrees of corruption commensurate with local tradition). Whatever Gorbachov may think of the successes (such as they are) of the self-management system, he cannot want to go down the road of Federal decentralisation.

DJILAS: No, he cannot. But I can quite see why those who want the Soviet Union to disintegrate encourage him to follow 'the Yugoslav model' Bids for various forms of national separatism are now openly made in Yugoslavia. In Slovenia, where criticism of the central government is strongest, influential people argue for an 'independent Slovenia' in the European Community. In 1971, some Croats, too, wanted autonomy under the UN, a separate currency and the reform of certain institutions—because Croatia, in their view, had become the paymaster of the poorer Republics. Even in Serbia, a feeling of disaffection with the Federal state is now gaining ground, partly because Belgrade has been unable to defend the lives and property of Serbs in the Albanian province of Kosovo, and partly for the reasons we have quoted from the memorandum of the Serbian Academy.

URBAN: I suppose Gorbachov would be equally ill-advised to take his cue from the state of the Yugoslav League of Communists?

DJILAS: Yes, he would. The Yugoslav League of Communists is in deep crisis, not only because of its poor social and economic performance, but because it is split, in reality, into eight parties. Each represents the interests of a national Republican constituency. The bonds uniting them in Belgrade are weak; they all pull in separate directions. They are united, though, in their distrust of what they call the Federal Party. On the surface they are not anti-Yugoslav or anti-Serbian, but their suspicion of the central bureaucracy does make it seem to many Serbs that they are hostile to the most numerous nation in the Federation. In short: the story of the decentralisation of Communism in Yugoslavia along national lines is bad news for Gorbachov.

URBAN: How is the spirit of Gorbachov's reforms going to affect the future of Moscow's East and Central European dependencies? The Soviet–Yugoslav Declaration (of 19 March 1988) appears to have repudiated the Brezhnev Doctrine. It contains, in Section II devoted to inter-Party relations, these words:

Proceeding from the conviction that no one has a monopoly of the truth, the sides declare their lack of any claim to impose their own ideas about social development upon anyone else whomsoever.

Even more important, in the inter-State section, the Soviet Union and Yugoslavia

confirm ttheir commitment to the policy of peace and the independence of the peoples and countries, their equality of rights, the equal security of all countries irrespective of their size and potential, socio-political system, the ideas by which they are guided and the forms and character of their associations with other states or their geographical position.

I would be surprised if some of the East and Central European nations did not conclude that the time was ripe for fresh moves to be made to free them from the apron strings of the Kremlin. And this feeling would, in some cases, be as strong within the Parties as with the public in general. In Hungary, for example, a bold but cautiously formulated 'social contract' has been drafted by one influential group of dissidents. It foresees what one might call 'Constitutional Communism' and some recovery of Hungarian independence within a more tolerant and economically weakened Soviet Empire. It would, above all, do away with the extra-legal status of the Communist Party and subject it to the control of a duly elected parliament. Another and more radical group ('Network of Free Initiatives') calls for a multi-party system and the removal of Soviet troops from Hungary.

The intriguing question is: have the Gorbachov reforms put the 'national question' on the agenda? In a recent lecture (in London on 28 January 1988), Zbigniew Brzezinski said that they have.

The region as a whole [Brzezinski observed] is experiencing today both political liberalisation and economic retrogression—a classic formula . . . for revolution . . . It is not inappropriate to pose the historically pregnant question of whether the year 1988 might not be initiating the new 'Spring of Nations' in Europe, a parallel to 1848. It is no exaggeration to affirm that there are five countries now in Eastern Europe, each of which is potentially ripe for a revolutionary explosion. It is no exaggeration to say that this could happen in more than one at the same time.

DJILAS: First, I do not take the 'repudiation' of the Brezhnev doctrine at face value. In 1955, Khrushchev and

Bulganin 'went to Canossa' in Belgrade. A Declaration was signed which was every bit as forceful in asserting each country's right to absolute sovereignty and to non-interference in each other's internal affairs 'for whatever reason', as is the March 1988 joint Declaration. Yet, one year later, the Soviet Union was threatening Poland and crushing the Hungarian Uprising, and in 1968 it suppressed the Prague Reform movement.[7]

Second, the national question is not yet openly on the agenda in Eastern Europe, but I have no doubt that, if the pace in Moscow continues, it will be put there. I do not, however, believe that the pattern of 1956 will be repeated. Khrushchev's revelations about Stalinism led to the rise of Gomulka in Poland, which in turn sparked off the Hungarian Uprising. Gorbachov appears to be a man of much greater intelligence, prudence and foresight than Khrushchev. He has, so far at least, not held up Stalin to national obloquy, although he and his supporters often speak meaningfully of the illegalities and the 'tragedy' of 1937–38. His formula is that despite the injustices of the 1937–38 period the story of Soviet socialism is one of overall success. To give those injustices undue emphasis would damage the self-esteem of the Soviet people and create unnecessary divisions.

Although my own convictions run absolutely counter to this tactic—because I believe the crimes of Stalin must be named and the Stalinists given no quarter—I recognise the prudence of Gorbachov's caution. This is one reason why I do not expect the Gorbachov reforms to be interpreted by the East European satellites in a manner that would lead to a violent rejection of the system.

URBAN: At the 19th All-Union Party Conference Gorbachov announced that a monument would be erected to the victims of Stalin. Will that not open up countless old wounds and raise the demand for figures to be given and the perpetrators to be punished?

DJILAS: It might, but I believe Gorbachov is strong enough to control any turbulence. This is a 'revolution' from above. Although Gorbachov would like it to become a more spontaneous affair, because that is what his battle with the bureaucracy now requires, it is not in his or in the Party's interest that de-Stalinisation should lead to a genuine revolution from below, for that would mean the end of the system.

My second reason for believing that the Soviet reforms will not cause Eastern Europe to go up in flames is that the Soviet leaders—all of them, from Khrushchev to Gorbachov—have learnt certain lessons from the bloody events in Hungary in 1956. They learnt that national sentiment is not to be trifled with—and however savage the retribution after 1956 may have been, the Kremlin would never again deceive itself into thinking that it could deal with the East European countries as though they were satrapies. Ordering the satellite leaders about by telephone stopped after the Hungarian blood-letting. Even the vice-regal role of the Soviet ambassadors changed, though I must admit it did not change in every case. We remember well enough how, in 1968, the Soviet Ambassador in Prague acted with the arrogance of a representative of an occupying power, and in Bulgaria the role of the Soviet Ambassador is still that of a governor-general.

But my forecast for Eastern Europe would be an evolutionary rather than a revolutionary loosening of the links with Moscow. The Soviet leaders now realise, even if they cannot say so loud and clear, that the national factor is much more decisive within the socialist camp than the ideological 'proletarian' factor, and will make concessions to it in order to keep the lid on the Empire. Indeed, they seem to be hoping that *glasnost* and *perestroika* will offer the satellites the kind of Europeanised up-to-date model of 'socialism' that the Prague reformers had on offer in 1968—but in the wrong place and at the wrong time.

URBAN: If so, their hopes may well prove to be unfounded. Learning from the Soviet model—even a 'liberalising' Soviet model—runs into deep cultural and historical resistance in most of East and Central Europe. It is, of course, quite possible that the spirit of 'Gorbachovism' will be used as a handy stick to beat the East European governments with (it is already being so used by the Hungarian writers); but only as a means to an end, and that end is national independence or, shall we say, maximum national independence compatible with Eastern Europe's geopolitical position. The fact is that public sentiment rejects any variety of Communist rule. I well remember how the brief flowering of 'Eurocommunism' in the mid-1970s had virtually no national impact (although it boosted the morale of dissidents within the Party and of some ex-Party members).[8]

DJILAS: There are, nevertheless, straws in the wind—and they are no more than that—that betray movement in the Soviet Union on a broader front than perhaps any of us expected; and this will have its repercussions in Eastern Europe. For example, the Belgrade magazine *NIN* recently published an interview with a Soviet person who uttered so harsh a critique of the shortcomings of the system that no Western Sovietologist could have done better. One of the solutions he offered—and offered in a context that made it clear that the idea was being quietly discussed in Moscow— was the replacement of the Communist party by *two* communist (or, as he called them, 'socialist') parties. The one-party system was a failure, he said; there was a need for some form of an opposition. A second 'socialist' party would supply the feedback, or words to that effect.

I don't have to add that a two-party system would fly in the face of everything that goes by the name of 'socialism' in the Soviet Union and would deal a body-blow to Leninism. Two-party socialism is probably no more than a thought floated, under the cover of 'openness', by a few individuals. Nevertheless it is a sign of the sort of forces Gorbachov is releasing within his own Party.

URBAN: That the question of softening, if not directly breaking, the monopoly of the Communist Party may now be on the agenda of Soviet thinking can be inferred from one of Gorbachov's own observations. Speaking to representatives of the media (on 14 July 1987) he felt it necessary to defend the leading role of the Party. Why defend it, if it is not under attack? No one, he said, should run away with the idea that

> it is possible to get by without the Party . . . If anyone thinks otherwise he is, at the least, mistaken . . . Social demagogues have found their way into some editorial offices . . . They are being particularly vicious in their attacks on cadres.

Only a few weeks earlier (23 May 1987) Georgi Arbatov was asked in the course of a Soviet–American telebridge programme whether the system could be widened under

Gorbachov into a multi-party system, and this is what he said:

> Our historical development has been such that we have one party. Actually, at the beginning of the Revolution there was not one party but there were two, and even a faction of a third party, I think—the internationalist Mensheviks. Then they withdrew from the coalition of their own accord and a one-party system was formed. . . . One can imagine in principle a system with the same property base and the same social relations as ours with not one party, but two, three or four. That is possible in principle and in theory. We have had debates about this and, in effect, have come to the conclusion that there is nothing in it that would contradict the system itself . . .

An even more intriguing account of how the one-party system came into being in the USSR was given by the *Novosti* spokesman, Rozental, in response to a request by journalists to fill in the 'blank spots of history'.

> The one-party system in the USSR is the result of the rejection by the leaders of the parties of Russian petty-bourgeois democracy, which formed part of the Petrograd Soviet of workers' and soldiers' deputies, of the proposal of the Bolsheviks that a multi-party Soviet government be formed. The Mensheviks, the Social Revolutionaries, the Popular Socialists and others came out openly against Soviet rule, unleashing a bloody civil war in conjunction with the bourgeoisie. . . . The West may, to a certain extent, regard itself as a co-author of our single party system.[9]

DJILAS: Arbatov was, shall we say, economising with the truth and speaking to gullible Americans who don't know their Soviet history. But it is certainly of some significance that he should have defended, at least in principle, the anti-Leninist idea of a multi-party system. The influential L. I. Abalkin raised it as well at the 19th Party Congress when he asked:

> Are we capable of ensuring the democratic organisation of public life, while preserving the Soviet organisation of society and the one-party system? Yes or no?

URBAN: If the question of what precisely the Party is for and how it should fit into 'democratisation' is now beginning to surface, Gorbachov himself is responsible for planting it. It was he who said in 1986 that, since under Soviet socialism 'feedback' could not reach the decision-makers through an Opposition, the Party itself would have to generate the criticisms and supply the feedback. This may well have been the idea that encouraged more sanguine spirits to talk about a two-party 'socialism'. But, in his formal pronouncements, Gorbachov has certainly given no encouragement to the multi-party reformers. At the 19th Party Conference he observed:

> Recently, we have seen attempts to use democratic rights in the pursuit of anti-democratic aims. Some people seem to think that in this manner we can solve all our problems, from opening up our borders to the creation of opposition parties. The Central Committee to the CPSU believes that such abuses of democratisation are in total contradiction to the aims of *perestroika* and go against the interests of the people.

DJILAS: The fact that a discussion of this formerly forbidden topic is taking place in the Soviet Union at all is an indication of the way the wind is blowing—and that wind is being carefully monitored by those sensitive minds in Budapest, Warsaw and Prague who seem to miss nothing.

So they must also have monitored the disappearance of '*partinost*' from Yugoslav culture. One of the most encouraging things about the Yugoslav model of 'socialism' is the return of culture to some semblance of normality. It is there that the satellite parties and the Gorbachov reformers could learn a thing or two to the benefit of Russian and East European cultures—and, come to think of it, to the benefit of the Communist movement itself.

Yugoslav culture is now as good as conducted *outside* the framework of the official ideology. Even in Croatia, where the Party is more orthodox than in most of the other Republics, literary culture is divorced from the Party. In Belgrade no self-respecting author would toe the Party line. Writers who joined the Party out of a sense of careerism write *away* from the tenets of official thinking and would be deeply offended if anyone suggested that they were 'constructing socialism'. Even in Bosnia, where the authorities carry in their baggage a heavy ballast of Stalinism, and punishment is still meted out for 'thought-crime' ('political gossip' and the like), culture has become a strictly non-Party affair.

The most important aspect of this relative cultural freedom is the liberty of our historians to write more or less objective history. There remain subjects that are delicately avoided—one does not attack Tito or the Communist Revolution in general terms—but the rest of history, including

Party history, has now become the sort of craft any respectable historian in the West would recognise as normal. Of course, Yugoslav historians offer wildly different and conflicting interpretations and are frequently at each other's throats. Surely, however, that is quite normal among historians and indeed a sign of the vitality of historiography.

URBAN: We mentioned that some of the more sanguine spirits in Moscow may have taken Gorbachov's 1986 call for a better feedback within the Party to be a call for the dilution of the authority of the Party or even a call for an 'opposition'.

DJILAS: They didn't have to be all that sanguine, though, because Gorbachov has given hostages to fortune. Note the sort of words he *avoids* using. There is nothing in his speeches about a classless society—about the advent of Communism, or even 'advanced socialism' (which was dogma under Brezhnev)—about the Soviet Union overtaking the US in per-capita production—or any of the other promises that had been made in Khrushchev's programme in 1961.

URBAN: There is a certain lack of passion in his speeches when he touches on the leading role of the Party; a difference of key from the one used by Ligachev, for example. In his talk to media-men (in July 1987) he used the curious phrase 'the Party must not lag behind the processes going on in society.'

DJILAS: Precisely. At the January 1987 plenum Gorbachov made a remarkable observation: 'The life of the working collectives is unimaginable without the party, the trade unions, the Komsomol, and other social organisations. . . .' This puts the Party on a par with the Komsomols and trade unions. In most cases he does insist on the leading role of the Party, but he tends to drop his predecessors' claim that Soviet society is homogeneous. At both the January and June 1987 plenums he argued: It is true that antagonistic contradictions have ceased to exist in Soviet society, but eliminating them does not mean 'levelling them out'.

   For me, this is an important admission. For it expresses the recognition that conflicts stemming from group interests, collective interests, departmental interests and Party interests exist—and that they have *stratified* society. It follows that these interests must be given expression, and that implies the quiet entry of pluralism.

In almost all of Gorbachov's articulations there are hints or statements that 'parasitic' groups within the *nomenklatura* are responsible for the present state of the Soviet economy—

URBAN: —a certain Milovan Djilas wrote a book along those lines thirty-odd years ago. . . .

DJILAS: Yes, in *The New Class* I anticipated most of Gorbachov's current findings. But even before that, in 1953, I wrote an article in *Borba* in which I argued: Of course, a single party cannot secure socialism and democracy, but even a homogeneous, single-class society couldn't do it. Conflicting interests would remain. Freedom and democracy would *not* be safe under the rule of the working class. That ended my political career; in January 1954 I was expelled from the Central Committee.

I find it, also, intriguing that Gorbachov should now want to vest power in *non*-Party cadres. Here again, we anticipated Gorbachov by well over 30 years. In 1952–53 some of us—for a time, Tito himself—felt that the leading role of the Party should be cut back and non-Party people given more influence. I personally urged that the power of the Party should be reduced—so did Kardelj and Bakarić. Tito, however, having looked at the idea, could sense the approaching dangers of a post-Stalin thaw and finally disagreed.

URBAN: What was his argument?

DJILAS: He was jealous of his personal power which he had wielded without opposition during and since the War. He told us that the long-term success of the Revolution required a strong man, that in the Soviet system the leading role of the Party was absolute and without it Communism would disintegrate.

URBAN: In Hungary Kádár did give a more emphatic role to non-Party people some years ago, yet the system has not disintegrated nor did his personal power suffer. His 'retirement' in March 1988 can certainly not be ascribed to the influence of the non-Party elements. Do you think these things are yet to come in Hungary and, perhaps, eventually in the Soviet Union too?

DJILAS: I would hesitate to predict. Certainly, Gorbachov's new deal represents the terminal phase of the Stalinist model of Communism—and, we may safely say, of the *Soviet* model of Communism, for, apart from a few years in the 1920s, there has been no other. That does not automatically mean the end of dogmatism and Leninism. In Yugoslavia and Hungary the Stalinist model has been dead for some time, yet the remnants of the past are alive. One-party rule and police control are, alas, in rude health.

URBAN: Your reading of the Communist system has certainly come in from the cold since those dramatic days when *The New Class* was written behind bars. . . .

DJILAS: I finished writing *The New Class* on the eve of my imprisonment for what I had said about the 1956 Hungarian Uprising. I was myself responsible for sending the first part of the book abroad (through the courtesy of a foreign journalist). The second part was first hidden by my wife Stephanie, and then smuggled out through the same channel some days after I had started my term in prison. It is poignant to remember those conditions, sitting as we are in your study in Brighton 30 years on.

URBAN: The main difference between Milovan Djilas and Mikhail Gorbachov is that Djilas followed his analysis of the Communist system to its logical conclusion and says '*No socialism*'—whereas Gorbachov's slogan is '*More socialism*'. It will be interesting to see whether Gorbachov will still say '*More socialism*' five years from now and what he will mean by '*More socialism*'—if he hasn't 'restructured' himself out of the leadership in the meantime. '*The anti-Party group led by M. S. Gorbachov . . .*' Can you see those words appearing in some future statement of the Central Committee?

DJILAS: Nothing is impossible under Soviet rule; but so radical a 'restoration' is, in my opinion, not on the cards. Political systems are not in the habit of committing suicide. In any case, Gorbachov, unlike Brezhnev, strikes me as a true believer—

URBAN: . . . so was Milovan Djilas—

DJILAS: . . . and I cannot see Gorbachov presiding over the liquidation of Communism. He is a man who has begun to recognise what ails the system and is trying to change an Absolute Monarchy into a Constitutional Monarchy. In that he may succeed, and gain a good deal of credit for it. Since the 19th Party Conference, it is clear that *he* wants to be the Constitutional Monarch.

His plans for the rejuvenation of the local Soviets and for a powerful executive Presidency, with himself, undoubtedly, as President, point to a new political arrangement whereby a much reinforced State apparatus would act as a countervailing force to the Party.

'Inform the People . . . Blow by Blow, Crime by Crime'

URBAN: You said you recognised Gorbachov's prudence in not presenting Soviet public opinion with a spate of sudden and dramatic revelations about the Soviet past. At the same time you want to see the whole of that past laid bare. But can the Soviet system reform itself even within those narrow limits which (as you have indicated) restrict the reformability of *any* Communist system, without unveiling everything there is to unveil about the Soviet past? Can a new future be planned without the lessons of Soviet history being first publicly assimilated?

DJILAS: In the long run, retrieval of the Soviet past is *the* essential prerequisite of Gorbachov's programme of reconstruction. Soviet historians have frequently falsified Soviet history. They excelled, as we know, especially in representing the 1917 *putsch* against the Provisional Government and the forcible dissolution of the Constituent Assembly as 'a Revolution'. The full truth about the 1931–33 Collectivisation campaign, and the man-made famine resulting from it, remains to be told. So does the story of the Show Trials, the Great Terror and the rest of Stalin's despotism. The Soviet people cannot hope to understand the reality surrounding them without being told the truth about the roots of that reality. In our age of television and short-wave broadcasting, the true history of the Soviet system can no longer be hidden from the people. The question is only whether they get it in dribs and drabs, with the periodic shock accompanying each revelation, or whether they are given the full story and let the blame fall where it will. Soviet history must be rewritten from Day One—rewritten, that is, with complete intellectual integrity.

Calls for the reassessment of the Stalinist record are now made openly by Soviet historians such as Alexander Samsonov—and opposed by others, Isaak Mints, for example. Yury Afanasiev, writing in *Sovietskaya Kultura*, urges the authorities to permit 'a full reassessment of Stalin's repressive rule', pleading that the suppression of historical facts deprives people of self-respect and spiritual strength. He argues that it is not enough to brush aside Stalin's terror as a 'mistake' or a 'personal shortcoming' as Soviet historians are inclined to.

These are significant developments, especially as they are accompanied by calls for the reassessment of the Khrushchev era too, which will have a direct bearing on Gorbachov's own. Fyodor Burlatsky's formidable essay on Khrushchev (*Literaturnaya Gazeta*, 24 February 1988) and Arkadiy Vaksberg's merciless critique of Andrei Vishinsky (*Literaturnaya Gazeta*, 27 January 1988) are pointers of great importance.

URBAN: There are a great many skeletons in the Soviet cupboard. Gorbachov is aware of this. I don't think he is against letting those skeletons haunt some of the living, but he seems to be anxious not to allow the soul-searching to turn into a night of long knives. His dilemma is neatly encapsulated in two antithetical articles which appeared, ironically, on the same day (23 July 1987) in the Soviet press.

The one in *Izvestia* criticised the 'distortions of historical facts in Soviet history text-books', and called for the compilation of 'an objective history book because reforms launched in the country can be made irreversible only by people who are not afraid of telling the truth, who have their own views and are capable of upholding them. . . .' *Izvestia* then inveighed against some—not all—of the same misrepresentations of Soviet history you have just criticised:

> In the period following World War II a trend towards embellishing the country's history emerged. Deleted were certain undesirable names and even many events, such as authorised abuse during Collectivisation when peasants were forced to join farm cooperatives; famine in the

1930s; the negation of genetics and cybernetics which were proclaimed pseudo-sciences. History text-books failed to assess Joseph Stalin objectively. . . .

A very different opinion was articulated in *Pravda* in the shape of a reader's letter from one Georgiy Vasylievich Matveyets:

We schoolchildren took part in subbotniks at construction sites and enterprises. We witnessed the building of socialism in our country. Our hearts and minds were moulded in this atmosphere of satisfaction with our ordinary working lives . . . All that—the Five-year Plans, Stakhanov, the success of the Collective farm peasantry, the flights of Gromoy and Chkalov, the Chelyushkin epic, the drift expedition by Papanin and his comrades, and many others—really happened, and Soviet people did it not out of fear but in conscience. People were inspired by the great idea. It mobilised them. They raced ahead. . . . It was a time when fairy tales actually became reality. . . . That was the actual and heroic reality of Soviet people and it cannot be erased by any miscalculations, errors and even crimes on the part of one man, even though he may have worn the uniform of a Generalissimo . . . It seems to me that those who are denigrating our history in such a fashion have no sense of respect or love of their country and their people. . . .

Gorbachov is clearly in an unenviable position. He would, as he has often indicated, be happiest if he could harness a truthfully-told past to *perestroika*; but the 'social base' for that truthfully-told past doesn't exist—at least not yet. There are many people in the USSR who vested their work and honour in the Stalinist period and do not want to see that period disowned and disparaged. Ligachev is one of their spokesmen and Nina Andreyeva's conservative manifesto, 'I cannot waive principles',[10] is as representative of their thinking as any we are likely to get.

DJILAS: It *is* a dilemma; but it is one Gorbachov will have to tackle even if he can do so only by stages. Suppose we shifted the scene of discussion to Hitler's Germany. Couldn't millions of Germans argue, in good faith, that in the 1930s they had put their work and enthusiasm into changing unemployment-plagued and inflation-ridden Germany into a welfare state and a great power—and that their achievements should not be denigrated because mistakes and crimes had been committed by one man, Adolf Hitler?

No one in a position of responsibility would accept that sort of an argument in Germany, much less anywhere outside Germany.

I don't want to stretch my analogy too far because the two systems are not comparable. I would, nevertheless, insist that leadership and statesmanship put very special responsibilities on a reforming leader of the cut of Gorbachov. If he thinks, as he clearly does, that the Stalinist past landed the Soviet Union with burdens it can no longer support either at home or in its foreign policy, then he must pick up the threads of 'de-Stalinisation' where Khrushchev left off, undeterred by the sort of sentiment (which I grant you may be quite widespread but no longer decisive) you have quoted from the pages of *Pravda*.

URBAN: Even General Jaruzelski has urged him in that direction, in the pages of *Kommunist*, to boot. He wants the truth to be told about the Soviet invasion of Poland in 1939, and the question of who was responsible for Katyn is now all but openly discussed.

DJILAS: Gorbachov is a populist radical and a very un-Russian one at that. He doesn't believe in the control of the people by Authority. He thinks the population ought to and can control itself once it has been given the facts. Speaking to the workers of Zelenograd (29 July 1987) he said:

> People say: control is necessary . . . But who should do this? If we are to count on controllers, then we will have to increase that apparatus still further. We have to do it through democracy, through the people participating in everything. This is the main guarantee of control and against all outrages, for the people see everything and know everything, and won't allow them . . .

These are unexceptionable sentiments, even though they show a trust in popular wisdom that is not clearly warranted by history, least of all Russian history. But if wisdom resides in a free and fully informed people, how can Gorbachov forego informing the people—blow by blow, crime by crime, lie by lie—about the long Stalinist past of which all of the Union's present troubles are the natural and inevitable consequences? It isn't enough to boast, as he did, that the Party was strong, that 'we criticise ourselves as no one before has criticised us in the West or in the East. . . .' If

the Party is that strong—give out the truth and nothing but
the truth. We must press for this because, when the chips
are down, the liberalisation of the Soviet system is more
important for the world than arms control agreements with
the Soviet state.

URBAN: Don't you think Gorbachov is checking his
impatience and proceeding by stages? He seems to have
decided to deprive, first, the Stalinist era of its aura of
heroism; and, having created a psychological neutral land
around Stalin, eventually, when he feels the time is right,
to out-Khrushchev Nikita Sergeevich by telling all. He
would, then, perhaps launch a frontal attack on Stalin and
link it to some move in his struggle for an uninhibited
mandate.

In doing so, he would certainly not be short of support.
'In order to compensate, at least morally, for past guilt
and to avoid a repetition of lawlessness in the future', the
Estonian Creative Unions say in their petition,

> . . . we consider it necessary for the Party Conference to make an
> assessment of Stalinist repressions as crimes directed against the Party,
> Soviet power and humanity. . . . Along with this it is necessary to
> complete and make public the rehabilitation of all the innocent victims
> of that period and to immortalise their memory.[11]

DJILAS: Cautious de-Stalinisation appears to be Gorbachov's tactic. Almost every day he, and the press that
represents him, keep inching forward to a full reckoning
with Stalinism. His position may be summed up in these
words: We never can or should forgive or justify what
happened in 1937 and 1938. Those who were in power are
responsible; but that does not detract from all we have
today, what the Party and the people accomplished while
undergoing those trials.

I can accept this as a formula of transition; and that, I
believe, is what it is meant to be, but no more than a
formula of transition.[12]

URBAN: Will the *apparat* stand for the final push, if indeed
it comes to one? I have my doubts. V. M. Chebrikov's
laudation (10 September 1987) of Felix Dzerzhinskiy to
mark the 110th anniversary of Dzerzhinskiy's birth—he was
celebrated as a great, humane leader—must have made

Gorbachov wonder whether he and his KGB chief were marching to the same tune.

> Imperialism's special services [Chebrikov said] are trying to find new loopholes through which to penetrate our society . . . with the aim of instilling in Soviet people a bourgeois understanding of democracy . . . splitting the monolithic unity of Party and people, and installing political and ideological pluralism . . . We have people who hold ideas and views which are alien and even frankly hostile to socialism. Some of them embark on the path of committing anti-state and anti-social actions . . . There are also those who are prepared to enter into direct cooperation with the imperialist states' special services and betray the homeland . . .

Then came Chebrikov's warning:

> Clear awareness is needed that restructuring is taking place under the leadership of the Communist Party, within the framework of socialism and in the interests of socialism. And this revolutionary process will be reliably protected against any subversive intrigues!

DJILAS: Well, this is a tough warning, especially as the speech appeared in *Pravda* under the ominous headline of 'Aspects that make him [Dzerzhinskiy] our contemporary'. Chebrikov might as well have said 'Aspects that make *Stalin* our contemporary'.

The strange thing is that Chebrikov, as we heard from Ligachev at the 19th Party Conference, was (together with Gromyko and Solomentsev) one of that small group of Politburo members who had helped Gorbachov into the saddle at the March 1985 Plenum of the Central Committee. Has Chebrikov changed? Has Gorbachov? Or is there some compact between reformers and conservatives that we cannot yet fathom?

Whether the *apparat* would stand for the final push, if indeed it came to one, remains to be seen. If Gorbachov's power-base elsewhere in the state is strong enough, if he can provide more food and consumer goods, and if the *apparat*'s personal interests are not dramatically affected, it might . . . but then it might not. The counter-attack encapsulated in Nina Andreyeva's manifesto is a signal he dare not ignore.

Gorbachov, a Djilas Disciple?

URBAN: You have said that Yugoslav historiography has become fairly independent and reliable. Does that reali-ability extend to its treatment of yourself?

DJILAS: Yes, it is beginning to. When they write about me in various papers and magazines, they quote from my speeches in 1949 or 1951 and publish the photographs that go with them. The quotations are correct and the comments neutral.

URBAN: For example?

DJILAS: Well, they might say that on such-and-such a day the Central Committee discussed higher education and Milovan Djilas said this or that. They neither embellish the official record nor distort what I had said.

URBAN: But you are far from being 'rehabilitated'?

DJILAS: Under the present régime, I'll never be rehabili-tated on the political level. You saw the Yugoslav Prime Minister's attack on me in *Spiegel* (23 March 1987). He called me 'a traitor *par excellence*'. That does not quite herald rehabilitation. In the press, however, I have been to some extent *morally* rehabilitated—as a former leading Communist who had a certain part to play and was, shall we say, no worse than the others. That's the line they take on me.

URBAN: It is not quite clear to me why, given the Gorba-chov factor in the Communist world, you should not be rehabilitated on the political level too.

DJILAS: Well, I am negotiating with certain Yugoslav publishing houses, and there is a vague possibility that my memoir entitled *Wartime*, which appeared in the USA and elsewhere some years ago and attracted much comment, will eventually be published in Yugoslavia. One historian who enjoys the confidence of the present leadership ventured the opinion after some hesitation that the book is not hostile to the Revolution, is rather well written, and offers an important testimony. If the book does, in fact, get published I will feel that my 'moral rehabilitation' as an author, not as a politician, will have been accomplished.

I do not, as I say, expect political rehabilitation because

that would imply an admission on the part of the authorities that I had been right all along, and that might, in their view, re-open the road to my ideas.

URBAN: But the plain fact is that you were substantially right in almost everything you had written. You were the first to expose the 'New Class', the corrupting influence of privilege, the gap between words and deeds in Communist practice, the lack of democracy in socialist society, the falsification of history, and so on. Perhaps you had the misfortune of being right before your time, but that should not be counted against you after three decades.

DJILAS: I'd be the last to disagree. It would be false modesty on my part to deny that the present 'Thaw' in the Soviet Union does give me some satisfaction. But, in the political world, being right is a long way from meaning that you will receive justice.

URBAN: Let me be quite open about this. Does the régime fear that you might, if you were fully rehabilitated, make a bid for power?

DJILAS: No, the régime is not afraid of that. It is just worried that my rehabilitation would cause turbulence in the Party. I have never been a threat to the political power of the Party . . . but I *have* been a force of opposition in ideology and could perhaps become one again. And as ideology is what justifies the existence of the Party and supplies its vocabulary, this danger is something the leadership dare not discount.

URBAN: Would you like to be in power again?

DJILAS: Every man of ideas would like to see his own put into practice. I have, from time to time, been led by a similar desire. I would have liked my ideas to have some influence because I believed they were right. But I was never *hungry* for power, and I am certainly not anxious to have any power now.

URBAN: Certainly your portrayal of Tito in your new biography[13] cannot be prejudicial to your political rehabilitation—since you paint a picture of him that is surprisingly favourable and even reverential. You depict him as a Communist of absolute dedication and a man of vision and integrity. No one can accuse you that, after Tito's death and thus without danger to yourself, you took your revenge on him by remembering him unkindly.

DJILAS: Well, you will probably be surprised to hear that some of the Belgrade opposition thought that my book was far too friendly to Tito. 'You were unduly fair to him,' they told me. 'He was a lot worse than you have shown him to be.' I do not accept that view. I described Tito as correctly as it was in my power to do so. I tried to dispel delusions but I also recognised the great qualities of the man.

URBAN: It crossed my mind as I was reading that book that you were, perhaps, lifting Tito on to a higher plane of history than he would deserve to be on in the eyes of disinterested historians—because by lifting him you were also upgrading your own stature. This may sound unkind, but isn't it an inclination we all have? If you show a fellow-writer or politician, with whom you had good or even bad relations, to have been a significant man, you are automatically showing yourself to be of his order of importance. You and Tito may have had your differences but—so the reader is given to understand—those differences were the differences of great men and of historical importance. Did this kind of consideration play a part?

DJILAS: It was certainly not a conscious consideration. Perhaps subconsciously it may have coloured some of my writings. But I flatter myself that my place as an intellectual is separate and independent from Tito. Not that I was politically as important as some Western commentators have tried to make out. I was not groomed to be Tito's successor. In the hierarchy of the Yugoslav leadership I was probably in fourth place—after Kardelj and Ranković, although I am vain enough to believe that I was a better writer than Kardelj and more original as an ideological thinker. But in terms of power politics I was merely number four, and I never thought of myself as the pretender. At the same time, to the end of Tito's days, I sustained certain basic sympathies for him as a Yugoslav revolutionary-leader and human being. This is probably the source of your impression that Tito comes out better in my book than his critics—and some of my friends—would have liked and expected.

URBAN: But you were, to my mind at least, the keeper of

the purity (if that is the right word) of the Revolution. You were a fanatical Communist when you felt the old Order and the new Invader had to be fought. You were suspicious of Stalin when he began to encroach upon Yugoslav independence. You became increasingly critical of your fellow-Communists in power when you discovered that the 'dictatorship of the proletariat' corrupts just as any other dictatorship. And when the cup was full, you declared that the Revolution had become a fraud, and that Communism could answer none of the world's really pressing problems.

So, whatever your official or unofficial place may have been in the Yugoslav leadership's pecking order, you do, in history, stand next to Tito as a kind of counter-Tito-of-the-Yugoslav-Communist-conscience, a heretic who may have saved the faith (at least to his own satisfaction) while consigning a corrupt church to the flames. That is, perhaps, too metaphorical a way of putting it. But it leads me to ask you whether you do, nowadays, look upon yourself as a heretic of the Revolution.

DJILAS: A revolution is always a tragedy in human affairs. I don't like to romanticise it, and dislike intensely people who do. The Yugoslav Revolution, too, was a great evil— although it would be erroneous to say that it could have been avoided. Our Revolution did resolve certain problems we had inherited from Royal Yugoslavia, but it didn't satisfy the aspirations of the revolutionaries. Revolutions never do. There can be no greater insult to my conscience and intelligence than to be told that the 'socialist' revolution was a 'humanitarian' event that 'changed the course of history'. There are no such sudden watersheds in history; and I cannot quite see how enormous blood-lettings and sufferings can be termed humanitarian even in the embellishing light of retrospect. Yet, from time to time, revolutions are inevitable because the guilt and corruption of certain ruling classes seem to be an ineradicable feature of human history.

I was, as you rightly say, a fully believing Communist. Communism for me was not just a social policy, not a means for manipulating people, not a stepping stone to advancement, not a way of acquiring and exercising power, but a deep, personal, moral commitment as strong as religion.

Only a true believer has the right to rise up against his own convictions and reject them at the risk of being damned as a renegade or a heretic. When I reject revolution and the dictatorship that follows it as great misfortunes, I speak as a man who believed in revolution fervently, but has learned from bitter experience and long reflection that while revolutions may be pleasing to the temper of revolution-aries, they achieve virtually nothing. That does not mean to say that revolution is not justified when enormous injustices pervade the lives of men and every peaceful means of putting them right has been exhausted. But they must be the last resort.

If you now describe me as the keeper of the conscience of the Yugoslav Revolution, a through-and-through heretic who now rejects Revolution—that's an identification I accept without demur.

URBAN: Looking back on your life at the age of 76, do you feel that you lost something vital when you lost power in 1953? Or did your writings compensate for that loss?

DJILAS: They did, and they did more than compensate because they were and are much closer to my real self than was the exercise of power. If you said to me: 'Choose between being the leader of Yugoslavia and writing books,' my answer would be: 'If I knew that I could do something essential for the freedom and prosperity of the people of Yugoslavia, I would choose to be the leader.' But if you asked me: 'Choose between being a leader under Tito and pursuing your vocation as a writer,' I would choose writing without hesitation.

URBAN: Would it be because writing itself is a form of power, or because writing gives you so much satisfaction?

DJILAS: It is more the latter. I am, as you know, not only a political writer. I am a belletrist as well. Circumstances pushed me into politics; but power has no attractions for me, least of all the day-to-day exercise of power.

The repercussions of whatever power and influence I had were severe when my spell in power ended. But the lion's share of the suffering was borne not by myself, even though I was twice sent to prison, but by my family and relatives. I had, after all, freely chosen to do what I did, but my dependents had not. My wife Stephanie and my son Aleksa were the real victims. My wife was a young and strong woman, and she could cope. But my son Aleksa was only about four when I was first sent to prison and about nine when my second term came. For a small boy it is an immense shock to have a father in prison. Boys heroise their fathers. To see a father behind bars and humiliated is, I feel, the worst thing that can happen to a child.

URBAN: An inscription you were kind enough to write for me into a copy of your book, *Rise and Fall*,[14] says: '. . . as further evidence that my "fall" was more "glorious" than my "rise", . . .' Should I read this as a summing up of your career?

DJILAS: Those who are seen by the world and the church to which they once belonged as heretics usually get better billing in history than those who are not. In that sense my 'fall' was more 'glorious' than my 'rise'. But I also meant that dedication to be read by you as a bit of a personal message because you have, in the course of our many conversations over the years, witnessed my 'fall' and given it a dimension I found new and challenging.[15]

URBAN: I said earlier that you were a keeper of the purity of the Revolution. Can I change my metaphor and say that you were in many ways a Philosopher who became King (even though you were only a Viceroy to Tito)? You found yourself in a position where you could, as a Communist intellectual, put many of your ideas into action because you had a good deal of power.

DJILAS: No, Tito alone was King. But he was King with a vengeance.

URBAN: But weren't you in reality Tito's mentor? When your teaching was abused, the philosopher's 'love of wisdom' induced you to part company with your charge. You discovered that your monarch wasn't true to his Kingdom—

DJILAS: No, I was not a philosopher even in the weak sense of the word in which you use it, but I did see the emperor without his uniform, without his crown, and without his decorations; and that was sobering.

The most I would say is that I was a thinker in Tito's court but one without pretensions. My ambition was, and still is, to put pen to paper and have some impact through the written page on my nation's destiny. There isn't a single

Serb writer who has not sought to involve himself in shaping the future of his people; I am no exception. To be so involved is probably characteristic of the intelligentsia of all small nations. But it is especially true of those nations that arrived late on the stage of history or are in danger of extinction. You could observe the same trend in Poland and Hungary both in the 19th century and nowadays. The realisation that your nation may be on the brink of disaster focuses the minds of its intellectuals wonderfully on the one thing that really matters—survival.

URBAN: You now clearly point to 'the Nation' as the focus of your loyalties. Isn't this slightly at odds with the support you gave 'Eurocommunism' in the 1970s, and now with your tacit approval of the Gorbachov round of reforms?

DJILAS: Not at all. Anything that dilutes a generically bad political system must be welcome. Anything that lessens the impact of a disease is still a great step forward for those suffering from it.

URBAN: But aren't 'Eurocommunism' and now 'Gorbachovism' likely to help those on the European and American Left who have always argued that there is nothing *basically* wrong with the Soviet system? Take away the accretions and distortions, they claim, and 'socialism' will stand out once again as the way forward?

DJILAS: There are precious few left who would now subscribe to that misguided idealism. The Soviet system has become an anti-model. Even 70 years of ceaseless Gorbachovism would not improve it to a point where it could *begin* to compare with the life-chances and freedoms offered by the liberal democracies. Only fools and scoundrels could be tempted.

So let me say it again without rehearsing my arguments: Communism as culled from Marx and abused by Lenin is totally unsound. It is ill-conceived in principle and does not work. You can alleviate some of its wrongs and patch up some of its defects, but you cannot turn it into an acceptable system.

We can say all this without denying that Marx was a great historical figure and an original thinker in some areas. I re-read his *Capital* for the last time towards the end of my spell in office in the spring of 1950. Our problem then was to find a way out of Stalinism. I found *Capital* a most relevant piece of writing. In volume II, I hit upon the idea of self-management and informed my comrades and Tito. Tito would, however, not immediately accept it, despite the respectability of the source.

URBAN: Why wouldn't he?

DJILAS: Initially he just didn't understand what I had in mind. Self-management was outside the standard Communist experience and there was no sanction or model for it. But being a practical and intelligent man he eventually understood that this might turn out to be a good idea. It didn't. But the two points I am making are: first, that Marx equipped us in our search for unorthodox economic solutions with a practical idea that the Soviets are only now beginning to embrace (having rejected it as 'treason' when it was first launched in Belgrade); and, second, that Tito was good at using other people's ideas but poor in generating original ones of his own. In this he was like Stalin. Even the concept of building 'socialism in one country' was Bukharin's not Stalin's (which may, incidentally, complicate or—who knows?—ease his full *political* rehabilitation).

URBAN: The need to refer to the sacred books was a real one even within the narrow circle of the top leadership?

DJILAS: It was. The question of presentation was crucial. In offering self-management to the public and the world, it was important that we should have canonical sanction for striking out in this new direction. Of course, you and I realise that every heresy has to stick to the revealed texts while actually giving them unorthodox meaning. With Marx we didn't even have to do that, because Marx contains so much that is ambiguous or genuinely 'anti-Communist' (in the Stalinist interpretation of Communism) that we could conveniently help ourselves to whatever served our purpose.

URBAN: A device Gorbachov has not, as yet, made use of but one he is surely familiar with. At the moment his reforms are all wrapped in Leninism in which he steers a similarly selective course; but who knows what the future may hold. If he wants to dilute the primacy of the Party, for example, he may very well go back to Marx and argue that the idea of a Communist party is rejected in the *Communist Manifesto*, and he may exploit many other loopholes and ambiguities in Marx to liberalise the system without erring from the original revelation.

DJILAS: Eventually, he might. Whether he could get away with it is another matter.

URBAN: What exactly did Tito say when you first put the idea of self-management to him?

DJILAS: Tito's first reaction was, as I say, negative. He felt the workers in Yugoslavia were too uneducated to run a self-managing economy. But when Kardelj, Kidrič and I explained that self-management might solve some of our worst problems and offer a model to others, he quickly understood and said 'Well, let's do it: we can advance it under the slogan "All factories to the Workers!".'

Initially, self-management did show certain successes. It opened our economy to the market, and gave us a weapon against Stalinism and the abuses of the bureaucracy. After a short time, however, it came unstuck for the reasons we have already discussed and is now the source of my country's present round of misfortunes. In a sentence: self-management without a free market economy, and that without political pluralism cannot be made to work. It is one auxiliary Utopia among many that Communists resort to when practical life repudiates the principal Utopia of Communism itself.

URBAN: Wouldn't you say that after his (March 1988) visit to Yugoslavia Gorbachov might nevertheless go down that Utopian road? He admired Yugoslavia's relative plenty, the well-stocked shops, and the absence of queues.

DJILAS: Compared to the economic situation in the Soviet Union, especially as far as consumer durables and food are concerned, Yugoslavia is, of course, a veritable paradise. But Gorbachov would be gravely mistaken if he mistook our auxiliary Utopia for a solution. We have what we have because we are parasites, in one way or another, on the really free market economies and parliamentary democracies of the West. Such political and economic 'successes' as we have had cannot be measured in terms of developing the un-used resources of 'socialism' (as Gorbachov is in the habit of saying), but only in terms of repudiating socialism in fact if not in language.

URBAN: The dominant Western conception of socialism appears to concern itself no longer with 'property relations' and the 'ownership of the means of production' but, rather, with equity and political decision-making. Would you agree with that change of emphasis?

DJILAS: I would indeed; and it is not merely a change of emphasis but a re-conceptualisation of socialism. The need of that re-conceptualisation within the Soviet system, too, is what Gorbachov's visit to Yugoslavia should have brought home to him.

The Fixed Addiction to Utopia

URBAN: You said earlier that Revolution must be 'the last resort'. Would, then, the Soviet people have been justified to rise against the tyranny of Stalin?

DJILAS: Absolutely. From the moral point of view a revolution to put down the monster Stalin would have been right and proper. Can you think of a *more* moral cause, with the sole exception of putting down the genocidal Hitler?

URBAN: Why, then, was there no organised opposition? Professor Sidney Hook, who has given this question probably more thought than any man alive, puts it poignantly (in his book *Marxism and Beyond*).

> Hitler's domestic regime was not as oppressive to the majority of his subjects as Stalin's was to the great mass of Soviet peasants and workers. Yet there were plots against Hitler and at least one failed effort. But there is no objective evidence of any movement directed against Stalin . . . Why no opposition despite the century-old traditions of revolutionary opposition to despotism?

DJILAS: A good question, and I cannot provide a good answer. Stalin's despotism did not coincide with the frustration and stagnation of the whole of Soviet society. The rapid pace of industrialisation, the cultural revolution and the spirit of dedication which had been inherited from Lenin gave the Stalinist system a certain dynamism and coherence

which would have made a revolution against Stalin impossible. The letter you quoted from the recent pages of *Pravda*
is a fair sample of the spirit of the 1930s. Vasily Grossman's
masterly novel *Life and Fate*[16] gives an almost Tolstoyesque
account of the same phenomenon. Although an uneven
book, it nevertheless catches those moments in Soviet
history when the duality of Soviet life was at its most
conspicuous: Stalin's terror and the concentration camps on
the one hand; and, on the other, an undoubtedly inspired
and heroic national effort first to industrialise backward
Russia, and then to protect it during the War.

URBAN: Would the Romanian people, on your showing, be
morally justified to rise against the rule of the Ceauşescu
clan?

DJILAS: Absolutely. Ceauşescu's is a terrible and shameful
dictatorship. It is heaping indignity upon the whole people;
in an even tolerably just world it should not be allowed to
exist.

URBAN: You said that revolutions almost never achieve
what they set out to achieve.

DJILAS: Not quite. What I do say is that Communism as a
system has shown itself to be completely unsuccessful, even
though in some countries it may have accelerated the pace
of popular education, industrialisation and modernisation.
It is, therefore, wrong to make a revolution if a Communist
system is going to be its direct or indirect result. In other
instances it may not be morally wrong to make a revolution,
but it is always wrong in terms of the suffering caused.
The sacrifices are always too high when set against the
achievements.

However, because the real world is what it is, revolutions,
like wars, will go on occurring. There is hardly a nation that
hasn't its roots in a revolutionary past. The price of the
Soviet seizure of power, of the Civil War and of the Revolutionary Terror was extremely high, so was that of the
Yugoslav Revolution, although it was proportionately
'cheaper' than the October Revolution. I cannot see how
either could have been avoided.

At the back of it all is Man's, and especially Communist
Man's, indefatigable preoccupation with Utopia. Reflect on
the resurfacing of Utopia in Gorbachov's rhetoric. If you

look at his or Rizhkov's articulations you will find the outlines of yet another 'New Jerusalem' emerging: a 'socialist' society supported by the gleaming electronic technology of the nuclear age.

URBAN: It isn't really new, though. The glamour of science has always been part of the dream of 'scientific socialism'. But earlier varieties had to make do with tractors, steel mills, canals and hydroelectric stations.

DJILAS: Yes, but what is remarkable is that the new rulers of the Soviet Union, turning over (as they say they are) a new page in their planning methods and economic philosophy, should maintain this slavish addiction to Utopianism! They realise that Stalinism, the 'command economy' and the conservative bureaucracy have made the system a permanent loser *vis-à-vis* the variously mixed economies of the world. Yet here they are, investing their energies in yet another grand design that will prove illusory—in the fallacy of thinking that one can apply high technology and modern science to a monolithic political system and make it work as though it were a free and self-correcting mechanism.

URBAN: But isn't Gorbachov taking the system to the very borders of the market economy and building (or trying to build) a great many suspiciously un-monolithic features into it?

DJILAS: He is, but his error is to imagine that the gleaming gadgets and the science-fiction thinking can be harnessed to the old 'socialist' wagon—as though 'existing socialism' were a jet aircraft with a Mach 2 capability.

URBAN: Won't Gorbachov sooner or later have to admit that maintaining a social system based on Karl Marx's analysis makes no more sense than claiming that 19th-century Darwinism should be our lodestar in zoology and biology in the year 2000? It is a point often made by Sidney Hook and quite recently by Deng Xiaoping's people in China. Hu Yaobang observed in November 1986:

Marx never saw a light bulb, Engels never saw an aeroplane.

The Soviets appear to be coming to similar conclusions. In 1987 Alexander Yakovlev admitted:

Not even 70 Marxes could have foreseen in detail the future of the new society. . . .

DJILAS: Perhaps in his heart of hearts Gorbachov realises that the Marxist conception of socialism is a museum-piece. We don't know. What we do know is that he behaves as though he believed in the basic soundness of the Soviet system and its reformability through technology, renewed dedication, and a selective and uninstitutionalised imposition of certain freedoms.

I sometimes wonder whether Gorbachov is reacting to Paul Milyukov's observation that, while in Western Europe technological revolutions always led to *more* democracy, they had the opposite effect in Russia. Certainly Gorbachov wants more 'democratism' in the wake of the new technology, and if he comes anywhere close to succeeding, he will have broken the spell Milyukov diagnosed. But this is something for the distant future.

I am ready to believe that Gorbachov will impart a certain *élan* to the Soviet Party, and that some of his reforms *will* make the system marginally more efficient. But I doubt whether he will achieve a fully-fledged 'restructuring' under existing conditions of 'socialism'. We have seen how very difficult it is in Yugoslavia, under our much-advertised but totally inadequate 'self-management system', to get private enterprise going and to lift the economy out of the trough it has now occupied for most of the three last decades. We have not succeeded because we have not mounted the necessary political reforms.

It is self-evident for me that you cannot mitigate the effects of the disease of Communism as a whole by excising or diluting some of its elements. And from this follows what is, to my mind, another iron law of Communism: every economic crisis of Communist society is, in fact, a political crisis—

URBAN: A crisis of the system, would you say. . . .?

DJILAS: Yes, this is the present crisis in the Soviet Union. It is, in reality, not about a sluggish economy, nor about a lazy population, nor even about a corrupt civil service, but about the political system that is responsible for the growth and luxuriance of these characteristics.

URBAN: These are strong words from a man who first

suggested the introduction of the self-management system to an unwilling Tito. Several decades later, Gorbachov, and now the Bulgarians too, are following in your footsteps, ignoring the bitter lessons of the Yugoslav experiment.

DJILAS: This is so and the reason is, as I say, the Communist obsession with Utopia. But it is a Utopia with a difference. If the Communist Utopia were of the purely airy-fairy kind it would not have survived or given the world too much to think about. But Communist Utopias combine the vision of a classless society, human fulfilment and eternal peace with cunning tactics and violent strategy, and a seemingly scientific problem-solving vocabulary that lends their Utopian imaginings a certain plausibility. The violence is real—the 'coming age of peace and plenty' is not.

This is undoubtedly a shrewd combination. Who would disapprove of freedom, equality, fraternity and peace? Who would be against Plato's benign 'totalitarianism' with which the Communist vision has a certain affinity? The problem is that the Communist Utopia cannot be put into practice without changing the nature of man, and that requires violence. Communism is Utopia in Power; it is the institutionalisation of violence. No economic reform, no 'restructuring', no temporary freedom of discussion can change that.

URBAN: You were yourself not reluctant to utter Utopian forecasts in your days as a Communist leader, as you ruefully admit in *Rise and Fall*. In 1948 you declared in the Cominform journal that in ten years Yugoslavia would catch up with Great Britain in per capita production.

DJILAS: That is why I want to see these words put on the mantlepiece of every free and intelligent person: 'You must oppose Communism.' It is the duty of those of us who come from the Communist movement and are familiar with the nature of the animal to make this truth clear and relevant again to the thinking of people captivated by the new Utopianism of Gorbachov. Our efforts will not have been wasted if we can persuade the West to remain strong, and to learn the art of dealing with the political crisis of the Soviet system within its own terms of reference.

URBAN: That's where the West has been most deficient. The Soviet leaders have always had the heretic's traditional advantage of being able to worship both at their own altars and ours.

DJILAS: Yes, and that's why it is of such great importance that Western politicians, journalists and other opinion-makers should now take the trouble of learning what exactly it is that has made the various Communist systems founder and how the Dengs and Gorbachovs are trying to make the leaking vessels seaworthy. The struggle in the world is not about the level of armaments; it is about political advantage and victory in the international political arena. The West is poor, and—what is distressing—increasingly poor at playing this game.

The advent of Gorbachov has brought with it a tremendous increase in the political sophistication and effectiveness of expressing traditional Soviet hostility to the Western democracies. Look at Gorbachov's speech to Soviet diplomats, his words to American teachers of Russian, to Western writers and intellectuals. Hardly a day passes without some nerve centre of the Western world being addressed, over the heads of Western governments, by the new Soviet leadership. The West is not paying back in kind except through its broadcasting stations, and these have their hands so stringently tied that their effectiveness, at least in the Soviet Union, is open to doubt. I can see no experts of Soviet affairs directing American or British or French foreign policy, but I *can* see Soviet experts of US and West European affairs—the Yakovlevs, the Dobrynins, the Falins—shaping the political and psychological policies of the Kremlin, and to signal effect.

Sooner or later Gorbachov's successes will have to induce Western governments to rethink the way in which they deal with Moscow. Why haven't Mrs Thatcher and President Mitterrand seen to it that people of the calibre of a Hugh Seton-Watson or Leonard Schapiro (both now late and lamented), Robert Conquest or Alain Besançon represented or represent their countries as emissaries in Moscow or Peking?

URBAN: The official Western conception of the USSR is still anchored in the assumption that the Soviet Union is a country rather than a cause. If it is a country, you deal with it on grounds of power and use a combination of power and diplomacy to keep it at bay. If it is a cause, or a cause *and* a country, we don't quite know how to deal with it. The age of faith is (allegedly) behind us. We are rather shame-faced about fighting ideological battles—and also very bad at it. We have, in fact, almost completely surrendered the political field of engagement to the Soviet Union.

DJILAS: And yet, it would be so easy to show up the hollow-ness of the Communist Utopias. Look at the way Mao's various Utopias collapsed: the 'Great Leap Forward' move-ment, the 'Hundred Flowers' period, the Cultural Revol-ution. What is left of them? Poverty, starvation and abysmal backwardness which Deng's 'pragmatism' is now trying to put right. Look at Khrushchev's 1961 Party programme which predicted that the Soviet Union would overtake the USA in per-capita production by the year 1980, that all rents and transportation would be free! What is left of all that? A ramshackle Soviet economy and a primitive agriculture which Gorbachov is attempting to rescue as best he can. The Soviet share of world trade is a mere 4 per cent and Soviet foreign aid no larger than that of Holland.

Look at the demise of the Yugoslav experiment which has now forced no less a person than Branko Mikulić, the Prime Minister, to admit in *Politika* (17 August 1987) that the 'self-management system' is responsible for his country's economic disaster. Yugoslavia has a foreign debt of $23 billion; inflation is running at an annual rate of over 150 per cent; our loss-making firms are now being allowed to go bankrupt, making thousands of workers unemployed; and there are serious strikes in the country.

Every variety of Communism that has been put to the test ended in economic bankruptcy. That Mikhail Gorbachov's remedies for the Soviet system sound like nothing so much as the nostrums of Mrs Margaret Thatcher, contains one message to the world about the failed Utopia of Marxism-Leninism. Another lesson on the doubtful blessings of central planning and nationalisation should be addressed to the West European Left. If the Soviet leaders are now being forced to embark on the 'privatisation' of the economy, can the West European Left cogently insist that socialism must mean *more* collective ownership?

URBAN: Your castigation of the Utopian element in Communism has, it seems to me, certain weaknesses. If Communism is a universal ideology, which it is, I cannot see how it could do without a coherent package of long-term goals as a magnet to attract followers. No one in the Communist movement would expect a classless society and universal plenty to be easily attained, or perhaps to be attained at all. But a level-headed Communist would probably argue (as, for example, Leszck Kolakowski did in his early Marxist phase) that the Utopian element is an essential part of all radical thinking. Without it no revolutionary movement could take off or keep flying. Melvin J. Lasky—no supporter of utopias or revolutions—wrote a big book about those radical thinkers who believed that 'the noble dream and the great deed have no real effective life without each other.'[17] One need not be a Communist to believe this to be true. All idealists of whatever political colour would subscribe to it.

DJILAS: Idealism is one thing; the institutionalised mendacity with which your ideals are turned upside down and the whole of reality is re-defined is quite another. If you went down the list of all the things Communist leaders have offered in their various speeches and programmes and wrote them down in one column on a sheet of paper under the heading of 'Pledges', and then made up a second column under the heading of 'Facts', you would merely have to write 'the contrary' after each of the pledges to get the second column right.

For example: the Communists offered a classless society but produced a privilege-ridden society and a class of monopolistic power-holders. They promised scientific efficiency but produced dismal backwardness and inefficiency. They promised economic plenty but created conditions that would shame some Third-World republics. They promised peace and the elimination of the conflict of interests among 'socialist' countries but produced the Sino-Soviet conflict, war between Viet Nam and Cambodia, the occupation of Hungary and Czechoslovakia and the diabolisation of Yugoslavia. They repudiated, with Marx, the 'cult of the personality' but produced in Mao, Stalin, Kim Il Sung, Ceauşescu, and other tyrants, the most monstrous cults of the personality history has known. I could go on. You would, I should imagine, agree that these crass repudiations of the Communist power-holders' solemn pledges rob their Utopia of any virtue it may have possessed—if indeed it did possess any—in the first place.

URBAN: The facts that are now coming to light about the Soviet system confirm point by point what Western critics have been saying about it—and have been derided for saying—for the last 40 years.

I noticed with some amusement that a Yugoslav Communist, disillusioned by the performance of his Party, returned his Party card and decided to sue the Party on grounds not very different from the examples you have just given. He said he had joined the Party and had been paying his membership fees for a great many years on the understanding that the Party would give him socialism—cheap housing, free health care, a decent standard of living, an inflation-free economy, full-employment, and so on. But seeing that the Party could supply none of these elements of the socialism he had joined it for, there was a breach of contract and he wanted his money back. The man had a nerve—but also a great piece of natural justice on his side.

DJILAS: Yes, Communism is not only the kind of science-lined Utopia we know about, it is a Utopia that can only exist *as* Utopia. Communism (or 'socialism') as a *realistic* blueprint for running human society is nonsense and dangerous nonsense at that. 70 years of Communist history make it incumbent upon us to record this simple conclusion as a fact and a warning.

URBAN: The history of ideas is replete with Utopias of one kind or another. Those that were put into practice usually caused destruction and carnage. The rest remained rather intriguing flights of the imagination with which we have little reason to quarrel, or do we?

DJILAS: In 1968 I was asked to meet a group of Leftist students at Princeton University. The unrest on American campuses was riding high. The students assured me that within four years the USA would be 'socialist'. American socialism, they said, would of course be different—it would be a *developed* kind of socialism, without censorship, without repression, without a bankrupt economy, and so on. This put me on my guard.

'I don't really believe that the USA will be socialist by

1972,' I said. 'In any case, I very much hope that it will *not* be.'

'How can you say that,' the students asked.

'Because,' I answered, 'a "socialist" America would be the greatest calamity for the future of mankind. America is a rich and advanced country, it has resources to make a temporary success even of "socialism". If it did, a socialist USA would send a false message to the rest of the world, for it would be telling us that there is such a thing as a good and workable socialism, whereas there isn't.'

If Gorbachov Falls

URBAN: However you and I may see the long-term chances of a socialist Utopia, Gorbachov seems to be determined to bring it about through modernisation, high technology and the motivation of his human resources. Given the enormous natural wealth of the Soviet Union and a long-suffering population, it would be extraordinary if he failed completely. We have to assume that, short of a sudden palace revolution (which is by no means impossible), Gorbachov will make some slow and painful progress. Is it in our interest that he should?

DJILAS: Before I answer your question, let me say that Gorbachov has so far tackled only the foothills of the mountain range he will have to climb. There has been a lot of sermonising, criticism, encouragement and some limited legislation, none of which has yet begun to bite. His difficulties will begin in three or four years from now when decentralisation, privatisation and self-management will confront him with the painful fact that none of these reforms can be made to become effective without revamping the *political* profile of Soviet society. That is the experience we have had in Yugoslavia and that is what the Hungarian Communists, too, are now discovering to their dismay. Up will go the demand for political pluralism.

URBAN: To well-schooled Marxists this should not come as a surprise. Some of Gorbachov's economic advisers are already saying that 'social relations' will have to be brought into harmony with 'production relations'. In plain language this means: you cannot have a free and productive economy without political pluralism.

DJILAS: Yes, and this is going to cause trouble, because while members of the Soviet *apparat* may well be forced, lured or cajoled into supporting reforms for a more productive economy, they cannot be lured or cajoled into underwriting the dissolution of the Party and the destruction of their own jobs and security. Economic reform without political pluralisation will bankrupt the system. Political pluralisation, on the other hand, would *end* the system. Gorbachov and his successors will no doubt choose the former. The Soviet system is economically bankrupt— perhaps after *perestroika* it will be slightly less bankrupt. But I cannot see how they could subscribe to political pluralism without giving up their title to rule.

URBAN: What you are saying again is that Gorbachov is a transitory phenomenon. . . .

DJILAS: Yes, I am. He may well be ousted from power when the full implications of his reforms dawn upon the hard-liners. Or he may, seeing the opposition, relinquish power as he once hinted that he might. The setbacks he suffered in the Yeltsin affair and on Armenia are tips of the iceberg.

Gorbachov could become a great figure in history if he had the good fortune to be toppled right now—or if, as I say, he gave up in despair. *Now* he is seen as a man of clear vision, a man of critical spirit, a man unafraid of the Soviet past, a man of un-Soviet language, a man who has seen what's wrong with the system and has tried to do something radical about it. A few years from now his zeal will drown in the mire of Russian life and the unredeemable contradictions of the Soviet system. Today is Gorbachov's finest hour; whatever comes next will be an anticlimax.

That brings me to your question. A greatly strengthened Soviet system would, of course, *not* be in the interests of world freedom. But that strengthening of the system is, in my judgement, not going to happen overnight, if it is going to happen at all.

URBAN: Aren't we writing off the power and elasticity of the system *as it is* in too cavalier a manner? I would have thought a conservative but unblinkered man of the *apparat* could make a good case for sticking out against Gorbachov.

We lifted, under Stalin, a backward Asiatic economy into the 20th century [he would argue]. Yes, we were using repression. Yes, we herded manpower reserves from the villages to the factories. Yes, we kept the standard of living low—but look at our results! We have won a terrible war, we have an empire, we are a superpower equal in strength to the USA. Our system—whether feared or admired—is spreading in the world, and the Russian nation is enjoying its long-delayed rendezvous with History. Why risk all that with your reforms? If we need reforms, as we undoubtedly do, why not proceed slowly and keep them strictly within the confines of the system? The One-Party state and the command economy have a lot of life left in them. They are *our* way of doing things.

DJILAS: That kind of thinking might have made sense—if you were willing to pay the price—in the 1930s. In the 1990s modernisation means educating and employing highly skilled manpower in small and self-managed units. The post-Industrial revolution is based on knowledge, individual initiative, and a high sense of personal responsibility. None of these things can be attained by central control, much less repression. The methods, therefore, that helped the Soviet Union to 'take off' as an industrialised power cannot succeed in turning it into a post-Industrial power.

For example, the use of the computer—to point to the most obvious obstacle to conservatism of the sort you have depicted—militates against any form of censorship and promotes, by its very nature, the dissemination of information. Not only that, but the whole social base of socialism, Soviet style (and, in fact, any contemporary style), has begun to vanish. The traditional working class is dwindling, and has already so dwindled in Germany and Britain, for example, that it can no longer hope to secure the election of socialist governments even if the whole working class voted socialist, which it never does. Soviet society, if it is to enter the post-Industrial age, is bound to follow suit. The state of the proletariat is destined to wither because there will not be enough proletarians left to sustain even that, false, sense of legitimacy which the Soviet state bestowed on itself through Marx and Lenin.

Gorbachov's conservative Soviet opponents do not, therefore, have a strong case. That does not mean to say that they may not get the better of him in the short run, but because the reforms of Gorbachov will have to be carried out sooner or later with or without Gorbachov, the conservative/Stalinoid argument is bound to be a loser unless, of course, the Soviet *apparat* decides that modernisation is not for them and that they'd rather face the dangers of stagnation than the risks of *perestroika*.

URBAN: Aren't democrats of the West-European liberal persuasion almost as self-righteous and indeed arrogant about the virtues of their system as the Soviet establishment is about its own? We find it self-evident that Soviet society should want what we want—that it should want to follow our curve of development from the supremacy of the Church or the aristocracy or an absolute monarch, to enlightenment, pluralism, liberalism, democracy and participation. But what if the Russian psyche is different? What if the Russian *apparat* and the people, too, should genuinely feel that the Soviet system, good or bad, is *their* way of doing things and that they don't want to be taught democracy by foreigners? We find it almost unimaginable that this should be so. Yet there are signs on every page of Soviet (as well, of course, as Russian) history that Paternalism, respect for Authority, even Regimentation are well-accepted features of Russian life and political culture. They express the ethos of the majority. Can democrats quarrel with that?

DJILAS: This is a tricky question. It could be turned around to read in a manner many Russians would regard as offensive, and indeed some have done so. It could be used to read: 'Democracy is for the culturally "superior" nations of the West. The Russians are used to serfdom of one kind or another. The Soviet system, perhaps some improved variety of the Soviet system, suits them rather well. No need to worry too much about their freedom, for they don't seem to be unduly agitated by the lack of it.'

   I do not deny that Russian reactions are, for whatever historical and cultural reasons, different from French or British reactions. But given time and political self-education, I don't think the differences are here to stay. You are, of course, right to suggest that the indiscriminate projection of Western values on to other cultures is a sign of Western conceit and parochialism and is politically dangerous. The Americans have been the worst offenders.

URBAN: But there are surely lessons to be learnt from the observable facts that Gorbachov's reforms proceed only very slowly and in the teeth of both bureaucratic and popular opposition; that popular 'extra-mural' organisations such as 'Pamyat' are in hot pursuit of Russian national traditions but not so much of civic freedoms; that the intellectuals who stand up for human rights are a small group and are looked upon with incomprehension, if not hostility, by the general public.

An American historian once told me that although he distrusted national stereotypes, he felt there was a sense in which the French in the Napoleonic period had a real liking, as a nation, for military service. Would it be too far-fetched to suggest, he asked, that the Russian people have developed, in the second half of the 20th century, a high degree of tolerance of an all-providing, egalitarian nanny-state?

DJILAS: Every leadership in the Soviet Union, and indeed all Russian governments under the Czars, were aware and afraid of the 'dark Russian masses'. Chaos and anarchy are never far beneath the surface of Russian tranquillity. If the purpose of your questioning is to show that it will be more difficult to instal democracy in Moscow than, shall we say, in Prague—I would agree because we cannot close our eyes to the facts of history. But if you question the suitability and ripeness of the Russian people to share the benefits— and risks—of liberal democracy, then I cannot agree with you. The Russians are endowed with the same human characteristics as any Italian or Swede. They do not enjoy the knout any more than you and I do, and we are doing ourselves, and them, no good by harping on the theme of 'Oh, but the Russians *are* different. . . .' That is the easy and irresponsible way out of a difficult but challenging skein of problems.

URBAN: Gorbachov is now trying to educate the Russian people in the ways of freedom and tolerance. He is doing it, in true Russian fashion, from above. Some think he is doing it too slowly, others that he is reckless and going too fast.

DJILAS: He is going at the right speed in my opinion. It is the speed I would take if I were in his position. His problems are immense. A few days ago I read an article by one of the senior journalists of *Pravda* in which the point was made that under its new relative freedom the Soviet press was launched on a no-holds-barred kind of fault-finding mission, and was creating too many 'anti-heroes'. This, it was argued, was wrong. The 'duty' of the press was not to indulge in dramatic feats of criticism but to remove the woodworm from Soviet society. Soviet journalists (it said) must concentrate on creating a sane moral climate and the right conditions for a more productive economy.

URBAN: Similar views were expressed by a number of conservative speakers at the 19th Party Conference—Y. V. Bondarev of the RSFSR Writers' Union, for example, who observed that a nihilistic, 'immoral press cannot teach morality to others'.

DJILAS: These are typical manifestation of the limits of 'openness'. The idea that the press has a 'duty' is clearly a remnant of Stalin and Lenin. At the same time, the media do enjoy some as yet undefined freedom which certainly extends to everything classified as 'negative', but not to the social order as a whole. Gorbachov's freedom, while laudable for what it is, is guided freedom based on the assumption that there is (as he often says) such a thing as 'socialist morality' which the freedom he is unleashing must promote. This is most unsatisfactory. The whole point about morality is that it can be neither a 'socialist' nor a 'capitalist' nor a Buddhist morality. It can, by the very nature of the concept, only be *Morality* without any kind of a coefficient.

URBAN: Again, you have come a long way from believing with Lenin that morality is what is good for the revolution and the proletariat.

DJILAS: I have. The same goes for Gorbachov's notion of democracy and 'democratisation'. You either have democracy which means rule by the people and therefore unrestricted pluralism, or there is no democracy. Under Gorbachov's transitional system there is a kind of guided democracy which is too guided to satisfy the real reformers and too democratic to satisfy the conservatives. He is on slippery ground.

URBAN: The confusion is genuine and gives us a fascinating picture of what happens to a prisoner who, having spent years behind bars, is suddenly told that he is free but must now look after himself. Such men are known to have collapsed under the strain—or asked to be taken back into the reassuring community of prison life.

To match your quotation from *Pravda*, I have one from

Izvestia in which the complaint is made that the average
reader does not know what to make of really free journalism. Our people, the article says, are accustomed to
thinking that whatever a journalist writes in his paper is
inspired by Authority. Now we are told that this is no longer
so, that he may very well represent neither Gorbachov, nor
the Politburo, nor even the local Soviet—but only himself.
How can people understand that? Whom does a journalist
represent if he represents no one but himself? I found this
article an incomparable introduction to the hazards of
liberty, but it would take the pen of a Dostoevsky to depict
its full impact on the souls of people unprepared for it.

DJILAS: This exemplifies one of the most baneful aspects of
the heritage of totalitarianism. It has never been true that
the Soviet public have been ill-informed about what goes
on in Soviet society. The truth is different and more
depressing. The Soviet people have never felt free to say
'Here is what I know—and here is what I conclude from
that knowledge'. No, they put their information aside and
wait to hear what Authority *expects* them to believe.

URBAN: We saw a wonderful example of this in March
1988. Nina Andreyeva's by now celebrated attack on the
Gorbachov reforms appeared in *Sovietskaya Rossiya* on 13
March 1988; the counter-blast from *Pravda* did not come
out until 5 April 1988. There was a three-week vacuum in
the central direction of public opinion. The man in the street
did not know which way to salute. 'Glasnost' was placing
too heavy a burden on him. Here is how one Ruslan Kozlov
saw his, and the country's, dilemma:

> I am ashamed to admit it today, but on 13 March I took that [Nina
> Andreyeva's] anti-restructuring stance to be the official viewpoint
> shared by the country's political leadership . . . I was not the only
> person who thought that way . . . What happened during those 'three
> weeks of stagnation'? Was there perhaps a succession of party and
> Komsomol meetings which angrily rebuked those committed to
> restoring the old 'order' in which servility and misrepresentation
> prevailed? No. Quite the reverse—in Leningrad, for instance, confer-
> ences were organized which were clearly in support of N. Andreyeva's
> article. One was even shown on television . . . The situation is undoubt-
> edly much easier for us now—the *Pravda* article convincingly and
> concretely guaranteed the Party leadership's loyalty to the course of
> expanding glasnost and democratisation . . .[18]

DJILAS: Yes, the successful or near-successful brainwashing of the Soviet public is one of those otherwise not very numerous features of the Orwellian nightmare that has actually come true. I do not envy Gorbachov his job.

URBAN: It is increasingly clear that the Gorbachov reforms require the complete transformation of Soviet thinking and manners in individuals as much as in institutions. *Perestroika* is assuming more and more the characteristics of moral-rearmament, or, if you like, of a Reformation of the Martin Luther type if we look upon Stalinist Moscow as the impure Papacy. Gorbachov's unceasing calls to the individual citizen to 'restructure himself', and his campaign against what one might call State indulgences (i.e. corruption), point to an analogy.

DJILAS: If that is so, Gorbachov might do worse than begin with the rehabilitation—resurrection he cannot guarantee— of those who have been cruelly wronged by an erring Pope. He really must have the Red Army generals of the 1938 show trials rehabilitated. He must rehabilitate Bukharin (he has partially done that already) and all the other Old Bolsheviks. Above all, he must see to it that Trotsky is restored to his rightful place in the Soviet pantheon as an historic revolutionary leader, organiser, and tribune. This is not to say that one Bolshevik faction or another would have done much better; it is the theory that is grievously mistaken, and the ruinous practice follows suit. But no history should be tampered with, distorted, censored.

URBAN: How should or would that affect the client states in East and Central Europe?

DJILAS: It would and should have its repercussions, but, as I said earlier, these should not lead to revolutionary upheavals if Gorbachov's plans are not thwarted.

URBAN: Should it mean the rehabilitation of Imre Nagy and Pál Maléter, for example, as Hungarian dissidents—and indeed the Hungarian nation—increasingly demand?

DJILAS: It should, it absolutely should. Now that János Kádár has retired from the exercise of real power and the members of the new Hungarian leadership have no personal responsibility for the suppression of the Uprising, the way should be open for the rehabilitation of Imre Nagy and the 400 people hanged by the Kádár authorities in the 1957–59 period. Kádár was personally responsible for the deception that led to Imre Nagy's arrest, and he must have acquiesced in his execution.

URBAN: Khrushchev, of course, always protested, while supporting the executions, that the execution of Imre Nagy and his associates was something the Hungarians had ordered—and said so, for example, to Ambassador Mićunović.

DJILAS: Imre Nagy and his friends were done to death on Moscow's orders and Kádár is co-responsible because he failed to intervene. Mind you, Kádár was a Soviet puppet at the time. He had come to power at the point of Soviet guns and bayonets. He had, nevertheless, enough influence as one of Khrushchev's favourite comrades to save the lives of Nagy and his associates if he had really wanted to.

Nagy's execution was, incidentally, one of Khrushchev's great mistakes—a function of the Soviet leadership's fresh suspicions of Tito. But Kádár made a miraculous recovery; the former Quisling apparently had a change of heart and was, for two decades, generally seen in Hungary as the guarantor of the country's relative freedom and economic well-being. He was highly esteemed in Yugoslavia too, and the general view was that he was a patriotic Hungarian more than a Communist.

URBAN: But the sharp turns in his career are exceptional even by Communist standards. Arrested and tortured under Rákosi, he was instrumental in securing a confession from László Rajk on the understanding that Rajk's life would be spared. It wasn't. A minister in Imre Nagy's 1956 revolutionary government, he betrayed Nagy, deserted the Revolution and returned as head of a Quisling government. Having settled accounts with the 1956 revolutionaries with great brutality, he proceeded to seek national reconciliation by his 'liberal' policies. In his old age he has been spared the need to make yet another *volte-face* because, in March 1988, he was removed from power. I should not like to be privy to János Kádár's conscience.

DJILAS: The careers of Nagy and Kádár are typical of the laws of feudal society. If a feudal baron rebels against his

King, or some provincial governor against the Sultan, he is put down as Imre Nagy was. If he falls in line, he is rewarded and sometimes given a measure of freedom—as Kádár was—provided that the King's rule is not endangered. If he becomes a hindrance or a nuisance, he is retired. The Soviet empire is entirely of that nature. We have had plenty of experience of it and should have no illusions about it.

End of an Empire—Rebirth of the Russian Nation

URBAN: Suppose Communist societies as we have known them gradually faded away under the pressures of modernisation or were brought down under less peaceful conditions— what sort of new 'governing themes' would the Russian, Polish, Romanian and the other Central and East European nations be most likely to embrace?

DJILAS: You are assuming that societies need 'governing themes'. I'm not so sure, but I can see what you are driving at. You are asking: what is going to replace the Utopian element, for example, in Russian thinking? Well, the new governing theme will have to be something more deeply rooted in the popular psyche than the egalitarian creed of Communism; and my candidate for that theme is a profound form of patriotism (not Nationalism) based on the loving care of national culture and especially language.

This theme is, in fact, already forming under the surface in every Communist country. In Yugoslavia, for example, people like the distinguished poet Matija Becković (a personal friend of mine) connect their fundamental criticism of the Communist system to a re-discovery of the national past. Dobrica Cosić, an excellent Serbian writer, has written a four-volume novel about the role of the Serb nation in the First World War. . . . Solzhenitsyn is trying to retrieve the Russian past in his own spectacular way, so is Valentin Rasputin. So are, each in their own way, the Armenians, Kazakhs, Estonians, Latvians and Ukrainians. A second theme will be the solidarity of human beings with their fellow men and women—the better off with the poor, and nation with nation. This will not be 'socialism', much less doctrinaire socialism. It will focus on the precariousness and preciousness of life on this planet, for no one has yet hit upon a worthier philosophy than the maintenance of life in all its forms. Religious leaders, philosophers and ideologues have all sought to give us a variety of answers to our quest for the meaning of life, but their nostrums tend to inflict more suffering than they manage to relieve. After the horrendous trials of Communism and Nazism, perhaps we ought to be content with the simple truth that the purpose and meaning of life is *life*—life loyally rooted in a nation and conducted with a maximum sense of solidarity towards our fellow creatures, whether walking on two legs or four.

URBAN: Wouldn't you have condemned all this in your earlier life as feeble 'bourgeois humanitarianism'?

DJILAS: Yes, I would—but we do learn from our mistakes and history, don't we? What I'm now suggesting is neither a bourgeois nor an anti-bourgeois philosophy, but a humane answer to human problems.

URBAN: What we have here is a philosophy of life which is patriotic without being nationalistic, socially responsible without being socialist, and respectful of human rights and all creation without calling itself Christian. I can hear some critics murmuring that it smacks too much of a general 'do-goodism' to attract robust nations such as the Russians, Poles or Serbs.

DJILAS: I don't think that is fair. If and when it comes to the post-Communist dispensation, every people or nation will have to find its own 'ideology' based on the reality of the nation. It would then be up to each to decide what collective personality it would want to assume. In Yugo-slavia, for example, the Slovenes would undoubtedly want to pick up their old ties with Central Europe, the Serbs might (or might not) want to emphasise their own strong ties with West European culture, and so on.

URBAN: Are you, in fact, assuming the disintegration of Yugoslavia? If Serbs, Croats, Montenegrins, Macedonians will all be free to cultivate and celebrate their own national identity. . . .

DJILAS: . . . which they absolutely must be—

URBAN: —then Yugoslavia is most unlikely to survive as a single state.

DJILAS: The assertion of national identity should not necessarily mean hostility among these nations. They may very well decide to maintain the present structures, or replace them with new ones. They will, however, fully assume their national personalities, as some of them are already doing.

URBAN: In the Soviet Union, then, you would envisage the emergence of strong Ukrainian, Estonian, Latvian, Uzbek, Armenian calls for national 'ideologies'. Would that not mean separatism at the end of the day?

DJILAS: Yes, it would, and it is, as we have seen, already under way, though not as noticeably as in Yugoslavia. But it would also mean the emancipation of the Russian nation from the present (and often unwillingly borne) burdens of empire.

URBAN: We are now talking about the break-up of the Soviet Union, aren't we?

DJILAS: We are talking about the natural expiry of an unnatural and tyrannical régime which is bound to come, as surely as the British and French Empires had to face their demise when the time was ripe. The Russian people would benefit the most. They would gain a free and more prosperous life and yet remain, undoubtedly, a great nation.

You see, the Communist system has forced the Russian people into a state of sulking introspection which seeks outlets in xenophobia, petulent demonstrations of national superiority—or, at the opposite end, maudlin admissions of national inferiority. I firmly believe that a reduced but self-confident, opened-up, democratic Russian state would induce much less brooding in the Russian people and make them a happier race to the extent that Russians can be happy. Imagine what it would mean for free men and women everywhere to see this last bastion of universal unfreedom go the way of all tyrannies!

URBAN: Gorbachov and the Politburo must have conducted a very thorough assessment of the world 'correlation of forces' before embarking on *perestroika*. They must have come to the unsurprising conclusion that the West was not threatening to make war on them and it was, therefore, safe to launch the reform movement. Seeing that the Soviet

Union is preoccupied with putting its house in order and diverting, or hoping to divert, resources from the military, is it your judgement that the West need not fear Soviet expansionism as long, at least, as the reform-movement lasts?

DJILAS: Yes, indeed. If 'restructuring' is to be seriously pursued, which it is, the Soviet Union will have neither the will nor the energy to embark on expansionist policies. But the West, and the Americans in particular, always misunderstood the nature of the Soviet threat. It has never been just, or even predominantly, a *military* threat, though it has been that too. The threat has always been political and *psychological*, and it is on that front that the Western world is in urgent need of rearming itself. I keep coming back to this point because it can never be stressed enough. Gorbachov and his friends are able propagandists. Note how brilliantly they have turned the 'Zero-option' affair to their advantage. If I were the President of the US I would continue to worry about the propaganda fall-out of my summit conferences with Gorbachov.

URBAN: When you say that the Soviet bloc expects no military threat from the West, or NATO from the East, are you putting, tacitly at least, an equation mark between the two alliances?

DJILAS: In one sense only. The Kremlin's inclination, indeed its ability, to be warlike in the foreseeable future is limited by the likely behaviour of Moscow's client states in Eastern Europe. America's inclination to be warlike is limited by the likely behaviour of its Allies in Western Europe. The Russians will not risk aggression because they realise that they could not count on the Poles, Czechs, East Germans and Hungarians except as sources of destabilisation. The Americans, on the other hand, will avoid taking risks, partly because they are, as a liberal democracy, extremely unwarlike, but also because they would not be able to carry the West European countries with them except in a dramatically clear-cut case of Soviet aggression on West European soil. This is disheartening because it betrays a lack of moral fibre, a loss of global purpose and a creeping sense of neutralism in once powerful West Europe, but it is a fact of life in 1988.

URBAN: For one reason or another, peace is, then, assured

and we can expect Gorbachov's revolution-within-the-revolution to go ahead?

DJILAS: Yes, I think we probably can, but the political struggle goes on, and it is with that in mind that the whole question of Arms Control has to be considered.

Arms Control is about political control; it is about the decoupling of Europe from America and especially the neutralisation of Germany. An INF-free Western Europe facing a conventionally superior Kremlin will mean a weaker Europe and a stronger USSR. It is, as I say, the political dimension of that weakening that the West should worry about. It is possible to redress an imbalance in nuclear arms. But the perception that the Soviet system has changed into something other than what it is, and is no longer a threat to the liberal democracies, is much more difficult to erase once it has got hold of the Western imagination. Mikhail Gorbachov is doing his best that it should.

URBAN: Are you suggesting that democracies should cease to be democracies—that German politicians should lift their sights above the next *Länder* elections, American Presidents above their ratings in next week's polls and Frenchmen above their willingness to fight to the bones of the last German Grenadier?

DJILAS: In a sense, yes, I am. We cannot, of course, fine-tune what is not fine-tunable; but the West should be able to coordinate enough of its interests to prevent NATO from degenerating into a suicide pact.

You must remember one thing: the Soviet Union is now talking to us from a position of great and openly admitted weakness. It is reaping the rewards of 70 years of economic mismanagement and the squandering of its human resources. It is trying, under Gorbachov, to shed its siege-mentality but cannot do so as long as it feels itself to be under Western pressure in terms of space defence, arms technology and the post-Industrial revolution. It wants the West to take the pressure off the Soviet system.

It is for the West to say *Yes* or *No* to that request. We should, in my considered opinion, not accede to it unless the Soviet state and the Communist Party provide a whole string of political guarantees, of the most tangible and enforceable kind, that international civil war, which they declared on the rest of the world in 1917, has ceased to be their objective. Seventy years after the Bolshevik Revolution it's not we who are the supplicants—it's the Kremlin.

Notes

1. Gorbachov's speech in Murmansk, 1 October 1987.
2. *Oni*, Stalin's Polish Puppets, London 1987.
3. *Sirp ja Vasar*, 15 April 1988.
4. On 23 July 1988, the *Estonian People's Front*, a new and officially recognised organisation supporting the Gorbachov reforms, issued an even more radical statement:
   'The Stalinist super-power policy destroyed Estonian state sovereignty. Even the right to self-determination, established by the constitution as the cornerstone of the Leninist nationalities policy, was left without any real guarantee . . . Estonians do not at present perceive the Estonian SSR as a sovereign state . . .
   The initiative centre of the *People's Front* does not consider separatist endeavours to be correct . . . In today's world the political sovereignty of Estonia can be realised only in terms of a socialist national state based on the right to self-determination. The most painless path in this direction would be to change the Soviet Union from a union of states into an alliance of states. It is necessary to work out and implement Union contractual foundations in the Soviet Union to this end. Likewise, one also has to create a mechanism which would function in practice and be juridically guaranteed and which would guarantee in real life the opportunity for national self-determination down to secession from the union. This mechanism would be an effective barrier to super-power chauvinism and to the arbitrary rule of the all-union departments . . .
   Promoting restructuring is at the moment the only realistic alternative to national pessimism, as well as to the national illusions which deny the realities of world politics . . . The *People's Front* can assume responsibility for implementing this perspective only with the continuation of radical restructuring. The victory of the anti-restructuring forces would force us to look for other possibilities in defence of the Estonian land and people. Tallinn, 23rd July 1988.'
   Sirp ja Vasar (5 August 1988)
5. Extract from a conversation between Stalin, Sergei Eisenstein, Nikolai Cherkasov, Molotov and Zhdanov, 25 February 1947. The occasion was Stalin's order to have the second part of the film about Ivan the Terrible, banned in February 1946, re-worked.

Stalin Did you study history?
Eisenstein More or less.
Stalin More or less? I have also a little knowledge of history. You presented a false picture of the oprichnina. The oprichnina was a royal troop . . . a regular army, a progressive army was formed. You depict the oprichnina as a kind of Ku-Klux-Klan.
Eisenstein They wear white hoods, whereas our men wear black ones.

Molotov This makes no fundamental difference.

Stalin Your tsar is irresolute, like Hamlet. Everyone prompts him instead of letting him make the decisions himself.

Tsar Ivan was a great and wise ruler . . . Ivan the Terrible's wisdom was that he championed the national point of view. He did not let foreigners in – he safeguarded the country against the penetration by foreign influences.

In this sense, the portrayal of Ivan IV is distorted.

Peter I was also a great sovereign, but he was too liberal in relation to foreigners, opened the gates too wide and let foreign influences into the country, having allowed Russia to become Germanised. Catherine allowed this to an even greater extent. Was Alexander I's court a Russian court? Was Nicholas I's court a Russian court? No. Those were German courts.

Ivan the Terrible was the first to introduce a monopoly on foreign trade – an excellent move. Lenin was the second to introduce a monopoly.

Zhdanov Eisenstein's Ivan the Terrible looks like a neurasthenic . . .

Stalin Ivan the Terrible was very ruthless. But you must show why it was necessary to be ruthless [sic]. One of Ivan the Terrible's errors was that he failed to knife through five large feudal families. Had he wiped out these five families, there would have been no Time of Troubles. But Ivan the Terrible executed someone and then he felt remorseful and prayed for a long time. God hindered him in this matter. Tsar Ivan should have been even more resolute . . .

The conversation ends with Comrade Stalin wishing success and saying: 'May God help you.'

Recorded by Eisenstein and Cherkasov
(*Moscow News*, No.32, 1988, pp. 8–9)

6. Lenin wrote (on 31 December 1922): '. . . not only formal equality is needed . . . it is necessary to compensate in one way or another . . . the non-Russian for that mistrust, that suspicion and those insults which in the historical past the government of the "great power" nation inflicted upon him.'

7. To mark the 20th anniversary of the Soviet intervention a Tass commentary by Aleksandr Kondrashov stated (19 August 1988):

The 1948 February victory in Czechoslovakia, when the people of that country chose socialism, alliance and friendship with the Soviet Union, has been and will continue to be close to the hearts of the Soviet people. So in 1968, when anti-socialist forces, taking advantage of the political irresponsibility and opportunism of some of the CPCZ leadership at the time, began to occupy more and more positions in society with the aim of carrying out their anti-February coup and tearing Czechoslovakia out of the socialist community, could all the friends and allies of socialist Czechoslovakia remain indifferent? . . .

At the end of August, alas, the Soviet Union and the other fraternal countries came face to face with the rise of a hostile power in Czechoslovakia, and Czechoslovak society faced the immediate prospect of a bloody settling of scores with honest communists . . .

All this obliged the Soviet leadership to take the decision to grant internationalist assistance to the Czechoslovak people.

Whether these views represent those of Mikhail Gorbachov or are a symptom of the power struggle in the Soviet leadership, must remain something for future historians to decide. [Ed.]

8. See G. R. Urban (ed.) *Eurocommunism*, London 1970.
9. 25 February 1988, Moscow briefing of the *Novosti* press agency.
10. *Sovietskaya Rossiya*, 13 March 1988. *Pravda*'s rejoinder appeared on 5 April 1988 and Fyodor Burlatsky's 'What sort of Socialism do the People need' in *Literaturnaya Gazeta* (20 April 1988).
11. *Sirp ja Vasar*, 8 April 1988.
12. De-Stalinisation has gathered momentum since these words were spoken. In an interview given to two correspondents of *Pravda* (19 August 1988), M. S. Solomentsev, Member, at the time, of the Politburo and Chairman of the Politburo's Rehabilitation Commission, stated:

Pravda The question naturally arises of those who deviated from democratic norms, violated socialist legality and perpetrated the repressions. Are they being called to account? This greatly worries readers. It is a matter of the specific people to blame for the abuses, those who organised and participated in the repressions. After all, there is no statute of limitation on moral responsibility for this . . .

Solomentsev Yes, of course, the inhuman deeds of the past can neither be forgotten nor forgiven . . . The guilt of those who abused power, who shook the democratic and moral foundations of our Soviet society, is immense. Those who carried out the repressions brought the people too much grief . . . There are many people guilty of abuses – those who have been named and those who have not yet been named. The degree of the responsibility of each will undoubtedly be determined . . .

Pravda It is sometimes said that Stalin and the people close to him did not know of the instances of lawlessness . . .

Solomentsev The documents in the possession of the Central Committee and Politburo Commission dispel the doubts existing on this score. The guilt of Stalin personally and of his immediate entourage before the Party and people for the mass repressions and acts of lawlessness allowed was truly monstrous. But, I emphasise, the guilt of the 'leaders' does not take away the responsibility of voluntary informers, obedient tools, the immediate violators of socialist legality or those who supported and blindly carried out the inhuman orders and perpetrated the tyranny . . .

Pravda Is it not paradoxical that revolutionaries who had been through Tsarist jails and exile, risked their lives more than once, accomplished feats during the October revolution and civil war, . . . were crushed, and that some of them had to reconcile themselves to the arrest of their friends and relatives? How can you explain this?

Solomentsev . . . From the great many letters we have received . . . we can get an idea of how people with strong characters were broken . . . Unable to withstand the prolonged torture which sometimes lasted many months, [they] 'confessed' to non-existent crimes.

To their credit, they stood firm, to the limits of human endurance . . . But the ordeals prepared for them often proved beyond human strength. For example, in the trial of the Right-wing Trotskyite bloc, going through the hellish round of 'inquiry', N. N. Krestinskiy fearlessly said to the court: 'I do not admit to being guilty. I am not a Trotskyite. I also did not commit any of the crimes imputed personally to me and, in particular, I do not admit to being guilty of connections with German intelligence . . .'

You can imagine the confusion of the court. At the proposal of Prosecutor Vyshinskiy, the court immediately adjourned and Krestinskiy's interrogation was postponed until the next day. It is not hard to understand the kind of 'processing' to which he was subjected if, at the next court session, he suddenly confessed to being guilty and denied the bold, true words he had spoken the day before.

13. *Tito: The Story from Inside*, Weidenfeld & Nicolson, London 1981.
14. Milovan Djilas, *Rise and Fall*, Macmillan, London 1985.
15. See George Urban, 'A Conversation with Milovan Djilas', *Encounter*, December 1979 and in *Stalinism*, London 1982.
16. London, 1985.
17. *Utopia and Revolution*, Chicago, 1976, p. x.
18. *Komsomolskaya Pravda*, 21 April 1988.

Appendix

Readers of this volume may find the following Introduction to an earlier symposium, Eurocommunism *(1978), relevant to the origins and prospects of the Gorbachov reforms.*

Trendy simplifications lie at the bottom of much historical misunderstanding. Is the Soviet system more Russian than Communist, or more Communist than Russian? Does the Soviet Union behave more like a cause than a country? Such tidy presentations of an untidy reality come easily to the minds of headline writers. We have tried in this symposium not to follow so simple a questioning, but rather to probe into 'Eurocommunism' precisely at those critical junctures where ideological commitment and the demands of practical politics mutually condition and react upon one another.

Inevitably, the result is disturbing, not because we are left thinking that Eurocommunism is the work of Soviet disinformation, nor because we have reason to suspect that it is a Latin-European device to deceive national electorates, but rather because Eurocommunism amounts to no doctrine, has created no centre, has (as yet) produced no generally accepted model—but has nevertheless earned the censure of the Soviet Union as though it had done all these things.

The shared 'model', such as it is, certainly rejects the Soviet type of socialism on grounds of irrelevance, but beyond that every Eurocommunist is the keeper of his own conscience and the maker of his own doctrine. Only in Spain has one variant been institutionalised, and even there the voices opposing it are powerful. In all other cases the Eurocommunists display a spectacular eclecticism, choosing and rejecting whatever bits of party history or ideological furniture fit their case or have ceased to support it. Whether so much sectarianism is more dangerous to the papacy in Moscow than it is to the future of Eurocommunism itself is a moot point. The 'movement' is in its infancy, and the iconoclasts are savouring the heady excitement of challenging the past, including their own.

Such are our immediate impressions of the state of Eurocommunism in the late 1970s. Taking a larger view, however, a question-mark hangs over the tenability of Eurocommunism as a *Communist* movement. Marxism on any interpretation means the dictatorship of the proletariat, and dictatorship (despite Marx's protestations to the contrary) requires a party. But no party can effectively impose dictatorship unless it is subject to rigorous discipline, which in turn invites the dictatorship of a ruling group and eventually of one man. The progression from Marxism to Leninism, and from there to Stalinism, inheres in Marxism itself. It stems from Marx's statement in the *Communist Manifesto*: 'The Communists . . . openly declare that their ends can be attained only by the forcible overthrow of all existing conditions. Let the ruling classes tremble at a communistic revolution.'

The Eurocommunists are attempting to unbutton the Marxist-Leninist-Stalinist straitjacket in reverse order. Under the impact of Khrushchev's report to the 20th Soviet Party Congress, they first read Stalinism out of the movement without (to this day) agreeing on the doctrinally crucial point of whether Stalinism had been an accretion or a systemic disorder. Next, some of the more outspoken Eurocommunists such as Jean Elleinstein, and before him the intellectual leaders of the Czechoslovak reform movement, and earlier still Djilas, proceeded to repudiate (though not always explicitly) certain aspects and then whole chunks of Leninism as a distortion peculiar to Russia's backward conditions. More recently the lure of electoral victory moved the French Communist Party, and is apparently also leading the Italian CP, officially to repudiate the dictatorship of the proletariat—unofficially it has been gradually abandoned since 1947—and with it (although this is as yet not admitted) Marxism itself.

Whether or not these moves have been merely tactical,

their political implications are significant. They reveal a geological fault running through the base of the Eurocommunist initiative—the logic of de-Stalinisation leading to de-Leninisation and that inevitably to the repudiation of Marx. If so, Eurocommunism to the extent that it really exists (and we have it on Giorgio Amendola's authority that it does not), is a freak which must either end in Social Democracy or revert back to some form of Leninism. In the first case it will cease to be Communist, in the second it will no longer be Euro.

Is this posing the dilemma too categorically? Recent West European elections suggest that the Communist vote is, and seems destined to remain, a protest vote rather than a vote for government. The abandonment of the myths of the Communist past and the Europeanisation of Communist ground-rules would, therefore, seem to be doubtful assets. The protest vote is attracted precisely because Communists are thought to stand for everything for which Social Democrats do not—a seamless world-view; uncompromising hostility to the existing order, authoritarian decision-making; firm guidelines and the will to enforce them.

But can such hopes be satisfied by a party which has cast doubt on the myth of 'Great October'; irreparably damaged the image of an all-just, all-successful and all-powerful Soviet society; and undermined the hope that somewhere, out there, dedicated and unyielding men have created a superior dispensation which, though no Frenchman or Italian would want to see it realised in his own backyard, can nevertheless be admired from a distance and, above all, held out as a threat to his rulers? The secret of the appeal of the Communist Party is its extremism, not its moderation. Take that away and the Party faces the sobering prospect of being overtaken on its Left.

Georges Marchais's insistence in his April 1978 Report to the Party Central Committee that both Eurocommunism and a return to orthodoxy 'would lead the Party into liquidation' fails to recognise this point. Eurocommunism would—Leninism would not, as it certainly did not in the past.

Where radicalism has a constituency, the Communist Party is strong because, rightly or wrongly, it is identified with Leninism. Where it has not and a viable Social Democratic Party exists to offer an alternative, the Social Democrats prosper. But there seems to be little room for a watered-down version of Communism.

None of this is admitted by Eurocommunists. Their drift towards Social Democracy is denied; so, of course, is any suggestion that self-preservation if nothing else may put them back on the Leninist road. Indeed, the Soviet variant of Leninism is derided as the 'anti-model of socialism'. No one has yet defined with certainty what socialism is, as Jean Elleinstein has argued in *Le Monde* (13 April 1978) but we know from the Soviet example what it is not—a far cry from the days when Elleinstein wept (as he tells us) on hearing the news of Stalin's death.

The Eurocommunist suspicion of Social Democracy is repaid, though not uniformly so, by Socialist suspicions of Eurocommunism. The West European Social Democrats are extremely conscious that the evolution of Eurocommunists propels them in the direction of Social Democracy, and they abhor the prospect on grounds of history as well as of electoral politics. ' "Eurocommunism" is becoming respectable,' Dr David Owen, the British Foreign Secretary, said in a lecture (18 November 1977).

> It is a term which socialists should eschew. We should give it no currency. . . . I reject the term because I do not wish to give communism anywhere, particularly in Europe, a coherent entity. I reject the term because it can easily mean lowering the guard of democratic socialists. It will not be long before we will be asked to link the British Communist Party with Eurocommunism. . . . The danger is that the Labour Party will be slowly turned away from its present outright opposition and traditional hostility to the Communist Party in Britain. We will be asked first to tolerate, then to associate and then to combine with the Communists under the broad banner of the left and embraced within the heady froths of Eurocommunism. We must resist, for it could spell electoral death for the Labour Party.

The Soviet rejection of Eurocommunism is less clearly worded but no less clear. It expresses the fear that the Soviet Party's remaining authority in its struggle with China and other 'splitters' of the world Communist movement will be further eroded, with incalculable consequences for the uncertain stability of Eastern Europe, especially if the Eurocommunists remain in opposition, retaining their freedom to criticise the Soviet system without the inhibitions of office. The Soviet leaders are shrewd enough to realise that where Socialism with a human face is made possible,

Socialism with a Russian face can have singularly few attractions. Their formula for putting the Eurocommunist heresy under anathema is to insist that Leninism, and especially the experiences bequeathed by the Bolshevik revolution, are 'laws' of international validity on which national parties may embroider, but which they cannot structurally change or ignore.

This is a feeble claim—indeed it is mendacious. Communism of the Western confession draws at least implied sanction from Lenin's own observation: '. . . after the victory of the proletarian revolution in at least one of the advanced countries things will in all probability take a sharp turn—Russia will soon cease to be a model country and once again become a backward country (in the 'Soviet' and the socialist sense) . . .' (*'Left-Wing' Communism—an Infantile Disorder*). The Eurocommunists contend that it is precisely the backwardness of the Russian example that has barred the proletarian revolution from victory in Western Europe and will continue to do so until Marxism is reclaimed from Slavic corruption and returned to its Western moorings. That the Soviet Union does not relish the prospect of being relegated to the status of a 'backward country'—even if this is done in Lenin's name—need not surprise us. Hence the counter-accusations that Eurocommunism is an 'imperialist plot'; that the Eurocommunists are conducting a 'crusade' against the Soviet Union and attempting to put the Communist movement 'under the control of the bourgeoisie'.

I have not gone into some of those immediate issues which Eurocommunism raises in respect of the future of parliamentary democracy, NATO, the East-West relationship and what remains of *détente*, because these have been amply dealt with in the pages that follow. A few points nevertheless need summarising.

No Italian or French Eurocommunist claims that he would, in office or out of office, unconditionally honour his country's obligations to NATO in an East-West confrontation—indeed, the Spanish Communists (Spain is, in 1978, not a member of NATO) are directly opposed to NATO.

The West European Communist Parties' links with Moscow have been weakened—not cut. Although most Eurocommunists insist that they and their parties (and it is uncertain to what extent Eurocommunists can speak for their parties) will attend no further international Communist gatherings of the East Berlin type, there is no institutional guarantee that they will not.

The Eurocommunist commitment to parliamentary democracy is ambiguous. The freedom of political parties, from far Left to far Right, to function outside the framework of 'socialism', more particularly to seek office with a mandate to *replace* 'socialism', is not clearly stated. Nor have Eurocommunists told us how exactly the application of Gramsci's 'hegemony' of the working class would differ from the dictatorship of the proletariat—whether 'hegemony' would be exercised under one-party rule or the aegis of a 'front' of some description, or in a genuinely multi-party system.

The internal organisation of the West European Communist Parties—'democratic centralism'—has not been liberalised. 'The Stalinist tradition survives in the Party apparatus,' Louis Althuser (no Eurocommunist) wrote of the French CP in April 1978. One consequence is that the balance of forces in the Party leaderships between Eurocommunists and conservatives cannot be reliably estimated. It is, from what we know, nevertheless clear enough that even in Italy and Spain Eurocommunism has an uncertain constituency. Among the establishment it is unevenly supported; among the rank and file it is barely understood, and to the extent that it is understood, it is opposed. In France, the process of de-Stalinisation, spectacularly set in train at the 22nd Party Congress in 1976, has made so little impact that Eurocommunist (and other) critics of Communist defeat at the 1978 general elections were not permitted to publicise their views in *L'Humanité* and were ostracised when they published them elsewhere.

Finally, the history of the Communist movement is a standing warning to us that the Communist reflex reaction in critical situations is to revert to dogmatism and strong-arm solutions. Lenin's call to 'use barbaric methods to fight barbarism'—barbarism being whatever stood in the way of the advance of Bolshevism—has sunk deep roots in the Communist psyche.

What are we to make of all this? Eurocommunism is the latest and for Moscow perhaps the most dangerous split in a once centrally controlled ideological and power-political movement. It is not a fraud even though its claims may turn out to be fraudulent if the Eurocommunists succeed in persuading Western electorates to support policies which the Eurocommunists themselves may eventually prove unable to control. Its leading proponents, though still hemmed in by the legacy of their Marxist-Leninist, and frequently Stalinist, antecedents, appear to be as genuinely convinced of the need to combine 'socialism' with liberty as were their ill-fated forerunners in Prague in 1968. And they have as hard a row to hoe, though of course with a better chance of success because, paradoxically, the prospects of renewing Communism in a bourgeois/capitalist environment are infinitely brighter than they are in the world of Soviet 'socialism'.

One lesson which I believe emerges from this symposium with reasonable clarity is that the obstacle to Communism is Communism—Soviet style. The spectre haunting Euro-communism (we may well say, *pace* Marx) is the spectre of Communism. Indeed, it is under capitalism alone that Communism can change and prosper.

G.R.U.

Notes on Contributors

Alain Besançon is Director of L'Ecole des hautes études in Paris where he teaches Russian history. He is the author of many books on Soviet culture and society including *The Rise of the Gulag: Intellectual Origins of Leninism; Court traité de soviétologie* and *Education et société en Russie dans le second tier du XIXᵉ siècle.*

Vladimir Bukovsky served ten years in Soviet prisons, labour camps and 'psychiatric' institutions. In 1976 he was exchanged for Luis Corvalan, a Chilean Communist Party leader. He is the author of *To Build a Castle: My Life as a Dissenter, The Peace Movement and the Soviet Union* and several studies on Soviet affairs.

Milovan Djilas was, until his fall from power in 1954, Vice-President of Yugoslavia, President of the Federal Parliament, and a Member of the Central Committee and the Politburo. He was imprisoned under the Monarchy (1933–36), and under Tito (1956–61 and 1962–66). His publications include *The New Class; Conversations with Stalin; Land Without Justice; The Unperfect Society; Wartime; Tito, the Story from Inside* and *Rise and Fall*,

Max M. Kampelman is Head of the United States negotiating team at the US–Soviet Arms Control negotiations, and was United States Ambassador and Chairman of the American Delegation to the 'Conference on Security and Cooperation in Europe' (Madrid, 1980–83).

Giorgio Napolitano is a member of the Italian Parliament

and is Head of the Italian Communist Party's Committee for Foreign Affairs.

G. R. Urban served with the British Broadcasting Corporation, 1948–60, and was the Director of Radio Free Europe, 1983–86. As a senior research associate of the School of Politics and International Relations, University of Southern California, he founded (with Roger Swearingen) the quarterly journal *Studies in Comparative Communism*. He was a Visiting Fellow at Indiana University (1975) and a Research Fellow at the Russian Research Center of Harvard University (1980). He is the author of *The Nineteen Days* and *Kinesis and Stasis*. He has edited and contributed to *Talking to Eastern Europe; The Sino-Soviet Conflict* (with Leopold Labedz); *Can We Survive our Future?* (with Michael Glenny); *Toynbee on Toynbee; Détente; Hazards of Learning; Eurocommunism; Communist Reformation* and *Stalinism*.

Galina Vishnevskaya is the author of the best-selling book *Galina*. She was a leading soprano with the Bolshoi Opera and is married to the cellist Mstislav Rostropovich. In 1978 they were both deprived of their Soviet citizenship.

Alexander Zinoviev is one of the Soviet Union's leading philosophers and author of many specialised works in the field of mathematical logic. His publications include *The Yawning Heights; The Radiant Future* and *The Reality of Communism*. He has held research appointments in the Soviet Academy of Sciences, and was for fourteen years a member of the Faculty of Philosophy in the University of Moscow. From 1970–78 he was Professor of Logic and Methodology of Science. After the publication of *Yawning Heights* he was deprived of all his appointments, expelled from the Communist Party and in 1978 was deprived of his Soviet citizenship.

Index

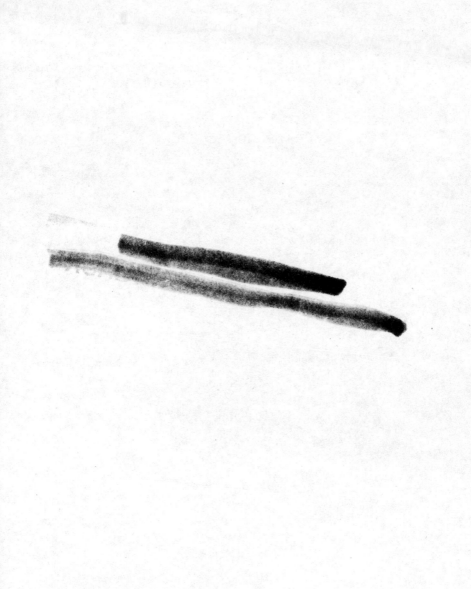